Drawing
for Interior Design

SECOND EDITION

First published in 2009
by Laurence King Publishing Ltd
361–373 City Road
London EC1V 1LR
Tel +44 20 7841 6900
Fax +44 20 7841 6910
E enquiries@laurenceking.com
www.laurenceking.com

Second edition published in 2014
by Laurence King Publishing Ltd

A catalogue record for this book is available from the British Library

ISBN 978 178067 177 2
Designed by John Round Design
Printed in China

Drew Plunkett

Drawing
for Interior Design

SECOND EDITION

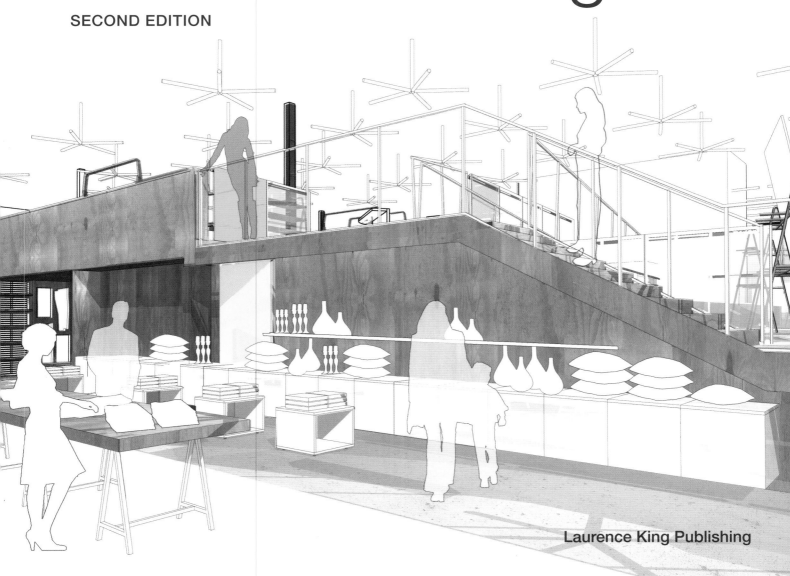

Laurence King Publishing

Contents

Related study material is available on the Laurence King website at
www.laurenceking.com

Introduction

Why we draw

Good interior design does not begin with a drawing but with an idea, an ill-defined image that exists for a moment in the imagination and continues to flit, evasively, across the mind's eye. Designing is, in effect, the pursuit of that image: a succession of attempts to define it more precisely, to give it form, to examine it and assess its worth, to make progressively more objective decisions that finalize ideas and to communicate those ideas to clients, collaborators and builders in the form of drawn and written instructions.

Drawing, at first broadly and speculatively and then with increasing focus and precision, is the means to test rigorously how a near-abstract concept can be viably translated into reality. It may be feasible to visualize and scrutinize concepts without drawing them, but it would be perverse to deny that the most immediate and effective way to design is to make drawings – and drawings may take many forms. With the advent of specialist hardwares and softwares they do not have to be, perhaps should no longer be, handmade pen or pencil lines on conventional papers. They should be made in the way with which each individual designer is most comfortable. They should change to suit the particular requirements of each project and, because they are a means to the end

Right
A computer-generated conceptual drawing, in which lines and blocks of colour are augmented by scanned artefacts and textures.

Below right
Most interiors depend for their success on two- rather than three-dimensional gestures. The computer allows the essence of these to be represented accurately and convincingly, with a little added drama.

Left
A hand drawing scanned and 'colour-washed' by computer.

Below
Detailed description of the relationship between new and existing structures is much easier to create by computer. In addition, the image – generated from plans and sections – may be rotated on-screen for selection of the best viewpoint.

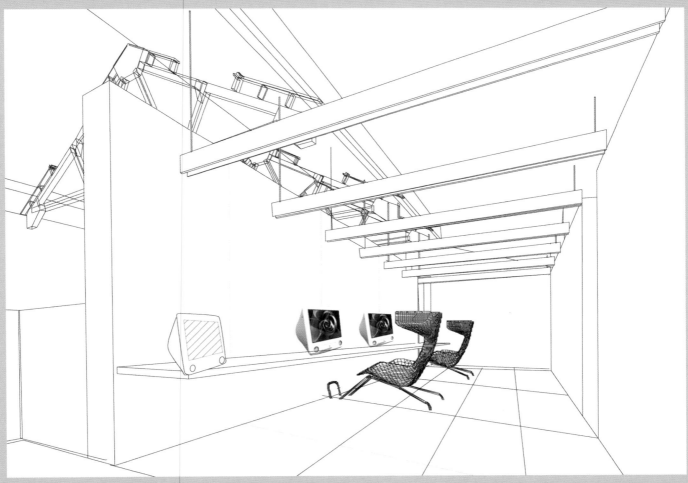

of expressing ideas, content should be more crucial than technique or style, which will take care of themselves.

As a designer becomes more experienced, making a drawing, the right kind of drawing, becomes automatic, instinctive, an immediate expression of thought. It need not be carefully refined but it does seem that when one is intensely focused, absorbed in thinking about possibilities, and when the imagination and eye are practised, then the drawings produced have a quality that gives them a particular authority. Effective and successful drawing bolsters self-confidence and confidence in the ideas one is proposing – and establishes credibility with clients.

The act of drawing structures thinking and the coherent progression of ideas. Paradoxically its particular potency is recognized in the caveat that one should delay making the first drawing in order to allow ideas to float freely in the imagination. A warning acknowledging that once the abstraction of thought is given tangible shape, wide-ranging speculation comes to an end, and the identity of the project and the direction of its evolution are as good as settled. Every designer experiences that moment of frustration when a fruitless idea is obsessively and repetitively committed to paper, as if the hand is stubbornly denying the imagination the chance to move on. At times like that the only way to progress is to stop drawing and to think, to allow the imagination the chance to start again.

In effect, all drawings but the final one made in the course of developing a project have some shortcomings. All are made in the optimistic expectation that they will encapsulate a final solution, but under objective scrutiny all

except the last – while they may offer some encouraging evidence of progress – will be found wanting. It is the identification of their shortcomings that will further inform not only the direction that the design process should follow but also the questions being asked in the brief, for these are inevitably modified and complicated as one begins to understand how the realities of an existing building determine what is possible. Clients' perceptions and expectations must also change as the nature of an appropriate solution changes. Their contribution and agreement is essential for the progression of any project, and the rationales for decision-making must be communicated to them clearly. Well-made drawings are the most effective way of doing this.

Making a good drawing requires practise and an understanding of how it may best convey information. While all drawings, like everything a designer produces, should aspire to be beautiful their first obligation is to convey information, and ultimately their success must be judged on their capacity to do this. Ideas need to be assessed objectively, regardless of the quality of the drawing that describes them. Evidence suggests that a good idea will generate a good drawing – one that, because the designer is immersed in and confident about a solution, will distil and convey the essence of an idea and its physical expression.

Different stages in the design process require different kinds of drawing. As the design becomes more precisely defined so the drawings become more exact; while initial sketches may be flamboyant and suggestive of an intense involvement with the creative moment, they are, because of their very spontaneity, more superficial than the prosaic plans, elevations and details that follow and explain in detail how the building will be made. It is in these precisely scaled drawings, showing little evidence of graphic gestures, that the designer becomes increasingly engaged with the reality of their proposal, the imagination is most intensely engaged and distractions are least intrusive.

The tools and materials with which designers make their drawings have always been in a state of evolution and the capacities of particular media have, inevitably, had an impact on the way designers 'see' their ideas and influenced how they, and others, appraise them. It is comparatively recently that the sedate evolution of the pencil, pen and felt tip has been abruptly and fundamentally interrupted.

Below
Drawings made to scale clarify precisely the interaction of elements within the project and allow final decisions to be made about proportions. Simple three-dimensional images, generated on computer, also help clients understand the composition and organization of a project.

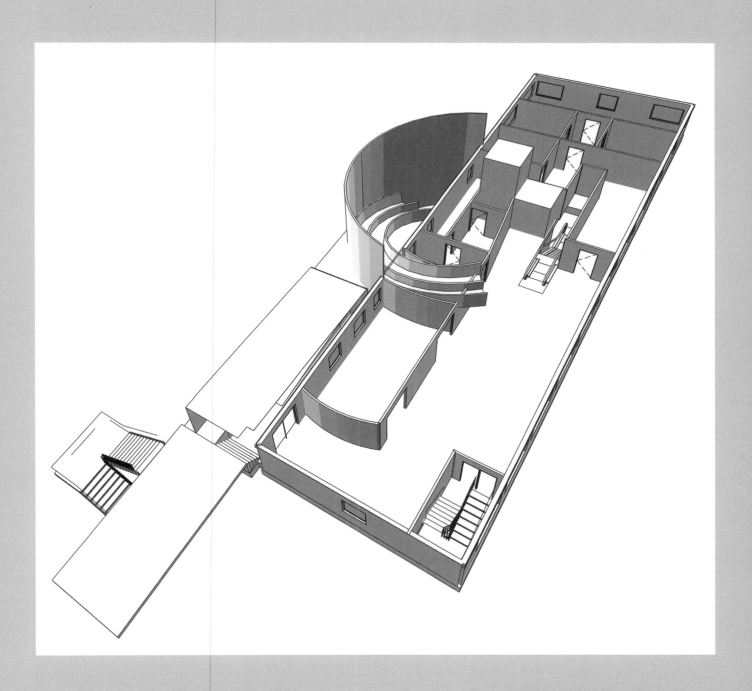

The impact of the computer

There is still some disagreement about whether images produced by computer can be described as 'drawings' at all. Those who harbour doubts have a visceral feeling that a drawing is something that must be made by the hand and that the communion of hand, eye and intellect has a power which offers the only true road to visual creativity.

There is a sentimental presumption that drawing by hand represents a more 'artistic' activity than drawing by computer, but this is an argument usually put forward by those with a vested interest in their own well-developed and polished drafting skills. It also denies the evidence of history. The pencil on paper is an improvement on the stick that scratched lines in the mud and sand, and on the quill that dripped ink onto parchment. It made possible a better standard of drawing and added to the capacity of those making drawings to express themselves more effectively. The computer does the same, but even more dramatically.

The computer, although it has only been widely used in the field of interior design for little more than ten years, has become the drawing tool of choice - because it is the most effective instrument available to support the practice of interior design, and the material it produces is inherently compatible with the new and ubiquitous digital mechanisms of global communication. It is becoming progressively more easy to use, and such development is likely to continue as long as producers of hardwares and softwares compete to offer more user-friendly – and, therefore, from their point of view, commercially successful options.

While the extravagant claims of the early supporters of computers – that the machines would take over the creative process – have gone unrealized, and are likely to remain so, the, only slightly, more modest reality is that they have had a fundamental impact on how people now engage with the process of creating interiors. Qualities that are essential in the making of a good interior – lighting, colour, texture, transparency and reflectivity – are all extremely difficult, some nearly impossible, to represent with traditional manual techniques. However, using computers it is comparatively simple to represent these essentials with a great – sometimes unsettling – degree of realism. Designers trained, and variously adept, in the use of manual techniques have been reluctantly compelled to acknowledge that the computer does those jobs better than they ever could. The fears that computer imaging would force uniformity of visualizing, and of the consequent built output, have been allayed by the evidence. The new medium has added to the creative palette, enabling rather than stifling creativity and diversity.

It is possible to make both good and bad drawings by either hand or computer. Merit is the result of refined technique and taste. A critical eye, rather than the computer or the hand, is what makes a drawing good. While the fear that all drawings made on computer and all interiors built from them would look the same has therefore been dispatched, but there is a generic look to computer-generated

Left
The computer has now become the drawing tool of choice for interior designers.

Above
The computer offers complex and complementary options for the rendering of three-dimensional images.

Below
The computer can introduce the extraordinary into the depiction of the (comparatively) ordinary.

Right
The computer-made image is the most effective way of representing materiality and atmosphere.

Below right
This image concentrates on the dominant elements in the space – the display system and products – focusing on them as the eye would and only hinting at elements of the existing building, which are of secondary, albeit complementary importance.

Right
Crucial construction details are identified,
considered in two dimensions at a small scale
(1:50 or 1:20) then drawn at 1:5 or full size
with explanatory technical notes. Often when,
as in this example, the construction process is
complex and ground-breaking, development of
the project will involve discussion with specialist
consultants and manufacturers and drawings
must initially communicate the designer's
aesthetic intention to them. Subsequent
drawings must incorporate information supplied
by them (see chapter on production).

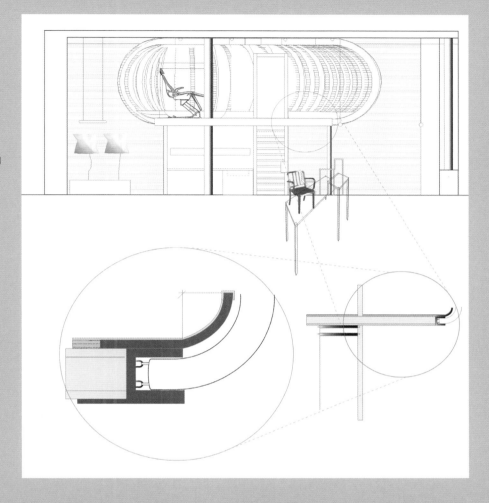

images. There is, of course, also a generic look to those made
by hand and, just as with handmade drawings, the more one
practises, and perfects the use of appropriate software, so
the more distinctly individual the computer-generated image
becomes. The maxim applied to traditional drawing, that the
identity of the maker is always clear in a good drawing and
that all bad drawings share an anonymous and unattributable
ineptitude, is equally true for those made by computer. The
mechanical, dispassionate and unadventurous implementation
of instructions in a software manual will offer only the most
prosaic description of reality, but the evidence suggests that
for every designer, regardless of the quality of creative design
work, the lowest level of digital drawing will be significantly
more acceptable than that of an incompetent hand drawing.

Designers who use software creatively offer
themselves, and others, the chance to consider a richer,
more accurate and informative representation of their
ideas. If one accepts that the opinions of a client are
an essential element in the evolution of a successful
project, then the more clearly and precisely ideas are
represented the more productive the dialogue will be.

If computers significantly extend the possibilities
of exploring and communicating the physicality of a

proposal, they have also impacted fundamentally on
the making of the production drawings that provide
builders with the information they need to construct
the designer's intentions. They ensure drawings of
extraordinary precision, to which text may be added
without the labour intensive tedium of stencilling and in
which the changes that inevitably become necessary as
the project evolves may be incorporated seamlessly.

Compatibility of drawing software with information
and communication technologies enables instant global
distribution of drawings and an exchange of ideas that
wholly supersedes the efficiency of any postal service,
making creative collaboration with specialist consultants
and manufacturers simpler and more spontaneous.
Problems on a site half the world away can be digitally
photographed and sent instantly to the designer, who
may identify and communicate a solution just as rapidly.
One reservation may be that the possibility, and perceived
obligation, to reply quickly will discourage the extended
consideration that a critical problem might require.

STEP BY STEP COMPUTER BASICS

Most drawing softwares offer a reasonable quality of three-dimensional image capable of meeting almost all requirements for developing and presenting ideas. However, in creating the most polished and realistic images it is often necessary to use a combination of programs, and, just as images made on different hardwares and softwares can appear very similar (as do drawings made by hand), so the basic steps in creating them are essentially the same.

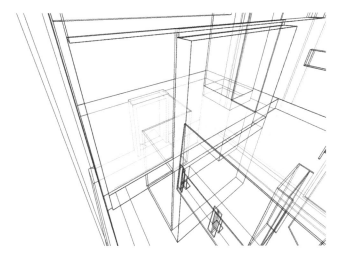

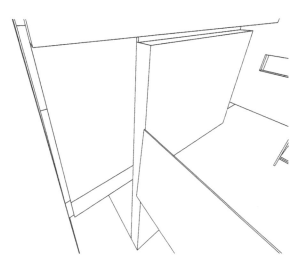

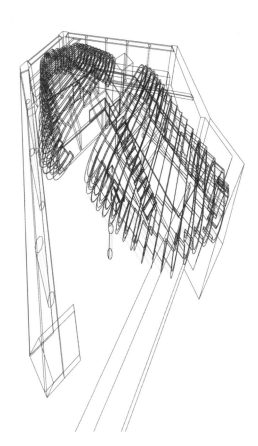

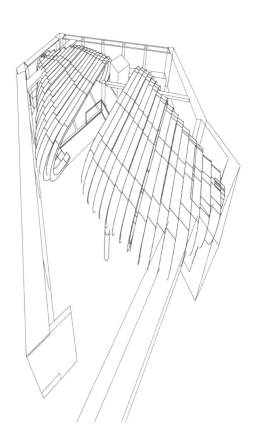

1 In the first step – the 'wire frame' – all lines generated by the projection of plan and section are visible.

2 The 'hidden' lines – those obscured by the built planes of walls, floor, ceiling and other solids – are eliminated to provide the first clear three-dimensional 'model' of the space.

Two examples demonstrate this: the upper sequence is primarily concerned with representing materials; the lower sequence with representing form. Each uses different hardware and a combination of different softwares.

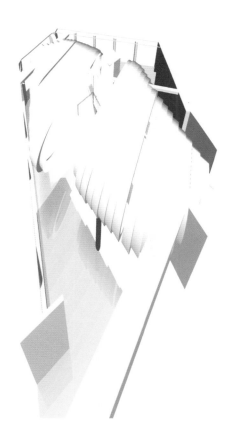
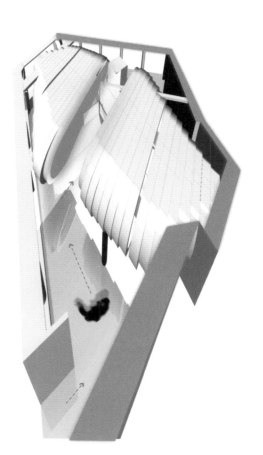

3 The first renderings of materials, textures and lighting are added. This stage allows an appraisal of the composition of the image.

4 The lighting and materiality are fine-tuned using compatible complementary software.

We are not, in this book, considering the particular merits of different software packages. Most of the specialist programs fulfil the essential requirements satisfactorily. Each is in a fairly constant state of flux as software designers create additions to their products, and often strikingly familiar, versions of successful rival softwares. Refinements to software packages almost inevitably make them simpler and faster to use and it is therefore increasingly easy for designers to move from one program to another. Comparisons of images made with different softwares, and combinations between packages, indicate that all can achieve a comparable level of refinement.

Those who first used computers in design practice were not only learning an unfamiliar way of working but grappling with equipment that was significantly more difficult to use than current (and, presumably, future) versions. They were also trying to disengage from the habits of drawing by hand, having to organize the way they put a drawing together in unfamiliar ways. Cumbersome early programs, untested in the fields of practice, did perhaps require a significant degree of induction and dedicated experience of use, but it would now be a short-sighted employer who would reject a talented designer on the grounds that they were unfamiliar with the practice's preferred software (although this may continue to be a useful diplomatic way of rejecting an unsuitable applicant).

Any good interior design school should be inducting students into the use of computers at the beginning of the course, allowing them to find and evolve their own way of thinking with this essential tool. Just as one should not be aware of the pencil in one's hand when drawing, so, ideally, one should not have to deliberate over procedures for making an appropriate computer image.

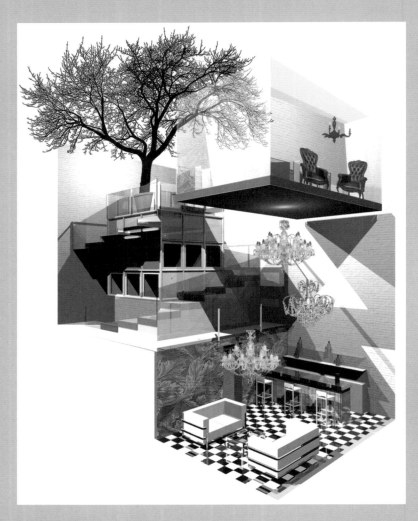

This page
The three-dimensional images for these three projects were generated by different software programs and refined using other specialist softwares, to import textures, materials, and furniture.

The essential skill in making an effective drawing, particularly one that attempts to represent an interior realistically, is to be able to visualize it accurately in one's imagination – the same skill that was necessary to make a good drawing by hand. Because the image in the designer's 'eye' is the crucial ingredient in determining the 'look' of a drawing, there is likely to be more variation in the work of two individuals using the same program than in two drawings by the same designer on two different software programs.

On this page drawings show how the computer makes possible the production of images that are distinctly different but that complement the style of the projects they illustrate.

When experienced designers have polished their computer-imaging skills, it becomes impossible to attempt to identify the programs they use and the impact of these on their work. Designers' individual ways of seeing become the determining factor in the expression of ideas. Rather than forcing graphic conformity as was, and is still sometimes, argued, the computer makes possible an extraordinary diversity of image. Examples on the following pages – each pair is the work of one designer – demonstrate this.

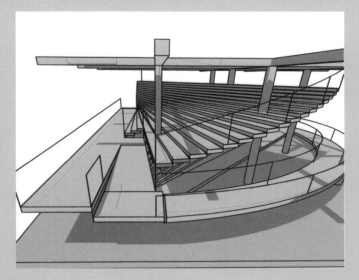

This page
Two images by the same designer. The limitations of hand skills do not allow such extreme diversity of expression.

Left and below
The unique character of two proposals, by the same designer, is distinctively represented, and complex detail convincingly realized.

Opposite, top
In the work of designers who are experienced in the use of computers it is sometimes impossible to identify which programs have been used because it is the designers' ways of imagining their proposal that become the determining factor in the expression of ideas, rather than the software itself.

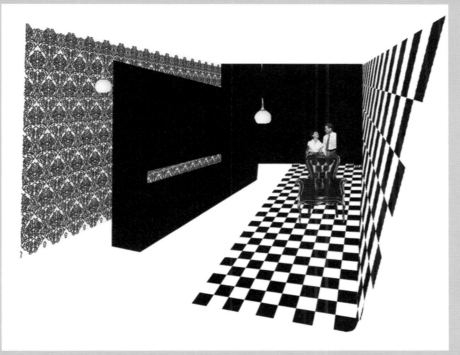

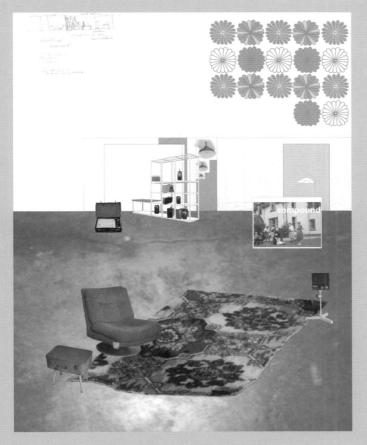

Above
Diverse, unconventional images, partly computer
generated, partly computer-scanned found
images and hand drawings, confound arguments
that computers lead to graphic conformity.

Left and below
Images of different areas of the same project, one dealing with the contrast of new and existing materials and textures, one dealing with the hard-edged precision of a new space.

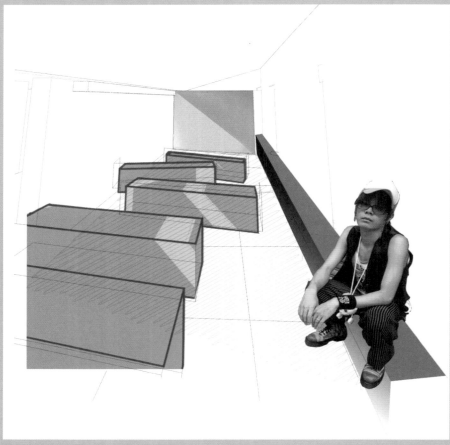

Above and right
Two drawings sit at opposite ends of the
graphic spectrum. In that above light
is harsh, colours are brash and sharply
outlined. In the other lighting is soft,
colours are muted and edges blurred.

The future

The often embarrassing history of predictions about future technologies suggests that dogmatic speculation is largely futile. The extraordinarily rapid development of computer-generated visualization suggests that the activity will continue to change significantly, but it is perhaps possible to speculate about the likely direction of emerging software and hardware.

It is likely that increasingly specialized programs will continue to evolve to deal with specialist needs but, as professional preferences and priorities become increasingly clear, operating systems are likely to become increasingly compatible. One significant example of this is BIM (building information modeling), a process for the generation and management of production information, the coordination of drawings made by all designers, working in all disciplines on a single project, so that, when any change is made, its impact on the project as a whole is identified and immediately communicated to all others involved so that they can respond to its implications. A mechanical and electrical engineer will immediately be aware of changes made by a structural engineer and be able to assess their impact, if any, on proposals for cable and ducting distribution. This changes the nature of collaboration. Meetings, involving teams of designers and consultants, that would once have been initially devoted to explanation and evaluation, can now concentrate on finding solutions.

As CAM (computer-aided manufacture) develops, its capacity to relate to CAD (computer-aided design) increases and the communication of instructions from designer to maker has become increasingly streamlined and refined. CNC (computer numerical control) technology now makes it quite feasible to link a designer's laptop in one hemisphere directly to a fabricating machine in the other. A computer programmed machine has no preference for straight or curved lines. Variations of lengths and radii, which would require time consuming manual adjustments to machine settings and templates, may now be infinitely varied and adjustment is made simply and definitively on the designer's computer. The maker whose job it was to interpret and implement drawn instructions is relieved of those time consuming obligations and, for better or worse, the quality of the finished object will depend primarily on the capacity of the designer not only to produce the drawings but to understand precisely the nature of the finished component, the appropriate range of materials, the nature of joints and fixings. Consultation with the maker of an artefact will be less important in the evolution of ideas and replaced by the advice of manufacturers about the practical and technical performance of their products. CNC software already ensures the most economical use of materials by maximizing the number of components, regardless of their size and shape, that can be cut from a standard sized sheet and, perhaps

it is reasonable to assume that software development will identify and incorporate other practical, economic and environmental data in the design/manufacturing processes.

So far CNC production has led to the, perhaps predictable, proliferation of spaces sculpted by horizontal and vertical ribs, which realize three dimensional form with a minimum of material. Inevitably, as designers experiment with the technology more subtle – and more extraordinary - proposals will emerge. Already there are examples of intricate CNC- produced mouldings that may encourage a return to the use of ornament in interiors. The old Modernist argument that machine production made intricate ornament obsolete is itself made obsolete by the capacity of digitally facilitated creativity and production, which allow the creation of intricate elements without the cost of highly skilled labour. 3D modelling makes it quite feasible to produce bespoke door furniture and other components hitherto sourced from manufacturers' catalogues. The caveat should perhaps be made that objects that are too easily produced may not be subjected to the same scrutiny as those that now evolve, often frustratingly slowly, in the collaboration and prototyping processes.

The computer's capacity to create animated 'walk-throughs' of interiors is an established, if expensive, presentation option. It can be initially spectacular but is compromised. Spectators' experience of movement through the space, particularly if the sequence is viewed on a monitor screen, is limited, and the images lack the three-dimensional depth of a physical model. This latter problem may be overcome by digital projection at a large scale, which makes interpretation easier for those unfamiliar with reading drawn images, and, increasingly, by the development of the software and hardware that generates three-dimensional images with perceived depth. Ultimately success will depend on the refinement of the representation of materials within the images and on the ease by which spectators control their movement through the interior. Ideally, the image should respond to the direction of the spectator's gaze, providing detailed close-up views. When such visual refinement is achieved the logical progression will be to complete the sensory repertoire by adding sound and sensations of touch, and perhaps when warranted, smell.

Something more extraordinary than these prosaic suggestions, as yet unanticipated, will materialize. Those who learnt and matured as designers in pre-digital times will fade away and ways of visualizing and, therefore, thinking about interiors will change. The creative process for interior designers is not about how you draw but about what you draw and the more effective tools have inevitably prevailed.

Above
The CAD data that creates the perfect repetition of
elements in two dimensions can be translated into
the CAM data that manufactures the same three-
dimensional components for the built interior.

About this book

This book concentrates on describing why drawings are
made, and the techniques and qualities that go into making
good ones. Any drawing technique can only improve with
sustained, self-critical practise but one also learns from others,
not only about how they made successful drawings but also
why they made them. The interior designer must be able to
create a number of quite different types of drawing, each
with its own conventions, which are the result of well-tried
and tested experience. While the conventions should be
respected it is possible to fine-tune them to personal taste.
Much of the text deals, inevitably, with the nature of the
design process. This is not to trespass into other territories but
rather to recognize that the act of drawing – in two or three
dimensions, by hand or computer – is so intimately a part of
thinking about design that the two must be discussed as one.

Designers have individual ways of drawing and making,
which are as distinct as their handwriting. These emerge
from personal ability and individual preference but, broadly
speaking, are personal variations on the universal battery of
skills and techniques that have been proven in professional
practice. Individual style tends to reflect aesthetic preferences.
Those who make flamboyant gestures within their interiors
tend to draw flamboyantly, avoiding technical precision
as long as possible – often longer than is productive.
Others will move quickly to a precise definition of their
proposal, and may miss out on some of the unpredictable
ideas that a less controlled exploration might reveal.

There appears to be a clear correlation between
the success of designers' work and the rigour of their
working methods. Natural talent can only be expressed
if it is backed by intense hard work. It is not difficult
to have an idea but it is very difficult to convert that
intangible thought into a built reality and mastery of
the range of drawing techniques underpins and refines
the process. This book makes suggestions about how
drawings can be most effectively made by hand, but does
not attempt to explain how to use particular computer
programs. These are in a constant state of development
and refinement, and instruction is most effectively and
comprehensively found for each in the relevant manual.

A good hand drawing can still prompt enthusiastic
appreciation but an elegant or flamboyant digital image
will stimulate the same response. The computer makes
the production of drawings a little more egalitarian than
hand-drafting in that one does not need the same degree
of inherent manual dexterity. However, the ability to create
a wonderful interior remains paramount, and perhaps there
is a different pressure on the designer in that the quality of
content, rather than the quality of the drawing, now falls
under greater scrutiny and credit is no longer given for the
successful grind of producing a decent handmade drawing.
The computer gives each individual a battery of techniques,
with an, almost, guaranteed successful outcome. Polishing
of skills requires individual commitment, but this book and
the analysis of the drawings it contains offers examples that
point to a diversity of rewarding directions to explore.

The drawings used in this book have been made in the
creation, presentation and realization of projects, some by
practitioners and some by students. Many of the designers
are familiar with each others' drawing style and some of
the drawings included will demonstrate how collaboration
can lead to productive cross-fertilization of ideas or, more
importantly, how a shared idea is developed in a distinctly
individual way by distinctly creative individuals.

It makes sense to look at the work of students,
particularly for presentation drawings, because they have
time to concentrate on the development of techniques
and to push these to the limit in order to explain proposals
that must, necessarily, remain on paper. Professionals
make such drawings intermittently and are therefore less
practised and less inclined to experiment, liable to fall
back on familiar techniques and unable to devote time to
exploring new directions. Students also tend to be more
relaxed when working with computers and therefore
more prone to experimentation. They have grown up
with them as an integral part of their everyday lives.

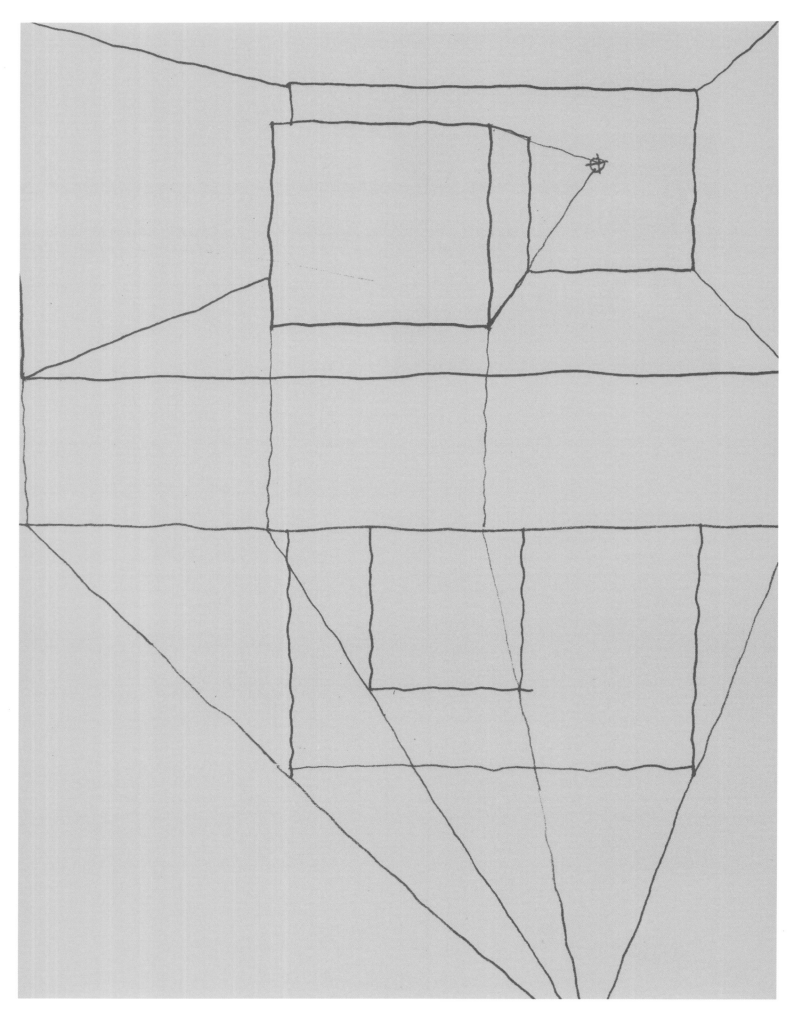

CHAPTER 1 THE BASICS

Measured surveys

It is important when designing an interior, particularly one that involves the complex subdivision of an existing space, to know the exact dimensions of that space because decisions about the location of new elements inevitably depend on the particularities of the original structure. While drawings of existing buildings may frequently be found and referred to, there are some for which no records exist, and others for which the drawings do not inspire confidence in their own accuracy. In such cases it becomes necessary to carry out a measured survey and to produce an accurate version of plans, sections and significant details. Even for recently constructed buildings it is worth checking the accuracy of dimensions on drawings because variations and discrepancies almost inevitably occur, and go unrecorded, during the building process. A very small discrepancy can often cause problems and embarrassment.

When no drawings exist it is normal to draw a plan on site, usually by hand, and good practice to record systematically all measurements because until design work begins it is impossible to forecast those which are likely to be crucial in the decision-making process. If the general outcome can already be anticipated with confidence, then it may be safe to take selective measurements, although, almost invariably, something will be overlooked, and only in the making of the measured drawing will this become clear.

Carrying out a survey

It is good practice to take 'running' dimensions rather than measuring and recording each element separately. Running dimensions are made by measuring sequentially all significant points on, for example, a wall from one clearly identifiable point, usually a corner. This prevents the accumulative error that is likely to occur when a collection of separate dimensions are aggregated on a drawing. The running dimension effectively offers the opportunity for correction with each individual reading. This is vital, particularly as the conditions on most sites are unlikely to support meticulous accuracy. Buildings in use are likely to be cluttered with inconveniently placed furniture. Unoccupied shells tend to be badly lit and possibly littered with building equipment.

There are circumstances in which it will be obvious that only a few isolated dimensions will be needed, and then it is enough to take a series of single measurements. This is also the easier method when working alone.

It is, however, better if two people collaborate to make a survey: one to hold the end of a long measuring tape and record, on the plan, the dimensions called out by the second, who will move along the length of the wall. Over a long distance the tape, if held in the air, will sag, increasing measurements. It is good practice, when possible, to lay the tape along the floor. When this is impractical because of clutter, it may be sensible over a long distance to measure in two or more sections to reduce weight and sag. Hand-held laser measuring devices, which provide a perfectly straight line at any height and eliminate this problem, are increasingly replacing the traditional tape measuring tools and, with their inbuilt digital programming, they can also calculate areas and volumes. The most basic models can measure lengths up to 100 metres (328 feet) with an accuracy of plus or minus 1.5 mm (¹⁄₁₆ inch). Most have built-in spirit levels for horizontal alignment and project a light spot onto the surface defining precisely the length measured, which avoids readings being made to inappropriate obstructions and projections. The laser tool allows one person to carry out the survey, with no need of an assistant to hold the end of the tape and call out measurements.

It is always unwise to assume that corners are perfect right angles because, although most will appear so to the eye, this, particularly in older buildings, is almost never true. It is obviously important that angles are accurate and, to establish these, one should measure the diagonals of the space surveyed. A diagonal, together with the two walls it connects, represents the sides of a triangle, and when these are drawn to scale the angle of the intersection of the walls is established automatically and accurately.

It is easy to overlook diagonals, just as it is to forget about measuring heights. It is always necessary to have heights of ceilings, door and window heads, window sills, steps in floors and ceilings, the depth of beams and other dimensions particular to individual spaces. To distinguish these from horizontal dimensions on the drawing it is usual to draw a circle around them and, as far as possible, place them separately from horizontal dimensions.

There are usually places in any building where a lot of dimensions must be recorded and it is better to draw these areas separately to a larger scale so that the new drawing has enough space to accommodate the density of information legibly.

It is advisable to try to make the accurately scaled drawing based on the survey findings as quickly as possible, while the realities of the site are fresh in the memory. It is always sensible to take photographs of a space, and particularly of complex areas or details. Digital photography makes prolific record-making easy.

It is sensible to assume that a second surveying visit may be necessary to check discrepancies and correct omissions, and it is diplomatic to warn an occupant or owner of the building of this probability. It is better to make this sound like a regular procedure than to appear to be correcting oversights.

TIP MEASURING TOOLS

The bottom tape, typically made of canvas or flexible metal and 30 metres (150 feet) long, is used to take horizontal dimensions. The top tape, typically 3 metres (10 feet) long and more rigid, is used to measure small spaces and heights. The laser measure can also calculate areas and volumes.

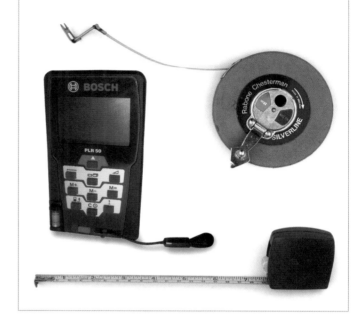

Case study The measured survey

Right
A notebook with initial freehand survey drawings. The drawing on the left page records dimensions of walls and diagonal measurements. The drawing on the right page records dimensions relating to a column and brick pier on the ground floor of the space.

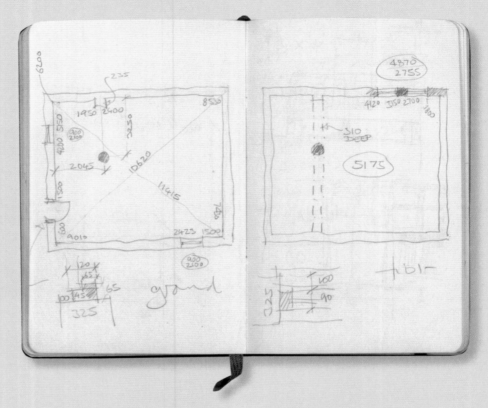

A freehand plan of the space is made in a small sketchbook. While it is good if this is proportionately accurate, it may be distorted to allow more space on the page where a number of dimensions need to be recorded in a small area. In this case, the drawing does not register the angles that emerge when it is redrawn to scale. Such discrepancies can be alarming when they first appear during scaled drawing in the studio and it may be necessary, for peace of mind, to return to the site for confirmation. If, however, the survey has been comprehensively done to allow cross-referencing dimensions one may be confident that the angles are accurate.

The 'running' dimensions for each wall are normally taken from the left-hand corner as one looks at the wall. When necessary, widths of individual elements along the wall may be calculated by subtracting the left-hand dimension from the right. The diagonals are measured. Heights are recorded in circles to distinguish them from horizontal dimensions. A few parts of the drawing are shaded for clarification, for example the windows on the top right and, for clear identification, the column in the middle of the floor.

The column position is established on the ground floor by the distance of its centre point, measured at right angles, from two walls. In this instance its diameter should be recorded and in the case of square or rectangular columns the length of sides. It is important to indicate that the measurement is made from the wall and not the face of the projecting brick pier. The depth of the pier's projection is not recorded. It may be that since it is a brick pier, and constructed in accordance with the module of brick sizes, it was assumed that the dimension would not need recording. It is, however, more likely to be an oversight needing to be checked later – particularly if the pier has a critical relationship to the proposed new construction.

The plan on the right records the location of high-level windows, overall dimensions of the walls having been determined by the data for the lower. The dotted-and-dashed line represents a beam overhead, and the note with it records its depth below the ceiling. A rigid wooden or metal calibrated measuring rod is the appropriate tool for making vertical measurements.

The two plans in the bottom left of each page record dimensions for the door and window openings. These elements are likely to be unaffected by the project work but their accurate depiction on the plans and sections will give credibility to later drawings and remind the designer about the depth of reveals, which may later play a part in decision-making about interior details.

There are projects, involving no new construction or where the location of new construction is already determined, for which the measurements may be anticipated accurately. In this example, on the right the few dimensions are enough to establish the position of an overhead beam towards the bottom of the drawing and the geometry of the window at the top.

When it is necessary to return to a site for additional information it will be very clear what this is and a few isolated dimensions will be enough. A return visit may not always be to take additional measurements but could be to confirm that the plan drawn from the original notes is accurate. With complicated surveys there are often ambiguities and apparent discrepancies that demand to be checked.

Right

The lower sketch records dimensions for a door frame, and because it is safe to assume that right angles would be cut very accurately for such an element, the dimensions shown are enough to establish the angle.

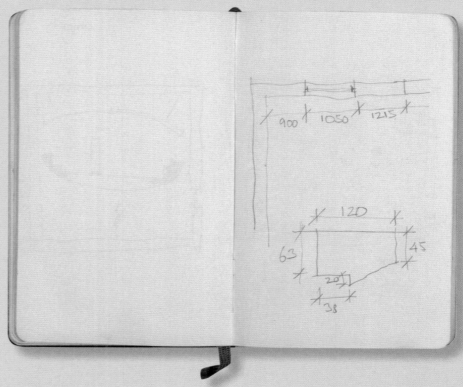

Right

A simple measurement sketch for a space where no new construction is needed.

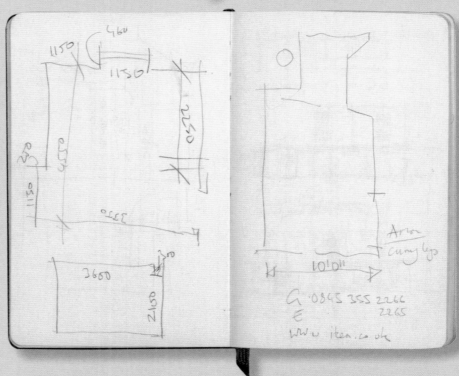

STEP BY STEP DRAWING A PLAN FROM SURVEY INFORMATION

When an accurate survey has been made of the existing building it is possible to begin the design process. The essential information about any project is communicated in a comprehensive set of plans. Plans are essentially horizontal slices nominally drawn at 1200mm (4 feet) above floor level, which means that they cut through most windows and therefore locate these crucial elements. A high-level window, with its sill above 1200mm, should be indicated with dotted and dashed lines, since its existence is likely to have a significant impact on design decisions. Dotted-and-dashed lines indicate the edges of high level elements. Dashed lines indicates the location of elements below floor level and therefore not visible. These should only be indicated when conveying information essential to understanding of the upper floor.

TIP SECTION LINES

The section line, which indicates the location of the cut, need not be drawn continuously across the plan because additional lines can complicate the reading of those representing built elements. It is sufficient to indicate its position on the edge of the plan, but arrows at each end of it must indicate the orientation of the section. These arrows are good examples of how personal taste may influence the graphic style of a drawing. They may take any form as long as they are unambiguous.

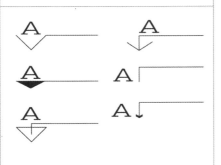

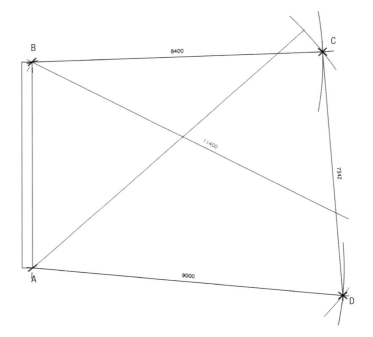

1 All lines are drawn to scale. The wall between corners A and B is drawn vertically, as an arbitrary starting point. The intersection of the arcs, which represent the length of the wall from B to C and the diagonal from A, locate corner C. The intersection of the arcs from C to D and A to D locate D. The whole may be checked by plotting the diagonal from B, which should intersect corner D. This is unlikely to be wholly precise, particularly if traditional hand-measuring techniques are used since the measuring process is subject to error and the computer will make a scrupulously accurate interpretation of the input data. Minor discrepancies are acceptable. Where precision is required, and this will become apparent when the design is developed, measurements may, and probably should, be checked on site.

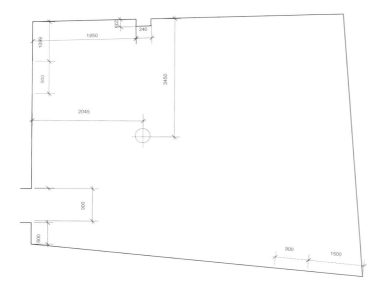

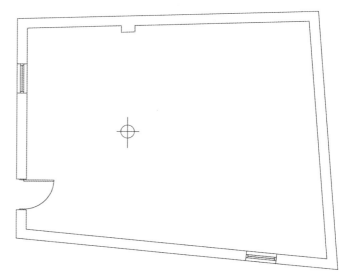

2 Dimensions from the survey notes locate the door, windows and column.

3 The drawing uses established drawing conventions for doors and windows. Minor variations may be made to these as long as they broadly retain their recognized configurations. Too much variation and the drawing will fail to communicate effectively.

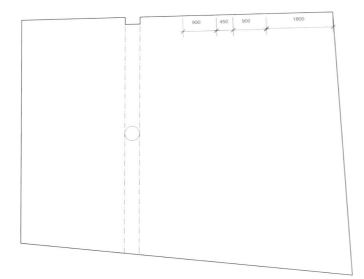

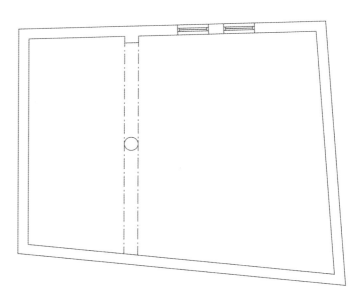

4 Surveyed dimensions locate high level windows. The position of the beam is determined by the pier that projects from the wall and the column.

5 The beam is indicated by a dotted and dashed line, which is the standard graphic convention for elements 1200mm (4 feet) above floor level, the height at which plans are conventionally drawn.

Graphic options

The essential information about any project is communicated in a comprehensive set of plans and sections. The number of plans is determined by the number of floors but the number of sections depends on the nature of the proposal. The section's function is to explain the interaction between levels, and so a decision must be made about the appropriate number and where each 'cut' may most effectively be made. The location of the cut determines how much useful information the drawing will yield, and it is important to indicate its position on plans with a 'section line'. The graphic interpretation of plans and sections is a matter of taste, and consideration should be given to their compatibility with the spirit of the project. Whatever that decision may be, when presenting new proposals, it is always sensible to distinguish new construction from old, by tone or colour, because this allows clients to see immediately the extent of the work envisaged. If no differentiation is made it is difficult for them to identify the new work, and their cautious assumption tends to be that it constitutes more than it actually does – which in turn suggests greater cost and may cause alarm.

Essential conventions

Plans are essentially horizontal sections nominally drawn at 1200mm (4 feet) above floor level, which means that they cut through most windows and therefore include these crucial elements. A high-level window should be indicated with dotted and dashed lines, since its existence is likely to have a significant impact on design decisions.

The drawings demonstrate standard conventions that

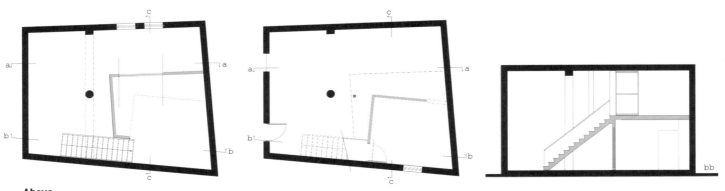

Above
In this sequence, two plans and a section use solid filled lines to indicate walls and existing elements, with new elements shown as lighter tones. The bottom section shows the standard way to draw stairs.

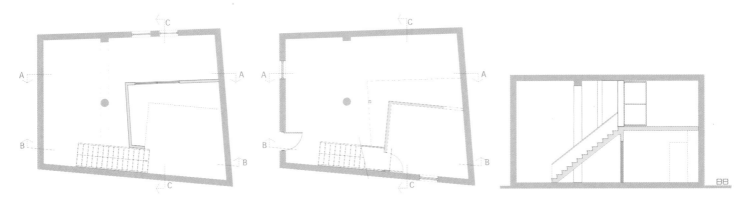

Above
In this sequence, existing walls are shown as a paler shaded grey, to allow the new elements, in yellow, to stand out.

are so fundamental that significant variation from them is counterproductive but, as long as coding is clear and the drawing easily understood, modest reinterpretation is acceptable. Plans represent proposed upper floor and lower floors. Sections are cut as indicated by the section lines.

It is worth noting the standard practice for drawing stairs: a stair, unless it is leading to a change of level less than 1200mm (4 feet) above the main floor, is inevitably cut through. The convention is that it be shown cut off, at an angle, approximately 1200mm (4 feet) above floor level. This allows some indication to be made of the construction below it. In the examples below, this shows a store entered from within the room in the lower right-hand corner. An arrow always points towards the top of stairs. On upper floors (on the left of each sequence) the entire stair is visible because it is below the level of the plan 'cut'.

Dotted-and-dashed lines indicate the edges of elements above the floor level. Dashed lines indicates the location of elements below a floor level and therefore not visible – these should only be indicated when conveying information essential to understanding of the upper floor.

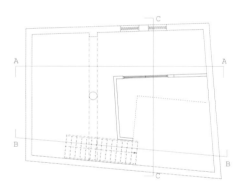
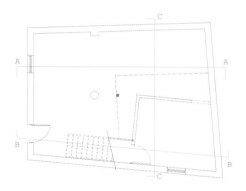
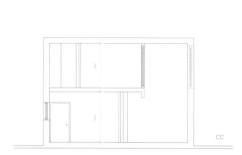

Above
The distinction between existing and new elements has been lessened in this sequence.

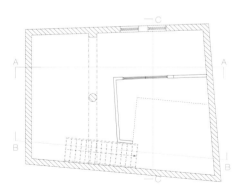
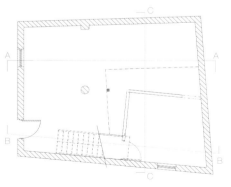
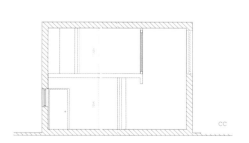

Above
In this sequence, existing elements are indicated by hatching.

STEP BY STEP MOVING TO THE THIRD DIMENSION

Once the plan and sectional information has been fed into the computer, it is simple to generate convincing three-dimensional views that can, in turn, provide a basic form to which colours, textures and lighting may be added.

There are a range of standard three-dimensional projections, all of which the computer produces with equal ease.

While it is still possible to conform to traditional axonometric and isometric forms, the computer offers a greater range of options and consequently invites experimentation, particularly with perspective. This facility with perspective produces images that are closer to reality and therefore easier for nonprofessionals to understand. There is, however, a danger that the temptation to distort perspective to produce a more dramatic image may confuse rather than clarify. The purpose of every drawing is to convey information clearly and not to be an end in itself.

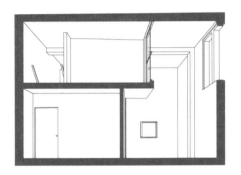

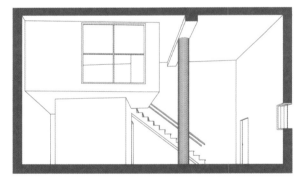

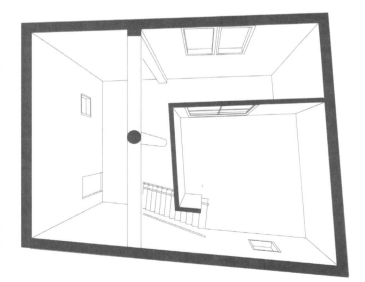

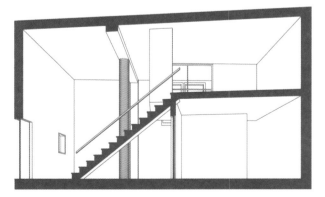

1 Plans may be projected upward in perspective, and this can make them more comprehensible. It is probably most effective for an interior on one level, in which all walls are visible.

2 With more than one floor level the conventional section, projected back in perspective, can sometimes explain the context of the section 'cut'.

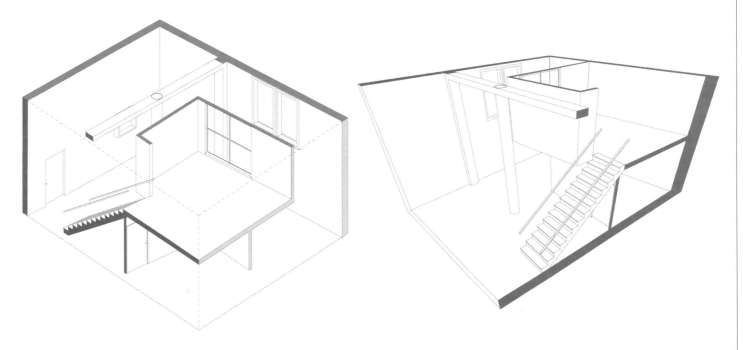

3 It is a matter of deciding which three-dimensional option works best for the project, and the computer allows options to be generated quickly and rotated on screen for consideration.

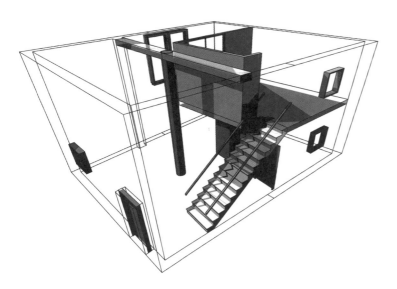

4 Further clarification of the three-dimensional may be achieved with the addition of tones and shadows, and the manner in which this is done again depends on the nature of the project.

Drawing by hand

Handmade drawings are normally made with either pen or pencil. The pen tends to be favoured when a more precise line is required, and this was particularly important in the days when dye-line printing, which produced a line that was soft and greyer than the original, was the most common method of reproducing drawings. The computer has now superseded the pen as the most effective means of making and reproducing precise drawings, in particular those providing technical information for building contractors. It is the more effective tool but, if drawings are any longer to be made by hand, it is perhaps logical that they should now be made in pencil because these have a quality that the computer cannot (yet) match and the significantly improved quality of photocopying equipment delivers a better line, which can also be adjusted in the copying process.

Hand-drawing tools

While there is no doubt that the computer has become the tool of choice and a necessity for large and small practices, there is no reason why hand drawing should not survive as an alternative, perhaps most viable for the slightly eccentric individual practitioner working on small-scale projects.

Freehand sketching provides an effective and immediate way to visualize concepts in the earliest stages of the design process, but to develop ideas it quickly becomes essential to work accurately to scale, to understand how plans and sections should be organized and to refine the interaction and relative proportions of new and existing elements. The tools and instruments illustrated on these pages, together with a drawing board with a T-square or parallel motion arm, ensure the necessary level of accuracy.

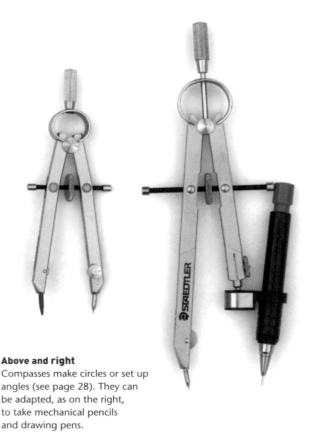

Above left
The wooden pencil remains viable but needs constant sharpening. More sophisticated, mechanical pencils offer consistent line width. Some, like that on the right, provide a thick heavy line for sketching. Others, like that on the left, offer precisely controlled line width and a choice of lead types.

Above right
Pens like that on the left use cartridges of dense, usually black, drawing ink and offer a choice of exact line thicknesses, which are useful in the articulation of drawing content. The thinnest nibs (0.1 and 0.13 mm) are vulnerable and expensive. Felt-tipped pens, like that on the right, come in a variety of line thicknesses but do not offer the same degree of precision, and, although cheaper, do not last long.

Above and right
Compasses make circles or set up angles (see page 28). They can be adapted, as on the right, to take mechanical pencils and drawing pens.

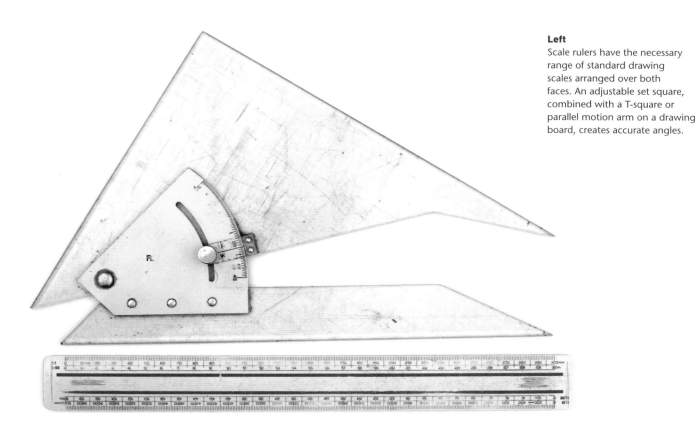

Left
Scale rulers have the necessary range of standard drawing scales arranged over both faces. An adjustable set square, combined with a T-square or parallel motion arm on a drawing board, creates accurate angles.

Below
Circle templates come with a comprehensive range of radii options and 'French curves' define more complex shapes. Stencils, for both pen and pencil, make clear lettering but are time-consuming.

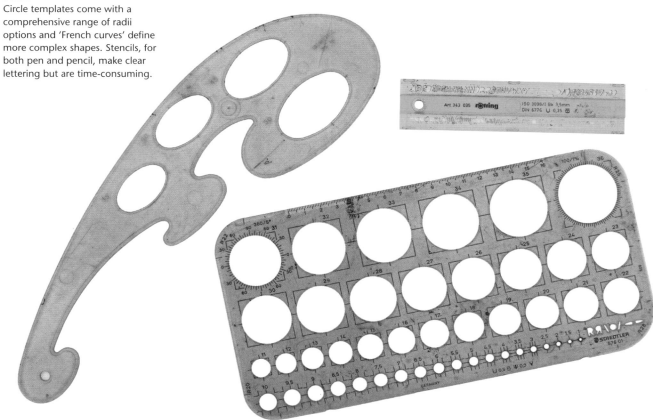

Above

A freehand 'perspective' can concentrate attention on its shortcomings rather than its content. It is better to make no pretense to perspectival accuracy and focus attention on content. If the parameters of the drawing are not formally established it is still possible to get a convincing approximation to perspective if all lines broadly conform to the principle of convergence to a shared vanishing point. A first drawing may be made and refined in a series of tracings, which if made quickly will retain a sense of spontaneity.

The first sketches

Handmade drawings may have been superseded by computer-generated images as the principle presentation tool but they retain their role as a first means of delineating and communicating ideas. Making such drawings does not require elaborate or sophisticated technique. In fact, too much reverence for the finished piece may result in time wasted in the refining of an image that has no value beyond the moment it delivers the information that is revealed in its making. However – since designers tend, by nature, to worry about the aesthetic merit of everything they do – it is difficult not to tinker with a drawing once it seems that it might have some merit in its own right, even though the act of refining it can divert the mind from consideration of its content. It is always difficult to know exactly when a drawing is completed and has no more insights to yield. Perhaps it is only when it appears to be complete as an artefact that it becomes clear that there is nothing to be gained from pursuing it further.

There is always a danger that if a drawing turns out particularly well it may cloud judgment about the quality of the idea it illustrates. It is difficult not to feel some loyalty towards something that embodies style and skill, but it is worth bearing in mind that any drawings made in the development of a project are liable to, and generally should, end in the waste-paper bin.

It is not surprising that it is difficult to find examples of simple, utilitarian developmental drawings. Those that are available are untypical, simply because they had particular significance or because they were particularly well made and their maker could not quite find the resolve to throw them away.

TIP HAND DRAWN LINES

Avoid broken 'artistic' lines. Isolated and inadvertent line variation, as on the left, will appear as a drafting error. Controlled variation, as on the right, will absorb errors in a more deliberate 'freehand' effect. The concentration needed to control the variation will help keep the line straight.

It is important to be able to draw a convincing freehand approximation to a right angle. This is not difficult with some practice, and it easy to make a credible approximation to 45 and 30 degrees by subdivision of the 90. Where accuracy is particularly important, or where the shapes to be defined are complex, lines and angles may be drawn first, lightly and precisely, with technical instruments and then overdrawn freehand.

Accurate proportions can be guaranteed by accurate measurements, and a measured drawing does not have to be technically constructed. The same rules used to construct a technical drawing may be followed to make a freehand version, and a freehand line can be drawn to scale.

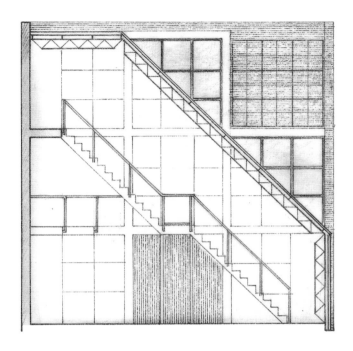

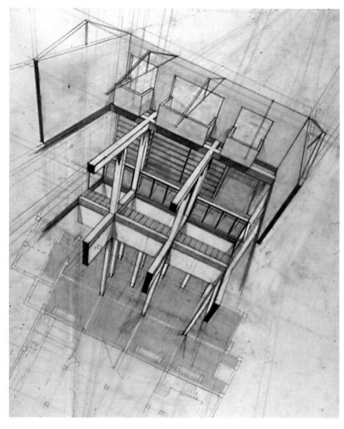

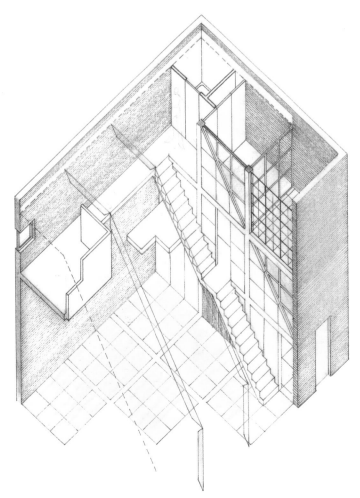

Above left and left
These pen drawings use varying thicknesses of line, hatching and adhesive tone for additional articulation. Lines have the constant density of ink.

Above
The pencil drawing has a richer patina. The plan and the construction lines used to set up the section and perspective have been retained, and the smudging that is inevitable in a complex pencil drawing contributes to the background texture. Weight applied to the pencil point provides variation in line quality and articulation of content.

The best way to make good drawings by hand is simply to make a lot of them, spontaneously, quickly, until it becomes something done almost without thinking. The intention is not to create a perfect set piece or a scrupulous observation of an existing object. There are no subtleties of light and shade to be captured. The thing to be drawn exists only in the imagination, and it is the serial act of trying to draw it that helps define its nature with ever increasing clarity.

The first drawings are likely to be crude, diagrammatic plans showing the subdivision of area and furniture layouts or simple perspective views with little indication of detail. These will become more detailed and precise as the design process progresses and as the designer gets increasingly clear insights into possibilities and limitations. It is important in every project that two- and three-dimensional drawings complement each other throughout development. The plans and sections allow the feasibility of the ideas expressed in the perspective views to be checked. Ultimately, the viability of any proposal depends on its relationship to the shell of the existing building in which it is to be located. In most cases the designer's ability to manipulate intricately the dimensions dictated by function in the context of the existing plan is key to success.

If a drawing is to be effective, its content should be credible but not necessarily precise. There are essential fundamentals and these should be aspired to and, if met, should ensure a convincing outcome.

Proportions and perspective should be accurate and plausible. Representation of light and shade should be kept

Above
This concise description of the curves that soften the lines of a stair is convincing because, although rudimentary, it has been made by someone who understands the mechanics of the stair, the proportional relationship of tread to riser and the essential structure. It does not solve the problems generated by those practicalities, but sets out aesthetic priorities.

Right
A very early, nearly abstract, exploratory drawing that holds meaning only for its maker.

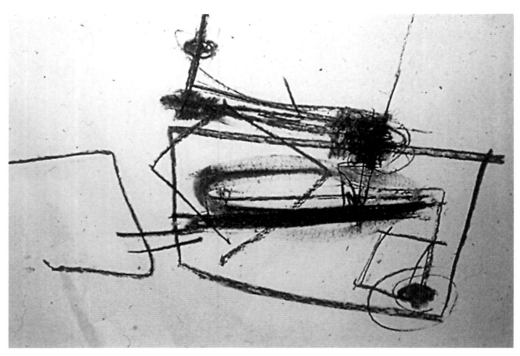

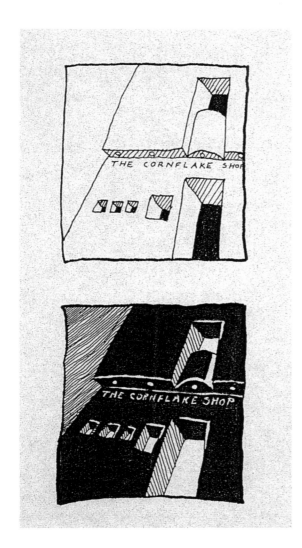

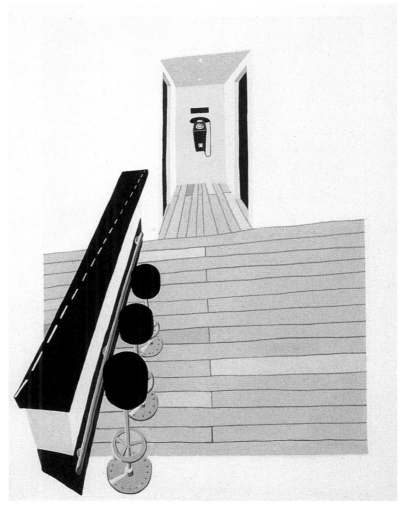

simple, used to define volumes with clarity. Wall tone will differ on either side of a corner because each will receive a different light, but the tone on each will be spread evenly – not in impressionistic textured blotches. The edges of shadows should be sharp. Each drawing should have one consistent light source so that the convention used to articulate form is easily understood. If the play of light and shade becomes too complicated the point of the drawing is likely to be lost in an incoherence of graphic effects.

There are two ways to make a freehand perspective look convincing. The first is to make the perspective so 'wrong' that it may be assumed to have no pretensions to follow the rules but this must be done with enough panache to confirm that it is deliberate. Alternatively, it should be near enough to being accurate to have credibility, and for this the proportions of the space drawn need to be accurate.

Above left
The same internal elevation by day and by night conveys information effectively because it is simple and precise.

Above
This very carefully composed image pays enough attention to perspective to be credible, but is more concerned to represent the detail of the simple elements that make up the interior.

STEP BY STEP MAKING A SIMPLE FREEHAND PERSPECTIVE

Establishing correct proportions is relatively easy. If the back wall of the space is drawn in elevation then, even when freehand, it can be made to scale for accurate proportions, and the image established using the principles of single-point perspective.

In perspectives drawn without measuring the tendency will be to overestimate the length of side walls, and this may be acceptable when the perspective is distorted to allow clearer representation of elements within the space. There comes a point when it is preferable to move away from a credible perspective to something more diagrammatic. In 'true' perspective, elements tend to be superimposed one on the other and the information may be communicated more clearly if they are separated out. If the 'distortion'

is handled positively, and clearly makes no attempt to suggest a true perspective, it will appear acceptable.

The same principles will convincingly set up volumes within the space and may be applied to the location of every element. However, there will come a point when there is no need for this degree of precision and further drawing may be made relative to the reference points provided by the first plotted locations. In fact, it is probably undesirable if too much deliberation is employed because the drawing will lose the charm of the freehand sketch. The same construction principles apply if technical drawing equipment is used for extra precision and straight lines.

Estimating the lengths of side walls

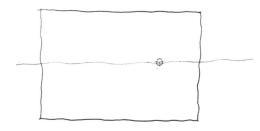

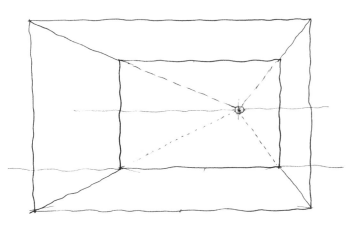

1 The back wall of the view is drawn freehand but to scale. A 'vanishing point' is established on the wall, generally at a height of 1500mm (5 feet) which corresponds to an average standing eye level. The height can be varied to dramatise or clarify the view.

2 Side walls are drawn, from the vanishing point through the corners of the back wall (all lines share a vanishing point). The length of side walls is determined by intelligent guess work. The tendency is to overestimate their length.

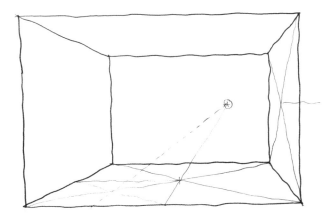

3 The centre point of walls, floor and ceiling will be at the crossing point of their diagonals. Further diagonal subdivision of the resulting quadrants, and if necessary further diagonal subdivsion will give accurate positions for corners of walls and locations of other elements.

4 All vertical elements are vertical in perspective and heights can be drawn accurately by scaling the height on the back wall and projecting from the vanishing point.

Plotting the lengths of side walls

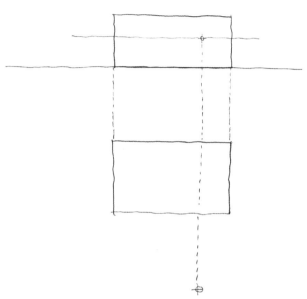

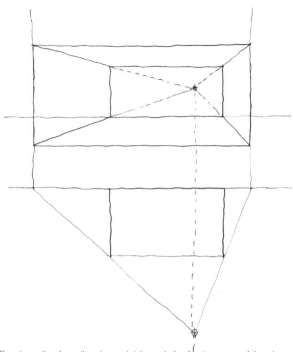

1 The plan and elevation of the back wall are drawn, to the same scale. A vanishing point is established on the elevation and a 'view point' on plan. Again preliminary experiment will establish the most productive position for both.

2 Drawing a line from the view point through the front corners of the plan until they intersect with the projection of the line of the back wall, which is called the 'picture plane', will set up the front edges of the walls.

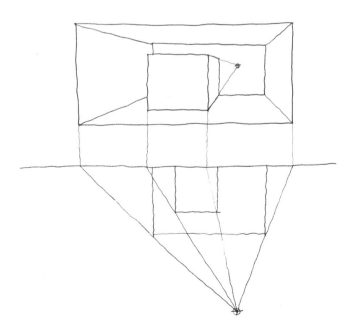

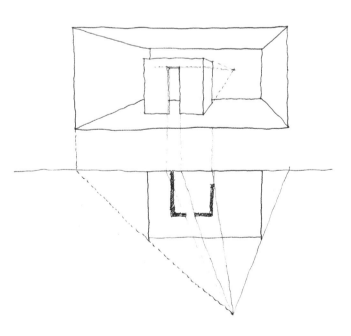

3 A solid within the room can be sized and located using the principles set out in the previous step. Its height can be established by plotting it, to scale, on the back wall and projecting a line from the vanishing point to intersect the verticals.

4 Elements, like openings and distance of the object from the rear wall can be established using the principles set out in the previous step.

Axonometric and isometric projections

While perspective drawings rely on lines converging to a shared vanishing point axonometric and isometric drawings rely on parallel lines and are therefore easier to set up without, or without instruments. An axonometric or isometric drawing, which relies on parallel lines, avoids this and is extremely easy to draw with or without instruments. Both are in effect formalized views of an interior from above, without roof or ceiling and have the advantage over a conventional perspective view of revealing at least a portion of all spaces within a compartmentalized interior.

The principles for constructing both projections are simple. Plans are drawn at angles, the axonometric at 45 degrees to the horizontal, as a true plan. An isometric is made with the two walls nearest to the viewer at 30 degrees to the horizontal, which results in distortion of the plan but opens the spaces up more in the final drawing. In both projections, vertical lines are drawn to the same scale as the plan. While neither method creates a true perspective, both give a convincing sense of three dimensions. The shallower angles of the isometric are considered to give a more realistic image. The results may be treated as diagrams or rendered to give a more realistic impression of finishes and lighting. The axonometric is easier to draw by hand because the plan remains a true rectangle and circular forms on plan remain perfect circles although circles in elevation become elliptical. The simple geometry and the consequential simplicity of drawing it make it useful as structure for making quick three-dimensional drawings, whether for one's own enlightenment or for making spontaneous sketches for clients, contractors or consultants. In isometrics circular forms become elliptical in both plan and elevation.

The computer deals equally easily with both but most users prefer to use the isometric because of its more realistic image or, since the computer is as comfortable making perspectives as it is with axonometrics or isometrics users also set up overhead views in perspective. When making a freehand axonometric or isometric it is important to concentrate on establishing one corner that conforms credibly to the fundamental principle, of the angle of the front corner between plan and the horizontal.. After those few lines are established, it is easy to follow the same rules to complete the whole. It is not difficult to judge angles and relative dimensions by eye if one concentrates and critically assesses the drawing as it takes shape. If an area is unsatisfactory it is easy to retrace over the flawed original and correct its shortcomings.

TIP DRAWING CIRCLES

Both axonometric and isometric circles are constructed by drawing a circle or ellipse, as appropriate, so that the line touches the mid point of the sides of the circle or parallelogram that would contain it.

In axonometric the circle on plan sits within a square.

In axonometric, elevation and, in isometric, plan and elevation, the circle sits within a parallelogram.

Axonometric

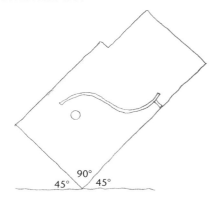

1 The plan is drawn at 45 degrees to the horizontal. Vertical and horizontal lengths should be drawn to the same scale if measured and, if freehand, as close as possible to a shared scale.

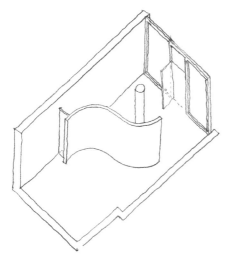

2 Walls are projected vertically and thicknesses may be added. If working freehand it is useful to set up a faint technically drawn floor grid, which may later be erased.

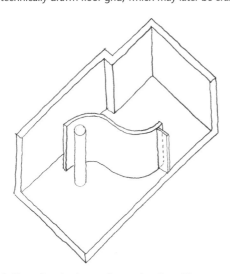

3 Since the plan is not distorted wall positions match those on the true plan and need only be projected vertically to their true-to-scale height.

Isometric

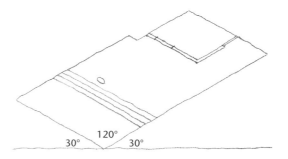

1 The near walls of the plan are drawn at 30 degrees to the horizontal. Vertical and horizontal lengths are drawn to the same scale if measured and, if freehand, judged as close as possible to a shared scale.

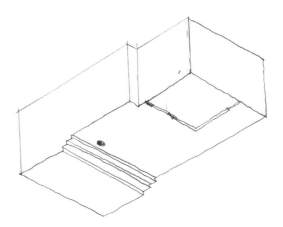

2 Walls are projected vertically and thicknesses added. If working freehand it is useful to set up a faint technically drawn floor grid, which may later be erased.

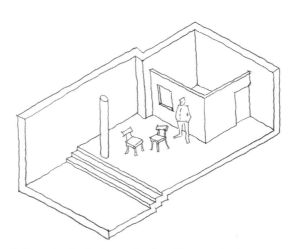

3 Since the plan is distorted wall positions need to be reconfigured to suit the splayed plan, vertical lines need only be projected to their true-to-scale height.

Overlays

When making design drawings by hand, a tracing of the existing building shell is particularly useful, precisely setting out the constraints within which the new interior must work. New elements drawn freehand will, given the restraints and guidelines set out the original drawing, be accurate enough, and significant measurements for new elements, such as the dimensions of rooms, width of doors and sizes of furniture can be checked with a scale rule. Such elements, which have a broadly standardized and recognizable size, give insight into the reality and feasibility of the proposed spaces. If measurements are not checked, there is a counter-productive tendency to be optimistic about sizes and lose track of the realities of restricted spaces.

Frequently, when an early proposal is drawn to scale, whether by hand or computer, shortcomings become obvious and rethinking is necessary, the rejected scaled drawing can be used as the underlay for a return to freehand sketching. Fresh exploratory drawings can be made quickly, and thinking once again expressed with a spontaneity that allows new ideas to flow and build momentum. The slower pace of making accurate mechanical drawings creates time for attention and the imagination to wander.

Whether considering a project for the first time or trying to reorientate thinking to solve an emerging problem, there is some virtue in repeatedly redrawing wall thicknesses and the locations of windows and doors for each new sketch because each reiteration reinforces awareness of the nature of the existing building. An interior contained within thick stone walls will suggest different interventions from one within less substantial construction.

When making overlays, tracing paper offers complete transparency. Detailing paper, which is thin and white, offers something which is less transparent, but through which the dark lines of an underlay will show. The semi-transparency of detail paper makes it easier to colour. Choice of material is, as always, a personal matter, but to reject a degree of transparency in favour of the more familiar texture of cartridge or another wholly opaque paper necessitates making a fresh, scaled drawing of the existing building shell for each new drawing. The grids of graph paper, available in different sizes representing different scales, offer an alternative measuring system, which is particularly useful when considering an element in isolation, when the context of the whole building shell is superfluous.

Below
A quickly traced section, in which new elements are identified by coloured felt tip pens.

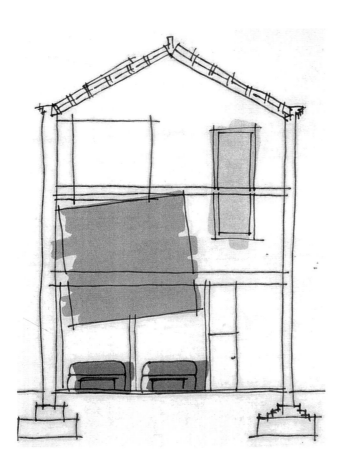

TIP DIMENSIONS IN FREEHAND DRAWINGS

A facility for mental arithmetic is useful when making freehand drawings. When the dimensions of rooms and wall thicknesses are known it is reassuring to check practicalities, such as circulation spaces, mathematically, even though the drawing itself may not be precise. A working knowledge of standard furniture dimensions provides useful visual indicators of relative scale. In this example circulation around and behind the curved desk looks restricted and suggests that the seat below the window should be flipped horizontally to create space.

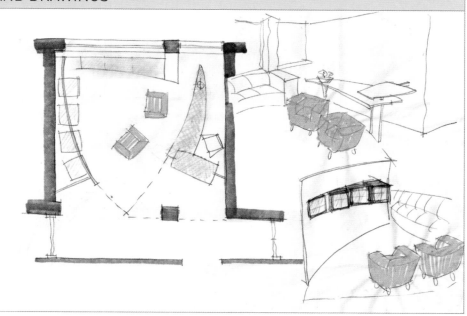

Below

This very ordered internal elevation may have been prompted by the decision to draw on graph paper – or may have influenced the same decision after the nature of the solution had emerged. Whatever the sequence, the grid makes the location and sizing of elements simpler.

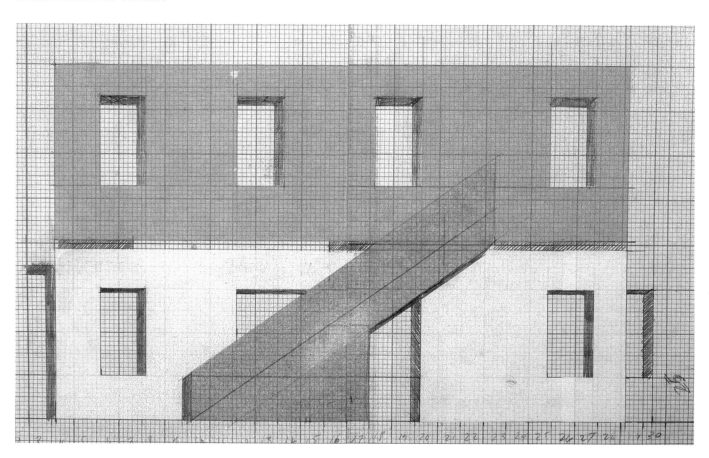

Freehand drawing for presentation

Freehand drawings can be useful for initial presentations, particularly during early discussions when it is more important to get insight into a client's preferences than to secure definitive approvals.

It is, however, seldom a good idea to confront a client with a collection of crude diagrams on scraps of paper, and it is unlikely that any preliminary sketches will stand scrutiny as serious presentation material. The inevitable weaker sections will undermine strong areas of drawing. By contrast, the computer may be initially slower but it tends to guarantee an acceptable outcome and, when essential dimensional information has been fed in, will quickly produce a battery of appropriate two- and three dimensional images.

While more polished versions of early drawings are preferable for presentation purposes, it is also desirable that the final version retains some of the flourishes and energy of the developmental sketches. Unsatisfactory freehand images, typically the result of deficiencies in perspective and proportion, may be corrected by

tracing again over the last version of the drawing and eliminating weaknesses. Areas that work may be retained. However, to sustain graphic consistency it is a good idea to retrace all the lines quickly to achieve a vigorous line that suggests creativity and to avoid an image that appears to aspire to precision and might have been made more effectively with technical instruments.

The photocopier and the computer scanner also allow the size of an image to be adjusted. Changes in size frequently seem to improve the quality of a freehand image and are also a useful way to suggest that a number of disparate sketches, when printed to a similar size, comprise a set. A reduction in size gives a density of drawing that may be missing in the original, and inflating the size reveals line textures, particularly when the original is made with a soft pencil, that will not necessarily be apparent in the original.

It is not usually good practice to draw large in the first instance. A large drawing will generally invite or require more detail and inevitably take, and therefore waste, more

Above
This apparently simple drawing nevertheless convinces because it is made vigorously – and the perspective is credible. The delineation of the seating makes it obvious that the designer has specific examples in mind. The representation of the glass table's transparency is particularly effective. The suggestion of panel joints on the curved form indicates that thinking is being shaped by an awareness of construction.

Right
A few of the pencil lines that initially set up this gouache sketch remain visible, but most are lost under the vigorously applied paint. The concern is more with describing atmosphere than detail, which is only hinted at in representations of furniture. The energy of the image was enough to persuade a sceptical client to commit to the project.

time. Credible perspective in particular is much more difficult to sustain in a large drawing. For most designers it is more physically comfortable to draw at a small scale, perhaps within the confines of an A5 or A6 page, but individual preference should determine sizes and media.

There is one category of drawing at which the hand excels, and that is the diagram. Interior design projects are very frequently complex and it is good practice to introduce clients to them in a series of steps, which make the salient points clearly and sequentially. These can be made using computer-generated views, but a too-simple computer image tends to be less effective. Like every other drawing tool it is most effective when its strengths are exploited, and the computer's strength is the generation of complex form and subtle rendering. Complex images do not necessarily make good diagrams. The handmade diagram that deals only with a single, crucial idea can exactly explain principles and intentions.

TIP PRESENTING SKETCHES

Presentation sheets are usually composites of a number of different drawings and, particularly with freehand drawing, it is difficult to place individual drawings together on a single sheet and next to impossible to sustain a compatible quality across the group. It is seldom satisfactory to present scraps of tracing paper to a client, and mounting them on card is a rather grandiose way to present modest scribbles. It is better to photocopy them, adjusting size as appropriate and to present them singly as, say, A4 sheets. This retains an appropriate informality. If it is considered worth presenting a number together, to make a sequential explanation, individual drawings may be arranged and copied on to a single sheet. Computer scanning is superior to photocopying in that it reproduces more accurately the quality of line, tone and texture.

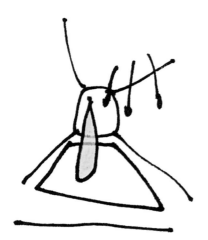

Above
An elemental diagram identifies crucial components in the strategy for the redesign of a space.

Right
Traced plans, in which the problem area is identified on the left by the hatched lines, and the proposed solution is shown in red on the right.

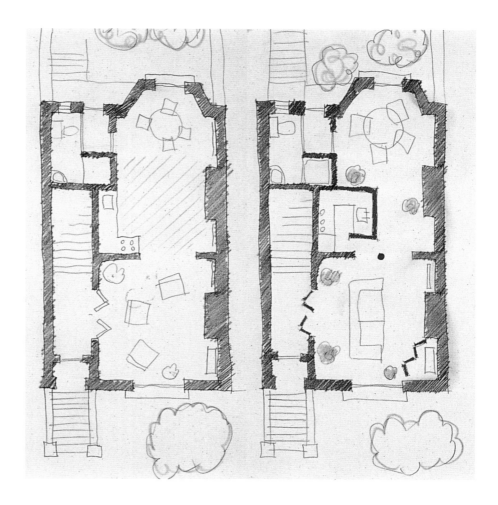

Collage

The majority of interior projects do not require elaborate manipulation of floor levels and walls, and while those that do may be superficially more spectacular, they are not necessarily more successful than those relying on the comparatively modest devices of carefully selected materials, colours and lighting effects. All these are notoriously difficult and time-consuming to represent by hand, and, early in the design process collage offers an alternative to the computer. Those who favour the technique build a stock of colours and textures, usually clipped from magazines that have been identified as reliable sources. Such images, however roughly pasted together, can, if confidently assembled, take on some of the characteristics and authority of the well-crafted object. Source materials may be scanned by computer

Far left and left
While a line drawing defines planes, it does not easily convey three-dimensional form. Collaged papers in different colours and tones, roughly cut to the shape of the proposed element, give a sense of solidity. The monochromatic version on the far right, created on computer, concentrates on form.

TIP COLOURED TISSUE

It is always difficult to represent flat masses of colour in any hand made drawing. Tissue papers provide blocks of colour, albeit limited in range, that indicate different wall and floor finishes. The tissues are applied to the back of the tracing paper, which filters the intensity of their colours. They are cut or torn roughly to shape and lightly sprayed with fixative in order to position them no more permanently than is required to survive the copying process. Since they have a degree of transparency it is possible, once they are fixed, to cut them with a scalpel to match exactly the outlines of planes.

and manipulated to take greater account of perspective and scale. With their deliberate lack of dimensional and perspectival precision, it will be clear that they intend to offer only an impression of the proposed interior.

Obviously, in collage-work the representation of colours is dictated by the limited range of papers and images available. However, if a handmade drawing is scanned on computer, then blocks of colour and texture may be matched accurately and further refinements – like representation of transparency, reflectivity and light – may also be added. Increasingly, it makes sense to resort to the computer, which copies and pastes more efficiently.

Collages, once cut and pasted, can be improved if photocopied to make a flat, integrated image. Digital scanning offers superior copying quality and the image created can be manipulated further on the computer.

Below
A quick line drawing on tracing paper is given solidity by collaged blocks of textured colour. The freehand drawing works particularly well because of the convincing perspective of both sets of curved steps.

Right
In this drawing on tracing paper, a black ink line roughly defines the space. The collaged photographs of pink stools give credibility to the more roughly presented elements. The sketched stools are finished with coloured pencils on the front of the tracing paper, which avoids damaging the tissue papers that provide the background colours of walls and floor.

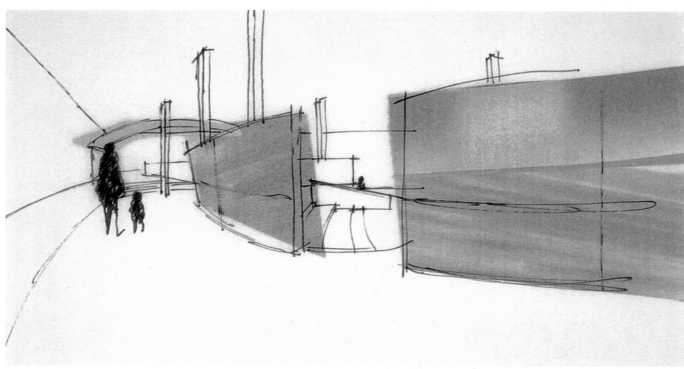

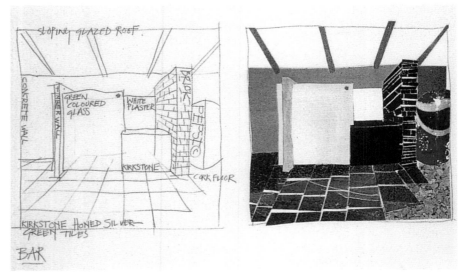

Above
A photocopy of crumpled white paper provides a random pattern that suggests marble.

Above
While precision in a collage may be difficult, ambiguities can be eliminated if the collaged image is paired with a line drawing that also provides a key to the materials proposed.

Left
A traditional cut-and-pasted collage was scanned and the colour tones were adjusted in the computer to get closer to the designer's intentions.

Opposite
This image uses the principles of collage but was achieved solely with scanner and computer. The green and grey receding planes were created purely as a computer image, but the yellow-and-black image on the left and the column on the right were scanned and digitally pasted. The figures were downloaded from an image website and pasted – or collaged – in, but adjusted for varying degrees of transparency.

Case study Hand drawn presentations

Below
Hand drawn sketches, such as this section, allow a degree of graphic flamboyance.

Opposite
In this composite drawing a plan is drawn on tracing paper. Underneath this layer red tissue paper indicates solid walls, and blue tissue paper indicates water on a location plan.

Technical drawings made by hand, particularly using a pencil, are comparable in accuracy to those made on a computer but they have a very different patina. Hand drawn lines are softer and will be slightly blurred as T-squares and set squares slide across them as the drawing progresses. In the section on the left the sky is achieved by rubbing pastel dust into the reverse side of tracing paper using a soft cloth or tissue paper. The ground is made with felt tip pen and the red of the brick with pastel. Colours and tone are varied in intensity to suggest changing light and textures. Denser colours, like the blue water, are made with coloured pencils, crosshatched and rubbed with a finger to eliminate directional lines. The finished product has character but is a one-off and, unlike a computer-made alternative, cannot be adapted or easily amended.

Some adjustment and development is possible during the making, however. Working with tracing paper allows drawings to be built up in layers and individual elements to be combined for a more complex presentation. In the plans on the right, a strip of blue paper, first fixed to a white base sheet, represents the sea and highlights the edge of the coastal site, represented by a fragment of map. The tracing paper with the red-walled building, drawn to one side, is fixed over the other layers. The whole may be shown within a transparent sleeve or photocopied to produce a single sheet. There will be some blurring – of the bottom image in particular – because of varying thicknesses within the composite sheet but if this is conveying less detailed information, the distortion is acceptable.

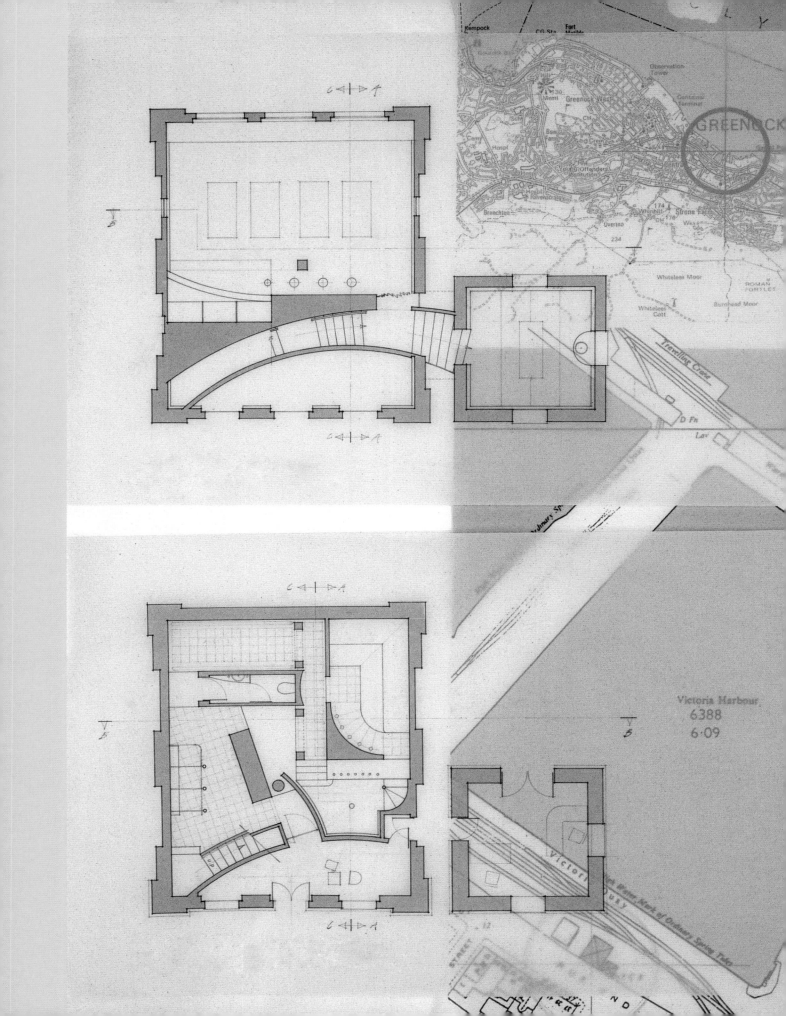

Victoria Harbour
6388
6·09

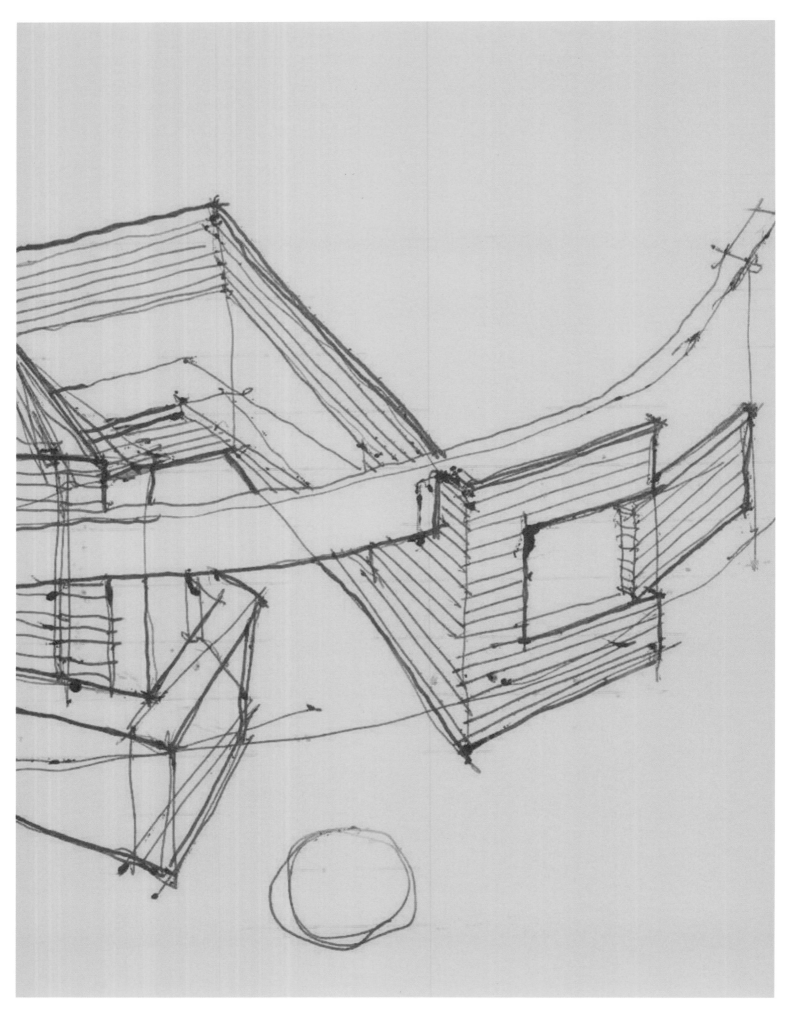

CHAPTER 2 CONCEPTION

Exploratory drawings

Every project begins with an idea, which must be defined and refined. That first idea is little more than an informed presumption, made with limited understanding of either the precise requirements of the brief or the quirks of the building shell, and is unlikely to survive intact to the end of the development process. The more ambitious the concept, the more difficult it will be to resolve – and the more time resolution will take.

The first drawings for any project may be no more than thoughts about a strategy for organizing the given space to accommodate its new function: a suggestion of where new walls might be located, or how furniture could be arranged. Alternatively, they might attempt to describe an atmosphere, perhaps in words or in a collage of evocative found images. First drawings should, in fact, be whatever they have to be to do their job: to record ideas, to examine them and to communicate them to others. They are likely to be very simple, perhaps no more than diagrams. They may well be – and perhaps are liable to be – quick, handmade scribbles, although, as computer software becomes easier and quicker to use and as designers emerge who are more adept at employing it, first images may increasingly emerge from the computer.

Such exploratory drawings tend to be esoteric because they are for the designer's own information and are made without too much concern for their aesthetic merit. Nevertheless, they provide the reference point that will orientate and reorientate thinking throughout detailed development, and are therefore particularly important when a team of designers is collaborating on a project. Most members of such a team will not be involved in the project's conception, and all will have not only different responsibilities but also different degrees of responsibility and will need to understand and share a common objective – which can be encapsulated in those early drawings.

While the first drawing may be the significant reference point, the intention it represents will develop as understanding of the project evolves. In fact, however clear and powerful a first idea may appear to be it ought to evolve. The longer one works on a project the more closely one becomes aware of the complexities of the interaction between requirements of the brief and the realities of the existing building shell. Early diagrams will, and indeed should, change. In fact, it should be a matter of concern if no changes suggest themselves. Every designer must be aware of the dangers of complacency or, as is more often the case, a stubborn commitment to sustaining a seductive first idea at the expense of practical priorities.

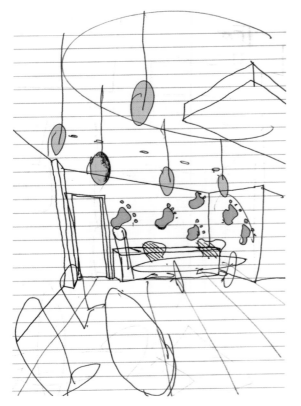

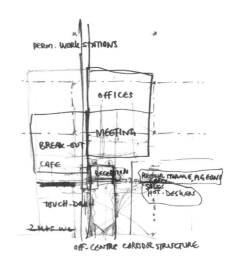

Left
A very early sketch, made with coloured felt-tip pens in a lined note pad, captures the essence of an idea to be refined and tuned to the specifics of the brief. The 'foot' motif is obviously the starting point and subsequent detail – the shape of the light fittings and foreground chairs – is sympathetic to it. Other elements – the curve on the ceiling, the parallel lines on the floor – indicate that ideas about massing and finishes are already taking shape. The recess that contains the desk and the projecting section of wall beside the door indicate awareness of the physical realities of the space.

Above right
An early attempt to define strategic planning: the dotted and dashed lines indicate the structural grid and column locations showing awareness even at this stage of practical imperatives.

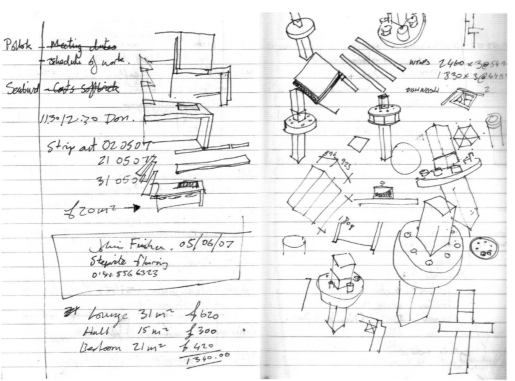

This page
Pages from a notebook
illustrate how ideas persist
and are explored obsessively
throughout the design process.

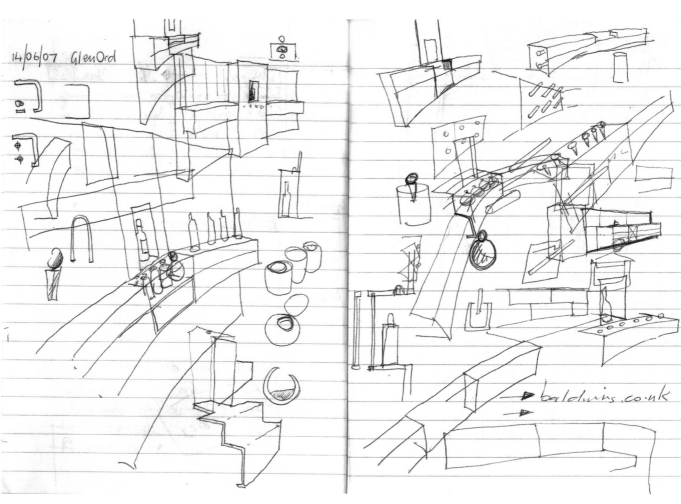

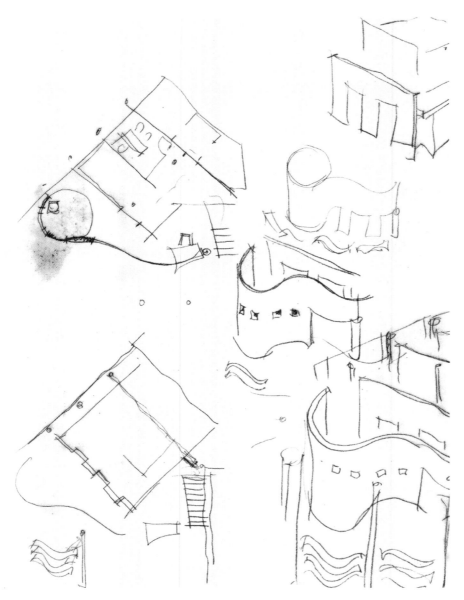

TIP WORKING TO SCALE

Every successful interior evolves in a search for a satisfactory balance of intuition and objectivity.

First ideas spring from consideration of a brief and its context and even when they are little more than an intuitive hunch, a designer will want to make them tangible and first expressions of this starting point and initial investigations of its viability are usually quick freehand sketches which begin to establish the physical shape that the untested proposition may take. As they sketch designers also begin to understand better, not only what they should do but what they can do. A good designer does not force an inappropriate concept but rather identifies how the requirements of the brief and the nature of the existing building can be reconciled so that each enhances the other. This understanding can only be properly achieved when details of both are dealt with precisely and, inevitably, this requires more controlled, scaled drawings, using conventions that allow the interaction of new and existing elements to be accurately plotted in two dimensions. While these drawings may deal with prosaic practicalities, they also allow fine-tuning of proportions. They may be made traditionally, by hand on a drawing board, or, as is now the norm, on computer. The latter also eases the conversion of data accumulated in plan and section to a rendered three-dimensional form.

Above
The ground- and first-floor plans on the left were made as overlays on the existing plan but the only evidence of the original building is in the circular columns that determine practical locations for new walls. The sketches on the right speculate about the extrusion of the plan. They are drawn from above to emphasize the relationship between plans and elevations.

Right
This sketchbook drawing records early speculation about how new elements might interact with the existing building. The bottom of the sketch explains how the footprint of the stair will be excavated from the existing concrete floor, and the drawing makes clear that the concrete treads will be supported on a delicate metal structure and that the 'excavation' will remain exposed.

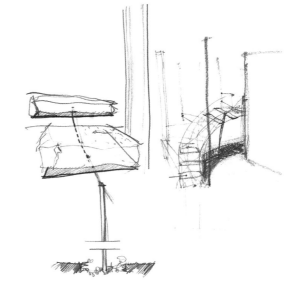

Left
Another quick sketch, made with pastels on white paper, showing clear thinking about how the elements – steps, small recesses and spotlights – will work together. Colour used in the drawing is determined by available pastels, so can only suggest the final hue.

Right
This computer-generated image remains quite abstract, and was made to distil the designer's ideas about form and materials but not intended to communicate very much to anyone else.

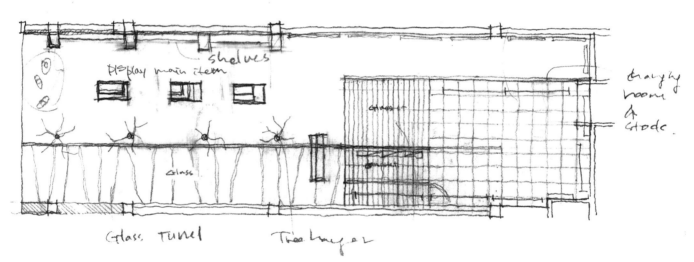

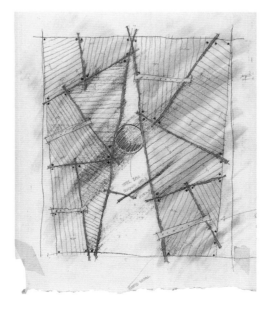

Above
One of a series of overlays of an existing plan of the building shell, made with pencil on tracing paper. The significant elements in the existing structure, particularly the columns projecting from the side walls, are indicated so that decisions about the location of new elements are made in response to them. Floor pattern identifies the mezzanine area, but while the whole is drawn comprehensively there is little attempt to make it comprehensible for anyone other than the designer. Notes are scribbled and meant to serve as aides-mémoires rather than sources of information. The drawing is not refined and might be enough to serve for preliminary discussions but is more likely to end up in the wastebasket.

Left
This drawing – pencil and pastels on tracing paper – describes clearly the timber and glass panels that will be used to make a façade and hints at the methods by which they may be assembled (nails and bolts). It suggests obvious questions about structural stability and the mechanics of the door, and in so doing points to the next step in the development of the project

The plan

A designer will normally begin to develop a concept by sketching and refining the plan. The images, on the opposite page, made by hand on sheets of A4 tracing paper give some idea of the progression of thoughts and the drawings which prompt and record them. Even when making the most rudimentary initial sketches, the dimensions and proportions of the building shell must be acknowledged.

Dimensions and proportions

Design drawing is really observational drawing but the subject exists only in the designer's imagination and it is easy for it to become unrealistic and for impossible ambitions to take over. Objective understanding of the realities of the existing space will give direction and discipline to decision making. Almost all interior-design projects require the insertion of the maximum possible accommodation into a space that was originally designed to contain some other function, and unstructured drawing can encourage counterproductive optimism. A solution conceived for a space assumed to be higher, wider and longer, or lower, thinner and shorter than it is in reality will not adapt readily or without debilitating compromise.

Getting the proportions of freehand sketches, whether two or three dimensional, correct requires no more than self-critical concentration. Freehand drawings may be used late in designing plans if they are (roughly) scaled and, if existing elements are located (fairly) accurately, they will provide constant reference points for the positioning of new features.

The earliest conceptual sketches are likely to be three-dimensional images, but once a strategy has been defined its development must be resolved in the two dimensions of plan and section. Ideas about form, materiality and atmosphere need to be precisely plotted, and that requires precisely scaled drawings.

The mind needs to be focused on the job of designing and it is good to allow momentum to build, so that one drawing follows the other with a minimum of interruption – no longer than it takes to place another sheet of transparent paper over the base drawing – so that thoughts flow effortlessly to and from each other. When an idea is being hotly pursued, drawings will flow spontaneously one from the other. However, sometimes it is important to slow the tempo to make time in which to marshal thoughts. Then it may be productive to draw the plan of the existing building again to refocus attention on its particularities, its wall thicknesses, its window sizes and door positions – and to test the relationship of new elements to the old.

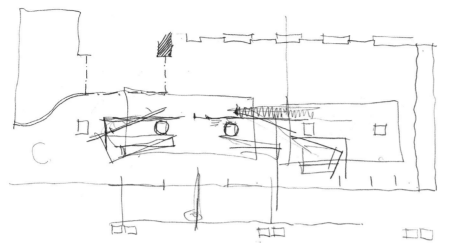

Left

In this overlay of the plan of an existing foyer space, the columns and walls are minimally indicated because the detail of the original plan was visible through the tracing paper. The existing balcony above is indicated using the established convention of a dotted-and-dashed line, and its supporting structures – the curved and the shaded walls – are drawn with a little more detail because they were initially considered crucial to the development of the project. Indication of the new elements is perfunctory because there is, as yet, no clear idea of their form.

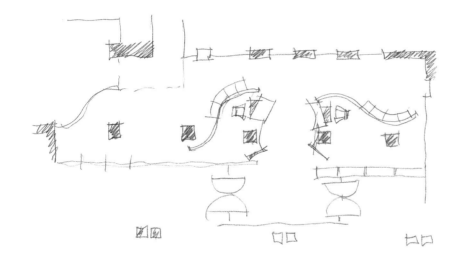

Middle left

The drawing remains rough and loose but the addition of furniture, and the more precise thinking about how new curved walls will relate to it, indicate more detailed thinking.

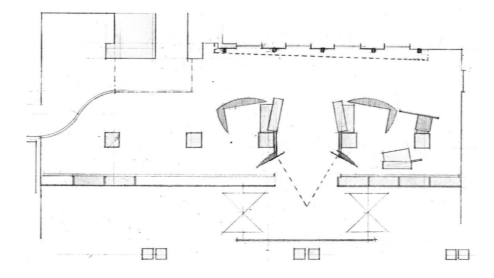

Left

In this later drawing, the existing building shell is traced accurately and the new elements placed precisely within it, to test their relationship one to the other. The drawing is made by hand, using drawing board, parallel motion and set square.

The section

The hand drawn section

The switch from loose freehand to precise scaled drawings is as vital for the development of a section as it is for a plan. As for a plan, drawings, however perfunctory, will record decisions made in the progression of a project, enable retrospective analysis and provide material for an examination of where momentum or direction has been lost.

While the ambiguity of the freehand drawing leaves room for creative interpretation, the precision of computer-generated images can also prompt fresh thinking. The hard facts of the first computer-generated plans and sections may be converted spontaneously into rudimentary three-dimensional expressions of the anticipated space, and these, in turn, may be explored further by rotating them in the virtual space of the monitor screen so that unanticipated possibilities may be glimpsed in the previously unexplored detail of the proposal, which the designer may consider with a degree of objectivity that is often lost to those drawing by hand who tend to have more emotional involvement with the drawing and are necessarily less self-critical about an idea that has already been anticipated and understood in their imagination.

The hand made drawings on this page show the development of the internal elevations for a cinema project and were created with pencil, pastels and coloured pencils on tracing paper.

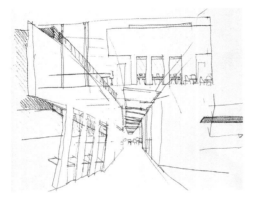

Left
Two- and three-dimensional considerations of how internal walls may elevate, and how areas may be physically and visually connected.

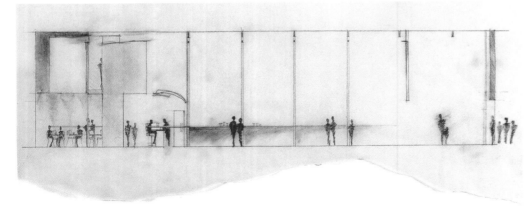

Left
The first (roughly) measured elevation of an internal wall. Ancillary or, as yet, unresolved elements are drawn freehand and figures are added for scale.

Left
As the designer's vision of the project becomes more detailed the drawing becomes more evocative of the possible end result. Ideas about lighting and materials are beginning to crystallize. Definitive decisions may be made.

The computer generated section

The digitally generated section, as an exploratory and decision making device, tends to be more definitive at all stages of project development than the hand drawn equivalent, because drawing by computer requires the input of more precise information in the first instance and produces, from that data, a primarily linear description of the proposal, which is factual rather than atmospheric.

The image on screen evolves as ideas evolve. The first delineation of planes can progress, with amendments and additions, into a final render, heavy with detail and unless the designer makes a decision to save or print it at a particular time in its evolution, there will be no evidence of the stages, critical or inconsequential, of its progression.

Once working with computer a designer's impulse will also tend towards converting the information accumulated in section and plan to produce, a three dimensional version of the proposal at a much earlier stage of the development process than with hand drawing, because what was hitherto a time consuming manual activity requires no more than a keyboard command.

One may argue that the protracted labour involved in making hand drawings leaves time for reflection and reconsideration or one may argue that the capacity of the computer to describe ideas in three dimensions necessarily offers more opportunities for appraisal. There is merit in both points of view but both require a designer to remain objective and see beyond the seductive image.

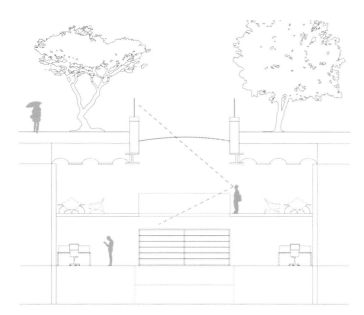

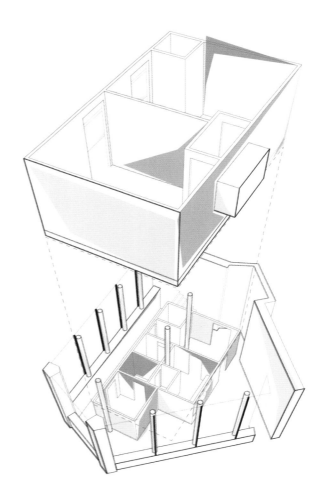

Above
A section sets out with restrained precision the visual connections between different levels and the rooflight. The figures, here selected and pasted from the designer's own reserve, give scale, as did those hand drawn in the previous example.

Right
It is simple to convert a plan and section into three dimensions and, in this example, consider the relationship between levels of the new elements and their relationship to the existing building shell.

Case study Evolving the idea by hand

Right
Information is edited to the minimum to concentrate attention on the essential subdivision of the existing building shell. Dimensional accuracy is not as important as clarity of information.

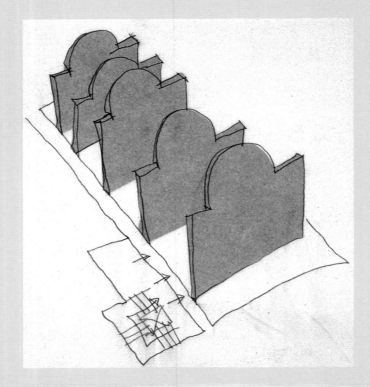

Below right
The precise relationship between the new and existing elements can only be effectively established with a drawing made to scale. Traditional instruments will produce an acceptable level of accurate detail.

Often the significant development of projects is initiated and resolved through handmade drawings. While the transition to computer for final presentation and production drawing is now almost inevitable, the point at which the transition is made depends largely on personal preference. In this example the designer, trained in conventional techniques and with a particularly strong drafting style, chose to exploit those strengths for an initial client presentation.

To develop the idea she had to work precisely, to understand the potential, and limitations, of the existing building, in particular the problem of how to relate the new multi-levelled structure to the vaulted ceiling and the rooflight within it. While a plan will determine the size of rooms and the circulation between them, it is the section that most effectively explores the potential of a dramatic volume – and identifies the peripheral and residual spaces where more utilitarian activities such as bathrooms and storage may be accommodated. Brown tissue paper fixed to the reverse side of the transparent tracing paper is used to define significant planes.

It is common practice to draw all or parts of a project to increasingly larger scales, to allow

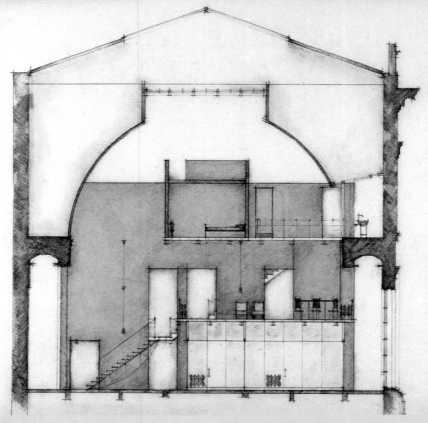

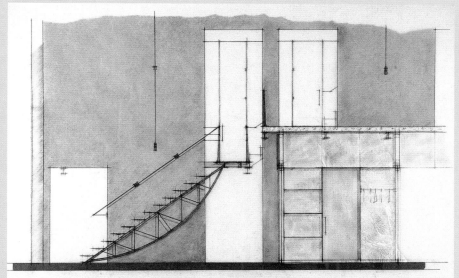

Above
This larger, scaled area of the elevation allows more detailed examination of the smaller elements: light fittings, handrail fixings, even door handles.

Below
Another three-dimensional diagrammatic sketch helps clarify the relationship of the three levels and the stairs that connect them. It is again simplified for clarity.

closer scrutiny of aspects of the design and to identify the areas where thought must be given to construction techniques. Often, as in this case, there will be few substantial changes, but drawing to a larger scale can point to areas that are potentially awkward to resolve visually and allow speculation about detail. Even if such larger scale drawing were not to result in any changes, which is unlikely, drawing and re-drawing would still be an important part of the design process because the repetitive act obliges a designer to reflect again on ideas evolved at the smaller scale.

While designers working on a project may understand very clearly the three-dimensional implications of their own plans and sections, it is less apparent to clients, and frequently to other designers. It therefore makes sense to produce freehand three-dimensional sketches that clarify the interrelationships. It is important to make sure, particularly in a domestic project, that clients understand exactly what is being discussed and its implications. Generally, as in the first diagram in this sequence, simplification of image is important for clarity.

It should also be acknowledged that making looser drawings, like the three-dimensional images, has a productively therapeutic effect on the designer. They offer relief from making detailed technical images that demand the simultaneous consideration and reconciliation of aesthetic and practical priorities, and a more disciplined and labour intensive drawing technique. They may also occasionally identify potential physical clashes between elements that were previously unsuspected in two dimensions. Most designers will quickly scribble three-dimensional views, for their own enlightenment, in the course of making plans and sections and these may, occasionally, be upgraded for presentation purpose. This habitual introspective scribbling is a useful way of maintaining a freehand drawing skill that can be useful when it is necessary to produce spontaneously an explanatory sketch in response to a client's question. Such ad hoc drawing may be the last hand drawing activity to be superseded by the computer and, if it is done well, it will always impress a client – or a colleague.

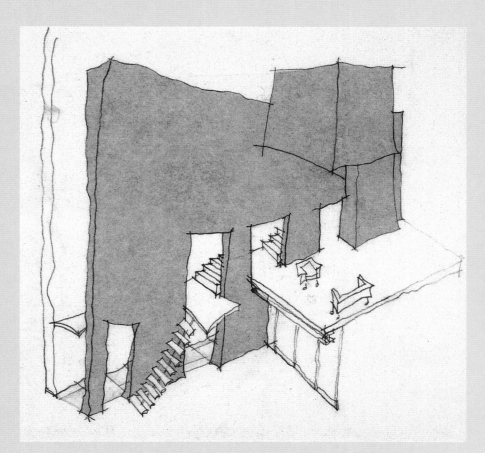

STEP BY STEP EVOLVING THE IDEA BY HAND/COMPUTER

When creating an interior within a conventional rectangular plan, it is often feasible to work on computer from the outset. However, if the proposal is three-dimensionally complex then it is more usual to record first moves in rough sketches that will establish viable starting points for the production of more complex and precise computer images.

This project is for the insertion of a complex multi-level interior, to sit within the shell of an existing building and to break through its roof. First a perfunctory diagram is created, which has no need to represent the existing plan and section in any detail. The second sketch, overlaid on a section of the original building, investigates the relationship of new levels to the existing section and, from that, a definitive section and its interaction with the original is established on computer. The computer's capacity to deal with curved lines is particularly useful for establishing a precise form. With the information contained in section, and plan, it is easy to generate the two three-dimensional images, one showing the new structure in isolation and one showing its relationship to the existing building. Both remain diagrammatic to an extent, with heightened shadows and the glazed cladding shown without indication of support or fixing, but the fundamental problems have been identified and solved. More detailed resolution can follow.

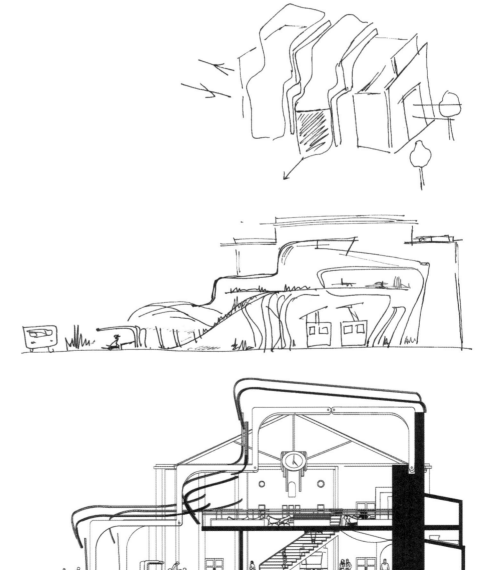

1 A spontaneous expression of the first idea, showing the cascading form set between the end elevations of the existing building but with no indication of its materiality. Arrows draw attention to a revised circulation strategy.

2 Freehand lines, overlaid for accuracy on a section of the existing building, begin to define the relationship of new to old. Hints of figures and equipment indicate that consideration of function is beginning to influence decision making and that the designer is remembering that the way in which users experience the building should not be sacrificed to the dramatic gesture.

3 A much more considered and resolved computer generated version of the section clearly sets out levels and new and existing structures but is most valuable as a definition of the geometry of new glazed cladding and the structure that supports it. The form rather than the transparency of the glazing is given precedence but the nature of the structure, its profiles and joints are clearly identified.

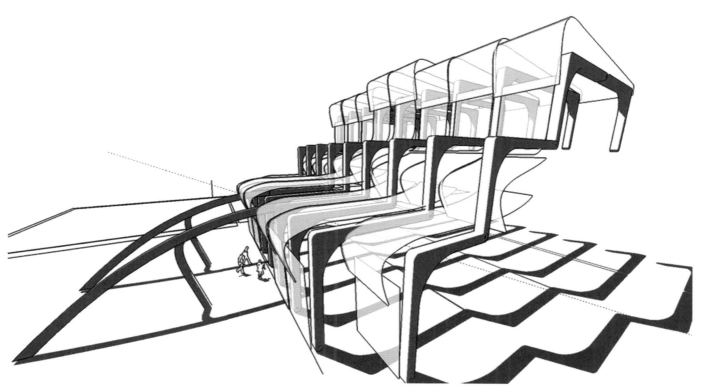

4 A computer-generated perspective clarifies the principles of the relationship
between the new structure and the overlapping glazing elements.

5 The contrast between solid structure and transparent cladding and the relationship
of both to existing gables is more clearly explained

STEP BY STEP EVOLVING THE IDEA BY COMPUTER

It must still be conceded that in the earliest stages of the design process one is likely to make quick freehand sketches, and for some designers – particularly those educated to use traditional techniques – this is, and will remain, true and they will adamantly defend their position, with a vigour that might suggest they may suspect that their argument is a shaky one. For those who have used computers from the beginning of their training, and as an integral part of their practice and daily lives, it has become as easy to 'doodle' and 'sketch' on screen as on a drawing board. It remains a matter of personal preference, but there are significant advantages to working digitally.

Once basic information has been fed into the computer, it becomes simple to generate outputs quickly and convincingly in two and three dimensions. The accuracy and clarity of the finished image ensure that, in contrast to freehand sketches, there is much less room for misinterpretation during discussion with colleagues, consultants and clients.

1 An early, diagram of an elevation suggests the idea of a ribbon stretching over a floor and up a wall.

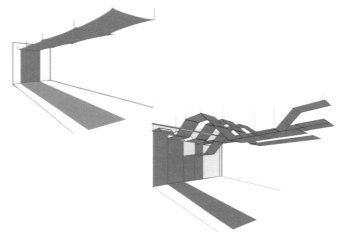

2 The idea of a continuous, undulating ribbon is developed in three dimensions.

3 Walls, furniture and figures are added to establish context and describe how the area might work.

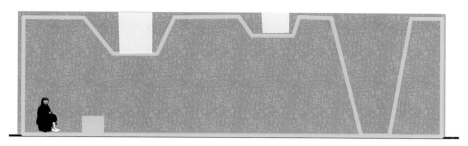

4 A first section, which relates profile to overhead structure, provides information from which all subsequent drawings are generated. The figure establishes scale.

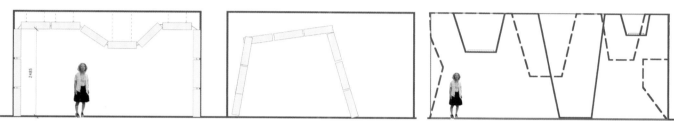

5 The basic form remains consistent, but inflated components replace the original fabric.

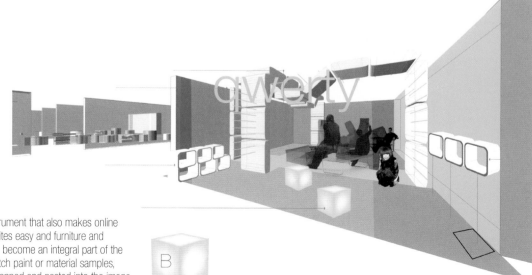

6 Sections extruded into three dimensions begin to explain spatial possibilities.

7 The computer is a drawing instrument that also makes online access to manufacturers' websites easy and furniture and finishes may be downloaded to become an integral part of the design process. Colours, to match paint or material samples, furniture and figures may be scanned and pasted into the image.

Detailed thinking

As a project progresses, a designer inevitably becomes increasingly concerned with detail. From the very beginning there will, or should, have been thoughts about materials and colour. Experienced designers will have evolved an instinct that prompts them to consider materials and appropriate construction techniques as they are making the most rudimentary first sketches. These ideas are very likely to change but they represent a first step towards the resolution of a project.

The most cherished drawings in any project are likely to be the earliest. They will have the purest expression of the purest idea and may, superficially, appear to be the most creative. However, it is in the later, more considered, detailed drawings that the crucial creative work is done. Such drawings may appear dry, but they contain more hard information about the real nature of the project for those who know how to read them and it is often in consideration of detail that designers are forced into unfamiliar territory where habitual solutions must be abandoned and something new is added to their repertoire.

A designer must learn to recognize the moment at which the means of investigating and progressing ideas must become more disciplined and it is often difficult to make the shift from the excitement of the first, comparatively unstructured, outpouring of ideas,

Right
Detailed ideas about materials and form will often emerge clearly in early drawings that are superficially concerned with an expression of atmosphere. Here lines made on tracing paper with a thin black felt-tip pen and thicker coloured felt-tips, express materials and surface qualities. The linear application of the coloured pens suggests floorboards and the hang of curtains. The grey tinting, particularly on the bar front and top suggests reflections on hard, shiny surfaces. The delineation of the bar is just enough to indicate how it operates Critical decisions are, necessarily, taking shape in the designer's imagination.

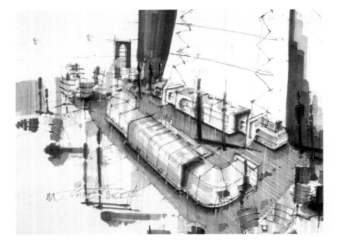

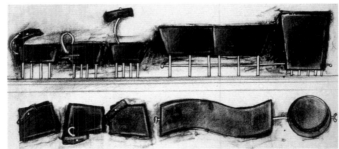

Left
Leather-covered furniture for a reception area was comparatively easy to draw both in plan and elevation. Technically constructed lines were loosely over-drawn in pencil. The dense semi-matt black of the leather-and-chrome structure was rendered with oil pastels, and overshooting of edges integrated the image into the paper.

Right
This sketch set out to create light fittings in a cafe and, while considering the context for these, the designer began to speculate about crockery and cutlery. It is very unlikely that such peripheral drawing will have a tangible outcome but, whether productive or not, such speculation will consolidate a richer understanding of the potential of the interior.

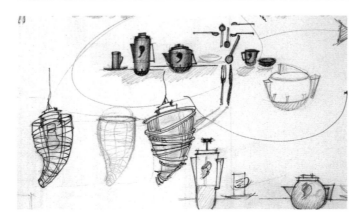

when things move with an exhilarating momentum, regularly hinting at exciting possibilities, to the more considered scaled drawings which offer fewer options and identify more practical problems. Such reconsideration will inevitably happen at a slower pace because it requires objectivity, and changes are likely to impact on every other decision made up to that point. Usually such problems, however great their potential effect on the overall concept, will be small-scaled, a matter of reconciling a misalignment or an inadequate dimension, but their solution will take a disproportionate length of time and without their satisfactory solution the project will not achieve the honed perfection to which any decent designer should aspire.

Often, solutions necessitate changes in materials and methods of construction with a knock-on effect that takes time to assimilate into the whole, and generally the work necessary to create and refine any project will fill more than the time nominally available. The identification of a solution and examination of its impact on the rest of the project will require a comprehensive collection of precise and detailed drawing. These may be freehand but even freehand lines in two-dimensional drawings may be sufficiently accurate if traced over a technically made scaled original or if line lengths are checked with a scale rule. Tracing over a gridded backing sheet also provides a regular module as a base reference. In three-dimensional drawings attention should be paid to proportion and this will ensure that the image is realistic enough to support decision making.

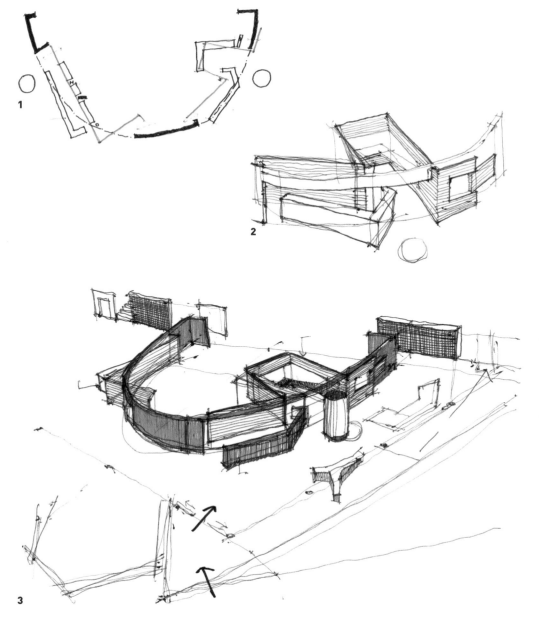

Left
The resolution of complex three-dimensional conditions requires particular attention, if a satisfactory balance is to be found between aesthetic ambition and practical obligations. Consideration of how elements should interact will influence, or be influenced by, the choice of materials. These drawings show a few of the freehand plans and perspective views made in such a process.

1 The plan is traced from an existing drawing. Elements are coded for clarity to define changes in levels and materials.

2 A first 3D sketch looks in more detail at the relationship between angled and curved walls. The existing round column is shown on plan, to remind the designer of its existence without its interfering with the view of the new elements.

3 A more substantial sketch explains the further evolution of curved and angled walls. Existing columns, peripheral walls and entrance point put the proposal in its wider context.

Case study Detail emerges

Two sketches, prepared for a preliminary client meeting, introduce strategies for circulation within a shopping mall. They recognize that all participants in the meeting will not necessarily be comfortable with two-dimensional technical drawings. Their informality confirms that the project remains at a formative stage and their cartoonish quality encourages relaxed discussion. However, the accomplished and confident handling of line and perspective lends the proposal credibility and its designer the authority to lead the meeting. The first drawing assists understanding of the crucial ideas, and ensures that everyone can contribute confidently to discussions. The second provides another layer of information.

Designers developing ideas do not require highly resolved images. As they evolve their drawings, they are inevitably considering the nature of the surfaces they propose, and areas – apparently 'blank' to anyone else – will trigger the appropriate association in their mind's eye. They will 'see' colour and materials in their black-and-white drawings. Freehand drawings such as these need not be big. Size can be adjusted with a colour photocopier or a scanner. Reduction will often lessen the impact of a weak area, while an increase in size can reveal enjoyable graphic incidents that are by-products of the media used.

Top left
Elements are reduced to essentials: the lift shaft is indicated but with a minimum of detail, 'customers' give scale, and those on the upper level explain how floors interact.

Left
Stylized figures again indicate scale and the figure with the pram leaving the lift gives reassurance that practicalities have not been neglected. Greater attention to detail is signaled by floor and ceiling patterns, cladding panel joints and light fittings at and between joints.

Case study Detail evolves

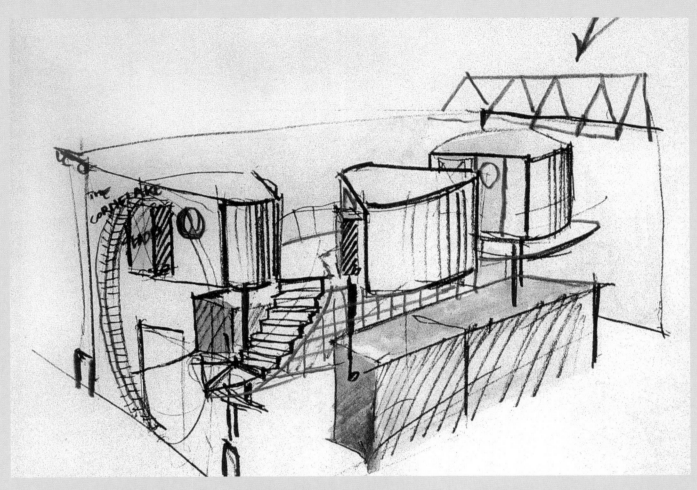

These drawings, made with pencil and coloured felt-tip pens on tracing paper, chart the three-dimensional evolution of how freestanding elements at an upper level would interact and be accessed. The obvious speed with which they were made, in an attempt to keep pace with, record and give shape to the thoughts that raced through the designer's imagination, convincingly demonstrates how thinking and drawing are symbiotic, the one feeding and driving the other as ideas merge spontaneously. The designer obviously draws with skill and authority but, at this stage, quality of drawing is secondary to the generation and examination of ideas.

The rough outline of the external walls defines the interior space and the two light sources – the circular window and the triangular roof light at the rear – are indicated. In the first drawing the form of the 'cabins', the walkway that connects

them and a distinctive stair structure begins to emerge. The geometry of the stair landing is the crucial element in the second drawing. The remainder of the stair is represented more precisely and there is a suggestion that the designer is also beginning to think about details of doors, windows and finishes to the 'cabins'.

Above
An exploration of how the raised elements sit within the rectangle of the existing shell, with the circular window to the street and the triangular rooflight indicated as aides memoires.

Right
A more detailed perception of the geometry of the stair establishes that the step incorporated into the landing is important to define how the stair flights mirror each other and can sit within the corner of the existing building.

'Sketching' by computer

There is an assumption that sketching is only done by hand, and that it remains the quintessence of 'artistic' creativity. Such a perception confuses technique with quality, and ignores the fact that drawings made on computer can have the values – and even the ambiguities – of a handmade sketch. It is possible to make 'freehand' drawings with a computer using a digital pen, a mouse or a finger on a laptop keypad and these options, like any other drawing medium, determine both the way the hand moves across the drawing surface and the quality of the line made. While the experience of making the drawing is comparatively close to that of using a conventional pen or pencil, there is a fluidity of line that is the product of a digital stylus not being directly in contact with the 'paper'. There is also a uniformity of line quality which it is almost impossible – and probably not desirable – to achieve in a handmade drawing.

Below
'Freehand' sketch made on a computer – giving a uniformity of line not found in handmade drawings but with the spontaneity of a handmade image.

Right
In this speculation about an enclosed volume within a stairwell, the immediate context – a stair below, a bridge, a glazed wall and the brown blob of an enclosure – are all delineated and rendered in convincing perspective. The retention of 'hidden lines' replicates some of the ambiguities of a handmade sketch, but the digital image may also be rotated and scrutinized from various angles and heights onscreen.

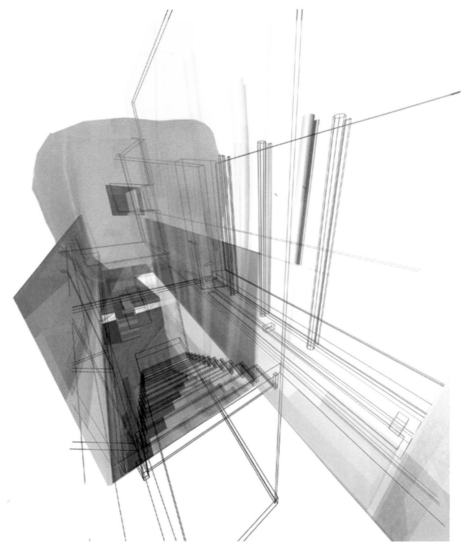

Composites

Handmade and computer-generated images can coexist very successfully if each plays to its strengths. The skilled hand will give a relaxed and simple line, focusing of necessity on representing broad essentials, but is unlikely to deal convincingly with perspective and the representation of materials and lighting. The computer's output, although having great potential for the accurate representation of complex form, materiality and lighting, is likely to appear bland at the same early stage in the evolution of a project when those qualities are unlikely to have been convincingly evolved. The strengths of the two techniques may, however, be combined most persuasively.

The computer translates two-dimensional information in plan and section into three-dimensional images more accurately, and significantly faster, than can be done by hand. The initial image it produces will be exact, but is also likely to be bland. The further refinement of that image by the addition of colour, materials and light using the computer will take time – particularly at an early stage in a project when definitive decisions that would justify fine-tuning have not yet been made.

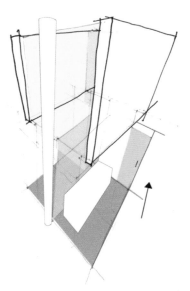

Above
The lines of the two-storey space are precisely sketched by computer, and blocks of tone and colour represent opaque floor planes and transparent glazing. The crossing and extending of computer generated lines gives them some of the informality of the traditional sketch, underpinned by the heavier freehand line, which also emphasizes the contrast between rough walls and pristine glass.

Above
The computer sets up the perspective which is then drawn over by hand, to enrich the thin lines of the original. Blocks of colour are added in the computer to the new scanned image.

Right
In the computer, it is simple to add colour, here graded to suggest three-dimensionality, to a scanned hand-drawn sketch.

TIP COMPOSITES

A computer creates the complex three-dimensional structure. The secondary content, the hanging garments that give it identity and explain its function, are suggested less powerfully with a substantial hand-drawn line that does not interfere with the strong expression of the primary form but shares its weight and directness.

'Base' drawings, created on computer, provide members of a team with an accurate perspective template, over which they may draw as individuals or as a team. When adjusting line weights for emphasis precision may be maintained by the use of ruler, circle templates and French curves.

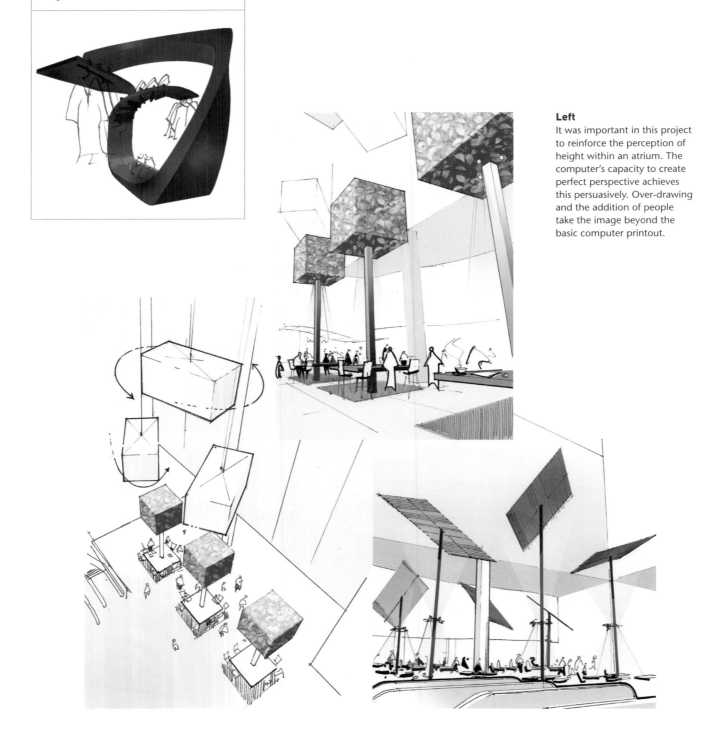

Left
It was important in this project to reinforce the perception of height within an atrium. The computer's capacity to create perfect perspective achieves this persuasively. Over-drawing and the addition of people take the image beyond the basic computer printout.

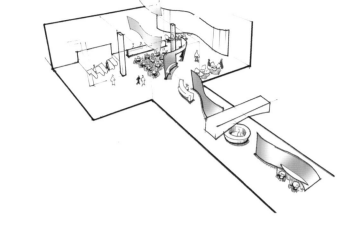

Top left
The computer sets up the complex three-dimensional elements, but lines are drawn over for variety and colours are added by hand. Stylized hand-drawn figures explain function and scale.

Left and below
These drawings, good enough for first presentations to clients, retain some of the character of the handmade image. The essential preliminary delineation by computer, including the scanning and pasting of advertising images, allowed a number of designers to add to the basic drawing without their individual freehand styles becoming discordant. The larger figures were traced from photographs to ensure convincing body language.

CHAPTER 3 PRESENTATION

Presentation to clients and others

Presentation images are made to persuade the client, and sometimes others, of the desirability and credibility of a proposal. Approval is also often necessary from the statutory bodies responsible for giving formal, legal permission. If this is refused at the first attempt, there is little opportunity to appeal against verdicts or to make adjustments because the timescale for interior projects is usually short. Planners will be primarily interested in street frontages, but they will, along with conservation bodies, also want to know about changes to protected historical interiors. A client will often rent premises, and the building's owners will want to approve proposed alterations and although their conditions are seldom onerous, they will be mandatory. Interiors within multi-occupancy developments will normally have to comply with conditions that apply to all leaseholders.

For most projects, however, the crucial approval is that of the client, who can make tangible ideas that otherwise only exist in a designer's imagination. A good designer should to be able to find a way of meeting a

Below and opposite
Two drawings from a set of 14, both showing different areas within a shopping development, focus client attention on the distinctive elements of each and provide comprehensive material for detailed discussion.

client's practical needs and aesthetic aspirations, however antipathetic they may at first appear. Presentations should take into account the knowledge, preconceptions and prejudices of those for whom they are intended. Some will be impressed by the 'artistic' quality of drawings, while others will be reassured by evidence of technological expertise. They all ought to be able to understand everything to which they are being asked to agree. Shortcomings may be glossed over temporarily, but they will become blatantly apparent when the work is complete and making them right will be expensive and embarrassing. The extent of a client's ability to understand the various types of drawings that can make up a presentation will become obvious in early conversations.

Presentation to a client, or any other interested party, is not necessarily a one-off event. It is prudent to talk to all individual and organizations during the progression of the design process in order to avoid protracted, unproductive work. Fine-tuning of a brief is frequently necessary. The nature of interior design, working within the restrictions of the shell of an existing building, means that, almost inevitably, the detail of an initial brief will have to be reconsidered in response to emerging realities. Clients who accept significant financial risks deserve to be consulted

at all stages and, as proposals are evolved and scrutinized, other possibilities will suggest themselves and changes of direction must be discussed and agreed. It therefore makes sense to set up a series of preliminary presentations in order to consider and agree on work in progress.

When a client is familiar with a designer's work – or when the two have collaborated before – it may be appropriate to produce fewer, and perhaps less-polished, drawings, but it must not appear that the client is being taken for granted and receiving less for their fee. Equally some may be concerned that they are paying for unnecessarily glamorous presentation and it may be sensible to agree at the outset what is included in a fee and what will be an additional charge. With new clients it is obviously important to make an impression – perhaps even to offer a little more than is strictly necessary, and certainly no less. Evidence of enthusiasm and ability will overcome most reservations. Some clients, old and new, enjoy the sense of collaboration in the development of ideas and will tend to prefer the less-polished drawings that suggest work in progress.

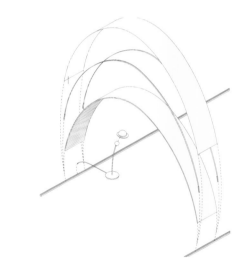

Above
The partially rendered perspective suggests the end result and the line drawing describes the construction of a free-standing 'tunnel' within a rectangular shell.

TIP DRAWINGS FOR INTERIM PRESENTATIONS

Drawings should be:

- Simple and informal
- Comprehensible without appearing definitive
- Realistic – don't hint at something that can't be delivered
- Quick – elaborate presentations consume time and therefore cost money

Successful presentation material

Designers tend to be fascinated by clients' response to presentations, particularly to individual drawings within the whole, and are always keen to identify the one illustration that swung the argument in favour of a proposal that met with initial scepticism – often reminiscing later about how a single, seductive image persuaded a client to find extra money.

The tone of any presentation, particularly during the face-to-face encounter with the client, depends very much on the personality of the designer. Some have natural gravitas and can easily convince clients of their serious intent and reliability, while others are instinctively inclined to humour and to finding a more personal level of communication. Whatever the inclination, it will be manifested in both visual and verbal presentations. Both positions, and any in between, will be drastically undermined by a blatant error in any drawing. It is prudent to have drawings scrutinized and text proof read by third parties.

Some projects are won in competition. In these cases, the strategy must be slightly different because the designers may not have an opportunity to talk to the judges.

Sometimes a commissioning client may not be a user of the space. Often, particularly with work for public bodies, the client will be a committee – not usually an easy body with which to negotiate. There is no single individual to respond to, and there may be tensions within the group which make differences of opinion – even differences unrelated to the proposal – inevitable. In such circumstances, things must be kept clear and simple. Often laypersons are concerned that they will be unable to understand specialist drawings and are anxious about looking foolish. Such anxieties can make them reluctant to engage with the material presented and hesitant about expressing opinions and approval. Accessible drawings supported by a relaxed, preferably good-humoured, verbal presentation can begin to overcome this.

Right
When explaining a proposal
it often makes sense to
start at the entrance.

Below
A three dimensional diagram
explains the strategy of the
entrance 'tunnel', a device
for leading customers to the
core of the interior, beneath
an existing rooflight.

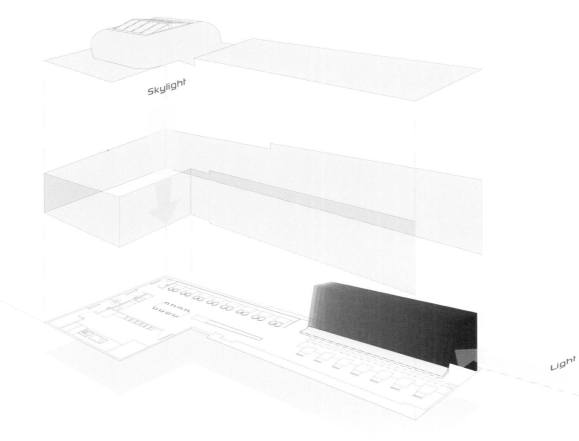

Skylight

Light

Case study Presenting concepts to clients

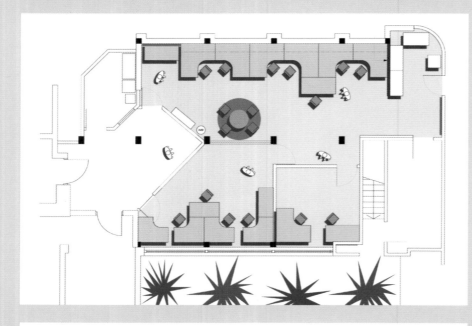

The following examples of presentation material resulted in the clients' agreement and commitment to the project.

On this page the plan offers the 'low impact concept'. The plan on the opposite page illustrates the more ambitious 'high impact concept'. The perspective views give an indication of how each option may look. They introduce ideas broadly but offer enough information to allow the client to feel confident enough to express opinions.

The computer provides credible perspective lines to define the planes of the interior. The hand-drawn details for furniture are necessarily simplified but are enough to suggest style and function. The quality of freehand additions, particularly of the chairs, suggest that the designer is in control of all aspects of the creative process.

Frequently, although not in this case, a client will suggest a solution incorporating elements of some or all of the options offered. This may irritate designers, but it helps identify a client's real priorities.

An alternative to the preliminary sketch, and one that may be useful in the very first meeting with a new client, is to present photographs of built interiors or collages of completed interiors and finishes and furniture that suggest some of the anticipated qualities of the project. There is however a danger that overindulgent use of found images will distort clients' expectations, and it is sensible to use illustrations from one's own completed projects where possible. Talented and ambitious designers are unlikely to countenance association with another's work.

Top
The 'low impact' solution, illustrating how minimal tidying up of the plan and the introduction of new furniture improves the workspace.

Above
The perspective view, set up on computer, is overdrawn by hand and blocks of colour and tone are then added by computer.

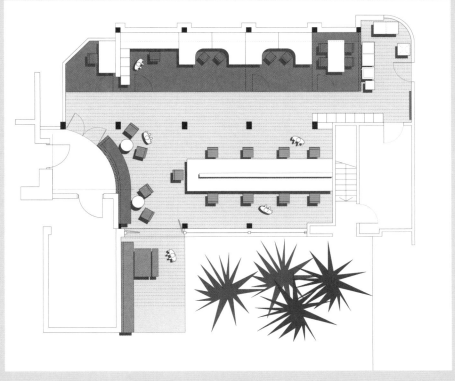

Right and below
Option 2: The perspective view now illustrates the whole of the office because the entire area is reconfigured, giving the outdoor area prominence. The designer's own preference for this version is perhaps indicated by the more extensive pencil work embellishing the raw computer lines. The clients also chose this option.

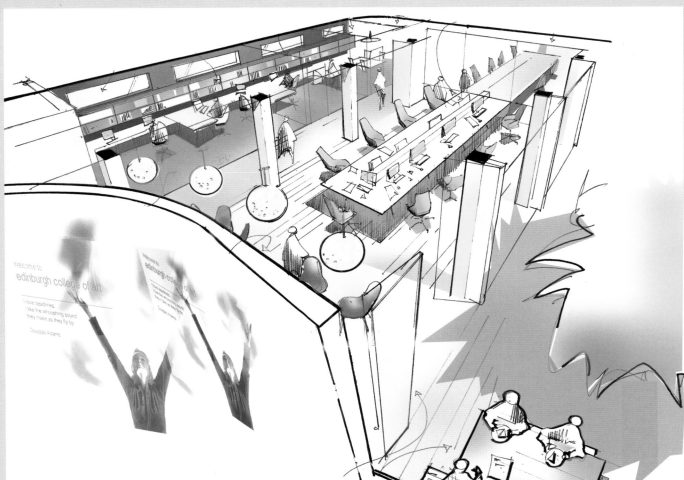

The components
of a presentation

Whether for preliminary or final presentations, there are a number of standard types of drawings – each with its own defining conventions – that will necessarily be produced for most projects.

The character of drawings, whether technical or not, is always determined by the medium with which they are made. Drawings for interior design must eventually be precise, in dimensions and finish.

When drawing by hand, different weights of line, in the case of pencil, and thicknesses, in the case of pen, help legibility. The use of colour was formerly restricted to one-off drawings until the arrival of effective colour photocopying. Definition of elements within the drawing required laborious hatching and toning. Computer drawing and printing now makes it easy to use colour and infinite shades of grey. The computer's richer palette offers a battery of options for the creation of more accessible drawings. However, it is important not to obscure crucial facts with an overload of colour

and texture, to remember what information the drawing is intended to convey rather than to become waylaid into creating a drawing that is an end in itself.

While the fully-rendered perspective view may be perceived as the quintessential presentation tool, other, less spectacular, two-dimensional drawings convey crucial information more clearly.

The plan

A plan is usually essential. It defines how the required accommodation will be set out and how furniture will be deployed, and confirms that the proposal will fit into and maximize the potential of the existing space.

Plans may, of necessity, be visually complex. It is, therefore, often good practice to use a diagrammatic version of the plan, explaining how the essential elements are arranged, as an introduction to a more complex version that incorporates more comprehensive and detailed information.

Right
The small plan defines the functional subdivision of the existing building. The detailed delineation in the bigger plan is enriched by the computer's capacity to deal with tone and colour. The addition of furniture and equipment confirms that the uncompromising planning strategy delivers efficient work areas.

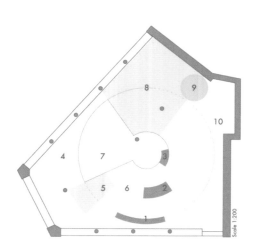

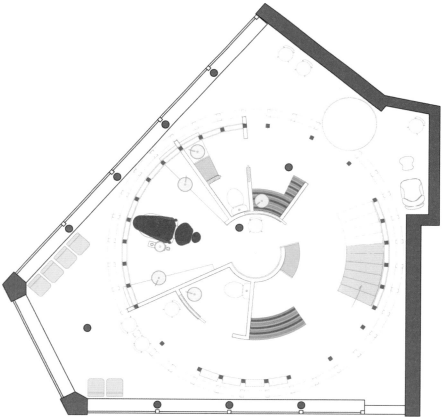

Right
This plan also works as a diagram, because the space is simple and contains few elements or items of equipment. The floor pattern dominates and identifies different areas, as it would in the finished interior. The furniture layout confirms that the spaces work.

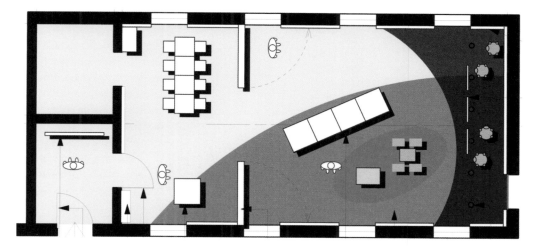

Right
Solid black represents existing structure, and white indicates new walls. Other colours refer to floor finishes. Tonal variations suggest the impact of artificial lighting. 'Shadows', cast by the round tables, and the graded colour on the green ramp add a degree of three-dimensionality.

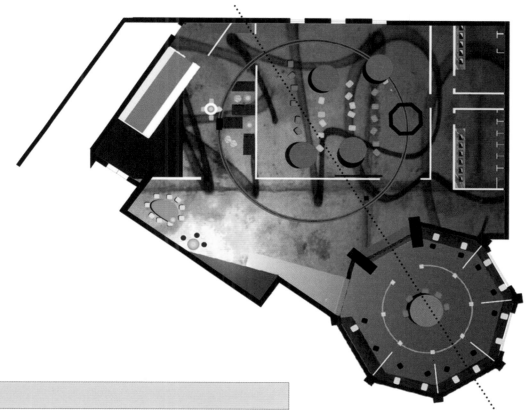

TIP SCALES

There are standard scales for drawings, recognized throughout the building industry. Generally, 1:50 is most useful for presentation plans: it is big enough to show a comprehensive amount of detail and to allow most projects to be contained on a single page. A scale of 1:100 is also capable of providing significant information, particularly with the precision and quality of line possible on a computer, but a 1:200-scale plan begins to lose important detail. If a comprehensive plan of a large project is necessary and may only be achieved at 1:200, then areas that are densely organized, or of particular interest, may be dealt with at a larger scale, say 1:50 or 1:20. The capacity of the computer to alternate easily between scales makes this conversion simple.

The scale of a plan should be declared on the drawing, but when a scale is used for which there is no 'ruler' – and therefore no way of measuring the paper copy – it should be declared to be 'not to scale' in a prominent position somewhere on the sheet.

Handmade plans

Near perfection of line can be achieved by someone constantly making technical drawings by hand, but the hand can never match the extraordinary precision of the computer, its consistency of line and its perfect corners. It is therefore logical, when drawing by hand, to aim for a more 'relaxed' outcome: to allow lines to cross, for example, and to apply hatching and toning vigorously, perhaps to suggest a certain creative exuberance.

For some simple projects drawing may be done freehand, without the use of T-square or set square. Corners, usually close to ninety degrees, may be judged by eye, and practice will improve this skill. Significant dimensions may be measured, even in a freehand drawing and, if these are comparatively accurate, other elements may be drawn credibly in relation to them.

For more complex plans, an alternative is to create a quick, technically constructed draft of the crucial elements and then to make a freehand overlay. It is not advisable to trace the original too carefully, because with most of the drawing being accurate the inevitable minor discrepancies will appear clumsier in comparison. It is generally better to trace quickly in order to sustain spontaneity. Technically constructed and freehand lines may usefully be employed in the same drawing – the first can define the precision of new elements, and the second the imprecision of existing features.

TIP EFFECTIVE SHARING

When designers sketch it is usually a private function in which they give some shape to their first thoughts, but the freehand sketch is also an efficient way of communicating with other members of the design team: colleagues and consultants. It therefore makes sense to observe drawing conventions when making even the roughest sketches, otherwise they are open to misinterpretation by those familiar with normal practice.

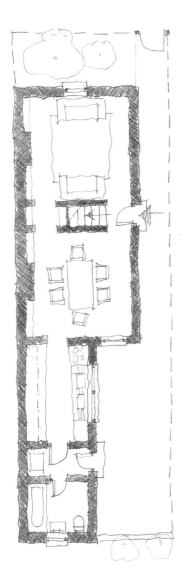

Left
Tracing over a measured survey ensures that dimensions are accurate to an acceptable degree. Fast freehand drawing makes shading and indications of furniture layout easy.

Right
This project involves more detailed work, and consequently the drawings are more accurate. A drawing pen was used in preference to a pencil, because it ensured precision and permanence of line. The black ink outline was drawn on tracing paper, which was then tinted on the back with coloured pencils. New walls and columns were coloured orange to clarify the modest extent of construction work. Other lines and colouring represented floor finishes and furniture layouts. The plans of the three floors were butted together, and distinguished by different densities of tone.

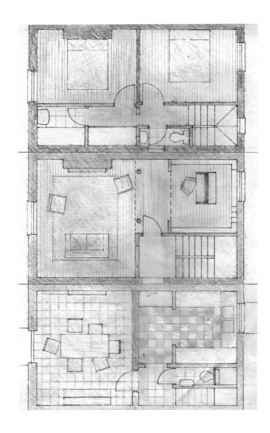

The section

All the observations made about drawing plans apply equally to the section. The section is the essential way to accurately describe changes of level, whether at floor or ceiling levels. If the plan allows a viewer to navigate and understand the subdivisions of a space, the section describes its vertical planes and allows an understanding of their composition as the viewer 'moves' vertically through the space. A section can offer a prosaic description of the physicality of a space or can evoke atmosphere with accurate depictions of colour, materials, lighting effects and furniture. The computer's capacity for precise representation of finishes makes it the ideal tool for this job.

It can be counterproductive to be overly conscientious when drawing sections. If too many lines are incorporated, in order to represent background detail, the whole becomes difficult to decipher. When planning the drawing, it is important to decide on priorities and to edit out insignificant information.

The crucial decision, which will determine whether a section is useful or not, is that about the location of its 'cut' through the building. This should ensure that the subsequent drawing includes the information most essential for describing the project. It is usually good practice to make a number of sections, each dealing with a significant condition, rather than to attempt the false economy of superimposing one on the other. Generally speaking, one section should cut through a stairwell in order to explain, practically and aesthetically, how floors connect. It is also imperative to cut through the edge of any mezzanine floor, to describe changes and visual links between levels.

There is also a choice to be made about the direction in which a section ought to 'look'. It should obviously be orientated to place elements in the most informative context or to incorporate information about an important background element.

Introducing people and props can give scale and help explain how the interior will be used. Well-chosen figures can assist in making otherwise forbidding technical drawings appear more accessible.

Below
Drawings are often peopled with glamorous models, and such superhumans sit incongruously in most interiors. In this meticulously detailed image there are many more eclectic and engaging characters.

Bottom
Developed rendering of finishes can give an impression of materiality, colour, texture and light.

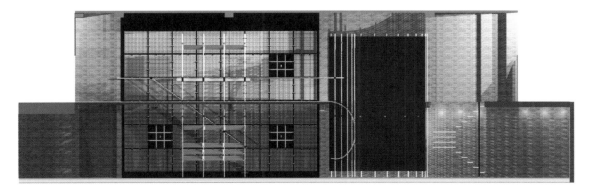

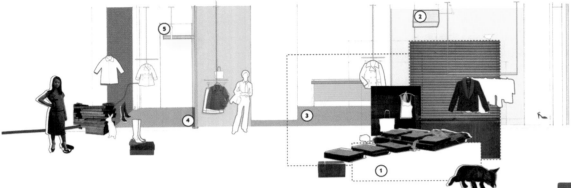

Above

While not a traditional section, the coloured elements describe the essential components of a minimalist clothes shop. The projection of these elements beyond the strict confines of the section plane introduces a sense of depth. The sparse precision of the whole is relieved by the ironic intrusion of wildlife.

Right

An even more reductive treatment in which the white furniture and fittings that sit against white walls are reduced to outlines. The areas of scanned materials and monochromatic pattern are shown in proportion to their proposed presence in the finished interior.

TIP CHOOSING THE BEST PLACE TO 'CUT' THE SECTION

While sections are useful ways to indicate wall finishes they also make clear changes in floor and ceiling levels.

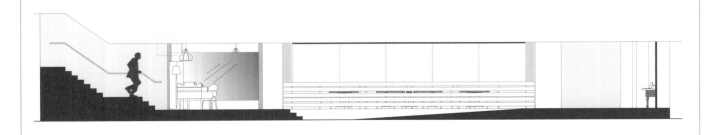

The axonometric and the isometric

Plans and sections provide the two-dimensional information that enables those who understand their conventions to inhabit an interior. The perspective offers a static image, a single view from a fixed viewpoint with no opportunity to 'move' through the space. Axonometric and isometric projections provide a method of constructing images that exhibit the virtues of both two and three dimensions. They are essentially three-dimensional views of all areas within a building, with roof/ceiling and at least two walls removed. They present information about adjacent areas, showing remaining walls and other vertical elements in the third dimension and, when rendered, materials, colours, textures and lighting effects.

They are simple to construct, and explain the translation of plans and sections into three dimensions. They allow the viewer to imagine moving around the space, or sequence of spaces; to understand how one area flows into another; and how the aesthetics of one evolve into another.

A viewpoint must be selected in order to ensure

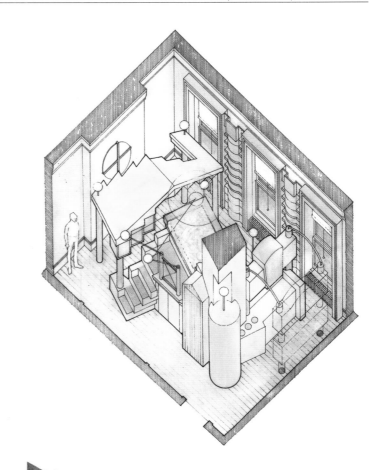

Below
In this computer-generated isometric the three-dimensional organization of vertical elements and levels is made clear, and meticulous rendering convincingly describes finishes.

Above
When made by hand, three-dimensionality is defined primarily by outline and, while every surface of this axonometric is rendered with pastels and coloured pencils, it is impossible to achieve an accuracy in the depiction of materials to match that achieved by computer.

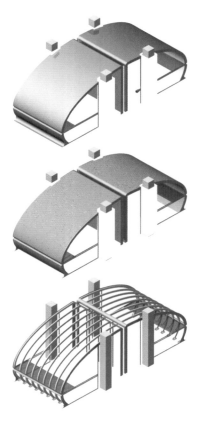

that the maximum information is offered, and it is often sensible to draw a project from more than one, usually from diagonally opposite corners, to provide an even spread of information. The axonometric is marginally simpler to draw by hand but the thirty degree structure of the isometric, which is no more difficult to draw digitally, appears closer to the more realistic format of the perspective.

Obviously, it is simple to generate a number of such images digitally, once information about plan and section conditions have been fed into the computer. It is also comparatively easy to set them up by hand because all horizontal and vertical lines are parallel rather than in the constantly changing divergences of the perspective view. This uncomplicated formula makes it feasible to draw both quickly and with a satisfactory degree of accuracy by hand and they can be an effective way of making spontaneous but controlled three-dimensional sketches during the course of a meeting. (For the principles of setting them up, refer to the section on 'Axonometric and isometric projections' in Chapter 1, pages 44-45.)

Above

This sequence of three computer generated isometric images documents a strategy for the construction of an enclosed office space, demonstrating that what is an apparently complex structure may be built using familiar materials and construction techniques.

Below

This isometric describes a continuous element that runs the length of a long, narrow building, progressively changing its function but not its character. The drawing is simplified, but remains detailed enough to explain the essential idea. The omission of external walls and floor focuses attention on the new elements.

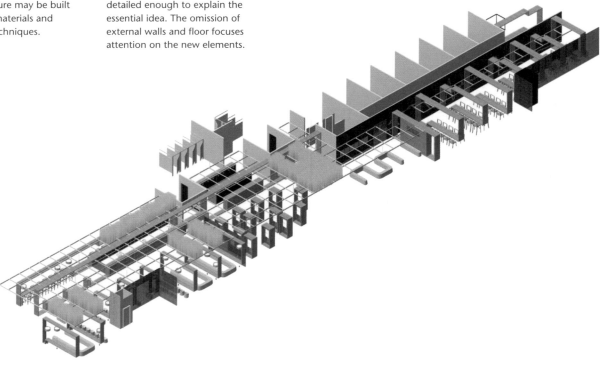

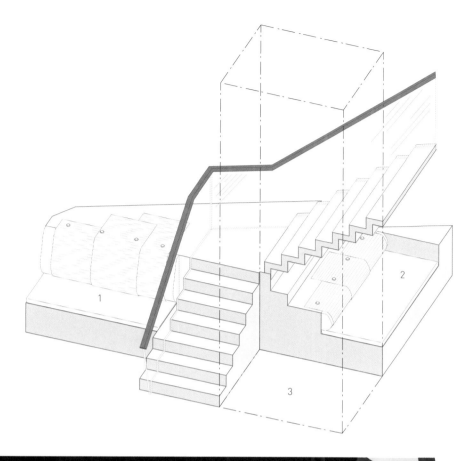

1. Waiting seating
2. Recovery niche
3. Lift

This page
An isometric provides a diagrammatic explanation of how fixed seating elements are tucked around and under a stair and lift tower, which is shown in dashed outline to reveal the stair behind and the heavy handrail helps explain the configuration of the flights and landing. The perspective adds materiality.

For a computer, it is no more difficult to draw a curved line than a straight one –a perspective is as simple as an axonometric. Working digitally it is therefore possible, when appropriate, to use the slightly more naturalistic overhead perspective view rather than an axonometricor isometric. For very complex spaces, however, the formal logic of the traditional configurations is likely to be more comprehensible and therefore more informative.

Below
This overhead perspective veers away just enough from the true plan to indicate how colour and materials are used to express the interaction of the walls. Furniture indicates room functions. Crucial elements of the exterior walls, such as windows and columns, are indicated on the edges.

Right
This overhead view explains how elements sit within a double-height space. The image is necessarily complex, but clearly contrasts the fragility of the stair and the bridges with the enclosed workplaces they connect.

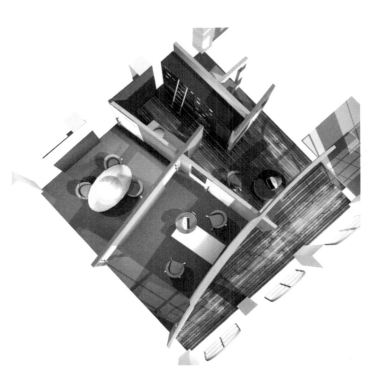

The perspective

Detailed and polished perspective views are generally the most accessible images in any presentation and a well chosen viewpoint will quickly convey the essential elements of the project. One comprehensive perspective may express all that needs to be shown, but it is always worth considering a number of views, each concentrating attention on different important elements. Such shifts of attention are, after all, the normal response to a built interior, the eyes focusing consecutively on particular set pieces. It is also worth considering incorporating large-scale views of details, junctions of materials and pieces of built-in furniture. Such detail can create a sense of intimate involvement with the project. (For the principles of setting up perspective views by hand, refer to the section on 'Making a simple freehand perspective' in Chapter 1, pages 42–43.)

The advantage of drawing by computer is that, once essential information has been fed into plans and elevations, it is simple to extrude as many complex perspective views as is necessary or desirable. However, with too many such views the impact of the whole may become diluted. It is better to identify those that are crucial, and invest effort in refining them.

Right
It makes sense to include a new street frontage as the first image in presentation material. In this example it is presented as a flat plane behind which the shop and its customers set up the idea of perspectival depth and the pedestrians and pigeons suggest a pavement, as a receding foreground plane.

Below
The street frontage as perspective. The computer makes it easy to manipulate a new elevation to match the perspective of a, preferably digital, photograph of surrounding buildings. These buildings may, in turn, be further manipulated within the computer to produce a more compatible alignment and graphic quality.

Constructing the real interior is necessarily a more difficult undertaking than generating an idealized image of it. If a rendering appears perfect, then a client may be entitled to assume that the materials and colours shown are precisely those that will appear in the finished interior – and any variations may lead to complaints. It is therefore sometimes sensible to offer a more impressionistic image of the proposal, one that expresses the essence of the project but is obviously not photographically accurate.

The conventional perspective view, neatly composed within a rectangle, tends, like a photograph, to give equal weight to all elements within it whereas, when in a real interior, one is more likely to focus on visually assertive elements. In a drawing it is sensible to concentrate viewers' attention on what will be, in reality, the most significant components, the impact of which may be lost if every surface is rendered with the same intensity. Content should be prioritized.

A strong argument can be made for computer-generated images that retain elements of the sketch. Sketches are always intriguing: they are not definitive, they leave room for the imagination to speculate – and they have spontaneity, energy and an intimacy that the perfection of the polished image inevitably loses. They remain accessible and appear to offer more evidence of a designer's creativity.

This page
The most complex proposals may be easily and endlessly rotated in the computer for critical appraisal and presentation.

Left

While, at first sight, this image appears photographic, its concern is to convey a sense of machined perfection, so the surfaces are hyper-smooth and the whole is dramatically lit. Such distortion is legitimate in order to express the spirit of the project – as long as the manipulation is obvious.

Below

Artificial transparencies indicate obvious stylization, and in this example also express the aesthetic intention.

Below and below right

These images explain how a palette of materials and colours runs consistently through a sequence of spaces. Created 'freehand' on computer, they describe finishes without the precision necessary to plot three-dimensional detail. Important elements, like the clothes-hanging recesses and sculpted ceilings, are delineated carefully, but the obviously deliberate discrepancies of size in the figures, as well as their extreme postures and costumes, confirm that literal accuracy is not intended. They suggest that the designer relished the creative process.

While it is standard practice to generate computer perspectives from plans and sections it is also possible to draw 'freehand', directly on to the screen. Program tools make it easier to delineate volumes with perfectly straight lines, rather than the undulations of the hand made, and to add blocks of colour, and to scan and paste in patterns, textures, figures and furniture.

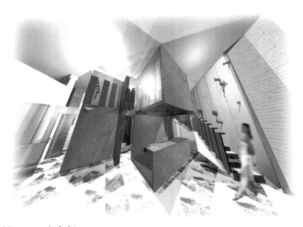

Above and right

Neither of these images aspire to accurate perspective, but they make clear statements about the nature of the spaces illustrated: that on the left is tall and airy, that on the right smaller and more intimate. Both are very clear about finishes.

This page
The flat, white planes of walls, floor
and ceiling are represented by the
white of the paper on which the
image is to be printed. Only crucial
elements are drawn. The stylization
of the view is acknowledged by the
obvious distortion of perspective,
which is confirmed by the view of
the street beyond the window

Image edge

In built interiors, the eye focuses on the area directly in the line of sight and registers less precisely elements at the edge of the cone of vision. It will be drawn to, and linger on, the dominant elements, and while areas of peripheral vision contribute to the impression of the whole they will not be scrutinized with the same intensity. There are a number of graphic devices that can begin to replicate this focus. Some break the rectangle others work within it.

An irregularly shaped image also breaks up the rigid grid, with its straight sided dividing strips, that results when a number of rectangular images are collected on a presentation sheet.

Left
The partial retention of wire-frame lines allows the intensity of rendering to reduce from left to right. The drawing fades into the paper.

Bottom left
The easing in, or out, of naturalistic rendering (as seen in the representation of the screen) dilutes the rectangle.

Below
The white dotted lines, like the framing device in a camera viewfinder, define the area of interest and, along with the floating pink rectangle behind and the figures overstepping the edges of the images, enhance the sense of depth.

Right

The projection of the lines of the wire frame integrate the image into the page. However, the lines, while they obviously belong to the project, are not aligned precisely with the image and their disjunction suggests that it floats above the surface of the paper. The legs of the chair, also projecting beyond the strict confines of the image, increase the sense of depth.

Below right

The centre of this image is the most solidly rendered area, and tones fade as they 'rise' from it. It is an impossible view, but it deals with a tiny space and the main purpose of the drawing is to describe the finishes.

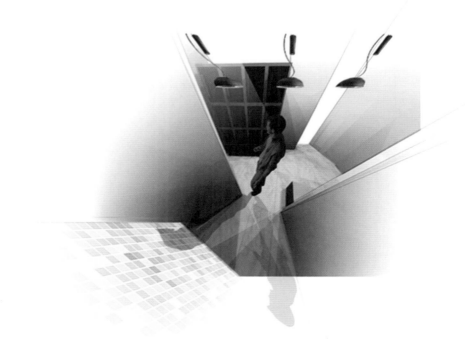

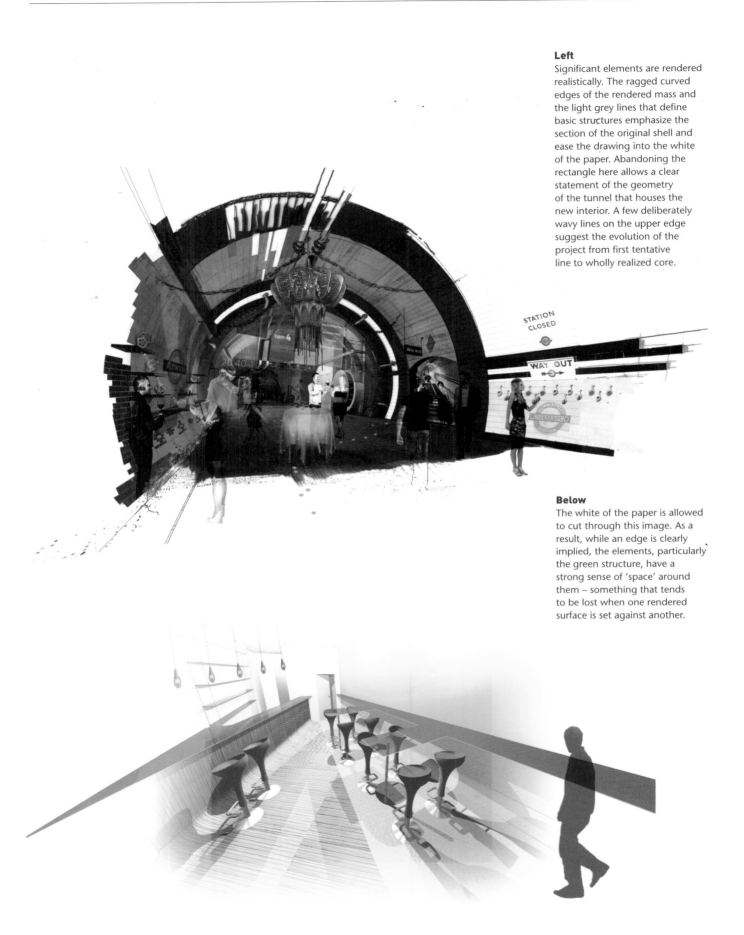

Left

Significant elements are rendered realistically. The ragged curved edges of the rendered mass and the light grey lines that define basic structures emphasize the section of the original shell and ease the drawing into the white of the paper. Abandoning the rectangle here allows a clear statement of the geometry of the tunnel that houses the new interior. A few deliberately wavy lines on the upper edge suggest the evolution of the project from first tentative line to wholly realized core.

Below

The white of the paper is allowed to cut through this image. As a result, while an edge is clearly implied, the elements, particularly the green structure, have a strong sense of 'space' around them – something that tends to be lost when one rendered surface is set against another.

Right

The angled linearity of stripes and shadows is focused on the curvilinear chaise longue, and held within a pale pink square that is just visible against the white of the paper.

Below

This image is stripped back to give an expression of finishes and a suggestion of planes. Colours and pattern are complemented by the foreground figure. The bottom brown line defines the floor plane. The heavier, right-hand, side is balanced by the floating shape on the upper left.

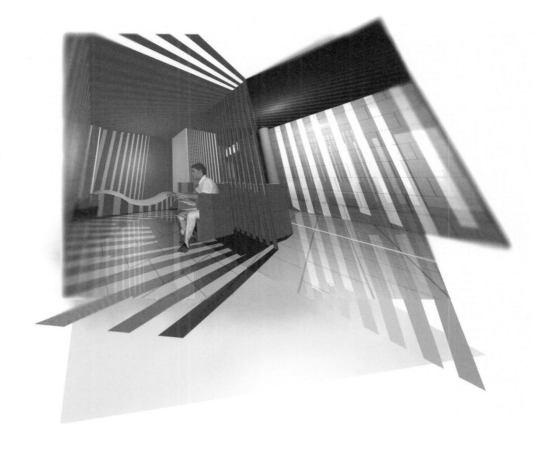

Below left and right
The computer deals objectively, as programmed, with the complexities of perspective, materiality and lighting within a precise three-dimensional representation of context. These images illustrate particularly its capacity to plot and represent the interaction of reflective surfaces. Realistic and objective depiction eliminates the necessary stylization and coding that were inevitable with hand rendering.

New finishes

It is common, and somewhat glib, to say that interior design is 'about space'. It is as much – and probably a great deal more – about surface, colours and textures. Since interior 'spaces' are usually rectangular and typically around 2.5 metres (8 feet) high, they depend for their success more on the creative handling of surface finishes than on dramatic sculptural gestures. Furthermore, no matter how well such 'sculpture' is handled, the way it is perceived will depend on the materials from which it is made.

When clients want hard evidence of what their interior will look like, it is sensible to produce images that focus on materiality. This should be apparent in conventional perspectives, but often it is worth making additional images that give priority to finishes.

No hand rendering method can rival the computer's capacity to represent materiality. Hand rendering relies on visual coding, with varying degrees of accuracy, to imply reality. Because such skills are highly specialist it was common to employ a consultant 'visualizer' – who, through constant practise, could achieve something close to reality – to produce a handmade perspective. Such specialists inevitably have their own style, and designers tend to employ those whose technique they consider most compatible with the spirit of their project. The disadvantage is that, regardless of how attuned designer

and visualizer may be, the former is at the mercy of the latter, who will inevitably not 'see' the proposal precisely as its creator intended. Now, with regular practise and appropriate computer software, designers can produce their own perspectives, expressing their vision exactly. Finishes, once the most difficult element of any drawing to make convincing, are now simple to represent and materials that would once have been presented as disjointed fragments on a sample board are now scanned and presented in context with photographic accuracy.

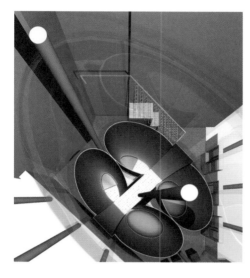

Left and above
More abstract evocations of transparent, translucent and opaque planes demonstrate the computer's ability to calculate and emulate the surface qualities of different materials, their interactions and the impact of artificial and natural light sources.

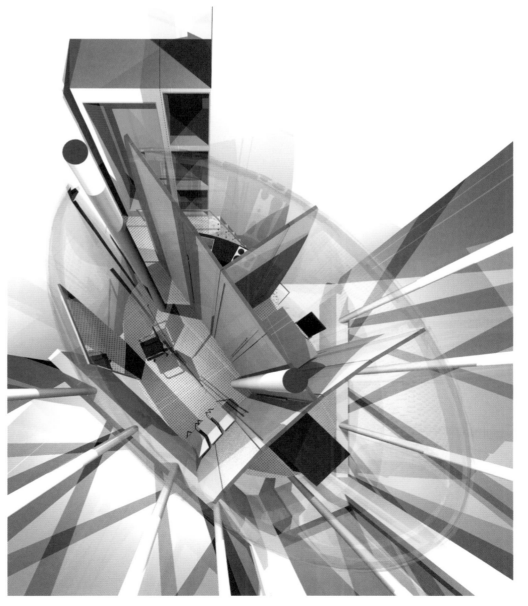

Existing finishes

A new interior should respond to the volume and the materiality of the existing building that houses it. Amongst the bare surfaces of a modern utilitarian shell there may be nothing worth retaining and integrating into the new but, particularly in older buildings there are surfaces or elements that have a quality that can add to the richness of the new and it becomes important that they are included in any representations of it. It would be laborious to recreate these elements by computer, and the solution is to photograph them – preferably digitally, to allow the manipulation that will match the perspective and tonal values of the rendered image. When taking such photographs it is sensible to position oneself as near as possible to the viewpoint of the intended rendering, so that the orientation and perspective of the existing feature is compatible with that of the virtual elements and require minimal adjustment in the computer.

Above
It is easier and more efficient to photograph existing elements and finishes (such as the decorative plaster ceiling in this space) and scan them into digital images, than it is to recreate them, from scratch.

Above right
In this digital collage the mundane, generic bookshelves – with their patchwork of book spines, scanned and pasted in with no attempt to refine them – transmute into outline, to match the representation of the existing masonry walls (depicted as a computer-made pastiche of a traditional architectural line drawing). The new stone floor with its irregular pattern is pasted in at an inflated scale to make its grain visible. None of the three principal elements makes any attempt to conform to a common perspective, and thus avoids the problems of compatibility.

TIP PHOTOGRAPHING EXISTING MATERIALS

The existing wall on the right was digitally photographed, scanned and manipulated. The problem of reconciling the perspective of the new drawing precisely with that in a photograph is dealt with by the exaggeration of both, so that conventional rules are seen not to apply.

This page

In many projects with large areas of windows the view to the exterior is, necessarily, an integral part of the interior, and 'pasting' in a digital photograph of the street puts the proposal into context. The intensity of the street image can be reduced to suggest its being 'diluted' through glass and problems of incompatible perspective may be solved by distortion of one or both originals.

Lighting

In hand drawn images the effect of light, both natural and artificial, has to be estimated and it is difficult to achieve a convincing complexity of highlights and shadows. In contrast light sources, natural and artificial have to be programmed into digital perspectives as an integral part of the information required to generate the image and the finished version has a wholly convincing subtle and complex reality. This process has the added advantage of allowing designers to appraise a convincing facsimile of their lighting proposals and to make adjustments to the position and intensity of sources. The examples illustrated on this page show proposed artificial lighting schemes, while those on the opposite page show proposals that use natural light.

Right
Spotlights, suspended and recessed into the floor, play on the folds of translucent hanging fabrics.

Above
Angled glass sheets rising through openings in the floor are lit from below.

Left
A representation of intense but concealed light sources on highly reflective surfaces.

Above
For projects in northern latitudes a cool, gentle light is more convincing.

Below left
Strong light spills through windows and is reflected appropriately on the various surfaces, reflective and absorbent.

Below right
Sloping rooflights light top edges and reflective surfaces of furniture and light fittings. The highlights on the dark floor finish are muted in comparison with the bottom corner of the lighter stone wall that just catches sunlight.

Furniture

Furniture is a fundamental component in any interior – the element with which users interact most directly – and it must be considered from the very beginning of the design process, because it is integral to the expression of a project's aesthetic.

Other than for one-off pieces, such as reception desks and bar counters, there is seldom a need to design furniture specifically for a project. A designer may enjoy isolated, inspired moments of creativity when a powerful idea springs tangentially from thinking about the entirety of a project and is worth pursuing, but these moments are rare and it is logical to select pieces instead from the superabundance of manufactured options. It could be argued that it demonstrates a lack of imagination or professional knowledge if one cannot find something suitable amongst the myriad variations of manufactured tables and chairs already available.

By and large, furniture conforms to strict size requirements and restrictions, and therefore familiar objects – such as chairs and tables – can be effective substitutes for the human figure in establishing the scale of an interior.

This page
This pair of images establishes a stylistic connection between the furniture and the interiors that contain it. The yellow-cube armchairs above reiterate the volume of the projecting floor above them. The charcoal 'blob' seats to the right match the colours and simplicity of their interior. The red unit acts as a focal point.

Left
Furniture is necessarily smaller in scale and frequently intricate and this can be lost in the complexities of an interior perspective. A few books explain how these bespoke library shelves operate without obscuring their configurations.

Because furniture has such an impact on the character of an interior, it is important that it is accurately represented in any images. This may involve the resizing and pasting-in, by hand or computer, of photographs from catalogues and appropriate adjustment relative to the perspective of the space that accommodates them. It may mean the laborious creation of a near-likeness by hand or computer. Alternatively, and most efficiently and conveniently, it may mean the downloading, where it is available, of data from a manufacturer's website that will provide exact images of individual pieces, which may be convincingly manipulated and integrated within the constraints of an overall perspective.

TIP USING FURNITURE TO DEFINE A SPACE

Meticulous detailing and setting-out of furniture, from data downloaded from a manufacturer's website, gives reality to an otherwise impressionistic rendering.

This page
Two extraordinary pieces of
furniture are wittily located in
context. The detail in the drawings
seems to acknowledge their
singularity. In the image to the
right, the circular window and the
face it frames echo the inflated
orange tube and the figure within
it. The contorted faces on the
screens in the image below seem
to despair at the extraordinary
seating that floats beneath them.

STEP BY STEP DOWNLOADING FURNITURE FROM MANUFACTURERS' WEBSITES

There is little need for a designer to create new pieces of furniture for any but the most unique projects. Many manufacturers, to encourage selection of their own products, provide digital versions of pieces in their range which may be downloaded and used in plans, sections and, most spectacularly and usefully, in perspective views. Since furniture and fittings have such a fundamental importance in the expression of the character of an interior, it is important that they be rendered with precision. Downloading ensures this and eliminates the laborious creation of less accurate facsimiles.

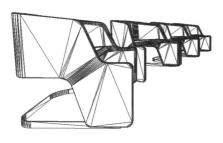

1 The data needed to construct a piece of furniture digitally is first downloaded as a wire-frame image, which allows the pieces to be precisely created compatible with the perspective of the intended finished image. It is in manufacturers' interests to supply this information free to encourage use of their products.

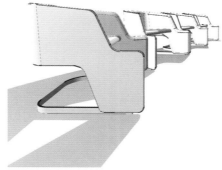

2 When the composition is acceptable, the elements may be made solid.

3 Or elements can be rendered with progressive refinement.

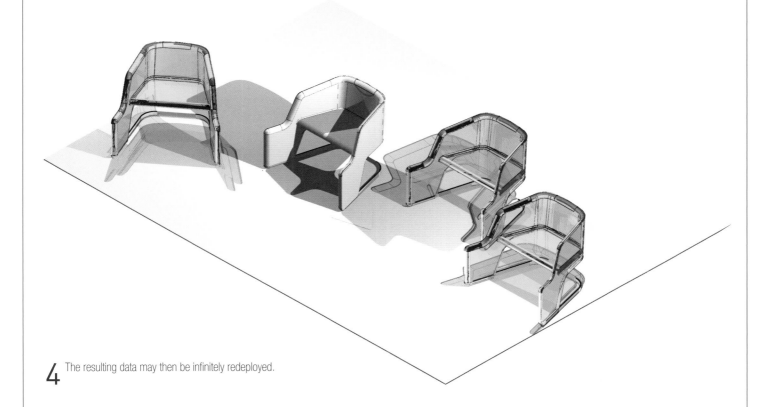

4 The resulting data may then be infinitely redeployed.

Case study Creating one-off pieces

This sequence of drawings, for a display system, serves to explain the proposal both to the client and the prospective maker, describing both the aesthetic intention and the method of construction.

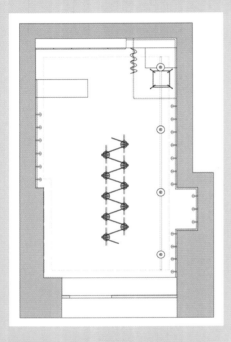

Above
Plan showing display unit in the centre of the shop.

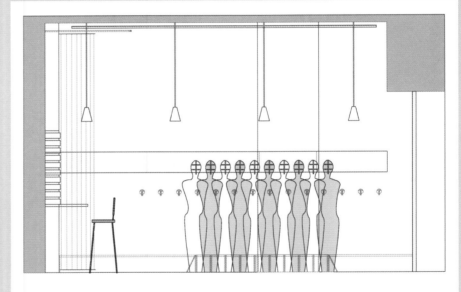

zig-zag structure 250mm (10 in) high

each MDF piece is placed at a 60° angle to the previous

MDF 'people' (1600mm [63 in] high) slot down onto base securing the freestanding structure

head pieces slot together to give a 3D form on which wigs are displayed

precise cuts ensure tight connections and structural rigidity

Above
Elevation of a side wall showing proposed 'people structure' display unit, with a detail below explaining the unit's construction and specification notes.

Pendant light

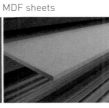

Wood flooring

MDF sheets

Colour palette

Above
In this presentation sheet a rendered perspective with
figures gives a sense of the proposed finishes and
scale, while below it are details of proposed materials.

Figures

Human figures give scale to an interior and help explain how it will work and be inhabited. Photographs of completed interiors are notorious for being bereft of people, which makes some sense because changing fashions in clothes and haircuts can embarrassingly date the most radical creation. Inappropriate dating is not however a problem for presentation drawings, which need, and should, only be relevant to the time of their making. The computer offers opportunities for including well-chosen figures that complement the aesthetic of the project. They can be witty or poetic, and may be particularly effective in engaging a client's imagination and sympathy.

Left and above
Figures give scale to interior presentations but it is not necessary, and often impractical, for them to be highly detailed or lifelike – the use of stylized figures is common practice.

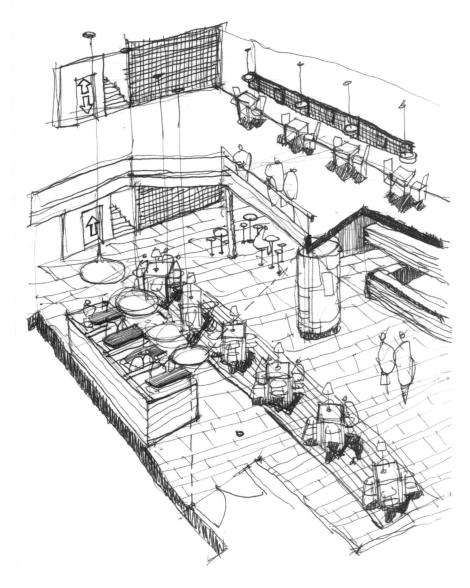

Left
These hand-drawn figures are traced outlines of photographs, made quickly to retain something of the spontaneity of a sketch. They are distinctly secondary to the finishes that dominate the image.

Left
Transparent figures give scale without obscuring the interior.

Below left
One way of ensuring that a figure is in sympathy with the perspective of its surroundings is to create a bespoke image, which is easily done with digital photography.

Below right
Figures can indicate the changing scale of spaces within one interior.

Left
Figures can clarify different levels and their function. The figure on the left identifies a stair, which is not itself visible, the figure in the bottom right obviously looks up through a void, the other two explain the booths and access to them. All four are deliberately in soft focus.

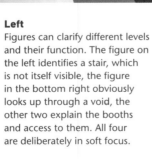

It is difficult, in interior-design presentations, to incorporate lifelike handmade drawings of people The body is too complex, and difficult to make the freehand lines of the drawing sit comfortably with the hard edges of interior elements and it is common practice to stylize the hand drawn figure.

Such manipulation of the size and quality of an image is easier, and can be taken further, on computer. It is also possible to download, from free and subscription websites, batteries of figures in wide ranges of age, character and posture. There are sites that supply wholly digitally generated figures that may be programmed to adopt appropriate poses, but these are disturbingly characterless and unconvincing.

Below
Figures provide witty confirmation of the interior's function (a hat shop).

Right
When making project-specific figure images, record a series of slight variations from which that most compatible with the perspective of the interior may be chosen. Final adjustment on the computer should integrate the figure convincingly with the elements of the building. In this example the shadow – made on a computer – suggests a convincing ground plane.

Below
Figures, such as those on the
right of this image, can identify
activities. Others, like those
on the left of the image, can
express the spirit of a project.
The exuberance of such an image
can only help seduce the client.

The most common practice among designers is to
build a personal library of figures scanned from
magazines, or to carry out project-specific searches
for photographs of suitable 'characters' in appropriate
positions. Generally, the figure should not dominate
the interior but a well-chosen and adjusted figure can
significantly influence perception of the design.

People obey the rules of perspective, and this is
the major problem in including them in any drawing.
Images culled from magazines are often difficult to
locate convincingly. They may, for example, be at
odds with the floor plane on which they are placed.
However, there are ways of dealing with this. It is
possible, with a digital camera, to pose volunteers to
meet project specific needs, and such digitally created
images may be extensively manipulated within the
computer for compatibility with the digital image.

Left

The isolated figures that give scale to most drawings, without obscuring large sections of the interior, are unsuitable to describe some activities and it is difficult to find appropriate ready-made images of groups. In this example a number of photographs, of individuals and smaller groups, were collected and combined. There are minor discrepancies in relative sizes and perspective but the image itself is composed loosely enough to absorb them.

Left and blow

Idiosyncratic figures and period costumes demonstrate wit - and avoid the possible alienating associations prompted by contemporary alternatives.

Samples

Selection of the right materials is fundamental to the success of every interior. Different choices and different combinations of colour, pattern, texture will radically alter perception of the same volume. It is therefore important, not just for the designer but also the client to see samples of unfamiliar, and familiar, materials at first hand. Traditionally this was, and continues to be, done with 'sample boards', which are usually cumbersome sheets of white mounting board to which swatches and swathes of fabric, pieces of wood, tiles and other components were glued. In the weaker examples individual pieces are stuck down arbitrarily, in the better the arrangement reflects the relative areas that each material occupies in the finished interior and its relationship to other examples. Card mounting boards tends to distort under the different weights and rigidities of different samples. Stiffer plywood baseboards add to the overall weight.

The necessarily limited size of sample boards meant that the effect of large-scale textures and patterns was not made clear. The traditional board originated to demonstrate finishes for traditional interiors, which tended to sport an expansive range of materials. While the modern interior can match that prodigality, generally, the number of materials used tends to be more modest and the impact of large unbroken areas is often more important. Whatever the inclination of the project it is now more usual to explain the orchestration, the areas and interactions of finishes in a rendered perspective, particularly since the advent of the computer as a presentation tool and the use of scanned images of materials, appropriately scaled, downloaded from a manufacturer's website or collaged from the designer's own photographs. However, no matter how accurate the reproduction, it always makes sense to obtain a generously sized real sample, particularly for all manufactured materials with textures and patterns and all natural materials with variable grains for precise reference during the design stage. And all should be shown to the client for formal approval. It is important that agreement is reached for all finishes, to guard against clients' misinterpretation of drawn images, which can lead to disputes and claims when the project is completed.

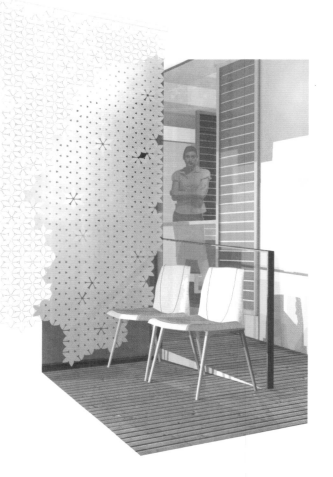

Left and above
An image explains how the thin cardboard sheets will look when sandwiched between sheets of clear glass. A full-size section of a proposed wall covering demonstrates how scored and cut lines may be adapted to make a decorative pattern.

This page
A drawing made to accompany a full size sample of the 'weave graphic' explains how it will be constructed and deployed (left). A perspective shows the mesh and weave in location (below).

Explaining elements and ideas

Below
The abstracted 'winged' image on the left expresses the concept that generates the tensile structure drawn in situ on the right.

Bottom right
A computer-generated structure superimposed on a digital photograph explains how the new 'maze' is accessed and its impact on the existing space.

It is always good practice to begin a presentation by explaining the thinking, whether conceptual or practical, ambient or organizational, that underpins a project, so that the rationale for subsequent steps is clear and convincing. Such drawings tend to be most effective when they are simple and, although simple images can be bland, the computer's capacity to be delicate and precise can ensure that they have presence and authority.

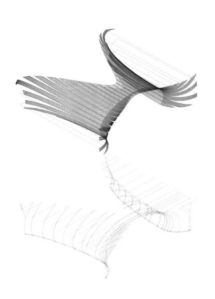

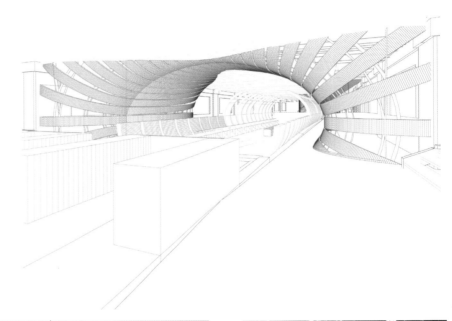

TIP CLARIFYING COMPLICATED ELEMENTS

The reduction of complicated or unfamiliar elements to their constituent parts can help in the understanding of the whole. Here, the separation of elements around a skewed wall opening explains superimposed layers.

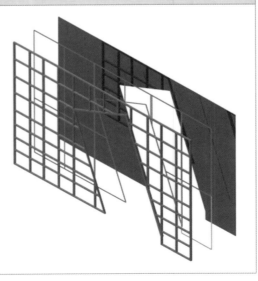

Linear and tonal clarity

The computer is an ideal tool for representing materiality. Most projects deal with modest rectangular single-storey spaces and therefore an accurate depiction of surfaces and finishes is all that is needed to explain the nature of the design proposal. There are, however, other projects when the character of an internal space is defined more usefully by the representation of more complex three-dimensional conditions and gestures. The clarity of these is often lost in elaborately rendered images that obscure the clear expression of form and depth. Information about complex volumes is more effectively conveyed in line drawings that strategically use the minimum of hue and tone, and then only where they help to clarify the expression of solidity.

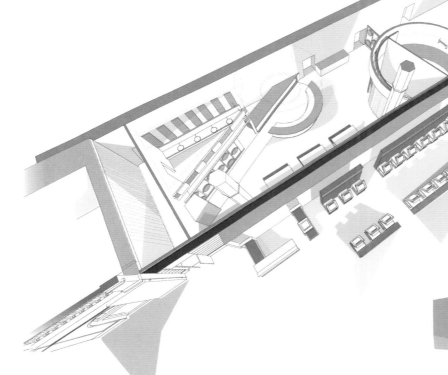

Above
Outlines clearly define the forms and explain how they interconnect. Toned planes emphasize vertical elements and coloured tints define changes in finishes and hint at likely materials. The substitution of a blue-grey line (similar to the shadow tone) for the traditional black helps unify the image.

Right
The same technique can be applied to more conventional perspective views where, again, the intention is to focus on the most important elements. The compatibility of the blue-grey used for both line and shadow reduces the strident contrast of black line on white paper and suggests the transparency of the space.

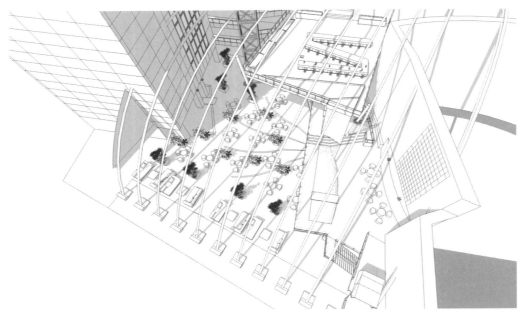

Left
Dramatic perspective drawing underlines the height of this internal volume and is emphasized by the lines of joints in the wall claddings. The single flat shadow tone is enough to give three-dimensional solidity. The recognizable elements of furniture and plants give scale.

Left
In this more conventional view of the same space the block of shadow is enough to convey the suspension of the foreground level, which would inevitably be less apparent in the complexity of a fully rendered view. Again, furniture and plants give scale and explain how the areas will be used.

Below left and right
The outline drawing defines three-dimensional form and the rendered version identifies finishes.

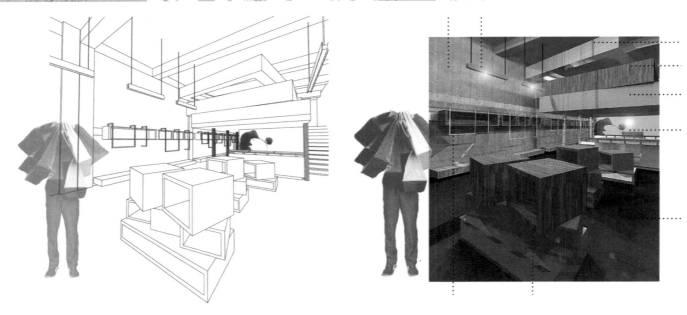

Text

While most presentations are made face-to-face with clients, with verbal explanations to support the images, it is still important to become adept at adding text to visual material. This is emphatically not about writing a long, supporting essay. Ideas should be defined with a minimum of evocative words – using well-crafted phrases rather than sentences, and words rather than phrases. It is productive to explain the evolution of ideas so that clients understand the rationale underpinning the final outcome. Clients usually have their own expectations of a project, and if these are not met they need to be persuaded that the alternative is the consequence of serious analytical thinking. It is generally good to leave presentation material behind after a meeting for a client to mull over, and text will prompt recollection of verbal explanation and focus attention on the essential messages. Extravagant, speculative claims should be avoided. They may goad a sceptical client into dissent.

Text may be used in any drawing – including perspective views, in which it can add a brief and useful commentary and suggest an invisible vertical plane that accentuates the receding perspective.

Before the advent of computers, and except for a small minority of designers with impeccable handwriting, applying text was a time-consuming process that involved stencils or rub-on transfer lettering. Consequently,

Right
Letters may be shaped and toned to respond to the composition of the image.

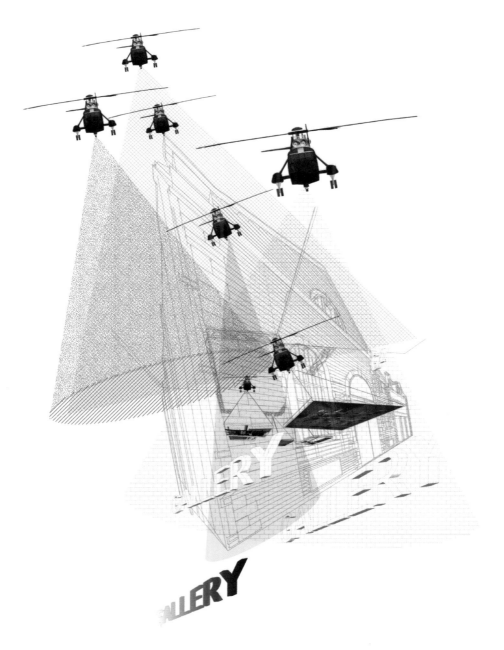

Below
A line of text is appropriately
distorted and connects the two
versions of the same drawing,
of which the desaturated lower
version acts as a backdrop
for the more significant text
that names the project with
a more assertive font.

written information tended to be strictly factual, confined
to the identification of floor levels and the naming of
rooms. Now it is as simple to add words as it is to draw
lines, and while this may encourage verbal excess it also
offers the potential to make drawings more accessible.

Before computers, text tended to be black on white.
Now options exist for infinite tones and hues. Size and
colour of letter may be adjusted. Fonts may be changed.
Styles may be varied. This presents fascinating possibilities
but demands editing, not only to keep text brief but also
to create hierarchies of information. The most important
information should be visually assertive. The impulse to
use too many colours and fonts is potentially dangerous,
randomly coloured text and a plethora of fonts is difficult
to read. Different colours and different fonts may be
used for emphasis and punctuation but the strategy must
be clear to the reader and adhered to by the designer.

Successful text will be an integral part of a drawing
and compatible with the style of the interior proposed.
Most clients will feel comfortable with words and
more confident about criticizing them than about
questioning the content of drawings. Crude grammar
and inept spelling will inevitably undermine a designer's
credibility. Always use spell and grammar checks, then
read the text again to be quite sure it is convincing.

Left
Text explains the
conceptual intention.

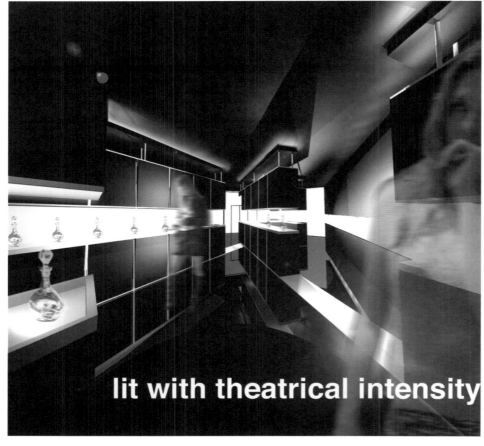

1

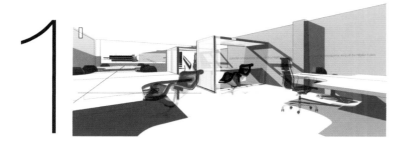

This page
Prominent identifying numbers
act as a clever visual feature of this
sequential client presentation.

2

3

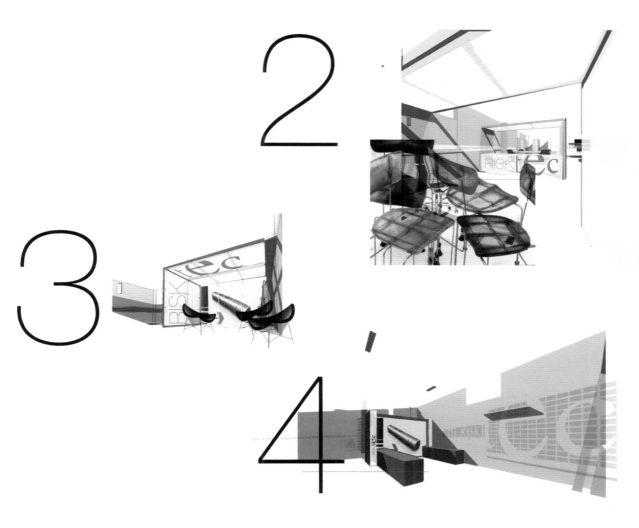

4

5

Designing the final presentation

A final presentation to a client may be perfunctory, the last in a series of discussions, structured around drawings which may be loose or roughly assembled into something resembling a book. When there has been less regular contact between designer and client or when the proposal must go for approval to a client group who will have a discussion amongst themselves about the proposals merits it is important to compile a presentation document that encapsulates the strategy and tactics that shaped the final outcome and a comprehensive representation of that conclusion, a document that provides a permanent record of the verbal presentation. It serves to remind clients of what was said and allows them to examine in their own time things about which they had doubts or that they did not initially understand.

The document should be beautiful to look at and elegantly put together. It makes the first impression. For most projects, there is no need to make big drawings. A3, often A4, sized drawings will support as much information as a client might be expected to assimilate without the punctuation of regular page turning. It is easier to discuss smaller sheets than large boards around a table, and much easier to carry them through the streets on the way to a presentation. It is also likely that an image, or collection of images, which work at A3 for a group presentation will also be legible in A4 format if left for individual perusal after the meeting. The computer is a drawing tool but it is also the tool of desktop publishing and simple specialist programs make it easy to produce ordered, elegant layouts. Odd drawings that need be bigger than A4 can be included as 'fold outs'.

A presentation should be the 'story' of the development of the project and, usually, it makes sense to start at the beginning and proceed logically to the end. It is normal to put more than one image on each page of a presentation – if they deal with the same area of the project. The order in which pages should be presented is usually self-evident – as is the issue of how images should be located on each sheet.

Each page needs to be composed. When images are organized methodically they tend to end up on a regular grid, which makes it difficult to establish meaningful connections or to get a balance of size and visual weight. A better rule of thumb is to identify the key image for each sheet, to locate that centrally – or just above or below the centre – and place supporting images around it, aiming to establish a balance by the manipulation of their relative sizes and distance from the central image. Like all rules this should be broken when events demand it

Images grouped together should complement each other. A perspective view might give an impression of atmosphere, but related plans and sections can contribute hard, practical information that will support and validate the aesthetic intention.

The closeup view in the circular inset at the bottom of this perspective explains the stair balustrade detail.

This page
Each page must be composed.
Here the fragment of inset plan
identifies the location within
the project of the dominant
three-dimensional image
and this is complemented by
information about finishes of
new and existing walls.

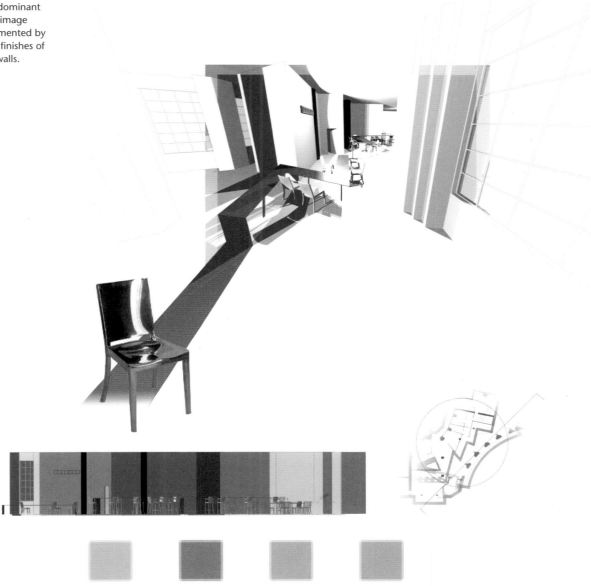

While it is often important to provide physical samples of materials, it is also logical – and, with computers, increasingly easy – to scan in images of materials and artefacts that complement the drawn information. Scans of finishes should be located close to the areas to which they relate and repeated close to every area in which they appear.

Comprehensive evidence, in image and text forms, eliminates the need for superfluous embellishments. Decorative logos and emblems are more likely to confuse than to clarify, and an elaborate and repetitive titling of each sheet is pointless and visually redundant. It may, however, be diplomatic to feature a client's corporate identity.

The pages that follow, which have been selected from much more extensive presentation sequences for each of the featured projects, illustrate particular approaches to the presentation document's mission to explain.

The illustrated projects demonstrate how each designer brings distinctive personal style to presentation techniques and image making that complements the spirit and intention of their proposal.

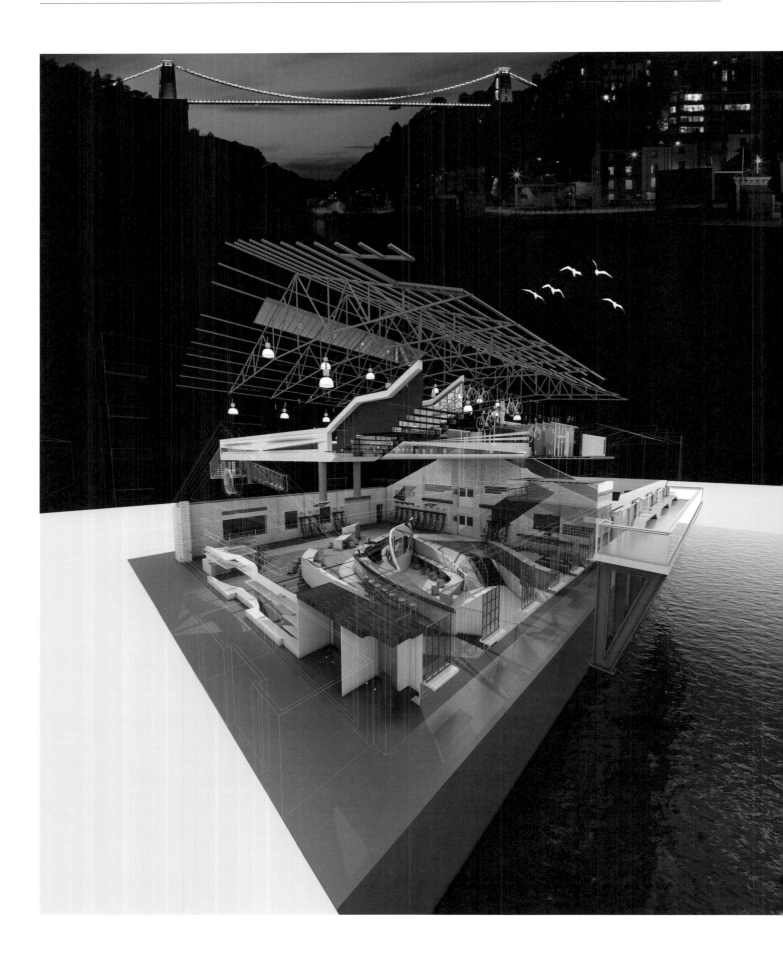

Opposite
This 'exploded' perspective view exploits the computer's capacity to make complicated and intricate forms to give a detailed description of the core area of the project. The floating roof structure and the water offer convincing reminders of the context.

Right and below
The 'exploded' top image here identifies and describes the individual elements that make up the complex display system that occupies the centre of the perspective below it.

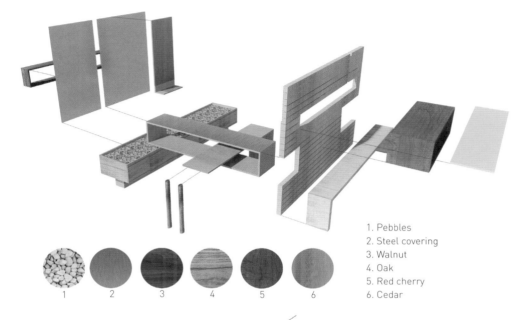

1. Pebbles
2. Steel covering
3. Walnut
4. Oak
5. Red cherry
6. Cedar

Case study Linking levels

The ground-floor plan and isonometric describe
this proposal in purely factual terms. The plan
demonstrates layout. The isonometric extrudes the
ground floor and relates it spatially to the upper
level and its lowered ceiling and light fittings.

The perspective view explains, in a
deliberately selective and mannered fashion, the
atmosphere created by materials and lighting –
and this is complemented by the scanned images
of materials and fittings, set out formally and
objectively at the bottom of the presentation.

Below
The isometric view explains the relationship of the
lower floor plan, on the left, to the upper floor.

Opposite
The three dimensional view and material samples
complete explanation of the lower floor.

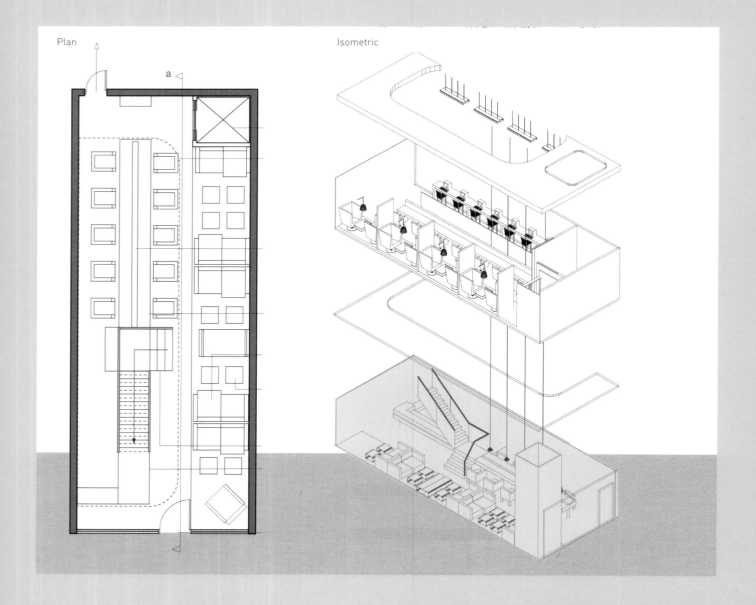

Plan

Isometric

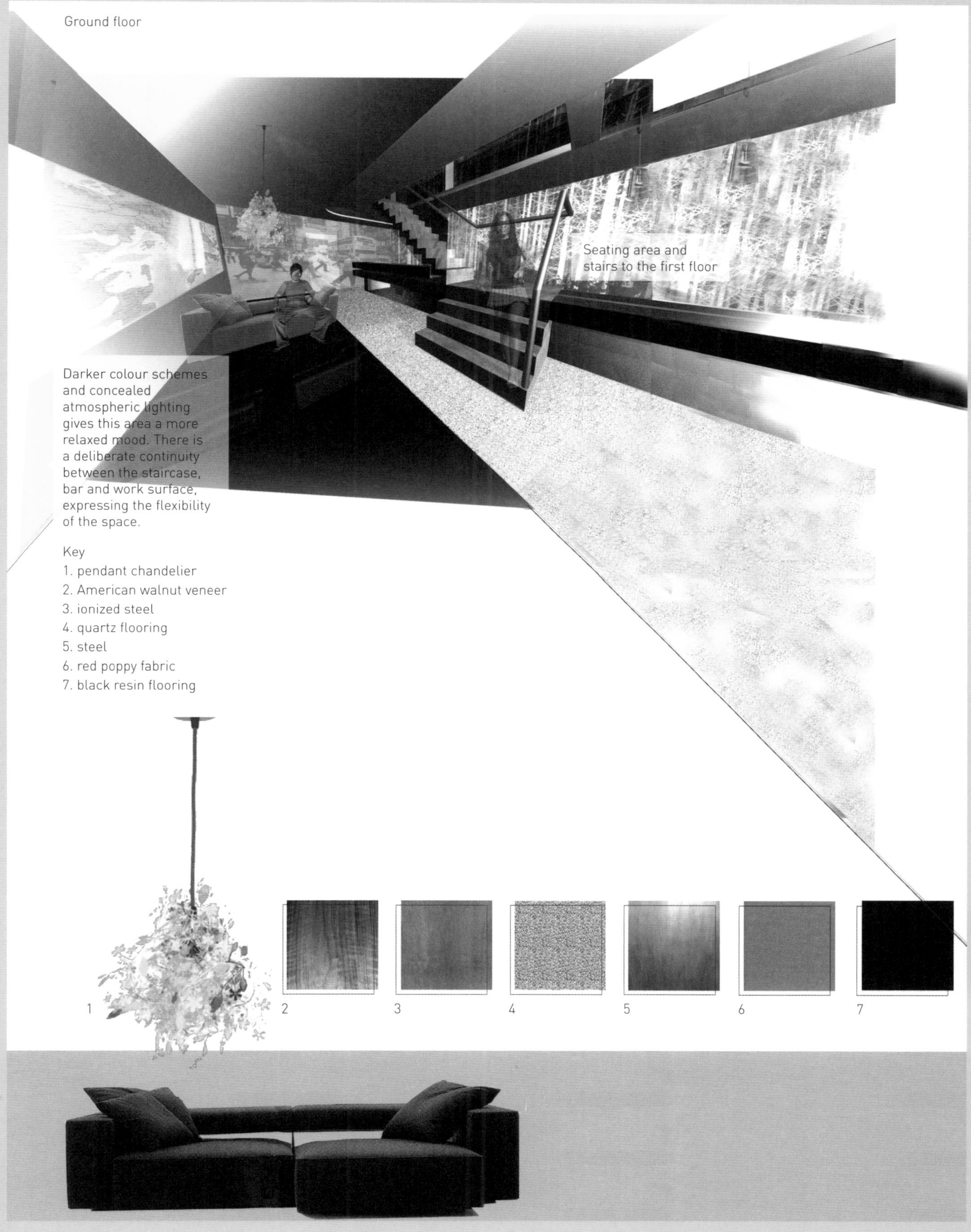

Ground floor

Seating area and
stairs to the first floor

Darker colour schemes
and concealed
atmospheric lighting
gives this area a more
relaxed mood. There is
a deliberate continuity
between the staircase,
bar and work surface,
expressing the flexibility
of the space.

Key
1. pendant chandelier
2. American walnut veneer
3. ionized steel
4. quartz flooring
5. steel
6. red poppy fabric
7. black resin flooring

1   2   3   4   5   6   7

Case study Explaining flexibility

Complex proposals may involve options for layouts or, as in this project, the use of movable partitions. For both a series of drawings, illustrating the range of conditions, is the clearest way of explaining things.

Right
Extruded plans show the three options and text identifies functional strategy for each.

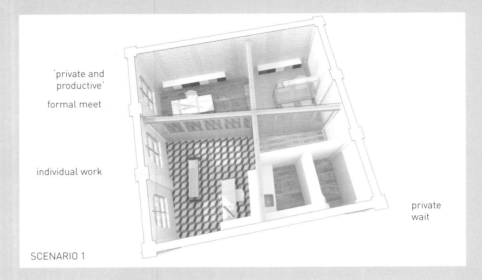

'private and productive'

formal meet

individual work

private wait

SCENARIO 1

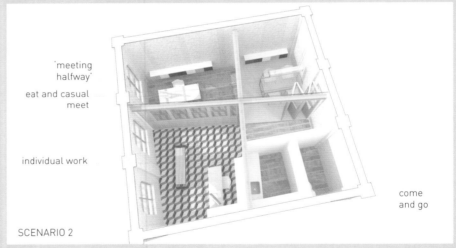

'meeting halfway'

eat and casual meet

individual work

come and go

SCENARIO 2

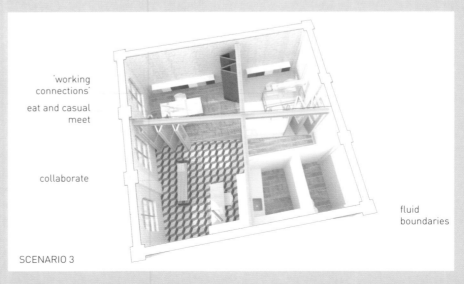

'working connections'

eat and casual meet

collaborate

fluid boundaries

SCENARIO 3

VIEW FROM OFFICE

VIEW FROM RECEPTION

VIEW FROM OFFICE

Left
Views amplify the explanation.

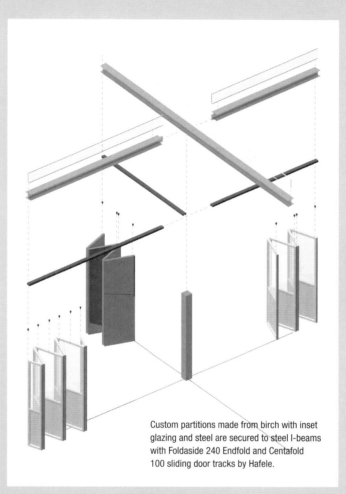

Custom partitions made from birch with inset
glazing and steel are secured to steel I-beams
with Foldaside 240 Endfold and Centafold
100 sliding door tracks by Hafele.

Above
A diagram illustrates structural principles.

Case study Context and content

A good presentation will explain a proposal from the very general to the very particular. Three drawings here illustrate the range of images necessary to describe a complex physical solution, within a complex existing building shell, to a complex brief.

Below
Location maps explain the geographical context and a photograph establishes the character of the existing building, drawing attention to the large window that defines the interior organization.

The residence is located in Inverness city centre, along the banks of the River Ness, with close connections to the city's services as well as the surrounding community. Potential clients (between the ages of 18 and 25) would require continued support throughout their adult life and would be unable to live independently.

Space is provided for two live-in carers who, with the potential help from additional day staff, provide 24-hour support.

The home is a social hub for the group, encouraging the building of a network of friends. Each individual finds their purpose and role within the small community, with their care network helping to equip them with life skills throughout their long-term stay.

The chosen site is currently home to the Highland Print Studios in Inverness. The long and narrow plot reaches to the river, with the front facade's large arched windows giving views of the river and hills beyond.

At the back of the site, there is a private walled garden that is level with the main living space.

THE WALL living sections

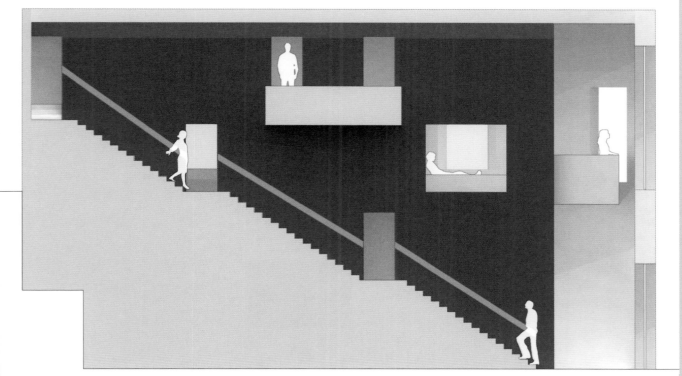

OUTSIDE THE WALL - Visual connections are created between extruding balconies and the main circulation route, giving people a sense of activity and movement outside of the space they are occupying.

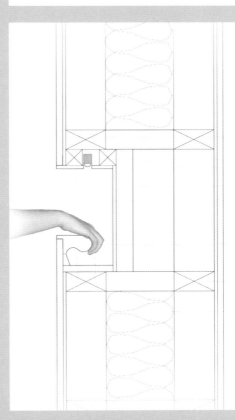

INSIDE THE WALL - living spaces are filtered between the bedroom levels avoiding the segregation of public and private, this allows the main living floor to occupy the building's centre

metal angle at edge of 18mm (¾in) (thick felt wall cladding

LED light strip in aluminium tray secured to 50x50mm (2x2in) timber

12mm (½in) plyboard

hardwood handrail (painted to match wall finish) is secured on to base plate and into timber stud frame

120x60mm (4¾x2⅓) timber stud framing (400 centres) between structural steel columns and I-beams

insulation

Above
A diagrammatic section illustrates how a stair rises through the building and balconies allow residents to look into the stairwell and across the void through the existing high window to the river.

Left
Detail of the handrail set into the thickness of the stairwell wall. This could be treated more diagrammatically with rendered colours and materials, but this drawing illustrates the principle and provides a means to draw attention to refinements of construction that might be lost in a rendered image.

Case study Sharing the creative process

This proposal for the flagship store of a mobile phone retailer demonstrates the analysis of the brief and the principles behind the solution. The key feature here is a 'paint wall', and this colour theme is carried throughout the store. The featured colours are those of the mobile phone casings on offer, and the colours are also used to represent the different downloadable apps that are available, updated sales for which are projected on to the store wall as a bar chart.

STORE PROCESS: MOBILE PHONE SHOP

STEP 1

→ Select Applications
Using the touch sensitive screen customers can drag the selected application onto the phone.

→ Select Price Plan
Customers then select a price plan to go with their phone.

→ Place Order
Once the customer is happy with their selection, they can place the order which can be collected in the basement level.

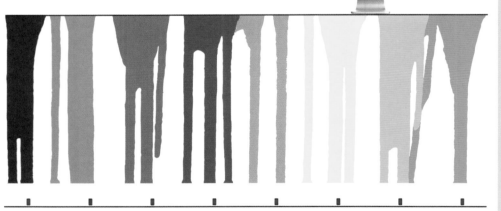

STEP 2
→ Chose Handset
Once the customer has customised their applications and price plan they can select the model of phone they want.

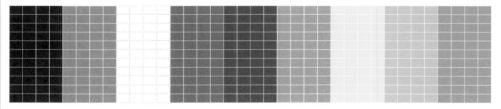

STEP 3
→ Choose Colour
The customer then chooses the colour of the handset

→ Make Payment
Once happy with their choice, the customer makes a payment to a sales assistant, and once activated, the phone's customised features will be updated via download.

Model exploring how paint is applied onto the glass wall [Scale 1:100].

Case study Explaining the hypothetical

These drawings illustrate devices to increase public awareness of schizophrenia. Light drawings and small text on generous white background suggest a scientific objectivity and the monochromatic perspective views show a similar restraint.

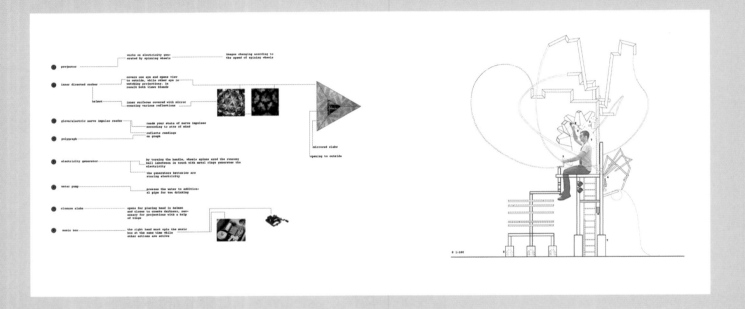

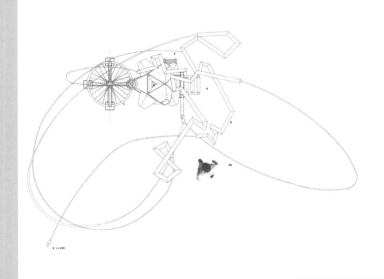

Case study Factual underpinning

Expressionistic renderings are given credibility by detailed rationales and analyses that are given equal weight in this presentation.

The proposal is for a restaurant serving insect cuisine in a disused tube station. The fantastical elements are given validity by the judicious use of factual information, structural data and technical drawings.

Right
Site plan and perspectival drawing alongside an unusual menu.

Below
Compelling facts and explanatory text provide gravitas.

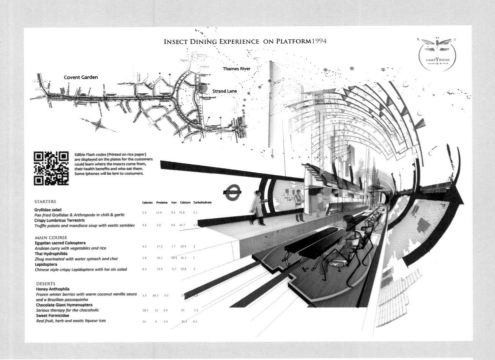

Right
Structural analysis of the site along with infographics and detail photographs ground the project in reality.

Below
Conceptual renderings alongside sectional drawings and conceptual information.

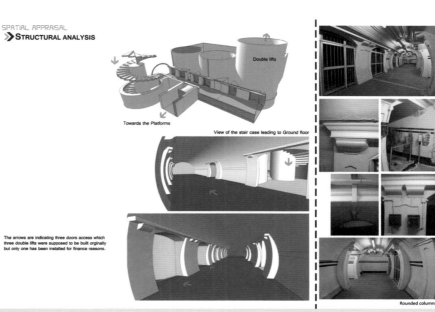

SPATIAL APPRAISAL
▶ **STRUCTURAL ANALYSIS**

Double lifts

Towards the Platforms

View of the stair case leading to Ground floor

The arrows are indicating three doors access which three double lifts were supposed to be built orginally but only one has been installed for finance reasons.

Rounded columns

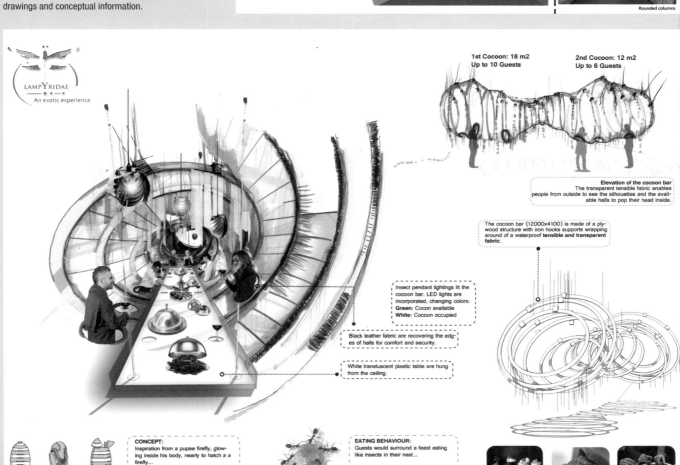

LAMPYRIDAE
An exotic experience

1st Cocoon: 18 m2
Up to 10 Guests

2nd Cocoon: 12 m2
Up to 6 Guests

Elevation of the cocoon bar
The transparent tensible fabric enables people from outside to see the silhouettes and the available halls to pop their head inside.

The cocoon bar (12000x4100) is made of a ply-wood structure with iron hooks supports wrapping around of a waterproof **tensible and transparent fabric.**

Insect pendant lightings lit the cocoon bar. LED lights are incorporated, changing colors:
Green: Cocon available
White: Cocoon occupied

Black leather fabric are recovering the edges of halls for comfort and security.

White transluscent plastic table are hung from the ceiling.

CONCEPT:
Inspiration from a pupae firefly, glowing inside his body, nearly to hatch a a firefly...

EATING BEHAVIOUR:
Guests would surround a feast eating like insects in their nest...

Case study Focusing attention

These drawings relate to the more complex image featured on pages 14 and 15 which illustrate steps in the process of digital rendering, and to the details on page 13. The more linear versions illustrated here emphasize the contours of the principal elements, their separation and interaction. While such details will be clearly visible in reality their impact may be diluted at the smaller scale of the rendered drawing.

Below
Two images, floating against a grey background tint, define individual ribs and their component pieces. The flat green tint identifies a glass wall.

Opposite top
Linear diagram gives way to linear perspective illustrating more clearly the separation of components and the nature of the internal space. Familiar elements, the stair and table, give scale.

Opposite below
This diagrammatic perspective image introduces materials, graphics and furniture and adds surface reflectivities and transparencies.

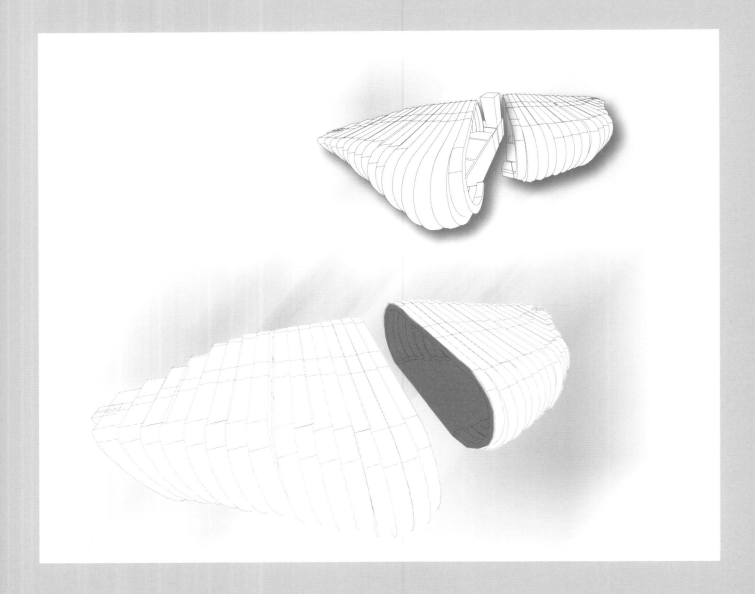

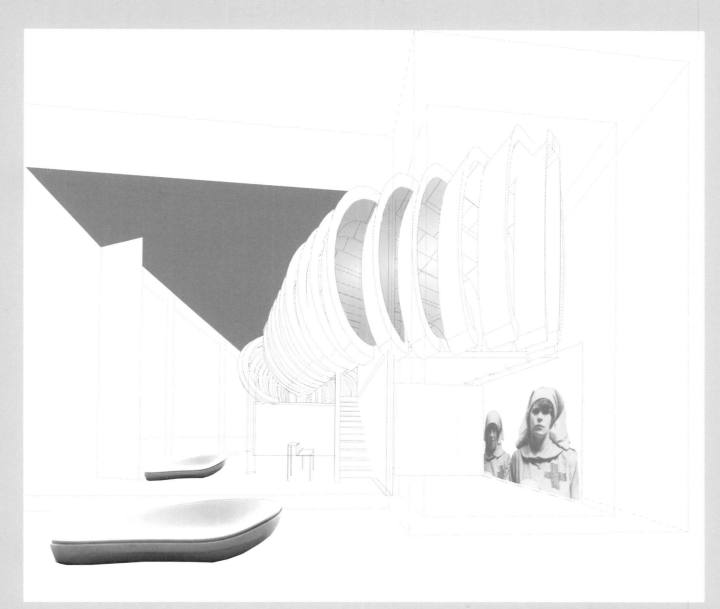

Case study Hard-edged thinking

These examples, selected from a more comprehensive set of presentation drawings, demonstrate how complementary two- and three dimensional, line and rendered images enhance understanding of a small but complex volume. The style of drawing is fine-tuned to suit its content.

Below
The blue three-dimensional images identify solid and void elements and locate principal activities within the building shell. The position of secondary elements is detailed on the plans which also establish the location of section cuts.

Opposite
The details provide enough information about materials, equipment and assembly techniques to enable a builder to construct the changing booth. With a proposal as particular as this it also makes sense to describe the aesthetic intention so that the builder is clear about the intended outcome. While the drawings provide a client with more technical information than they might wish, they make clear that the proposal has been well considered and its aspirations can be realized.

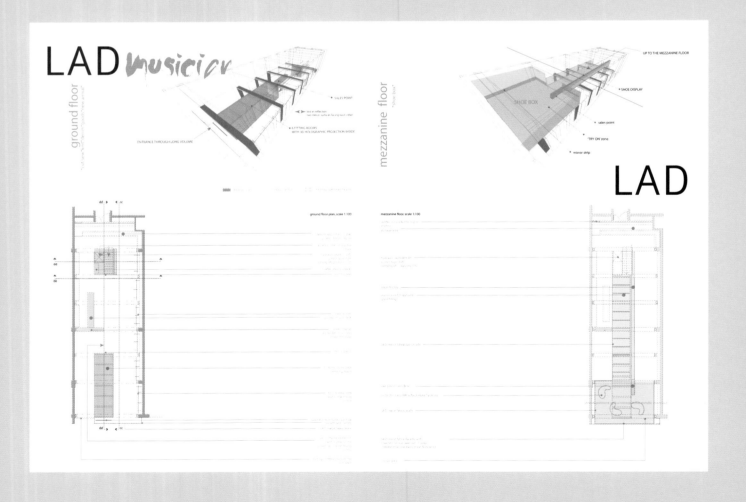

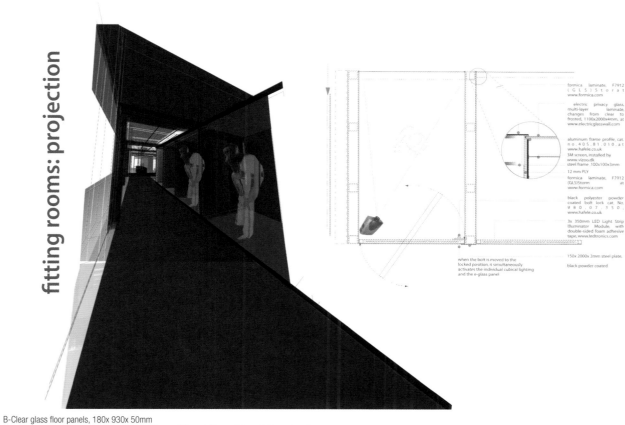

fitting rooms: projection

formica laminate, F7912
(GLS)Storat
www.formica.com

electric privacy glass,
multi-layer laminate,
changes from clear to
frosted, 1100x2000x4mm, at
www.electricglasswall.com

aluminum frame profile, cat.
no.405.81.010.at
www.hafele.co.uk
3M screen, installed by
www.vizoo.dk
steel frame .100x100x3mm

12 mm PLY

formica laminate, F7912
(GLS)Storm at
www.formica.com

black polyester powder
coated bolt lock cat. No.
980.07.350.
www.hafele.co.uk

3x 350mm LED Light Strip
Illuminator Module, with
double-sided foam adhesive
tape, www.ledtronics.com

150x 2000x 3mm steel plate,

black powder coated

when the bolt is moved to the
locked position, it simultaneously
activates the individual cubical lighting
and the e-glass panel

B-Clear glass floor panels, 180x 930x 50mm
www.mykon-systems.com

steel beam, 203x133mm,
clear varnished

18mm MDF, painted black

power supply for the projector

power supply for LED light strip
and electric glass

exposed neon tubes mounted on
1600x250mm toughened glass
by www.business-signs.co.uk

Rixson 370 pivot set ,
top screwed to steel frame
www.doorcloser.com

R 25mm door stopper

steel frame , 100x100 x 3

ceiling mounted projector,
installed by www,vizoo.dk

sliding security panel

Rixson 370 pivot set ,
bottom plugged and screwed to
to existing screed
www.doorcloser.com

holographic projection inside every fitting room

free-floating hologram looks absolutely true to life.

The film merges with the foreground and background to create an
illusion in a real-life setting. technology developed by www.vizoo.dk

Case study Towards abstraction

As designers refine and become more intensely involved with the development of a project, so the nature of the drawings they make to describe it often take on a particular identity that strays from the strictly factual but is singularly appropriate to the underpinning concept. Such drawings can be the most effective way of communicating, perhaps subliminally, the spirit of a project to a client. These two drawings demonstrate that creative and practised use of computer imaging allows the designer to deploy, with equal facility, distinctly different drawing styles, inspired by – and complementary to – the spirit of the project itself. Both are intended to explain the concept that underpins each project and their distinctive vigour suggests a creative confidence that has grown from an immersion in the design process that has taken the designer a long way beyond the obvious and the familiar.

Left
The same trompe l'oeil pattern used on the ceiling of the lower level and floor of the upper, dominates the image as it would the built interior. Single-point perspective is employed independently on each level, but the combination of two viewpoints adds ambiguity to the image and greater significance to the illusion. Each level demonstrates variations on shared themes: star patterns on similar but different padded backgrounds, the hemispherical chairs, resting on the floor above and hanging from the ceiling below, the silhouettes of animals and birds. The stars floating on the edges of the drawing repeat an important decorative motif and help give the illusion of depth. Black and white figures emphasize the mirroring of planes.

Opposite
The conceptual essence of the project again determines the nature of the drawing. The interior of a simple cellular structure is made extraordinary by an eclectic collection of elements, all of which, including wall finishes, are crucial in establishing the character of each level. Each object is set, with equal status, against a black background to establish its character. The colours of the figures, which give scale and explain function, complement and augment those of the levels they inhabit. The image of the moon relates to the building's function as a predominantly nocturnal place. The word 'perspective', which is itself in perspective but describe a drawing which is not a perspective, confirms a provocative wit determined to provoke reaction and encourage speculation.

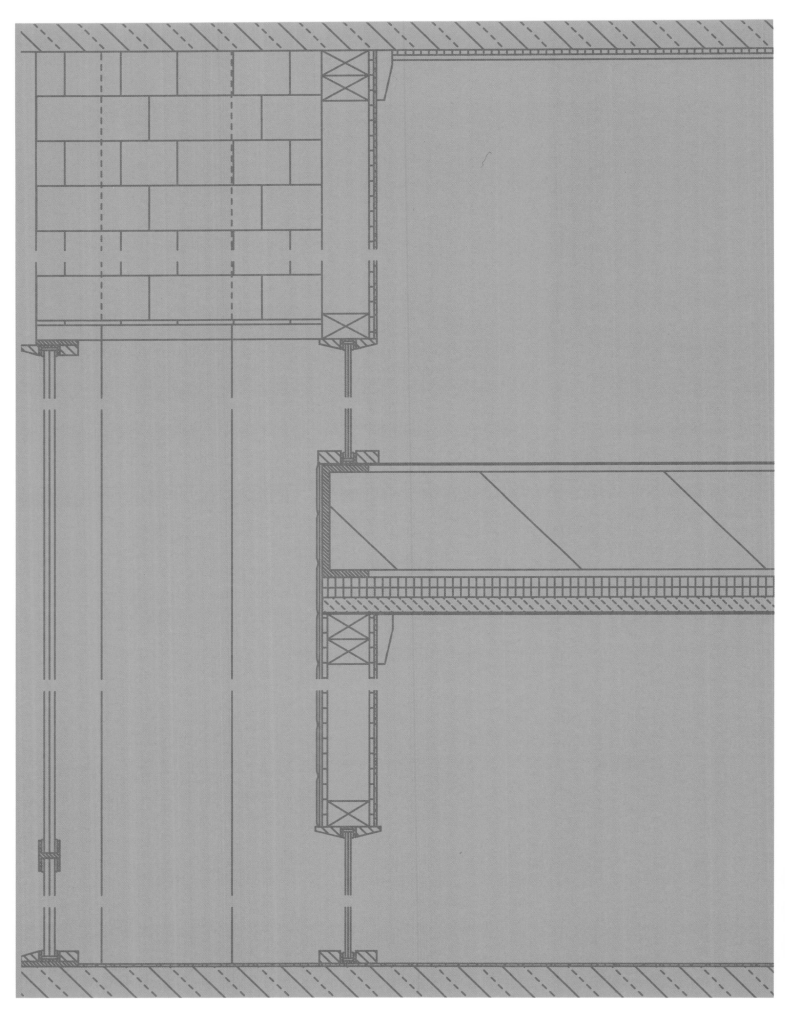

CHAPTER 4 PRODUCTION

The designer's role

After formal presentation, and once the client has approved the final design drawings, it is the designer's job to produce a set of 'working drawings' or 'production drawings'. The number of these will vary from project to project, but their function remains the same. They will provide the building contractor, and anyone else involved in the construction process, with a comprehensive description, in drawings and words, of the full extent and quality of the work necessary to complete the project satisfactorily and this information will also become the basis of the contractual agreement between client and builders. The designer must provide plans and sections of the complete project and of every element within it, to describe in detail the materials to be used, the sizes of components and the method for their assembly. Words are as important as drawings at this stage. The two are mutually supportive. The words, and numerical dimensions, will describe materials and methods of fixing components, large and small, that make up the finished elements. Plans, sections and elevations, provide the means to link written notes with the items and areas to which they refer. Most projects also require general notes about the standard of work and quality of materials that apply across the job and these may be added to a drawing or, if extensive, treated as a separate document.

It is usually desirable that a designer also takes responsibility for the supervision of work on site if quality is to be assured and the unforeseen difficulties that often come to light during construction are to be dealt with successfully. Almost inevitably with any interior project, particularly one in an older building, conditions will be discovered in the course of the work that require changes to the designer's original intention. It may be a structural problem that demands additional work or the uncovering of an extant element that is worth incorporating into the new. If discoveries require extra work then the contractor is entitled to be paid for that. If, as occasionally happens, the volume of work is reduced then the client is entitled to a reduction. If disputes arise it is the designer's role to act as an arbitrator to ensure, on the client's behalf, that the extent and quality of the job matches that quoted for; and, on the contractor's behalf, that payment is made for completed work and for extra, unforeseen work that may have become necessary during the course of the contract. While this may be the result of site conditions that were not apparent during the initial surveys, which are necessarily completed before it was possible to carry out exploratory demolition it may also result from changing requirements on the client's side. Occasionally, it may be the result of designer error, and, although it may be painful to admit shortcomings, it is usually sensible to do so since

it will be fairly obvious who is to blame, and stubbornly maintaining innocence in the face of contradictory evidence can only lead to a loss of credibility and trust.

A completed set of production drawings will allow a builder to estimate the cost of the building work and produce a 'tender', which is an estimated cost of all necessary work, including labour and materials, and the total sum for which the builder is prepared to carry out all the work. Sometimes clients will nominate a contractor, usually on the basis of a previous successful collaboration, and it will then be the designer's job to advise on the fairness of the uncontested tender. This has the advantage of allowing the designer to discuss costs during the development of the project, and so control the budget. If the client and contractor have a well established relationship and mutual trust then the nature of the designer's role changes slightly and some of the responsibility for maintaining quality is reduced. It is, however, more usual for at least three contractors to tender for a job, and for the one offering the lowest price to be given the work. It then becomes the designer's responsibility to check that the successful contractor is capable of carrying out the work to a satisfactory standard. This applies particularly if the tender is lower than anticipated, which can suggest that the contractor has miscalculated or is over-anxious to get the work and may not have the reserve resources to deal adequately with complications that arise in the course of the contract, or, at a more fundamental level, to pay initially for materials and labour.

Designers should not expect to know everything. As the individuals ultimately responsible for the success of a project, it is more important for them to be able to bring an intelligent, critical eye to bear on its development and to control the interaction between aesthetic intentions and practical priorities.

It is often difficult to estimate the cost of an interior project accurately. When operating in new buildings the nature of the work may be clearly defined and easily estimated, and it is very unlikely that unanticipated work or significant amendments to the first contract will occur. With work to existing buildings, cost estimation is more difficult. Complications are often unforeseeable, emerging only as existing finishes are stripped back and problems are exposed.

It is also in the nature of interiors projects that the finishes and construction details that make up the bulk of the work will be unique to the particular scheme, and therefore an accurate price depends on the contractors' perception of the intrinsic difficulties involved in meeting unfamiliar demands. In large contracts it may be possible to have a quantity surveyor estimate costs but the scale

Right
This detail, for sloping glass panels, demonstrates the interdependence of written notes and drawing.

Vertical Section
[Scale 1:10]

1. Touch sensitive LCD monitor

2. 50mm (2 in) solid acrylic shelf

3. Ø 30 mm (1¼ in) steel fixing bracket

4. Floor construction:
   5mm poured resin 'pearl Grey' flooring finish by Teknai
   50 mm (2 in) screen
   240 mm (9½ in) reinforced concrete floor slab

5. Scott Amir an 10 mm (⅛in) laminated safety glass

6. Ø 30 mm (1¼ in) rubber spacer

7. Ø 50 mm (2 in) pignose polished steel screwhead

8. Mobile phone display unit w. charging dock

9. 5 mm (⅛ in) white acrylic sheet

10. Plinth construction:
    5 mm (⅛ in) acrylic sheet
    20 mm (¾ in) MDF board
    160/80 SW batten

11. Floor construction:
    70/19 mm ((¾ in) ash boarding
    50 mm (2 in) screed
    245 mm (9¾ in) reinforced concrete floor slab

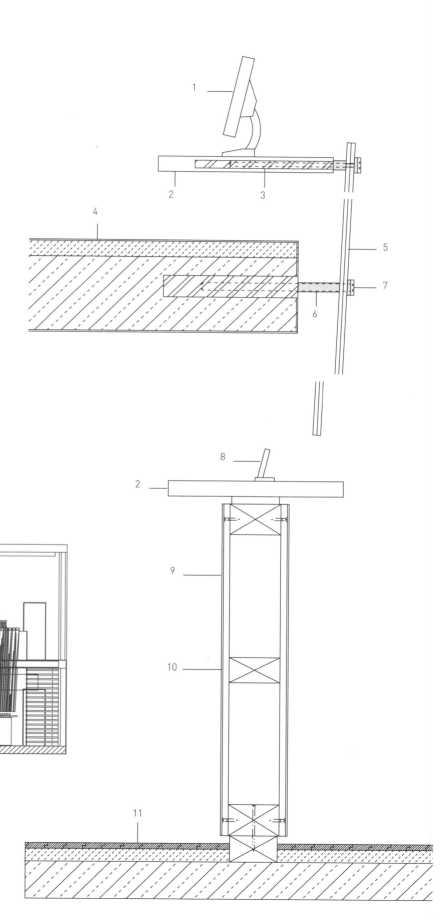

Below

An exploded isometric explains, visually, the assembly of a framing piece and helps understanding of the two-dimensional section, with notes that specify components.

and speed and short building period for most projects rule this out. Contractors inevitably prefer to work with familiar materials and techniques and will submit an expensive quote for complicated work to ensure that undertaking it will be rewarded and unforeseen costs will be covered. A project that strays from the familiar will also require extra commitment from a client, who may be inspired to agree to an expensive option by a seductive presentation but whose initial enthusiasm will weaken if there are a succession of expensive, unanticipated or unacknowledged complications. It is normal, and logical, that the designer will be blamed for practical inefficiencies and overspending if creative ambition has contributed to difficulties. A designer persuading a client to commit to an ambitious or innovative project must be prepared to spend more time detailing and supervising its construction, for the same fee as a more conventional solution.

Clients always have a budget beyond which they cannot or will not go. While they often have some capacity to extend this, there is usually a point at which it becomes apparent that it will be necessary to negotiate with the contractor details of the work, whether to eliminate whole elements or simplify construction, in order to reduce the overall cost. The designer is crucial to this process because decisions must be made about how savings will least prejudice the aesthetic and practical efficiency of the finished work, and only the designer has the overview and knowledge to resolve such compromises successfully.

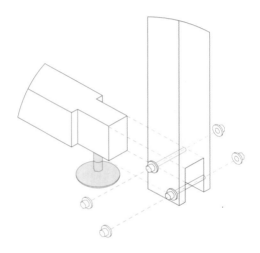

Detail: Shelves 1

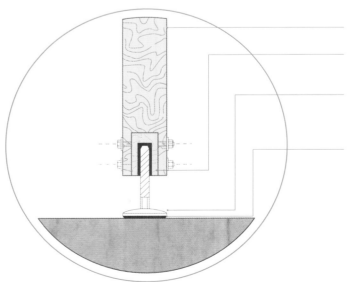

50mmx50mm (2x2in) dressed douglas fir posts

Mortise and tenon joint fixed with no. 2 M5 bolt and nut

M10 adjusting foot screw into threaded sleeve in horizontal bottom post

3mm (⅛in) rubber disk bonded to bottom of screw foot

Detail: Shelves 2

Developing detail

Normally the plans, sections and finishes for a project will have been finalized during the development of the design and been approved by the client, and an experienced designer will have considered, from early in the developmental process, the feasibility of constructing the more elaborate elements and visual impact of the likely detailing solutions. Often the first proposal for a construction detail, particularly if it uses familiar materials in a familiar context, will adhere closely to initial expectations and will be known to work. However, unanticipated problems, including necessary variations on well-tried solutions, will often emerge because the precise characteristics of each project are different, and aspects of the solution to one problem can very often have an impact on the resolution of apparently unrelated details. The admirable impulse on a designer's part to establish a stylistic compatibility between elements of a project will prompt a necessary variation on a standard and well-tested detail.

Detail drawings, like all others in the design process, begin with a designer's first thoughts, and, like them, are likely to be scribbled in a notebook or sketchpad. The process for developing them is also essentially the same. After initial, informed but unstructured thinking, the transfer must be made to scaled drawing in order to test ideas rigorously before producing the final version.

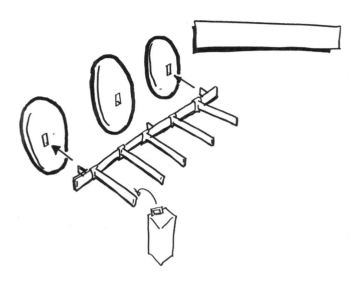

Above
A first speculation about bracket supports for wall-mounted shelving.

Below
First thoughts are likely to be made on any convenient scrap of paper. In this double page spread from a lined notebook calculations for setting out components and a list of equipment dominate the perfunctory sketches that are more about clarifying perception than finalizing an idea.

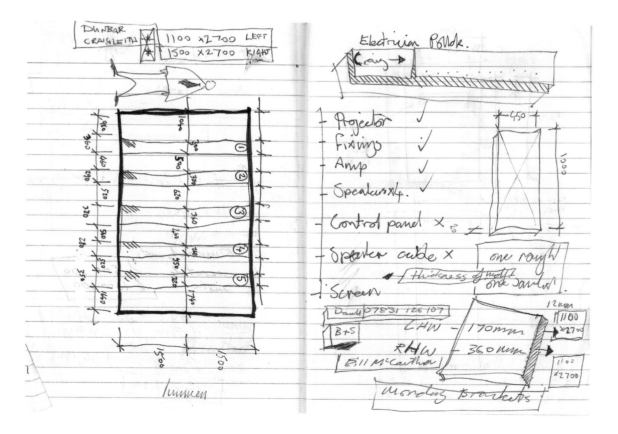

Accurate scaled drawings ensure an accurate perception of the relative sizes of individual components and their exact relationship one to another. While scaled drawings are sometimes still made by hand, on a drawing board with technical drawing instruments, normally they are now made on computer, which also allows the designer to magnify a drawing, which may eventually be issued to the contactor at 1:5 scale, to full size to get a more accurate understanding of the size of the finished detail.

While details, particularly those that will be visible in the finished building, must always be considered in three dimensions, it is standard practice to draw options and present conclusions, as two-dimensional plans and sections. This isolates and simplifies particular aspects of the problem and its solution, and so helps clarify thinking during development. It also presents information to the builder or maker in a more comprehensible form. It may be useful to add three-dimensional projections in order to clarify how parts relate, but unless the forms are very simple it is generally difficult to read dimensions and notes against three-dimensional images. The computer generates three-dimensional views much more quickly and efficiently than the hand, and those produced for earlier presentation work may be easily transferred to production documents in order to clarify the intended outcome.

There is perhaps an instinct amongst traditionally trained designers to be suspicious of the introduction of more accessible, superficially frivolous drawings during the production phase. However, if it is accepted that drawings made for a client should be as accessible as possible then the same should be true of drawings created for use on site. It was the difficulties involved in adding colour, tone and a third dimension – because of the drawing instruments and reproduction equipment available – that, until recently, have excluded them from the repertoire of production drawings. The computer makes their inclusion simple and their exclusion foolish.

It is obviously worth taking advantage of the advances and variations that the computer makes possible. Tones can effectively replace hatchings, which tend to be visually strident. Various coloured lines may be used because they are as easy to reproduce as a black one. However, it is important that the potential for variations is treated intelligently. Too much will result in incoherence. Differences in line thicknesses and tones must be readily distinguishable to the eye if they are to contribute to clarity. Probably a drawing should feature no more than three thicknesses, thin, medium and thick with clear differences between each.

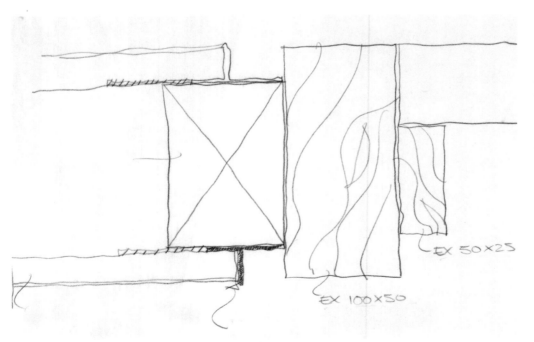

Left
Being able to draw a fast freehand detail remains a useful skill when discussing options with colleagues or instructing contractors on site for an unanticipated variation. This example, for a door jamb, was made roughly to scale with a pencil in an A4 tracing paper over an A4 gridded sheet that facilitated control of dimensions.

This page
A selection of notebook and
computer sketches speculating
about fixed seating units.

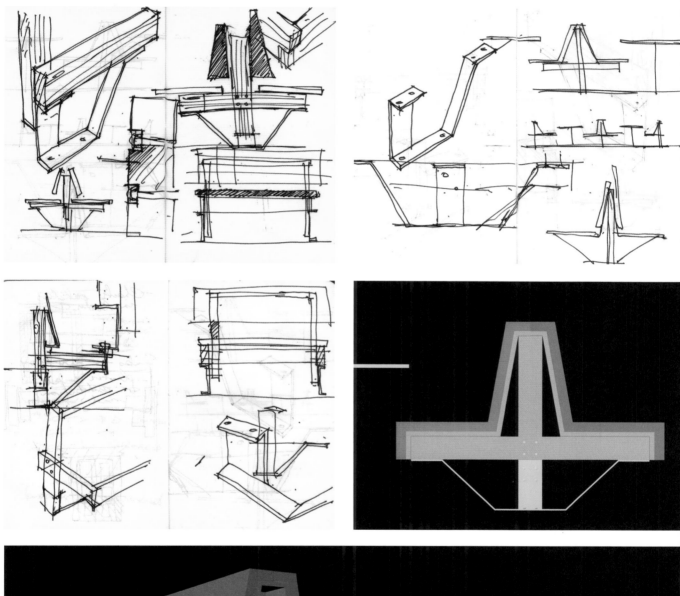

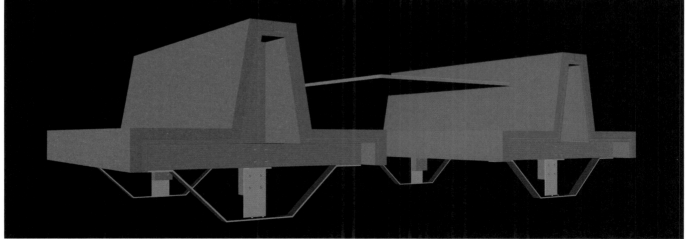

Collaboration

Contractors, particularly those responsible for highly specialist work, will frequently suggest simpler and cheaper ways of achieving a desired outcome, and if the designer is confident that the result will be aesthetically acceptable and will meet practical requirements, then there is every reason to accept the alternative offered. It is important under these circumstances to ask contractors to provide a guarantee of quality, and to agree, perhaps, to a reduction in cost.

With specialist trades, such as furniture manufacture, it is common practice to select a contractor on the strength of a quotation based on the drawings produced by the designer, which establish precisely the configuration and specification of finishes of the elements required but do not specify construction techniques. This is a recognition that a better and more economical job is likely to result if manufacturers are able to use the techniques most suited to their work force and machinery. Such specialists should provide what are, in effect, their

Below
The drawing and notes clearly explain the designer's intention and are enough to allow a conversation with the builder about construction tactics, such as the material and method of fixing for the curved ribs.

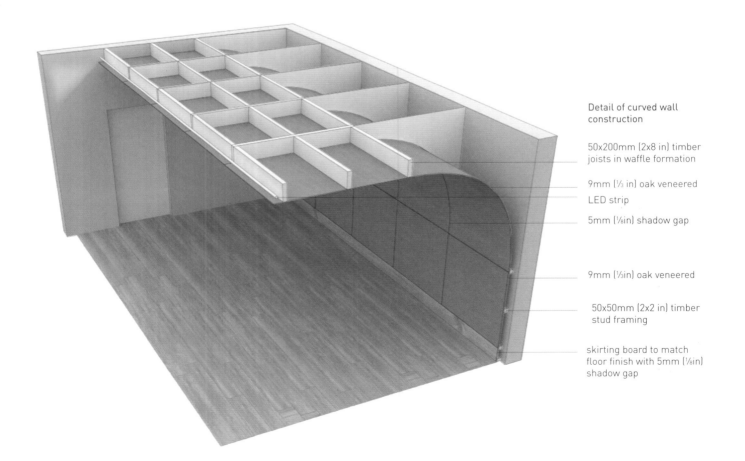

Detail of curved wall construction

50x200mm (2x8 in) timber joists in waffle formation

9mm (⅓ in) oak veneered LED strip

5mm (⅛in) shadow gap

9mm (⅛in) oak veneered

50x50mm (2x2 in) timber stud framing

skirting board to match floor finish with 5mm (⅛in) shadow gap

own detailed production drawings, and they should give these to the designer for approval before beginning the work. The designer will, in these circumstances, be primarily checking that there have been no changes that affect the aesthetic intention, because the specialists will have taken responsibility for practical performance.

It is a good idea to visit a factory or workshop in order to see and understand processes. Knowledge gained is liable to go beyond the immediate project and broaden creative horizons.

Manufacturers of fittings and materials, are constantly refining their products and it is obviously sensible to consult manufacturers for technical advice about performance and appropriate assembly techniques before making a definitive drawing. It is in manufacturers' interest to be supportive because it helps sell their products and many now provide precise and detailed digital drawings of their components, which may be downloaded and incorporated into finished production drawings. These also allow designers to design around the component – and give credibility to the drawings.

TIP THREE DIMENSIONS CLARIFY TWO

While dimensions are most effectively conveyed in two-dimensional drawings it will often help a contractor understand the nature of the proposal better if a supporting drawing, like this isometric, digitally generated from the two-dimensional data, is also supplied.

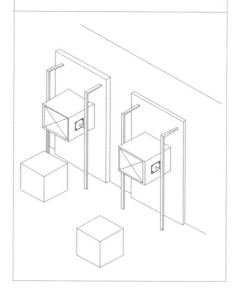

Below
The drawings provide the fabricator with all the information about dimensions needed to create a drawing for the designer's approval.

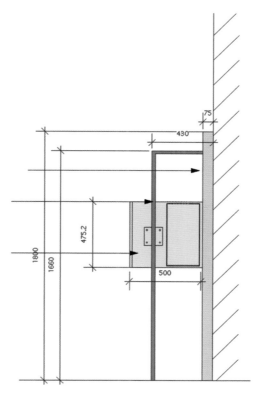

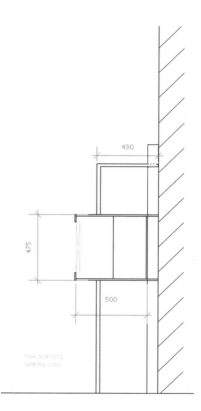

This page
These drawings, prepared by the designer
and sent to the nominated subcontractor/
fabricator, indicate dimensions of the
proposed pieces, and the small scale section
at the bottom of the drawing indicates
their eventual location. Structural framing
is indicated but this is as much to indicate
hollow elements as it is to suggest a definitive
fabrication method. The figures confirm
scale and presumably served to amuse the
designer and (perhaps) the contractor in
the midst of otherwise serious work.

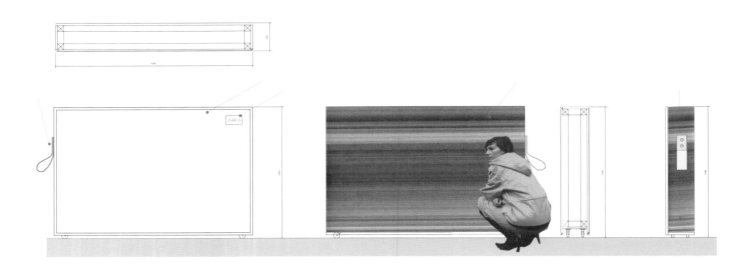

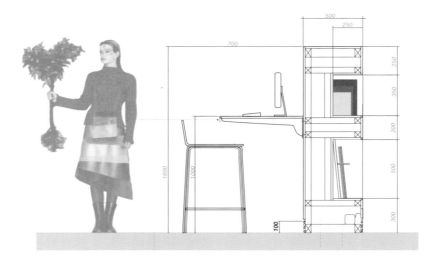

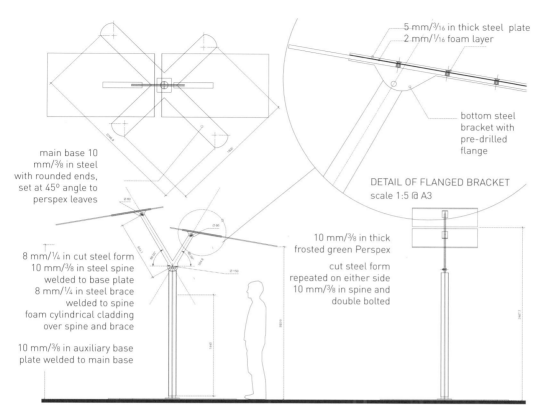

5 mm/³/₁₆ in thick steel plate
2 mm/¹/₁₆ in foam layer

bottom steel bracket with pre-drilled flange

main base 10 mm/³/₈ in steel with rounded ends, set at 45° angle to perspex leaves

DETAIL OF FLANGED BRACKET
scale 1:5 @ A3

10 mm/³/₈ in thick frosted green Perspex

cut steel form repeated on either side 10 mm/³/₈ in spine and double bolted

8 mm/¹/₄ in cut steel form
10 mm/³/₈ in steel spine welded to base plate
8 mm/¹/₄ in steel brace welded to spine
foam cylindrical cladding over spine and brace

10 mm/³/₈ in auxiliary base plate welded to main base

Left
While decisions about the construction and production of simple pieces of furniture and equipment may be left largely to the selected fabricator (with the proviso that they seek approval for those decisions), it is important when unfamiliar and possibly unprecedented objects are proposed that the designer draws and describes them in more detail. When possible, collaborative discussion with specialist suppliers and makers will still usefully enrich the process.

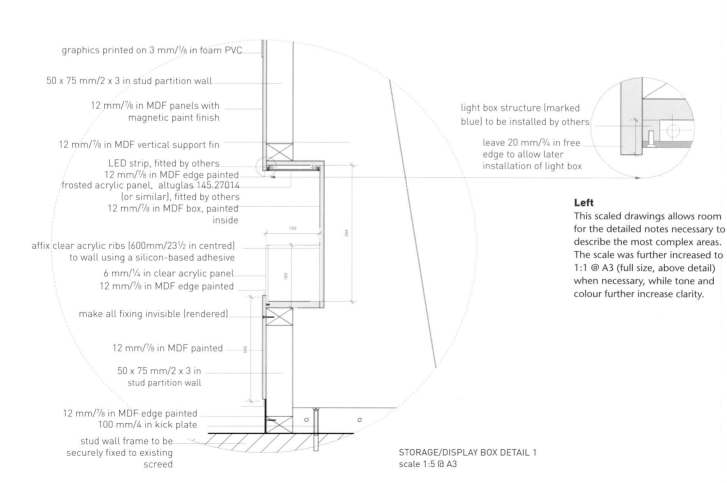

graphics printed on 3 mm/¹/₈ in foam PVC

50 x 75 mm/2 x 3 in stud partition wall

12 mm/⁷/₈ in MDF panels with magnetic paint finish

12 mm/⁷/₈ in MDF vertical support fin

LED strip, fitted by others
12 mm/⁷/₈ in MDF edge painted
frosted acrylic panel, altuglas 145.27014 (or similar), fitted by others
12 mm/⁷/₈ in MDF box, painted inside

affix clear acrylic ribs (600mm/23¹/₂ in centred) to wall using a silicon-based adhesive
6 mm/¹/₄ in clear acrylic panel
12 mm/⁷/₈ in MDF edge painted

make all fixing invisible (rendered)

12 mm/⁷/₈ in MDF painted

50 x 75 mm/2 x 3 in stud partition wall

12 mm/⁷/₈ in MDF edge painted
100 mm/4 in kick plate

stud wall frame to be securely fixed to existing screed

light box structure (marked blue) to be installed by others

leave 20 mm/³/₄ in free edge to allow later installation of light box

Left
This scaled drawings allows room for the detailed notes necessary to describe the most complex areas. The scale was further increased to 1:1 @ A3 (full size, above detail) when necessary, while tone and colour further increase clarity.

STORAGE/DISPLAY BOX DETAIL 1
scale 1:5 @ A3

Making production drawings

There is no room for ambiguity in production drawings. They should be clear and, as far as possible, simple. Even for the most complicated project, simple drawings will usually signify well-resolved thinking and an economical and effective solution, easily built and robust. While they should not set out to be complicated they must carry enough information to ensure that, with a number of contractors competing for the tender, the extent of the work and the quality of its execution is clearly stated, leaving no room for misinterpretation, no ambiguities that might lead later to disputes on site.

It is important to appreciate that, while drawings are produced in a comfortable studio environment with instruments designed to maximize accuracy, they will be interpreted and implemented in the confusion of a building site. They should therefore be as easy to understand as possible. Workers on site are not necessarily familiar with the potential of the materials specified and the techniques required to use them and need to be given support.

All project information can be distributed digitally, and this cuts out the delays and uncertainties that were previously an inevitable aspect of postal delivery. The advantages are obvious, in that delays that affect the price or completion times can be diminished. The disadvantage is that the designer is under greater pressure to respond quickly to unforeseen complications and, given that such revisions can have a significant and not immediately apparent impact on the whole project and its cost, it is sensible to agree a reasonable amount of time for consideration of each development. If a designer has given evidence of general efficiency, been sympathetic to the contractor's problems and is confronting an unforeseeable dilemma, then it is reasonable to expect understanding in return.

TIP BREAK LINES

When drawing details to a large scale it is often expedient to compress certain lengths to save space on a drawing. The solution is to shorten the length and acknowledge its truncation by leaving a gap, normally bounded by two thin lines, which show that the break is deliberate. In the example the important construction of the wall on either side of an opening is shown in full. The unimportant opening between them is condensed but the dimension confirms its real width.

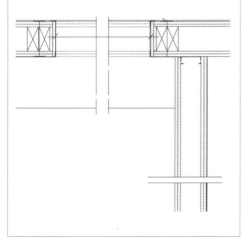

Conventions

There are two distinct categories of production drawing: plans and sections, which are likely to be at 1:50 or 1:100 scale, perhaps at 1:20 for small projects; and details, which explain the construction of typical elements or which isolate and explain complex conditions. Details are likely to be drawn at 1:5 or 1:10, and sometimes full size or half full size – although the latter is considered potentially misleading because it is easy to confuse half with full size, and the misinterpreted drawing can then imply a more elegant solution than will be achieved in reality.

The scale of details created on computer may be inflated on-screen during development, to allow examination at full size – or larger, if required – in order to give an accurate appreciation of the sizes of the elements involved, and then reduced to a more concise scale for distribution. Written notes may be added at typing speed, without the clumsy complications of stencils or the potential chance of misinterpreted handwritten notes. Corrections to lines or lettering in corporate drawings may be carried out without trace whereas corrections, whether to pen or pencil originals, damages the paper.

Because computer drawings may be developed in separately saved layers, it is now more feasible to produce drawings specifically for individual trades and specialisms. While it was once expedient to use one drawing to communicate information about a number of separate activities, it is now as easy to produce a dedicated drawing for each and to deliver instructions with focused clarity.

Below
Pale tints colour code materials – brown represents wood and green represents glass. Silhouetted figures give scale. The wheels are downloaded from a manufacturer's website.

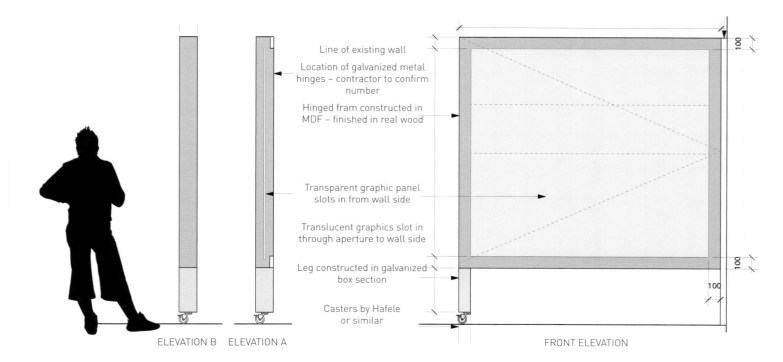

Line of existing wall

Location of galvanized metal hinges – contractor to confirm number

Hinged fram constructed in MDF – finished in real wood

Transparent graphic panel slots in from wall side

Translucent graphics slot in through aperture to wall side

Leg constructed in galvanized box section

Casters by Hafele or similar

100

100

100

ELEVATION B   ELEVATION A   FRONT ELEVATION

This not only reduces the likelihood of potential errors but, by providing a trade-specific drawing, eases the individual specialist's job and eliminates the uncertainty that can result from complex composite instructions.

While it is desirable that the nature of production drawings evolves in response to the improved capacities of the computer, respect for established drawing conventions is worthwhile. A shared visual language is vital if the complexity of construction information is to be communicated precisely to contractors and other building-industry professionals.

Graphic conventions evolved in response to the materials available for making them. When drawings were almost exclusively made with ink or pencil line on tracing paper, for reproduction by dye-line and photocopying, the articulation of components within the drawing was achieved by varying line thicknesses, hatchings and cross-hatchings. This process was time-consuming and, because the drawings were made in conformity with strictly established codes, it was viable and common practice to employ specialist technicians and 'tracers' to draft the volume of drawings necessary for the more substantial projects. These assistants tended to have responsibility for evolving and finalizing work initiated by the designers who led the team. They did not take responsibility for final decision-making, but often had valuable practical knowledge: the result of sustained involvement with technical detailing.

The switch to computer production reduced the need for repetitive hand drawing, and consequently the number of individuals engaged in the compilation of production information. The content of such drawings, however, has not changed much. Variations are small, but they have significantly changed the look of the final drawing. Lines, because specified into the computer rather than plotted by hand, are wholly precise. Quality of reproduction is standardized and perfect. Mistakes are now intellectual rather than manual.

Handmade drawings were invariably reproduced as black lines on white paper. The computer allows the use of colours and the colour printer allows their reproduction. This allows greater articulation of parts of a drawing, which can greatly assist understanding. It is particularly useful for identifying glass, areas of which were previously left blank or denoted rather unsatisfactorily by sloping broken lines.

Cross-referencing

Production and detail drawings must be intelligently ordered, numbered and cross-referenced. Plans and sections constitute ways in which to communicate the overview of a project. They will show the precise locations and lengths of walls and other major elements in the case of a plan, and heights in the case of a section. When setting out dimensions, it is standard practice to relate measurements to significant existing points within the structure. Some generic specification information – such as materials for wall construction, and floor and wall finishes – should also be communicated on plans and sections. However, when very specific information about the materials and construction of, for example, a junction between a new wall and an existing structure, is called for, then this should be drawn at a larger scale – and probably on another sheet. It is then standard practice to identify the location of that detailed condition, and to cross-reference it by giving it a unique number and by citing the sheet number on which it will appear (for example: 'detail C, drawing 53'). Other details, such as those for skirtings and architraves, which may have an application throughout a project need not have their locations specifically cited, but should also be numbered for efficient referencing during communication between designer and site workers.

Opposite, top
Hand drawn plans (originally A3 size) that give critical dimensions (and only critical dimensions), notes about materials and construction techniques (indicated by recognized graphic codes which are confirmed in the key on the drawing). Details that will be drawn to a larger scale are circled and given a reference letter (there is only one sheet of details for this modest project).

Opposite, below
Critical details, each with its identification letter, cover general and specific conditions. Notes describe the size of component pieces and, where appropriate how they are fixed.

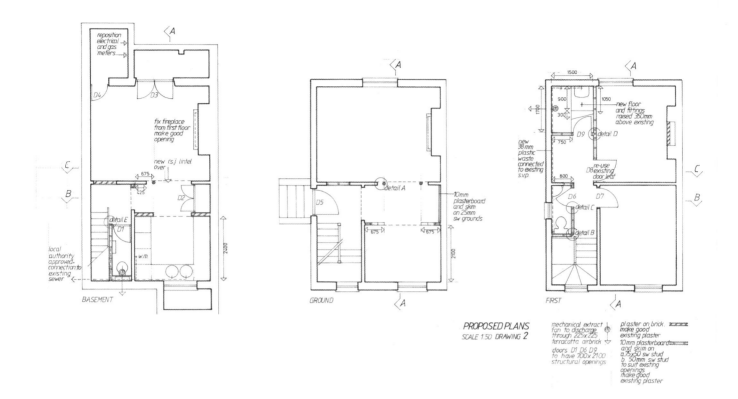

BASEMENT

GROUND

FIRST

PROPOSED PLANS
SCALE 1:50 DRAWING 2

reposition electrical and gas meters

fix fireplace from first floor make good opening

new r.s.j lintel over

local authority approved connection to existing sewer

detail E

675

25

2100

D4

D3

D2

D1

w.m.

detail A

675   675

2100

D5

10mm plasterboard and skim on 25mm sw grounds

1500

900   1050

300

750

800

new floor and fittings raised 350mm above existing

new 38 mm plastic waste connected to existing s.v.p.

re-use D6 existing door leaf

D9   detail D

D6   D7

detail C

detail B

mechanical extract fan to discharge through 225 x 225 terracotta airbrick

doors D1 D6 D9 to have 700 x 2100 structural openings

plaster on brick
make good existing plaster

10mm plasterboard and skim on
a 75 x 50 sw stud
b 50 mm sw stud to suit existing openings
make good existing plaster

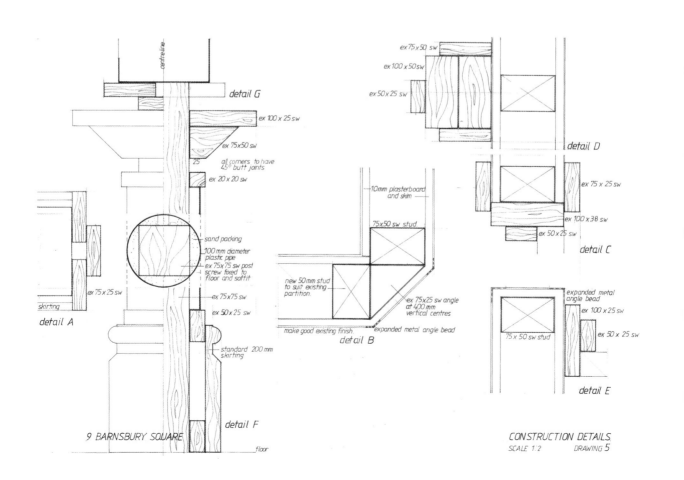

detail G

centreline

ex 100 x 25 sw

ex 75 x 50 sw

25

all corners to have 45° butt joints

ex 20 x 20 sw

sand packing

100 mm diameter plastic pipe

ex 75 x 75 sw post screw fixed to floor and soffit

ex 75 x 25 sw

ex 75 x 75 sw

ex 50 x 25 sw

standard 200 mm skirting

skirting

detail A

detail F

floor

9 BARNSBURY SQUARE

ex 75 x 50 sw

ex 100 x 50 sw

ex 50 x 25 sw

detail D

10mm plasterboard and skim

75 x 50 sw stud

new 50mm stud to suit existing partition

ex 75 x 25 sw angle at 400 mm vertical centres

make good existing finish

expanded metal angle bead

detail B

ex 75 x 25 sw

ex 100 x 38 sw

ex 50 x 25 sw

detail C

expanded metal angle bead

ex 100 x 25 sw

75 x 50 sw stud

ex 50 x 25 sw

detail E

CONSTRUCTION DETAILS
SCALE 1:2   DRAWING 5

The computer generated plan and section shown here utilizes recognized conventions. The existing structure is hatched or outlined in thicker black lines to distinguish it from the new, which is drawn in grey and includes more detail, showing construction information such as the framing for the plasterboard clad partition walls. Blue colour wash indicates glass shelving and is intensified where it represents vertical glass supports. The location of section cuts are clearly indicated and the grey rectangle next to the letters explains the direction of the view.

This page
The fragment of section is that defined by the line AA on plan. The red circle locates a crucial element of the construction that was drawn separately as a larger scaled detail. The flat plane of the image does not – cannot – represent the angle of the right hand section of the plan.

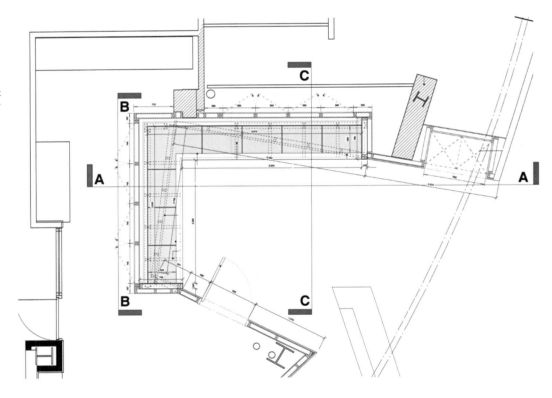

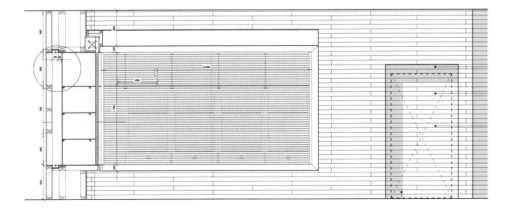

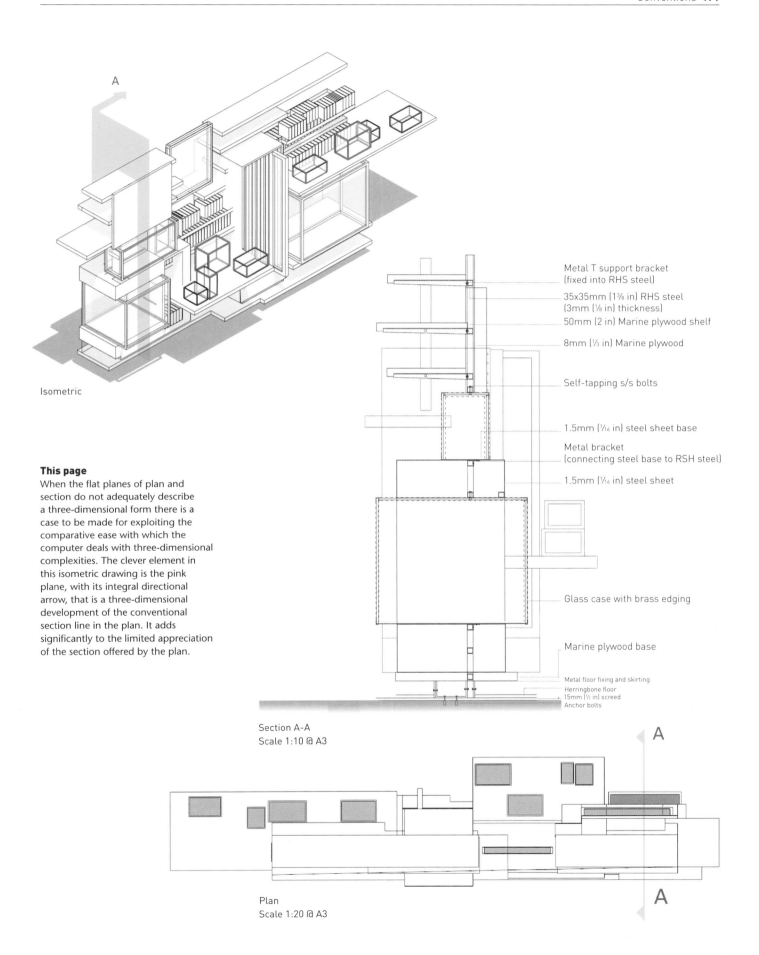

Isometric

This page

When the flat planes of plan and section do not adequately describe a three-dimensional form there is a case to be made for exploiting the comparative ease with which the computer deals with three-dimensional complexities. The clever element in this isometric drawing is the pink plane, with its integral directional arrow, that is a three-dimensional development of the conventional section line in the plan. It adds significantly to the limited appreciation of the section offered by the plan.

Metal T support bracket
(fixed into RHS steel)

35x35mm (1⅜ in) RHS steel
(3mm (⅛ in) thickness)

50mm (2 in) Marine plywood shelf

8mm (⅓ in) Marine plywood

Self-tapping s/s bolts

1.5mm (¹⁄₁₆ in) steel sheet base

Metal bracket
(connecting steel base to RSH steel)

1.5mm (¹⁄₁₆ in) steel sheet

Glass case with brass edging

Marine plywood base

Metal floor fixing and skirting
Herringbone floor
15mm (½ in) screed
Anchor bolts

Section A-A
Scale 1:10 @ A3

Plan
Scale 1:20 @ A3

These two pages show some of the drawings necessary to explain fully the construction of a very small entrance space. While this example is further complicated by the angles of walls, it is broadly true to say that production drawings for small areas are more complicated than those for larger spaces for the simple practical reason that the same information must be conveyed in a much reduced drawing area.

Below right
The section cut is defined by the cranked red line that joins the two letters B on the plan. This is a recognized convention where one straight line cannot efficiently take in crucial parts of the construction. It is important in this instance that the line is continuous to define the localized conditions.

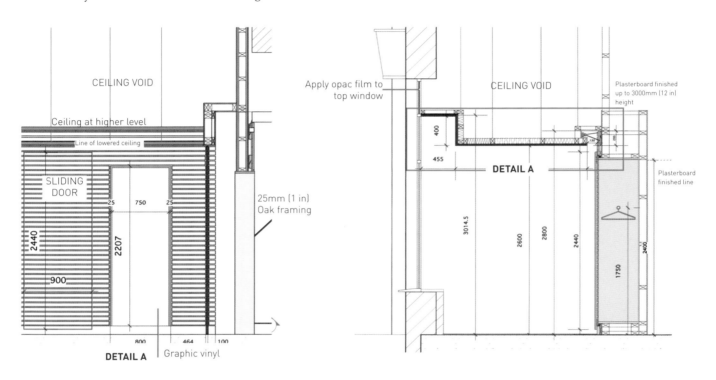

FOYER ELEVATION A
Scale 1:20 @ A1

FOYER SECTION B
Scale 1:20 @ A1

Above left
The location of the elevation is identified on the plan by the letter A in the small circle superimposed on the solid triangle, the apex of which indicates the direction of the view.

Right
The plan is principally concerned with identifying areas and conditions (of the lowered ceiling for example) and the dimensions necessary for its setting out. Existing walls are indicated by solid tone. New walls are distinguished by the structural framing shown within them and this also explains which have an insulated core.

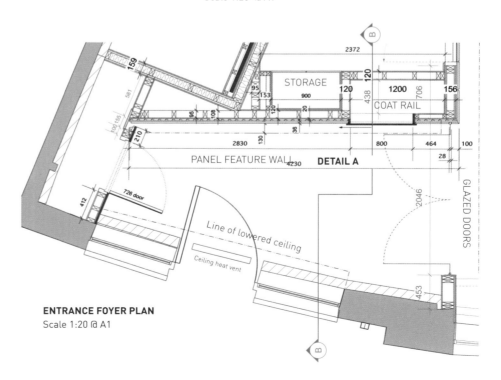

ENTRANCE FOYER PLAN
Scale 1:20 @ A1

Below
The red rectangle identifies the area to be drawn at the bigger scale.

Bottom left
Section C shows the broad construction of the coat storage cupboard. Tone defines its interior and helps understanding of the drawing. The coat hanger symbol is an elegant alternative to words. The two circles identify areas that need to be dealt with at a larger scale.

Bottom right
Details of the crucial door head and base conditions identified on section C.

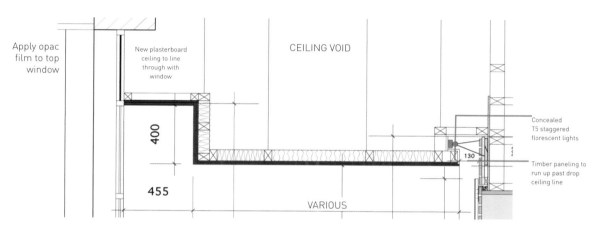

Apply opac film to top window

New plasterboard ceiling to line through with window

CEILING VOID

400

455

VARIOUS

130

Concealed T5 staggered florescent lights

Timber paneling to run up past drop ceiling line

BULKHEAD DETAIL A
Scale 1:10 @ A1

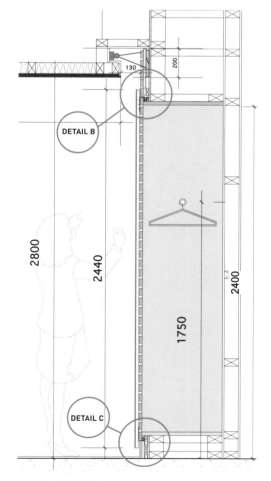

130   200

DETAIL B

2800   2440   2400   1750

DETAIL C

CUPBOARD SECTION C
Scale 1:10 @ A1

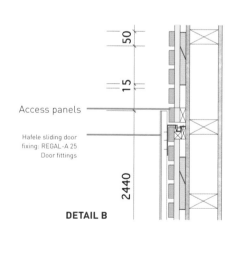

50

15

Access panels

Hafele sliding door fixing: REGAL-A 25 Door fittings

2440

DETAIL B

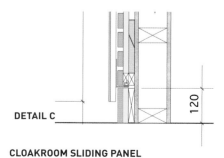

120

DETAIL C

CLOAKROOM SLIDING PANEL
Scale 1:5 @ A1

Annotation

There is a vocabulary and grammar particular to writing notes on drawings that should be mastered and adhered to. Technical terms and phrases should be learnt, because using incorrect, 'unprofessional' words or lay terms can seriously undermine credibility on site.

Notes should be brief: they should be phrases rather than sentences, and purely factual. They are instructions to the contractor, and so should not be explanations of aesthetic intentions or anticipated effects. Generally, they need to make three factual statements: they should name the material or the object to which they refer, they should state its size, and concisely describe the method of

installing it (for example: '10mm (⅓ in) plywood screwed to 94 x 44 sw stud'). It is safe to assume that three such pieces of information should be added to every individual element within a detailed drawing. If one of them is unnecessary, that will be clearly evident and it may be omitted. If additional information is required, this is likely to be less obvious and, for all details, the designer needs to visualize the process of assembly and decide if it is comprehensively, but concisely, described in the notes. It should then be apparent if something needs to be added.

This page
This section shows details of the meeting of a new upper floor with secondary glazing above and below it. Break lines shorten the vertical elements to fit the drawing size. The notes describe concisely but comprehensively all components, materials, sizes and fixing methods. Its location is shown on the small plan and complete section.

Vertical Section A-A
[Scale 1:10]

1. 10mm (⅓ in) plasterboard w. plaster skim coat,painted white

2. 20mm (¾ in) double glazing in cedar white painted frame

3. Wall construction:80/50mm (2in) wooden batten, 20mm (¾in) MDF, 10mm plasterboard w.plaster skim coat painted white

4. 200/100/5mm black and white metro tiles

5. 70/20mm (¾in) SW skirting painted white

6. Floor construction: 3mm (⅛in) poured coloured polyurethane finish, 30mm (1¼ in) screed, 20mm (¾in) impact-sound insulation, 20mm (¾in) polystyrene rigid foam, 14mm (⅔ in) MDF sheet, 197mm (7¾ in) timber floor joists

7. 225/89mm (3½ in) steel channel

8. Floor construction: Carpeting, 20mm (¾in) insulation, existing concrete floor slab,

9. 1700mm (67 in) high brickwork sill

10. Ø 250mm (10 in) cast iron column

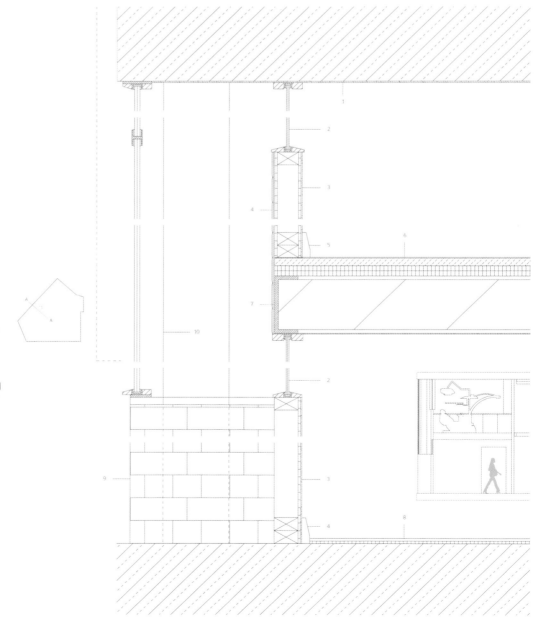

Drawings for specialist trades

It is good practice to provide separate drawings for each of the different trades that are involved in the building of a project. While the work of specialists, such as plumbers, electricians, heating and ventilating engineers, will be integrated with the work of all others on site it makes sense to provide drawings which deal only with the activity for which they are wholly responsible so that they do not have to extract the information they need from a much more complex general drawing. The computer's capacity to make a drawing in separate layers allows bespoke specialist information to be added to a general base layer that incorporates only the information common to all. The clarity of the specialist drawing reduces confusion and mistakes.

This page
The complexity of drawings depends on the complexity of the project – and a small project can be very complex. These two drawings, each for an electrical contractor, carry different degrees of information but each are very focused and clear on the layout of light fittings. The top plan shows the location for three different fittings, each shown with a different symbol and identified in separate specification notes, and links those on the same switch circuits. The lower plan deals with two different fittings and provides setting out dimensions. It is customary to use a 'reflected' ceiling plan, drawn as if the ceiling is mirrored at floor level, for all plans relative to the ceiling. By retaining the orientation of the floor plans correlation between ceiling and floor elements is kept simpler.

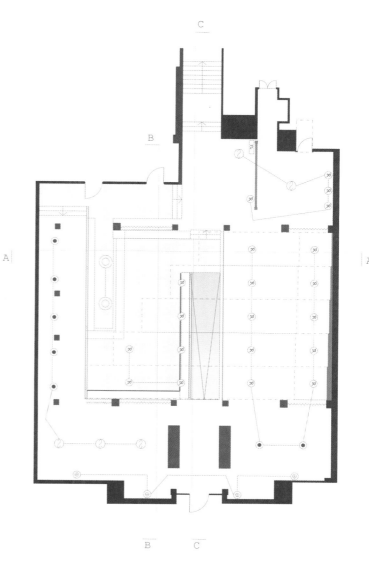

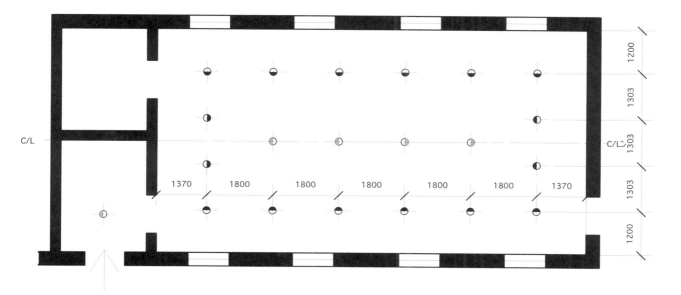

Specification

A specification is a written description of the quality
and performance of components and the standards
expected in their construction. It is written in purely
factual language. For bigger projects, it may be issued as
a self-contained booklet or, for smaller projects, added
to a drawing. This example, part of a more extensive text
printed on the bottom of a sheet of plans, offers a good
model for appropriate language. It is normal practice to
refer to local building regulations, trade standards and
manufacturers' installation instructions in a general
introduction as definitions of required quality.

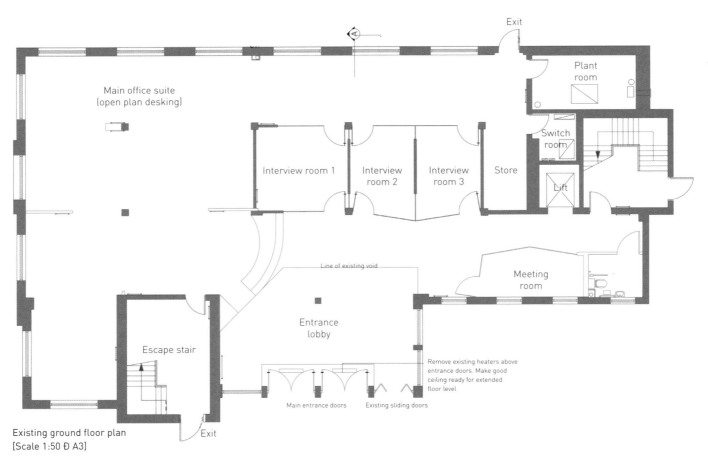

Existing ground floor plan
[Scale 1:50 Ð A3]

eneral Notes & Specifications

ll operations to comply with the Current Building Scotland
egulations and all current amendments.
ll electrical operations to comply with part 4 of the Building
egulations and be in accordance with BS 7671: 2001
ll drainage operations to comply with Part 3 of the Building
cotland Regulations 2004 and be laid and supported as per
anufacturers written specifications.
ll glazing to be in accordance with BS 6262: Part4: 2005
ll water service pipes and overflows to comply with BS 6700
nd Water Authority Regulations and bylaws.
ll sanitary pipe work to comply with BS EN 12056-2.2000.
nsulation of pipes & vessels to be in accordance with BS 5422: 2009
ny & all penetrations to ceilings / walls & floors to be
einstated as existing, intumescent collars / seals or fire
ampers to be fitted to new services / pipes / ducts as they
ass through separating compartment floors & walls.
ll Structural steelwork retained as existing. Walls being
emoved are of non load bearing nature and no lintels will be required.

erimeter walls

xternal perimeter walls to be insulated with 80mm insulated
lasterboard.

nternal Partitions (Lobby Walls)

lew lobby wall to be formed using 50 x 150mm dressed stud
artitioning at 600mm centers. Install 150mm insulation quilt
nd apply 19mm gyproc plank to both sides with 12.5 mm
lasterboard. Refer to structural engineers drawings for detailed
pecification.

Internal Partitions (Toilet Walls)

New sound proof walls between accessible toilets and
corridor formed using 95 x 50mm s/w framing at 400mm
centres with 50 mm Crown GP sound insulation quilt.
Partitioning to be taken above suspended ceiling level to
the existing structure to form sound proof room. Partition
finished either side with 1x12.5mm & 1x19.5 mm TE
plasterboard lining with filled joints both sides. Apply matt
emulsion paint to all new partitioning. Patch perimeter
walls as required. Apply satinwood paint
to all new wood work.

Glazed Partitioning.

12.8mm toughened glass silicon jointed floor to ceiling
glazed partitioning and doors as indicated. Door sets to
have recessed floor spring hinges. All doors to have
minimum opening of 850mm.
All glazing partitions to have film applied manifestations to
client design and to comply with Part 4.8.2 of the building
regulations. Glazing should be designed in accordance with
BS6262 part 4:2005 to resist human impact.

New First Floor Balustrade.

New 1200mm Balustrade & part hight partition. Refer to
structural engineers drawings & specification.

Circulation

Circulation to escape route to be kept to a minimum of 1200mm.

New Floor Extension / Void

Form new structural flooring over part of the existing
void with a new meeting room and first floor reception
area. Flooring made from treated s/w joists at 400mm
centres, floor finished with 22mm chipboard ready to take
new floor finish. New flooring to tie in with with existing.
Refer to Structural Engineers drawings and specifications.

Windows

All existing window roller shutters to be retained.
Where existing lobby doors have been removed and
replaced with new windows, make good existing shutters.

Doors - General

New accessible entrance door to comply with 4.17 &
4.18 of the building regulations. Door to be powered
by a motion sensor or by a wall mounted activation
device such as a push pad. New internal doors to
comply with 4.2.5 of the building regulations. Doors to
have a minimum clear opening of 850mm. All new
doors to have vision panels.

Access Facilities General

All access facilities should comply with the current
Disability and Discrimination Act. All relevant doors to
have a clear space 300mm from leading edge of
door to wall. As far as practically possible
contrasting colours to be used to distinguish between
finishes and fittings.

New Reception

New reception desk to allow for wheel chair access and
to comply with 4.2.10 of the building regulations.

Flooring - General

Existing floor to be retained. Lay new carpet floor tiles
throughout new office.
Altro non slip flooring within wet areas / kitchen areas.
All new flooring to be laid in accordance with the
manufacturers written specification.

Breakout / kitchen Area

Install new kitchen units and work surfaces.
Kitchen to have: Integrated dishwasher and Integrated
fridge.
Water & drainage from kitchen appliances to connect
into existing drainage system.
All walls to be filled and prepared ready to take new
paint and s/s splash back finishes.
Install new non slip flooring plywood base throughout
kitchen area.

Ceilings: (Refer to drawing BW (00) 002)

Retain existing ceiling grid and lighting, alter to suit
new partitioning layout. Allow for additional & new
lighting as required. Supply and install new ceiling tiles
as necessary to patch existing.

Amendments

Once a drawing has been issued, whether before tendering or after work has begun on site, it is not unusual for some changes to be necessary. Making such amendments, or 'revisions' once involved laborious erasing of pen and pencil lines, and this invariably resulted in deterioration of the drawing surface. Now computer drawings may be changed leaving no trace of the original error, but all those involved in the building operation need to be alerted to the fact that changes have been made and be made aware of what they are.

When changes have been completed on all the appropriate drawings, they should be described verbally in an 'amendment box', usually a vertical column on the right-hand side of the drawing, be dated and given an identifying number or letter (for example: 'amendment C. relocation of office door').

The number of the sheet, or sheets, on which the revision appears should then take on the letter or number of this last amendment as a suffix. For example, a drawing numbered 23B, because it has already been amended twice (A and B), will take the revised number 23C when amendment C is added. It is normal and efficient practice to issue a copy of the amended drawing to everyone involved in the construction process. All involved must be made aware of every change because of the potential, sometimes unanticipated, impact on other activities on site.

Below
A table of amendments is normally integrated in the production drawing to which it refers. The letters in the left column identify the revisions made. The middle column describes the amendment and therefore identifies the relevant area, or areas, of the drawing. The right hand column records the date on which the revision was made and issued to contractors and other consultants, which may be important in later disputes about responsibility for delays.

	DETAILS	DATE
A	Site sizes applied. Feature wall amended. Fire escape reconfigured.	08 02 07
B	Fire safety symbols shown	21 02 07
C	Fire escape reconfigured. New furniture sizes shown. Builders' notes amended.	01 03 07
D	Fire escape corridor enlarged. Escape doors enlarged. Electrical note added.	30 03 07
E	Ramp between areas shown.	23 04 07
F	Fire door U valve and vision panel shown. Floor height difference accommodated.	03 05 07
G	Ceiling detail amended. Flooring rake relocated.	18 05 07
H	Dead end to fire escape reduced in depth.	23 05 07
J	Fire escape redirected.	01 06 07

Case study Designing the drawing

Deciding on the detailed plans and sections necessary to describe the construction of orthogonal buildings is comparatively simple, with proven precedents and, when made, such drawings are readily accessible to anyone familiar with technical drawing convention. Non right angles offer some problems but, because they are defined by straight lines, can be rationalized. A curved or circular structure poses more problems and requires not only analysis of how it may be constructed but also of the type and nature of drawings necessary to describe that process.

The following drawings were made in order to describe the construction of a display area within a museum. While analytical deconstruction of the visually complex whole identified a comparatively simple basic rib component it was also necessary to rethink the conventional drawing package. The plan became a series of plans that traced the build up of elements. Perspectives of the finished structure and its ribbed skeleton replaced conventional flat sections, which could not have dealt clearly with the foreshortening of angled components.

This page
The basic plan is explained in layers, which are overlaid sequentially to produce finished, composites, each of which present an aspect of the project in isolation.

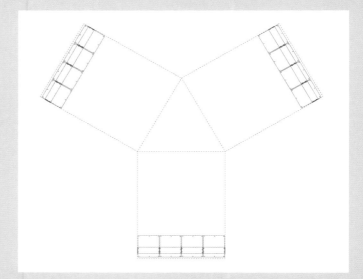

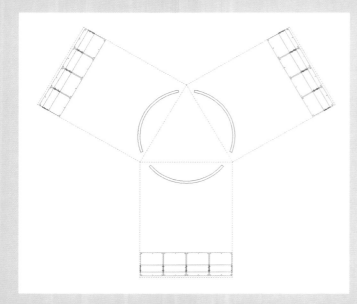

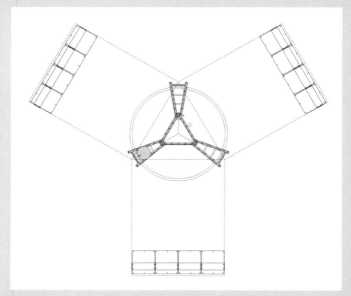

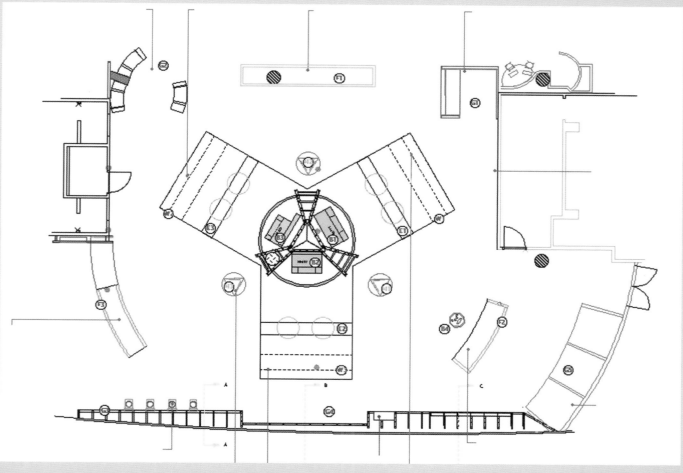

Above
The three-sided element in the context of other exhibition structures.

Below left
Critical dimensions for determining the footprint of the central structure.

Below
Setting out floor finishes. The simplicity of making a bespoke variation on the basic plan provides clear information for the flooring specialist, which would once have been communicated as notes on a much more complicated general plan issued to all contractors and subcontractors.

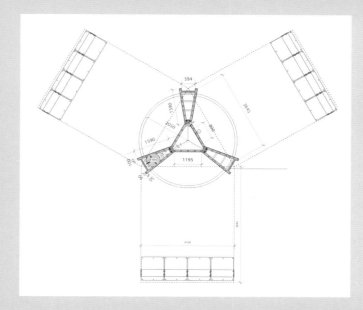

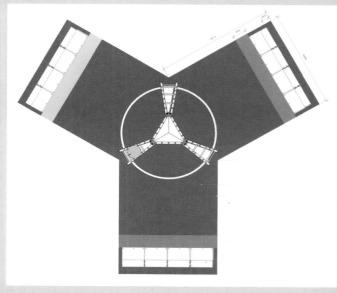

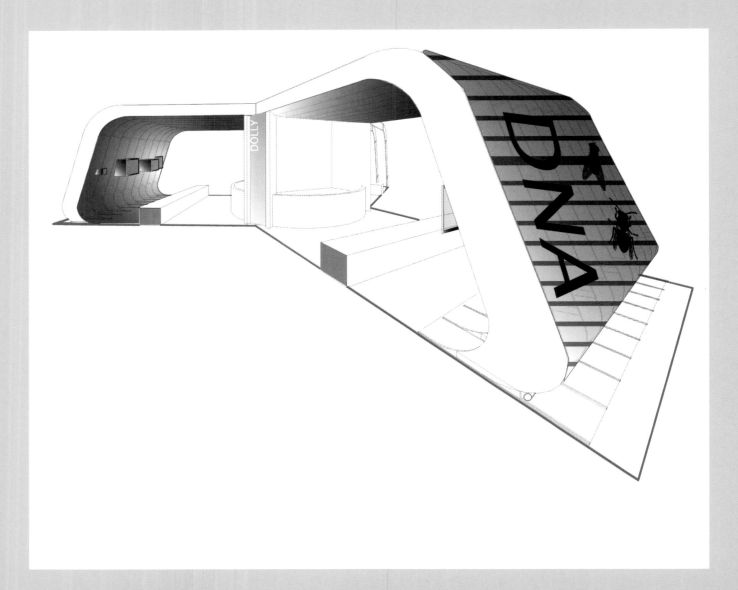

Above
One diagrammatic perspective
introduces the end product.

Once the three-dimensional drawing had established the nature of an individual rib it was appropriate to revert to two-dimensional rib profiles, as the clearest way of establishing dimensions and radii.

Had the drawings been made manually it would have been possible – indeed, essential – to provide the same information about profiles and construction techniques, but considerably more difficult and time-consuming to deal with the radiused sections. The three dimensional drawings would certainly have been prohibitively time consuming to make but without them even an experienced fabricator would have taken time to understand the intention. There would have been considerable opportunity for misinterpretation. The easy adaptation of digital drawings also allowed the tuning of base drawings to convey specialist information directly to the appropriate recipient, to allow them to concentrate solely on the section of the work for which they were responsible. The breakdown of the complicated whole into comprehensible stages and components illustrated the comparative simplicity of the construction and encouraged lower tender prices.

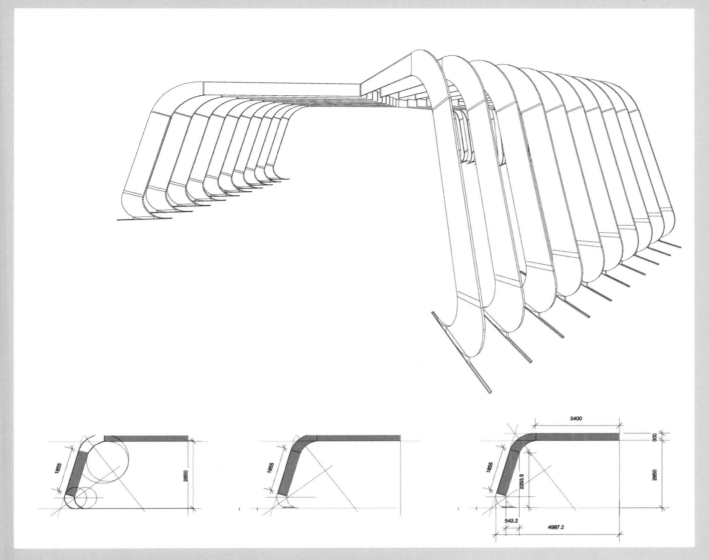

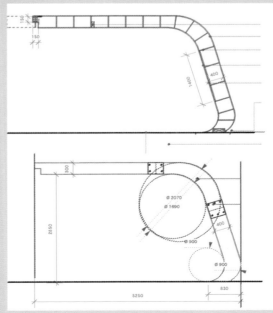

Above

A skeletal perspective reveals the rib structure and its joints and the red sections set out critical dimensions for straight lengths and angles.

Right

The upper section establishes spacings for cross ribs and the lower defines radii.

RESOURCES

Glossary

There are a number of words relating to the practice of drawing within interior design that are more or less understood by everyone but are open – and vulnerable – to individual interpretation. Ambiguities are further complicated by words that have necessarily been imported from new technologies. For the sake of clarity, it is worth defining a few of the more crucial words and phrases used in this book.

Drawing

A dictionary definition of a drawing is 'a picture or plan made by means of lines on a surface, especially one made with a pencil or pen a sketch or outline'. Such a definition held true for interior designers until the advent of the computer and more or less remains true if the computer is added to the list of drawing instruments. The same dictionary defines the activity of drawing as '*the art of making drawings, draughtsmanship*' and this applies very satisfactorily to interior design. So, while the word will continue to trail the idea of the hand-made behind it, it will serve very well to categorize the activities that concern us here.

The word 'drawing' can be used to describe everything, from a perfunctory scribble to the most highly refined artefact. It can describe something that is abstract, impressionistic, realistic or technical, which may be freehand, made with technical instruments, or made with computers all are graphic artefacts, created with the single intention of creating and bringing to completion an interior design project.

Of course a drawing may also refer to the sheet of paper on which a number of individual drawings, however generated, are collected, usually for distribution to those involved in the process of commissioning, creating and constructing an interior project. Everything that emanates from an interior designer's studio, other than a letter, tends to be described as a drawing and that convention is accepted in this book.

Drawings may be further classified by the following terms:

Digital drawing

Made using a computer.

Freehand drawing

Refers to a drawing made entirely without technical instruments and judged by eye, or to a drawing for which the essential delineation is made by instruments but which is finished by hand.

Image

A drawing, primarily three-dimensional, created on a computer.

Manual drawing

Made by hand, with or without technical instruments.

Model

There are two types of model:
- **Physical** or **'real'** a three-dimensional representation, made to scale. A physical construction as opposed to a drawing.
- **Digital** or **virtual** a three-dimensional, computer-generated **image** or **drawing**, usually rendered to achieve a high degree of realism.

Rendering

A drawing, usually three-dimensional and made either on a computer or by hand, which uses colour and tone.

Technical drawing

There are two types of technical drawing:
- Made to scale, on a computer with appropriate drawing software, or by hand, using the traditional range of instruments a scale ruler, set squares, compasses, pencils or pens.
- A drawing, usually made to scale but occasionally freehand, made to communicate technical information.

Visualization

An accurate three-dimensional, usually colour-rendered, representation of an interior, once hand made with technical instruments but now more likely to be computer-generated. who introduced so many to the fundamentals of digital imaging, to Jason Milne, whose virtuosity across media proves that great drawing depends on the maker and not the medium, and to Olga Valentinova Reid for her exploration of the far reaches of digital imaging and her generosity in creating so many drawings especially for the book.

Index

Page numbers in *italics* refer to picture captions

Picture credits

Front cover: Top **Drew Plunket**; Main **Grace Patton**
Back cover: Left **Tess Syder**; Right **Amanda Youlden**
1 **Matthew Maréchal**
3 **Hyun Hee Kang**
5 **Paula Murray**
6 Right **Louise Martin**
Below right **Ali Stewart**
7 Left **Jason Milne**
Below **Olga Valentinova Reid**
8 Left **Jason Milne**
9 Below **Xander Gardner**
10 Left **Simon Capriotti**
11 Above **Stuart Gordon**
Below **Emma Wynn**
12 Right **Neil Owen**
Below right **Stephen Noon**
13 Right **Olga Valentinova Reid**
14 Top left and right **Richard Smith**
Bottom left and right **Olga Valentinova Reid**
15 Top left and right **Richard Smith**
Bottom left and right **Olga Valentinova Reid**
16 Left **Robert Harvey**
Top right **Olga Valentinova Reid**
Bottom right **Richard Smith**
17 Top and bottom **Yoon Si Yoon**
18 Left and below **Roseann Macnamara**
Opposite top **Claire Roebuck**
19 Above **Louise Martin**
20 Left and below **Olga Valentinova Reid**
21 Top **Cassi Alnwick-Elliott**
Bottom **Rachel Burns**
23 Above **Lorna Midgley**
25 **Drew Plunkett**
27 **Drew Plunkett**
28 29 **Drew Plunkett**
30-31 **Olga Valentinova Reid**
32/33 **Olga Valentinova Reid**
34-35 **Olga Valentinova Reid**
36-37 **Drew Plunkett**
38 Above **Drew Plunkett**
38 Tip **Drew Plunkett**
39 Above and left **Drew Plunkett**
Above **Zaheed Khalid**
40 Above **Zoe Tucker**
Right **Paula Murray**
41 Above left **Patrick Macklin**
Above **Patrick Macklin**
42-43 **Drew Plunkett**
44-45 **Drew Plunkett**
46 Below **Amanda Youlden**
47 Tip **Drew Plunkett**

Below **Robert Millar**
48 Above **Angela Pignatelli**
Right **Jason Milne**
49 Above **Paul Revie**
Right **Drew Plunkett**
50 Far left and left **John Gigli**
Tip **Vivien Maxwell**
51 Below **Amanda Youlden**
Right **Vivien Maxwell**
52 Above **Robert Millar**
Above **Gina Leith**
Left **Lucy Galloway**
53 **Lucy Galloway**
54-55 **Robert Millar**
56 **Paula Murray**
58 Left **Jason Milne**
Above right **Louise Martin**
59 **Jason Milne**
60 Above **Drew Plunkett**
Right **Louise Martin**
61 Left **Arlene MacPhail**
Right **Nicky Bruce**
Above **Hyun Hee Kang**
Left **Grant Morrison**
63 **Drew Plunkett**
64 **Emma Franks**
65 Above **Michael Maciocia**
Right **Ashley Mooney**
66-67 **Tess Syder**
68-69 **Claire Probert**
70-71 **Olga Valentinova Reid for the Curious Group**
72 Right **Craig Tinney**
Left **Helen Davies**
Lower right **Val Clugston**
73 **Paula Murray for Graven Images**
74 **Jason Milne**
75 **Kevin MacLachlan**
76 Below **Joe Lynch**
Right **Lisa Donati**
77 Above left **Louise Martin**
Above right **Jason Milne**
Right **Jason Milne**
78 Tip **Nicky Bruce**
Left **Jason Milne for DMG Design**
79 **Jason Milne**
80 **Api Tunsakul**
82/83 **Hyun Hee Kang**
84 **Naomi Prahm**
85 **Zhang Yifan**
86/87 **Jason Milne for Contagious**
88 Right **James Connor**
89 Right **Jason Milne for Contagious**

Right **Melba Beetham**
90 **Drew Plunkett**
91 Below **Jennifer Laird**
Bottom **James Connor**
92 Above **Louise Martin**
Right **Ashley Mooney**
Tip **Gillian Polonis**
93 Above **Drew Plunkett**
Below **Robert Harvey**
94 Above **James Connor**
Below **Ezra Paris**
95 **Naomi Prahm**
96 Below **Simon Capriotti**
Right **Petra Probstner**
97 Right **Jennifer Laird**
Below **Stephen Noon**
98 **Somya Singh**
99 **Kathryn Taggart**
100 Below and below right **Emma Wynn**
Above **Julie McFadden**
Right **Sharon Kane**
101 **Morena Marchetti**
102 Left **Martyn Cotter**
Bottom left **Vili Tangalova**
Below **Api Tunsakul**
103 Right **Aminah Habib**
Below right **Emma Campbell**
104 Left **Mathieu Maréchal**
105 Right **Jenni Riach**
Below **Sharon Kane**
106 **Robbie Crocker**
107 **Api Tunsakul**
108 Above **Stephen Noon**
Above Right **Claire Roebuck**
Tip **Julie Mcfadden**
109 Top **Grace Patton**
Bottom **Petra Probstner**
110 Right **Kathryn Taggart**
Above **Monica Gromek**
Left **Emma Montgomery**
111 Above **Claire Robinson**
Below left **Vili Tangalova**
Below right **Laura Midgley**
112 **Rachel Glue**
113 Left **Hok Chun Chau**
Tip **James Connor**
114 **Lisa Donati**
115 **Olga Valentinova Reid**
116/117 **Grace Patton**
118 Left **Jason Milne**
Right **Paula Murray**
119 Left above **Carolyn Maxwell**
Left below **Rachel Munro**
120 Below left **Christine Myers**

Below right **Scott Mason**
Left **Scott Mason**
121 Below **Naomi Prahm**
Right **Richard Smith**
122 **Jenny Leach**
123 Left upper **Jean Paul Tugirimana**
Right lower **Petra Probstner**
124/125 **Naomi Prahm**
126 Below **James Connor**
Below right **Lisa Donati**
Tip **Jenni Riach**
127 **Xander Gardner**
128 Left upper and lower **Hannah Parker**
Below left and right **Annmarie Murphy**
129 **Olga Valentinova Reid**
130 Below **Laure Derolez**
Left **Jill Rodger**
131 **Olga Valentinova Reid**
132 **Michael Maciocia**
133 **Gillian Polonis**
134 **Kyle Tetley**
135 **Chanette Hansen**
136/137 **Karen Hamilton**
138/139 **Grace Patton**
140/141 **Grace Patton**
142/143 **Michael Maciocia**
144/145 **Ramona Bittere and Nikol Pechova**
146/147 **Mathieu Maréchal**
148/149 **Yoshi Sugimoto**
150/151 **Olga Valentinova Reid**
152/153 **Olga Valentinova Reid**
154 **Michael Maciocia**
157 **Michael Maciocia**
158 **Naomi Prahm**
159 **Jason Milne**
160 **Drew Plunkett**
161 **Patrick McKinney for Ben Kelly Design**
162 **Grace Patton**
163 **Olga Valentinova Reid**
164 **Nomad**
165 Upper left **Nomad**
Lower left **Olga Valentinova Reid**
166 **Sam Booth**
167 **Jason Milne for Contagious**
169 **Drew Plunkett**
170 **Martyn Cotter for Graven Images**
171 **Claire Robinson**
172/173 **Arka Design Studio**
174 **Michael Maciocia**
175 Top **Lesley Michie**
Bottom **Jason Milne for Contagious**
176 **Arka Design Studio**
178-181 **Olga Valentinova Reid for Arka Design Studio**
182 **Petra Probstner**

Author's acknowledgments

I am grateful to everyone who has allowed me to use their drawings in this book but in particular to Digger Nutter, for sharing his views on the future of digital drawing, to Jason Milne, whose graphic virtuosity proves that great drawing depends on the maker and not the medium, and to Olga Reid for her exploration of the far reaches of digital imaging and her generosity in creating so many drawings especially for the book.

With Compliments

DENT ST

FLOOD
HORROR AND TRAGEDY

Published: 2011 (First Edition)

Compiled by a committee of parents and friends of Agnew School, which serves the Plymouth Brethren Christian Church community in Queensland, often referred to as the Exclusive Brethren.

All monies for the printing, distribution and marketing of this book were raised through pre-orders or from parent and friends of the school. No government funding was used on this project.

Published by: Southern Education Managements Pty T/As ProVision Marketing

Designed by: Alison May Graphic Art and Design

Printed and bound by: Craft Print International Ltd

Promoted and distributed by: PAN MACMILLAN AUST.

PUBLISHER'S NOTE:

This book represents a lasting memento documenting the trials and tragedies experienced by Queenslanders in the extraordinary summer of 2010-2011.

This huge natural disaster, we believe, deserved recapture of its magnitude by creating a gripping book that would help satisfy public thirst for information on the catastrophic series of events.

As the book reveals, tens of thousands of Queenslanders suffered from the unleashed forces of nature. Flood Horror and Tragedy has endeavoured to capture first hand many of the stories of shock and despair from those who endured the ordeal. There were thousands of different experiences and thousands of varied accounts, each with its own unique story and each with its individual coping mechanisms. We have attempted to provide a diverse cross-section of accounts, which actually created its own unforeseen challenge. The experiences of some were such that they warranted books in their own right! Yet many accounts are missing - some could not face re-telling their stories, others are no longer here to do so.

Sadly, the magnitude of similar disasters in 1893 and 1974 had long been forgotten by some, and were little understood by others. We hope this book will serve as a reminder to future generations that these natural forces are beyond human control, but, at the same time, tragedy can be averted through greater preparedness and a keen appreciation of what can, and surely will, happen again.

Title: Flood Horror and Tragedy / Agnew P & F Association Inc.

ISBN: 9780646559650 (hbk.)

Subjects: Floods--Queensland.
                            Disaster victims--Queensland--Anecdotes.
                            Natural disasters--Queensland.

Other Authors/Contributors: Agnew P & F Association.

Dewey Number: 363.349309943

FLOOD
HORROR AND TRAGEDY

Her Excellency Ms Quentin Bryce AC
Governor-General of the Commonwealth of Australia

Message from Her Excellency Ms Quentin Bryce, AC
Governor-General of the Commonwealth of Australia

for the book *Flood: Horror and Tragedy*

Queenslanders lived through a summer that will never be forgotten. Australia watched as devastating floods swallowed communities and enormous regions of our country. I saw firsthand the grief people faced, continuing long after the waters had abated.

From the horror emerged heroes - neighbours, friends, and strangers - all working together and displaying fine examples of the Australian spirit. Vivid images of their deeds are etched in our minds; Defence personnel hovering above island properties while winching people to safety; emergency services personnel working beyond exhaustion to sandbag roads and homes; volunteers counselling and restoring hope for flood victims.

This book archives moments that echo in the memory of all Australians. It is an account of events that affected students, parents and teachers of Agnew School campuses across the State, and is a tribute to the strength of Queenslanders who faced pain and loss, now rebuilding with true courage and resilience.

I give my greatest support for this important and historic publication.

Quentin Bryce   2·9·2011

GOVERNMENT HOUSE CANBERRA ACT 2600 AUSTRALIA

TELEPHONE +61(2) 5285 3525 FACSIMILE +61(2) 6285 5595

CONTENTS

WHEN THE
WILD WATERS
INVADED QUEENSLAND

By the spring of 2010, Queensland had been drought-stricken for so long that the forecast of a wet summer was a welcome relief. The critically low levels in many dams had been the cause of much study and expense in exploring other options to increase or conserve supplies and many farmers had faced crippling losses and ruin. When the first summer showers started to fall, the cracked and parched earth greedily soaked it up.

Then followed the wettest summer on record for Queensland! An active cyclone season and a strong La Niña event in the Pacific Ocean contributed to the heavy and prolonged rainfalls experienced over most of the state during December 2010 and January 2011. After the parched ground became saturated, the dams filled quickly and overflowed; rivers swelled and broke their banks and by mid-January seventy-five percent of flood-ravaged Queensland had been declared a natural disaster zone.

SOME RECEIVED WARNING

In some places the rivers have fairly predictable habits and residents had timely warning. With the benefit of past experience they were able to employ planned strategies of sandbagging, elevating stock and equipment, or evacuating if necessary. It was not just a matter then, of waiting for the water to go down, however long that might take; foul smelling layers of sticky mud and silt had to be cleaned off everything before it hardened; there was debris and damaged property to remove and repairs to be made, often involving new electrical fit-outs, before the tedious process of moving back in could be undertaken. It would be weeks before heavy machinery could be driven onto the farms.

Whilst some were soon able to face the daunting task of picking up the threads, coping with their losses and moving on, there were many whose whole life savings and labour were utterly destroyed or washed away. To see homes and possessions - products of lifelong struggles and hard work - severely damaged or completely destroyed, was enough to plunge the strongest people into overwhelming despair. Many older citizens, who rebuilt after earlier floods, no longer have the courage to start again. People have been very kind, but life has lost its meaning as their long-treasured memories stored in photographs, heirlooms, family gifts and other possessions have been heartlessly stolen by the flood.

TRAGEDY STRUCK WITH UNHERALDED FLASH-FLOODING

Most rivers in Queensland's sub-tropical areas reached major flood levels at some stage, but the most violent flash-flooding resulted from torrential downpours over the Great Dividing Range. On the western side, floodwaters surged out of the creeks at an incredible rate, engulfing much of Toowoomba's CBD, while on the eastern escarpment the torrential downpour fell on the already saturated steep slopes, cascading into creeks and gullies and thundering downward with unbelievable volume and force to demolish the landscape and townships below on a scale that has never been witnessed before. Tragically, precious lives were lost in what has since been described as an 'inland tsunami'.

The heroic efforts of rescue teams, who in some cases put their own lives at risk, were all that prevented greater losses and supplied the initial support and reassurance for the injured, bereft and homeless. We may well appreciate the myriads of volunteers from not only Queensland, but many other places also, who responded immediately with generous donations, as well as broad shoulders on which to weep. The caring and unselfish traits of Queensland's youth were clearly evident in the volunteer armies who pitched in willingly to help anyone in need. Whilst feeling deep sympathy with those unfortunate victims of tragedy, what they endured in this catastrophe we will never really be able to take in. When the initial rallying of kind supporters has dwindled and the numbness of shock gives way to the unbearable pain of agonising memories and unanswered questions, the risk of depression and its possible consequences becomes very real. We cannot presume to measure the mental torment suffered by residents whose home towns were all but obliterated. Neither can we assuage the grief of those bereft. There are gaping holes torn in the close-knit social fabric of some small communities that can never be repaired.

Who can describe the horrors that will continue to haunt people through the terrible scenes they have witnessed? Who can feel the excruciating anguish of those whose loved ones were taken from them violently and who can explain it to the children? Who can even begin to imagine what it felt like for those who had to watch the bodies of friends and neighbours being swept to destruction while, powerless to help, they clung to comparative safety in trees or on roof-tops? Who can then understand their awful feelings of guilt, however unreasonable, when they themselves were rescued?

There is no joy for anyone, particularly bewildered children, in seeing their dearest possessions piled in a sodden and mangled heap in the gutter awaiting final disposal at the Council dump. The ongoing heartache that ensues as a result of these devastating events simply cannot be told in words; neither can photographs do much to reveal the harrowing experiences suffered by many victims of the floods.

For some, talking openly about their traumas has provided an emotional outlet, while for others relief is sought in looking for somewhere to place the blame. Others have found refuge in prayer, trusting God and recognising His right to use elements of His own creation to arrest man's attention.

There are many wonderful people who shone in different ways through these adversities. Those with hard-earned qualifications not only made use of their training, but laboured far beyond the normal call of duty where lives were at stake and people were suffering, sacrificing their own comfort to help others.

Then there were those that came forward as volunteers; those that emerged as natural leaders to organise the evacuation centres; those who made room in their houses to provide accommodation for homeless families, and those who donated whatever they were able, from substantial gifts of money down to a kind, sympathetic smile. Unfortunately, the real picture is not complete without reference to the despicable acts of looters and bogus trades people, who, to give them the benefit of the doubt, may possibly be victims of some illness that does not evoke sympathy because of the anti-social way in which it manifests itself.

When all causes, results and responses have been thoroughly investigated by Government Inquiries and the sagacious critics have voiced their opinions with the inspiration of long-pondered hindsight, there will certainly be lessons to learn and some serious re-thinking to be done. Men may not be masters of the weather but experience can teach us how to anticipate and respond to its challenges.

In perusing the first-hand accounts of those who were confronted with these challenges in the summer of December 2010 and January 2011, we may take the opportunity to develop a greater understanding and appreciation of all that entered into the devastating weeks when the wild waters invaded Queensland.

Esk-Hampton Road

QUEENSLAND

FLOOD STATISTICS

THE FLOODING THAT DEVASTATED QUEENSLAND DURING THE SUMMER OF 2010 - 2011, AFFECTED AT LEAST 1.3 MILLION KM² OF THE STATE, WHICH IS GREATER THAN THE COMBINED AREAS OF FRANCE AND GERMANY.

- 70% of Queensland received well above average rainfall, whilst for 30% of the state, the rainfall was the highest on record.
- 72 Councils were affected, involving 411 schools.
- 25% of Queensland's businesses were disrupted to varying degrees.
- 50,000 houses were either destroyed or required a significant degree of rebuilding.
- 54 coal mines were flooded.
- $5.8 billion damage was done to public infrastructure.

FLOODS ARE NOT ALL BAD....

THE EXTREME LA NIÑA EVENT OF 2010 - 2011, BROUGHT DRAMATIC RECOVERY TO THE ENVIRONMENT AND WATER STORAGES WITHIN THE MURRAY-DARLING AND LAKE EYRE BASINS.

THE MURRAY-DARLING RIVER SYSTEM

The Murray-Darling is Australia's largest river system and many rivers in Queensland are its tributaries, a large number of them having their headwaters in the western slopes of the Great Dividing Range. The Murray-Darling Basin covers an area of over one million km² and, passing through five states and territories of varying climate types, includes twenty-three major rivers.

Following the floods in Queensland in 2010 - 2011, the floodplains and wetlands of the Murray-Darling Basin are teeming with new life, including River Red Gums and many other species of flora and fauna, such as the yellowbelly and silver perch, which rely on the seasonal droughts and flooding for their survival and reproduction. Other species such as yabbies, birds and frogs are responding to the increased food and habitat, as well as micro and macro invertebrates that inhabit the sediments and remain dormant through long periods of drought.

Regular follow-up flooding will be required, however, to maintain the health of the remarkable estuary environment near the river mouth (in South Australia) called the Coorong.

LAKE EYRE

Further west in Queensland, the floodwaters of the Diamantina and Georgina Rivers, Cooper and Eyre Creeks, along with other watercourses, travelled over a period of three or four months, and contributed to the filling of the Lake Eyre waterways for the first time in more than thirty-five years. Many water birds, including seagulls and pelicans, flocked in to take advantage of the plentiful food in the swelling lakes. Most of the time Lake Eyre is almost dry, large areas being covered with a crust of salt, but following floods, this huge wetland system teems with aquatic life and the plains bloom with colourful wildflowers. Goyders Lagoon and the Coongie Lakes, which are listed as wetlands of international significance, also filled, and the Diamantina and Cooper Creek channel country produced rich cattle fattening pastures.

Lake Eyre is the fifth largest terminal lake in the world, its basin covering 1.2 million km². It has great conservation significance, supporting several rare and endangered species of flora and fauna, including the Bilby. The rivers in this system experience highly variable flow, many of them dry for long periods of time, forming a chain of clay pans, waterholes and channels.

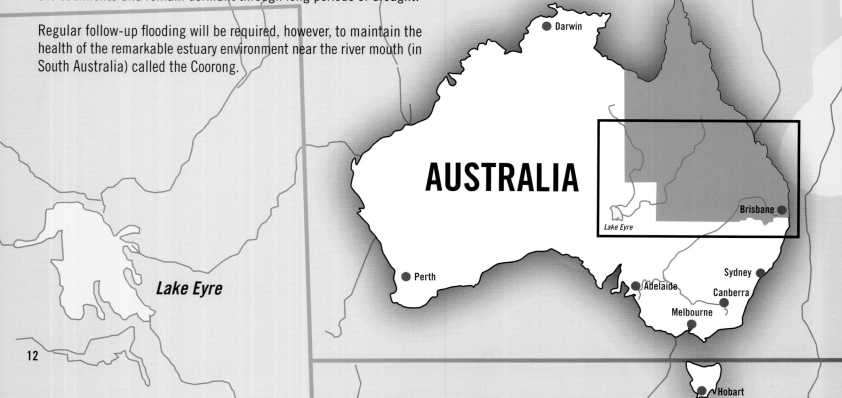

Lake Eyre

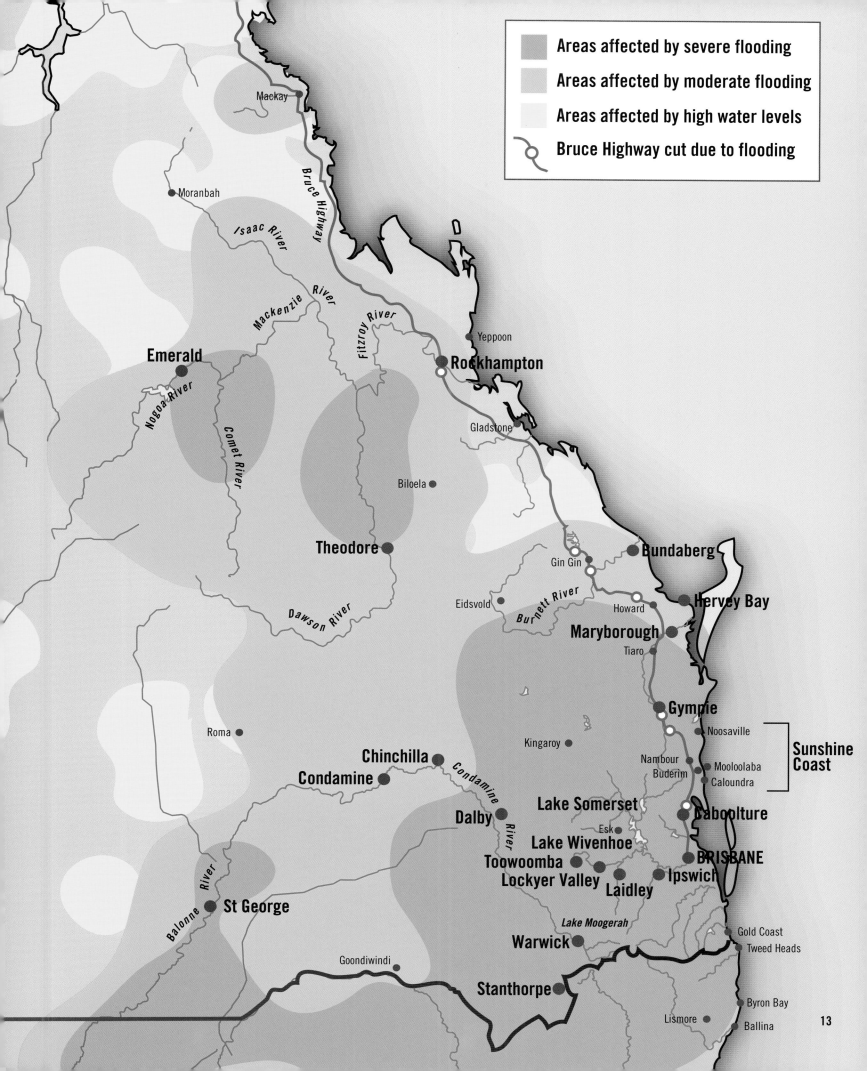

Areas affected by severe flooding

Areas affected by moderate flooding

Areas affected by high water levels

Bruce Highway cut due to flooding

Mackay

Moranbah

Bruce Highway

Isaac River

Mackenzie River

Fitzroy River

Yeppoon

Rockhampton

Emerald

Nogoa River

Comet River

Gladstone

Biloela

Theodore

Dawson River

Gin Gin

Bundaberg

Eidsvold

Burnett River

Hervey Bay

Howard

Maryborough

Tiaro

Gympie

Roma

Noosaville

Kingaroy

Sunshine Coast

Chinchilla

Nambour

Mooloolaba

Condamine

Condamine River

Buderim

Caloundra

Lake Somerset

Dalby

Esk

Lake Wivenhoe

Caboolture

Toowoomba

BRISBANE

Lockyer Valley

Laidley

Ipswich

St George

Balonne River

Lake Moogerah

Warwick

Gold Coast

Tweed Heads

Goondiwindi

Stanthorpe

Byron Bay

Lismore

Ballina

13

Lockyer Valley in Drought (Atkinson Dam in foreground)

Lockyer Valley in Flood

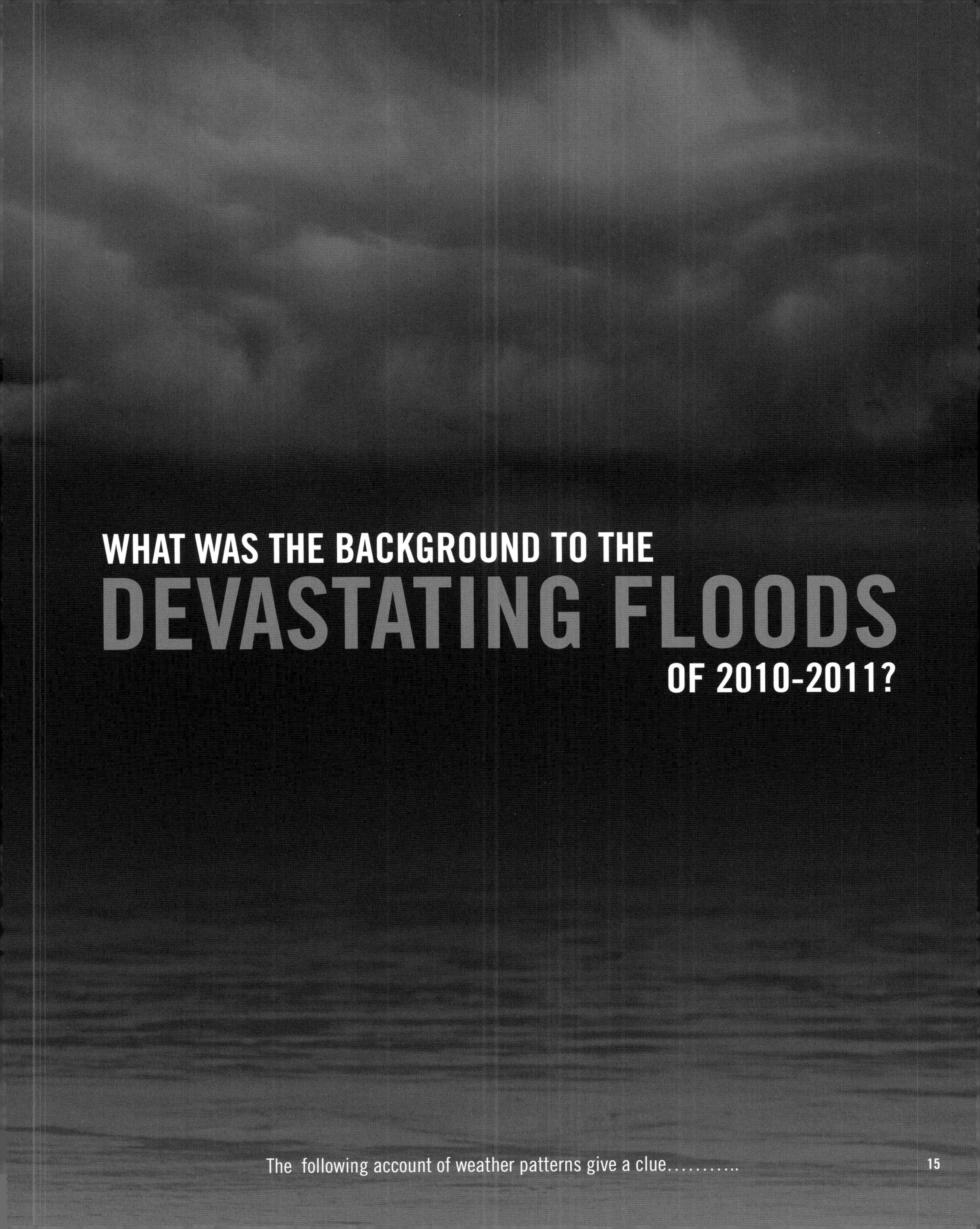

WHAT WAS THE BACKGROUND TO THE
DEVASTATING FLOODS
OF 2010-2011?

The following account of weather patterns give a clue..........

IMPACT OF THE SOUTHERN OSCILLATION ON AUSTRALIA'S WEATHER

THE SOUTHERN OSCILLATION IS A TERM GIVEN TO THE PERIODIC CYCLE OF ATMOSPHERIC CIRCULATION PATTERNS, WITH A CORRESPONDING MOVEMENT OF VAST AREAS OF WARM AND COOL WATERS, BACK AND FORTH ACROSS THE PACIFIC OCEAN.

WALKER CIRCULATION

Sir Gilbert Walker's studies of monsoon patterns led to the observation and understanding of the relative air pressures over the Indian and Pacific Oceans. He observed that high pressure over the Indian Ocean corresponded with low pressure over the Pacific Ocean, and vice versa. He called this pattern of oscillating pressures the 'southern oscillation'. Further studies have established the existence of a circulatory pattern involving changes in rainfall, wind and temperature, which has increased the understanding of global climate as a whole and has become known as the Walker Circulation.

Under normal conditions, a large area of high pressure lies over the eastern edge of the Pacific Ocean, along the South American coast; and southern trade winds blow from this high pressure zone towards the other side of the ocean where the pressure is lower, over Indonesia. The cool water that lies off the coast of South America is dragged westwards by the strong steady winds and becomes warmer through contact with the atmosphere and the heat of the sun. This westward flow of water raises the sea-level in the western Pacific, where it is about 40 centimetres higher than the eastern parts adjacent to South America, resulting in a thick layer of warm water in the western Pacific. The warmed water then gently flows back in a mild, deeper counter-current, cooling as it reaches the South American coast to begin the cycle again.

During this cycle, moist air rises into the atmosphere from the evaporating warm water, adding to the monsoon rains, and when farther aloft and drier, the air is carried rapidly to the east, cooling and descending to the high-pressure area off South America, where the cycle begins over again.

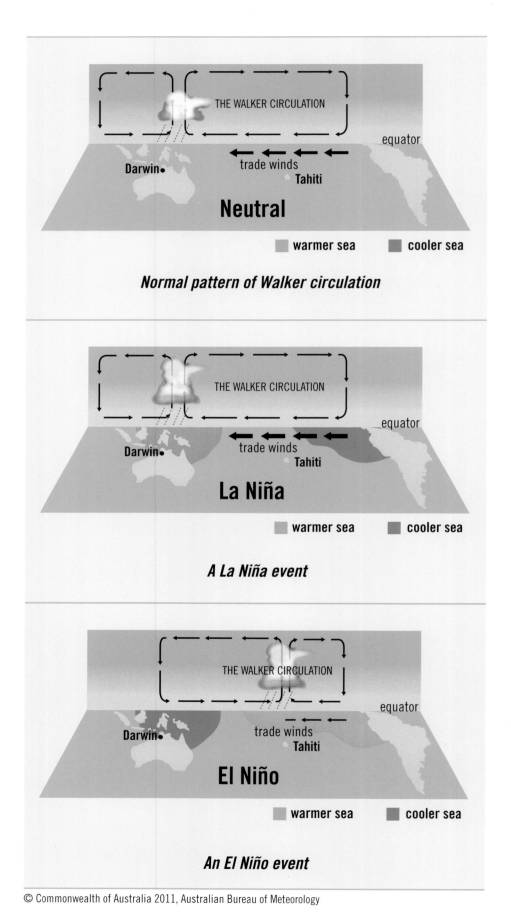

Normal pattern of Walker circulation

A La Niña event

An El Niño event

THE SOUTHERN OSCILLATION INDEX (SOI)

The Southern Oscillation Index relates to the fluctuating pattern of surface atmospheric pressures between the Asian and east Pacific regions, measured at Tahiti and Darwin. It is calculated on a monthly or seasonal basis and is used as an indicator of "El Niño" and "La Niña" events.

Sustained negative values indicate an El Niño event, with a reduction in the strength of the trade winds. The lower the SOI value, the stronger the El Niño event. In El Niño years the air-pressure is higher at Darwin than at Tahiti.

Sustained positive values indicate a La Niña event, with stronger Pacific trade winds. The higher the SOI value, the stronger the La Niña event. In La Niña events the air-pressure is lower at Darwin than at Tahiti.

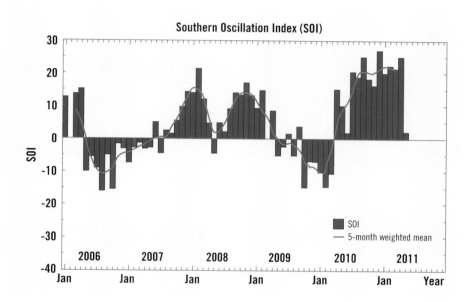

RECENT SOI VALUES – SUSTAINED NEGATIVE VALUES OFTEN INDICATE AN El NIÑO EVENT AND SUSTAINED POSITIVE VALUES INDICATE LA NIÑA. A STRONG LA NIÑA EVENT HAS OCCURRED IN LATE 2010 AND EARLY 2011.

© Commonwealth of Australia 2011, Australian Bureau of Meteorology

HOW AN EL NIÑO DEVELOPS

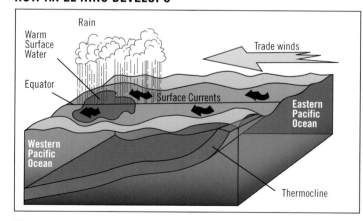

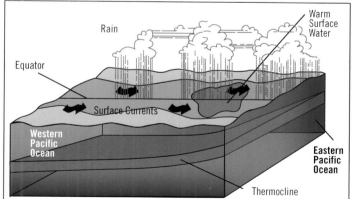

The boundary between the warm surface waters and the deeper cold waters is called the thermocline. In normal weather conditions the thermocline is pushed downward in the western Pacific by the pool of warmed water, with a resultant up-thrust of nutrient-rich cold water in the eastern Pacific.

An El Niño event occurs when the trade winds weaken and the warm surface current slows. The thermocline flattens, thus reducing the amount of cold water being brought to the surface in the eastern Pacific.

EL NIÑO

THE NAME EL NIÑO IS SPANISH, IT WAS SO NAMED BY THE ANCHOVY FISHERMEN OF PERU WHO DREADED IT, AND TRANSLATES AS 'THE CHRIST CHILD' AS IT APPEARS AROUND CHRISTMAS TIME.

It is associated with a significant warming of sea surface temperatures in the central and eastern Pacific Ocean, whilst the ocean temperatures close to eastern Australia are cooler, leading to the probability of reduced rainfall and drier conditions over northern and eastern Australia.

El Niño events can be expected to occur every three to eight years, and may last up to three years, and strong negative values in the Southern Oscillation Index are associated with these events.

An El Niño event is triggered by a slight relaxation of the trade winds, immediately resulting in a feed-back loop. The winds cease to drag the surface water and the mass of warm water in the west surges eastward, bringing warmer water closer to South America. The air above is warmed by the warmer water which reduces the atmospheric pressure and weakens the winds even more. More warm water surges towards the east as the air-pressure decreases, resulting in higher surface temperatures over the whole Pacific, and the winds change direction, beginning a new pattern in the opposite direction. The deep warm water comes up against the South American coast and evaporates, bringing welcome rain to farms inland, but driving away the fish which depend on the nutrient-rich cooler waters. The resulting failure of the anchovy catch then leads to a world shortage of fishmeal for animal feed. The disturbance of the globe-circling jet-streams during a strong El Niño event can affect weather patterns world-wide. No two El Niño events are alike.

A powerful El Niño event can cause severe drought in Australia, while it is causing storms and flooding on the eastern Pacific coasts (South America).

DECEMBER - FEBRUARY EL NIÑO CONDITIONS

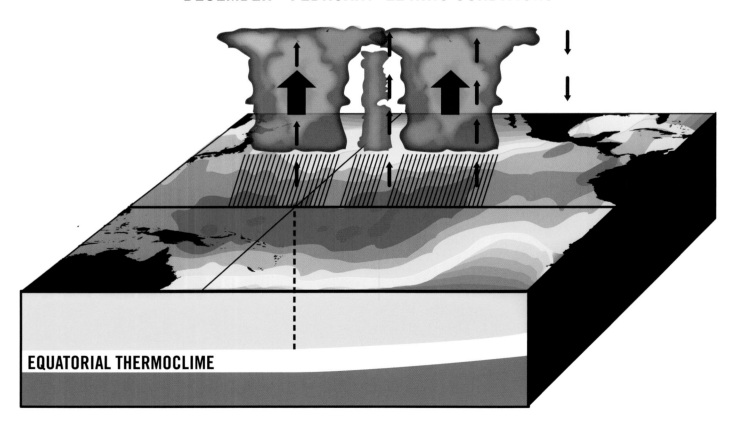

EQUATORIAL THERMOCLIME

LA NIÑA

THE NAME LA NIÑA IS SPANISH AND WAS NAMED BY THE SAME PERUVIAN FISHERMAN WHO NAMED EL NIÑO. IT TRANSLATES AS 'THE GIRL CHILD', BEING THE OPPOSITE OF EL NIÑO.

La Niña is associated with a significant cooling of sea surface temperatures in the central and eastern Pacific Ocean, whilst the ocean temperatures close to eastern Australia are warmer, leading to the increased probability of wetter conditions over northern and eastern Australia. It can also lead to an increased incidence of tropical cyclones.

La Niña events can be expected to occur every three to seven years, but not always after an El Niño, and may last one to two years.

Strong positive values in the Southern Oscillation Index are associated with a La Niña Event.

A La Niña event is triggered by the over-compensation in the ocean and skies, following an El Niño event as the trade winds strengthen during a return to the normal Walker circulation. This time the trade winds become exceptionally strong causing warm water to pile up in the west, increasing the strength of the counter-current so that there is a huge upwelling of the deep cool waters along the South American coastline which create excellent conditions for anchovies. The jet stream weakens, drawing cooler Arctic air into North America and a different set of weather extremes is generated globally. A La Niña event does not always occur following an El Niño. During the last century it is thought that only fifteen of the twenty-three El Niño events, which are thought to have occurred, have been followed by an over-compensation, or La Niña event. Where the build-up of warm waters in the western Pacific causes the sea-level to rise, low-lying islands can almost disappear. No two La Niña events are alike.

A powerful La Niña event can cause flooding and cyclone activity in eastern Australia, whilst drier conditions prevail along the eastern Pacific coasts.

DECEMBER - FEBRUARY   LA NIÑA CONDITIONS

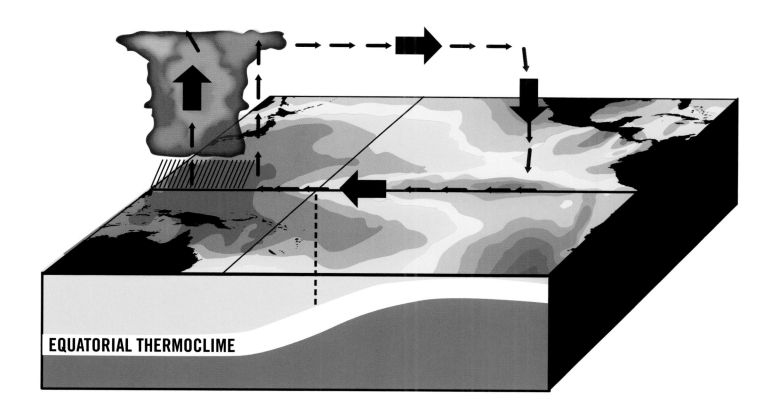

EQUATORIAL THERMOCLIME

The La Niña event of 2010-11 has been one of the strongest on record, in which most of Australia has received above average rainfall, with widespread flooding occurring , particularly in Queensland, between September 2010 and February 2011. The Southern Oscillation Index for December 2010 was +27.1, which is the highest December value on record. For Queensland, December 2010 was the wettest December on record.

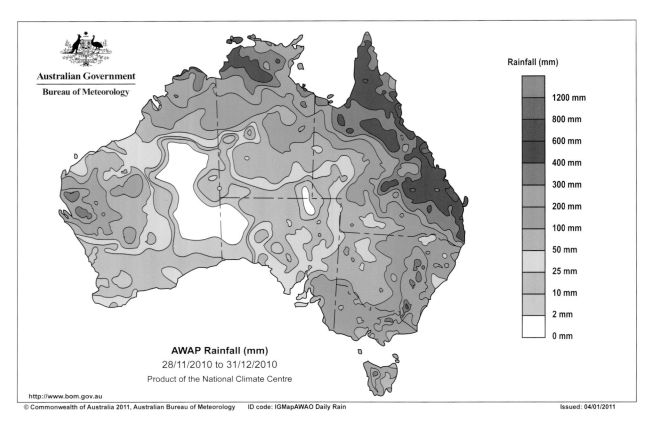

Australian total rainfall between Nov 28th 2010 and January 17th 2011

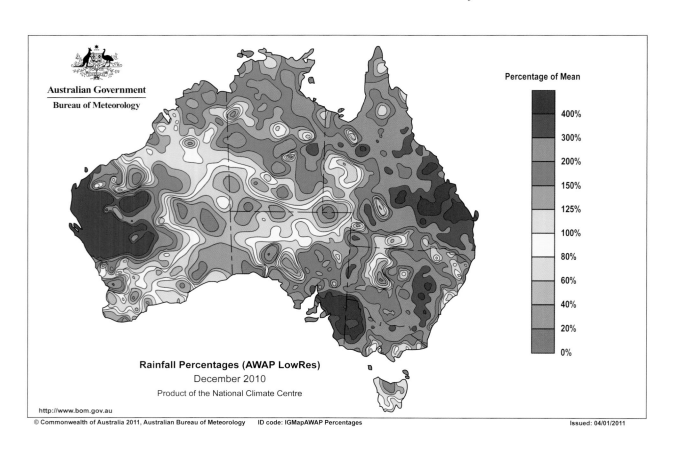

Australian rainfall - percentages of normal for December 2010.

BRUCE HIGHWAY
CUT DUE TO FLOODING

Water over Bruce Highway at Caboolture

THE BRUCE HIGHWAY IN QUEENSLAND IS THE MAIN HIGHWAY BETWEEN BRISBANE AND CAIRNS, PROVIDING ACCESS TO MANY TOWNS AND CITIES ALONG THE EAST COAST. IT IS THE CONTINUATION OF THE SOUTHERN COASTAL HIGHWAYS; THE PRINCES HIGHWAY BETWEEN MELBOURNE AND SYDNEY AND THE PACIFIC HIGHWAY BETWEEN SYDNEY AND BRISBANE. IT IS REGARDED AS THE MAIN ARTERY BETWEEN NORTH QUEENSLAND AND THE SOUTH. THE HIGHWAY IS CONTINUALLY BEING UPGRADED IN AN ATTEMPT TO KEEP UP WITH THE EVER INCREASING VOLUME OF TRAFFIC.

Numerous instances of flooding between January and March 2011 led to closures of the Bruce Highway at many different locations, causing major disruptions to towns and cities, and in some cases, periods of isolation. (See map on page 12). Travellers were stranded unexpectedly and delays in transport caused considerable havoc. One truck driver travelling to Brisbane from the north tried the back roads when the Bruce Highway was cut, with some success until he reached Toowoomba, where landslips on the range had closed the road! He spent the next three days parked at the top of the range until eventually one lane was cleared, but even then, traffic travelling down the range had to alternate with traffic coming up.

The patience of many holiday travellers was tested

Essential supplies ran out in many shops, although in some instances food was not far away, but could not be distributed because commercial agreements necessitated it being distributed via Brisbane, and the road to Brisbane was cut! Large quantities of milk were dumped when dairy farmers' tankers were unable to get to the depots. The tourism industry suffered severely from the disruption to travel, and even after floodwaters receded, frequent delays occurred while damaged roads were repaired.

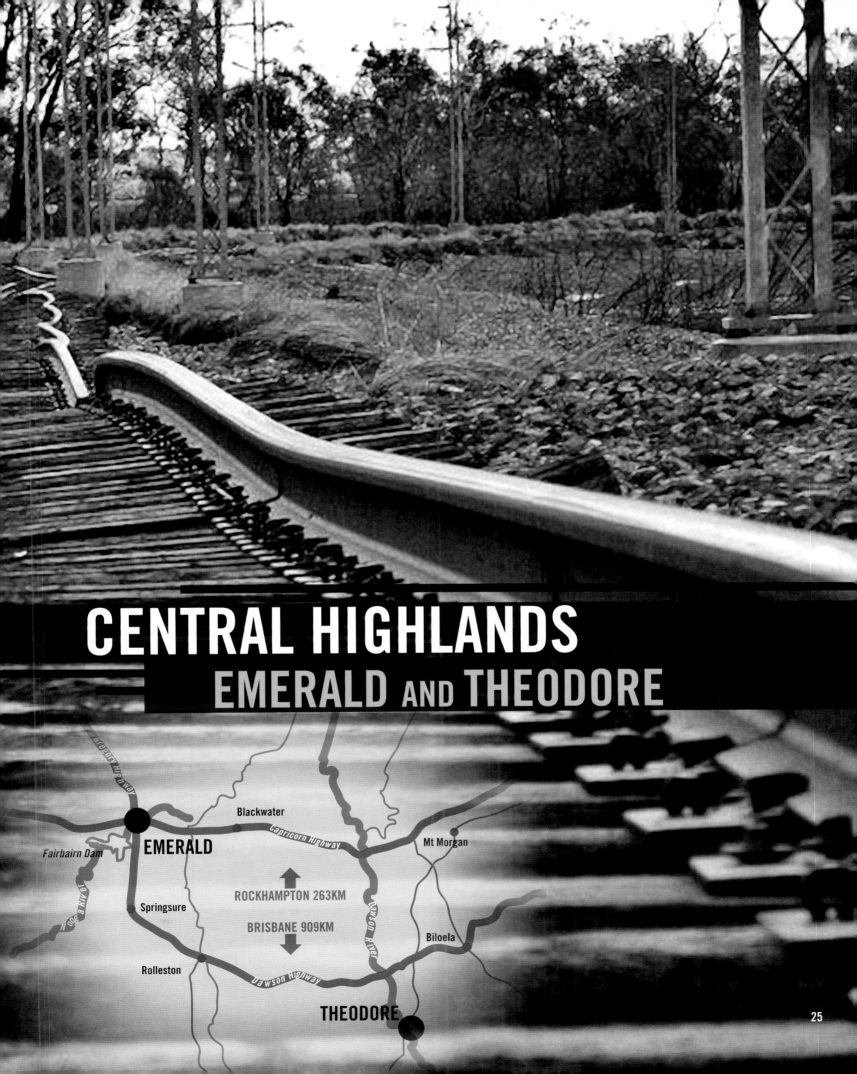

CENTRAL HIGHLANDS
EMERALD AND THEODORE

Blackwater

EMERALD

Fairbairn Dam

Capricorn Highway

Mt Morgan

ROCKHAMPTON 263KM

BRISBANE 909KM

Springsure

Dawson River

Biloela

Rolleston

Dawson Highway

THEODORE

THE TOWN OF EMERALD POPULATES BOTH BANKS OF THE NOGOA RIVER AT THE JUNCTION OF THE CAPRICORN AND GREGORY HIGHWAYS WHICH, ALONG WITH A NETWORK OF RAILROADS MAKE THIS THRIVING TOWN A BUSY 'HUB' ON AN IMPORTANT TRADE CORRIDOR. COAL MINING IN THE AREA HAS LED TO A SUBSTANTIAL INCREASE IN POPULATION WHICH NOW NUMBERS MORE THAN 14,000. ALTHOUGH IN PROXIMITY TO THE GEM FIELDS, ITS NAME IS DERIVED FROM THE SURROUNDING LUSH GREEN HILLS. THE FAIRBAIRN DAM ON LAKE MARABOON SUPPLIES WATER FOR THE TOWN AND ITS PROSPEROUS AGRICULTURAL INDUSTRIES. TWENTY-FIVE PERCENT OF QUEENSLAND'S COTTON IS PRODUCED IN THIS AREA.

Emerald is no stranger to catastrophe. Four major fires have destroyed much early history, but the railway station, now listed on the National Trust, has been restored and is the chosen setting for many tourists' photographs.

The town of Emerald has grown rapidly in the last two decades, and has been inundated twice, in 2008 and again in 2010. Emerald residents were kept informed of the progress in the Nogoa River's flooding situation in December 2010, by means of SMS messages, a strategy recommended following Victoria's Black Saturday bushfires.

Evacueees from flooded areas numbering 2,500 people were evacuated from the flooded areas and cared for in five evacuation centres. Power was cut off from 125 homes as 80 percent of the town flooded. The Nogoa River reached its peak of 16.05 metres on December 31st but by January 2nd some were able to return home to embark on the daunting task of cleaning and recovery. Pallet loads of cleaning products were supplied by the flood recovery centre.

Through the traumas the people in these communities have suffered together, the social fabric has been strengthened and enriched, which has enabled them to support each other in facing their distresses courageously and in tackling the challenges of restoration.

Bitumen works in Emerald

Jodi Harrold

THEODORE
EVACUATED IN THE CENTRAL WEST

THE TINY TOWN OF THEODORE, WITH ITS WIDE PALM-TREE-LINED STREETS, IS LOCATED ON THE LEICHHARDT HIGHWAY WHERE IT CROSSES THE DAWSON RIVER, AND IS AT THE SOUTHERN END OF THE COAL-RICH BOWEN BASIN. THE RICH BLACK-SOIL FARMING AREAS ARE IRRIGATED FROM THE DAWSON RIVER, WHICH ALSO LENDS ITSELF WELL FOR FISHING AND WATER SPORTS. THE NOGOA AND DAWSON RIVERS BOTH HAVE THEIR HEADWATERS IN THE CARNARVON RANGES AND BECOME TRIBUTARIES WITHIN THE FITZROY RIVER SYSTEM.

HISTORY WAS MADE IN THEODORE

THEODORE'S ENTIRE POPULATION OF 390 WAS AIRLIFTED USING FIVE HELICOPTERS ON DECEMBER 28TH 2010, MAKING IT THE FIRST QUEENSLAND TOWN TO BE COMPLETELY EVACUATED. AS MOST OF THE TOWN WAS FLOODING, THE ONLY DRY PLACE FOR THE HELICOPTERS TO LAND INVOLVED THE REMOVAL OF POWER LINES AND CUTTING DOWN OF THE POLES. PETS THAT HAD BEEN LEFT BEHIND WERE RESCUED BY POLICE AND EVACUATED, AND SES FLOOD BOATS WERE USED TO PATROL THE DESERTED TOWN.

The residents were allowed a rather disturbing brief visit back into the town more than a week later to view and assess the damage. Most were able to return home by January 9th, although some houses were still unlivable. Although the Dawson River had peaked at 14.7m on New Year's Day, it was in no hurry to relinquish the territory it had gained, which meant that the evacuated inhabitants of Theodore were out of their homes for longer than anyone else in Queensland.

Photos supplied by Qld Police

9 cats and 111 dogs evacuated by helicopter

THEODORE
AIRLIFTING THE ONLY WAY OUT

Powerlines and poles were removed to permit the helicopters to land in Theodore's streets

FLOOD

EMERALD

- **Dec 26th 2010** - Rain falling in already saturated catchment of Nogoa River. 200mm falls overnight.

- **Dec 27th 2010** - Mild flood warning issued to residents.

- **Dec 28th 2010** - Evacuation centres prepared.

- **Dec 29th 2010** – Evacuations start.

- **Dec 30th 2010** – 2,500 evacuated. River rising.

- **Dec 31st 2010** – Nogoa River peaks at 16.05m.

- **Jan 1st 2011** – Emerald isolated. 80% of town flooded. 125 homes without power. Water level beginning to drop.

- **Jan 2nd 2011** – Some residents return home. 44 interstate SES volunteers arrive to assist recovery process.

- **Jan 3rd 2011** – Co-ordinated clean-up begins.

- 95% of business properties damaged.

- Fairbairn Dam reached 151% capacity.

Michael Vale

Jodi Harrold

FACTS

THEODORE

- **Dec 25th 2010** – Dawson River rising. Police and SES door-knocking. Some residents evacuated.

- **Dec 26th 2010** – River at 13.4m

- **Dec 27th 2010** – Heavy rain over Dawson River catchment. Some relocation of residents in low-lying areas.

- **Dec 28th 2010** – Mandatory evacuation of all residents. 150 homes affected.

Ann-marie Joubert

- **Dec 29th 2010** – Power lines and poles removed to make way for helicopters. Five Helicopters evacuate the 390 residents.

- **Dec 30th 2010** – Police guard empty town. Pets in town rescued and evacuated.

- **Dec 31st 2010** – Dawson River at 14.4m.

- **Jan 1st-9th 2011** – Residents remain evacuated. Cotton crops destroyed.

- **Jan 9th 2011** – Premier visits Theodore's residents.

- **Jan 10th 2011** – Repairs being made to infrastructure in view of residents return.

- **Jan 11th 2011** – All residents now in town. Cleaning supplies issued. Some homes still unlivable.

Stephen Marshall

JUDI LIOSATOS

Emerald

THEIR STORIES WERE
HEARTBREAKING

EMERALD IS A SMALL TOWN OF FRIENDLY PEOPLE WITH A GOOD COMMUNITY SPIRIT, LOCATED IN QUEENSLAND'S CENTRAL HIGHLANDS. A CENTRE FOR EXTENSIVE AGRICULTURAL AND MINING OPERATIONS. THE LOCALS ARE USED TO THE WET SEASON AND MINOR FLOODING, BUT THE LARGE FLOODS OF RECENT YEARS HAVE PROVED EXTREMELY TESTING. BECAUSE EMERALD IS USUALLY THE FIRST DOMINO TO FALL IT GETS THE MOST ATTENTION. AS OTHER TOWNS GO UNDER IN TURN, THEIR CITIZENS ARE OFTEN LEFT WITH THE FEELING THAT THEY DON'T GET THE HELP AND SUPPORT THAT EMERALD GETS, OFTEN FEELING FORGOTTEN WHEN IT IS OVER.

Having experienced a large flood in 2008, the people of Emerald and the nearby towns had learnt how to get back on their feet quickly, although the emotional effect was still there when the 2010 - 2011 floods occurred. Many were caught unawares because of the unusual way the water rose. It came up quickly in some areas, but rose slowly in others, and people in areas that had not experienced flooding before found themselves under water.

As well, many people were out of town for the Christmas holidays and found it difficult – or even impossible- to return to protect their homes and properties. Those who did remain did what they could for their friends and neighbours. People banded together to rescue others as well as support each other as water rose around them. The council called for as many vehicles as possible to be moved to higher ground outside of town, which created an enormous car park.

I was asked once again to publish a book on the area's flooding and for this purpose met and spoke with many people from the Central Highlands. Their stories and photos, some of which are in this book, were heartbreaking, and I still don't know how some of them kept their sanity. I flew over the flooded land at its peak and saw friends' houses completely underwater with only TV antennas visible. I saw people boating down their street able to see only their roofs. I was told stories about houses with water running through them with the furniture floating on top of it. Others who did not have the time to remove their belongings and even if they had, there was nowhere safe to put them, and children had to leave their toys, school clothes, Christmas presents etc behind as they moved to the safety of the evacuation centres. Day and night helicopters, including Blackhawks, covered the sky as they ferried people and equipment out of the town.

The floodwaters divided the town up into many small islands. Most people did not realise the extent of it as they could only see the water lapping around their own places, their view blocked by buildings and other infrastructure. It was only when all the photos were collated afterwards that the damage caused by the flowing waters could be appreciated. Horses and cattle struggled to find high land as paddocks and crops went under. Some were lucky enough to be given hay via boats; others just had to starve with no food then or for some time into the future as their food had all disappeared. Crops were demolished and farmers were stranded for weeks on end. Emerald and the other towns ran out of food with the usual panic buying by the residents. Food was helicoptered in on pallets with volunteers helping to deliver the foods to stores.

The evacuation centres which included classrooms filled quickly. Children found a new way to look at their mundane school rooms!

Both main plazas in town flooded, as did most of the businesses of the area, and uncertainty based on previous experiences returned quickly. When was it going to end? How high will this flood go? Will the town be evacuated? What do I take with me? What about my pets? Will I have enough food for my children? I can't contact my friends; are they OK? Where can I get some food? When will there be money in the ATM's again? People were in despair; many had lost their homes, others their jobs or businesses as well. Without warning they had nowhere to live and no wage coming in.

When the water receded, everybody pitched in. People walked into strangers' houses and businesses and started cleaning up without being asked - they knew what had to be done. Volunteers came from everywhere to help. But some properties were so damaged that many will be unable to return to their houses until later in the year - if ever. Insurance companies knocked back a large percentage of claims, leaving people with no resources to repair or rebuild. As I write this the winter is upon us and many families with small children are still living in tents. As the clean-up period is still underway, people have not yet had time to deal with the emotional side of such an impact.

Children returned to school to find some of their friends no longer had school uniforms or other necessities. Schools from other areas sent gratefully received school items to help out. People continue to help wherever they can but the towns in this area are still broken and in need of much help.

Farmers with thousands of dollars' worth of repairs still cannot afford to employ people to help. Many businesses remain in temporary locations, and one of our plazas has not yet reopened, causing a great strain on the one remaining. Anger and frustration rear their ugly heads in these situations and only add to the difficulties of dealing with the aftermath of the event.

Our townsfolk who remain have to live with the question – when will this happen again? It surely will. While no actual lives were lost out here, many lives have been badly scarred, and some will never recover.

KAY SCHULZ

Emerald

THE WATER WAS RAGING
UNDERNEATH

WE WERE AWAY FOR CHRISTMAS AND TRIED TO GET BACK TO EMERALD ON 27TH DECEMBER. AT THIRTY MILE CREEK, ON THE OTHER SIDE OF COPPABELLA, WE WERE STOPPED BY WATER OVER THE ROAD. WE SLEPT IN THE CAR AND IN THE MORNING WERE ABLE TO CROSS THE CREEK SO WE GOT TO EMERALD.

The flood waters entered both our business premises (Emerald Autoglass) and our residence so we were prevented from living in our own property. Thankfully we were able to move in with friends nearby who were high and dry. The late afternoon of the 30th we went down the road by boat to see our business and it was just so quiet. It felt like a ghost town. Words cannot describe the appearance. The only sound was water and current flowing, in parts gushing, like someone turning on a tap. The current became too strong for the boat so we walked the rest of the way. The water was so still on the surface but raging underneath and we had to hang onto things to keep our balance, walk very slowly and be careful about the next step. The current was so strong that the fence was leaning, items had floated into the gate, forced away from their normal locations. The premises filled up overnight.

On the Saturday (1st January) we came back for another look. The water still hadn't peaked. We walked down to check on a friend in his house and found that the water was running through it. We nearly had to rescue some men in a boat who were zooming along the channel in front of our business. They didn't realise that there was a road that crossed the channel underneath the water, which the motor hit sending the boat sideways. The occupants managed to move it back into the deeper water and they decided they should put their lifejackets on!

Once the water started going down we all got to work, hosing out friends' places and businesses doing what we could until the owners were able to get across to do things themselves. When we were finally able to get into our business, the clean-up began. Friends, family and strangers all turned up to help. Although we hadn't asked for help we were all so stressed that it was obvious we needed help desperately and urgently. The QFRS also came with their fire hoses to help remove the mud and debris from our building and the others surrounding it.

.........KAY SCHULZ, EMERALD AUTOGLASS

All photos supplied by Kay Schulz

ARMY 'HABITAT' HOUSES EVACUEES AT
EMERALD

WHEN ON DECEMBER 27TH 2010, THE TOWN OF EMERALD WAS FACED WITH THE RISK OF SIGNIFICANT FLOODING, RESIDENTS WERE WARNED TO STAY TUNED TO REGIONAL BROADCASTS AND TO PREPARE THEIR HOMES FOR POSSIBLE INUNDATION. THEY WERE ADVISED TO PREPARE AN EMERGENCY KIT AND MAKE PLANS FOR EVACUATION, INCLUDING CARING FOR PETS. PEOPLE WERE ASKED TO KEEP A CHECK ON THE SAFETY AND NEEDS OF THEIR NEIGHBOURS ALSO.

By December 28th it was clear that some houses and businesses, particularly on the western side of the Nogoa River were at risk of flooding, and evacuations were recommended by the Disaster Management Group, whose operations centre was being manned 24/7. Bedding was sourced for the evacuation centres, which were set up at the Emerald Town Hall, and the Emerald Agricultural College. The centres were run by the Red Cross, with assistance from volunteers and other organisations such as the Salvation Army.

A further evacuation centre was set up at St Patrick's School on Thursday December 30th, and by the next day, when the Nogoa River had peaked, a total of five Evacuation Centres were operating. An army-designed 'habitat' was flown in to Emerald Airport from Amberley to operate as an additional evacuation centre to accommodate another 150 people. It was equipped with ration packs, sleeping bags and showers, and came with nine support staff. It was relocated from the airport by a Black Hawk helicopter to St Patrick's school on January 2nd.

As floodwaters receded, the numbers at the evacuation centres decreased and the Red Cross closed all but the Town Hall and Agricultural College centres on January 5th. Evacuation provisions, however, continued to be made available as long as they were needed.

Nadine Kennedy

A FEW POSSESSIONS SAVED

Kellie Williams

Town Hall evacuees

Tracey Dolzar

The habitat

Kellie Williams

Kellie Williams 35

Pet evacuation from Dawn Crescent

Jodi Harrold

Lachlan Winten

Lynn Bartle

Flood Relief Aid Centre

EMERALD
AND THEODORE

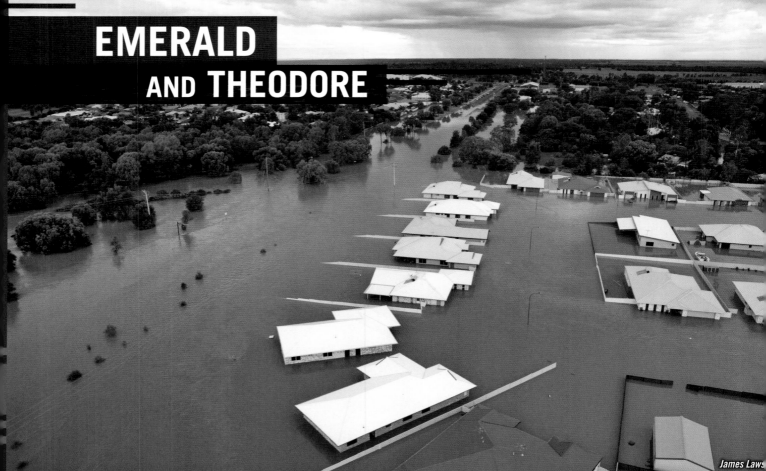
James Laws

Tracey Dolzan

Prepared to "wait-it-out"

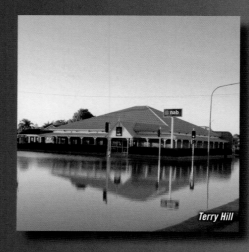
Terry Hill

Murray Herwin

Judi Liosatos

...esidence totally immersed

Const. Michael Banasiak

Judi Liosatos

Lynn Bartley

Recovery Centre

...rigation Lines

Nadine Kennedy

...aleyards Dump

Nadine Kennedy

Stephen Marshall

Foliage standing in 8ft water - Springsure 'Nandowrie...

Judi Liosatos

Judy McDonald

Terry Hill

Nadine Kennedy

Judi Liosatos

Terry Hill

THE ARMY AND SES VOLUNTEERS CAME TO EMERALD'S AID

AS A RESULT OF THE HEAVY RAINS OF DECEMBER, 2010, THE SES BOAT FROM THE CENTRAL HIGHLANDS REGION WAS FORCED TO CROSS A NUMBER OF FLOODED CREEKS IN AN EFFORT TO GET TO EMERALD. BY DECEMBER 28TH FLOODING HAD INCREASED TO THE EXTENT THAT SES VOLUNTEERS WERE KEPT BUSY ASSISTING WITH SANDBAGGING AND EVACUATIONS AND THE GEMFIELDS SES BOAT WAS ALSO RELOCATED TO EMERALD AS THE NOGOA RIVER PEAKED.

A Recovery Group was established on January 1st 2011 to initiate waste collections and organise volunteer work crews. Another 44 SES volunteers arrived from New South Wales and Victoria to assist with the clean-up of the shopping centres, Centacare, the showground

Terry Hill

Nadine Kennedy

Terry Hill

Terry Hill

Terry Hill

Terry Hill

Terry Hill

Michael Vale

other buildings. They also organised the supply of cleaning products to residents.
her crews of SES volunteers arrived from other places, including Cairns, to assist in
huge recovery operation.

ause of the road cuts and the inundation of Emerald's two main shopping centres, food
plies had to be flown in, and were distributed at several locations; all co-ordinated by
Army using Black Hawk helicopters. Several drops of food and grocery supplies were
de, mainly limited to bread, other essentials and non-perishable items, with SES and
l volunteers, in some instances, forming a human chain to convey boxes and packages
n the aircraft. The Army also arranged the delivery of a 'habitat' from Amberley, to
vide additional accommodation for evacuees.

e most of the Central Highlands region was in recovery, the Army and SES personnel
tinued to operate in the area, supporting towns such as Rolleston, which remained
solation.

Michael Vale

Judy McDonald

Michael Vale

Terry Hill

Comet

SUPPORT COMES DURING
TRAUMATIC TIMES

I LIVE IN COMET, 35KMS EAST OF EMERALD. AFTER 51 YEARS OF MARRIAGE, MY HUSBAND, ALAN, PASSED AWAY ON THE 28TH OF NOVEMBER, 2010. HIS FUNERAL WAS ARRANGED TO TAKE PLACE IN EMERALD ON FRIDAY DECEMBER 3RD FROM THE UNITING CHURCH. SOME FAMILY MEMBERS FLEW INTO EMERALD, OTHERS HAD DRIVEN IN WHEN THE ROADS WERE STILL OPEN AND OTHERS (FROM THE SOUTH) WERE STAYING IN NEARBY TOWNS. ON THURSDAY NIGHT SANDHURST CREEK FLOODED AFTER HEAVY FALLS IN THE CATCHMENT, PREVENTING US FROM DRIVING TO EMERALD FOR THE FUNERAL SO IT WAS POSTPONED FOR A DAY, AND JACKIE MACKAY OF ABC RADIO MOST KINDLY ADVISED FOLK OVER THE AIR OF THE CHANGE OF PLANS. TO ADD TO THE PROBLEMS, THE FUNERAL DIRECTOR WAS UNABLE TO BRING MY HUSBAND FROM ROCKHAMPTON BECAUSE OF FLOODING.

By the next day (December 4th) road access to Emerald had been blocked from all directions. With no other form of transport available, I rang Reverend Russell Reynoldson and he immediately contacted Donna and Mark Reid at Reid Heliwork, who came to our rescue, getting family members across the flooded creeks to Foley Road, where Rev. Russell met my daughter and son-in-law and drove them to the church. After a helicopter ride to Sandhurst Creek hill, my elder daughter and I were met by Ken Self, who took us by car into town for the funeral. Because of road closures, however, it was not possible to bring my husband from Rockhampton, so he wasn't able to attend his own funeral!

Marie Reid housed members of my family as well as myself. Donna and Mark Reid again helped us by flying us back to Comet. Rev. Russell agreed to conduct a memorial service in Comet Hall on 16th December for those friends who were unable to make it into Emerald. This was advertised in the media and it was lovely to see so many friends come to farewell my husband Alan.

My daughter made a beautiful DVD of her father's life which was played at his funeral and again at the memorial service. I am very grateful to Russell Reynoldson, Donna and Mark Reid, Ken Self, Marie Reid and all the people who attended the Memorial Service. Many thanks to everyone who has been so supportive to my family and me during this most traumatic time.

The recently widowed Rosemary McLeod

Judy McDonald

SENIOR SERGEANT
GRAEME REEVES
Emerald

THE ESTIMATE WAS
16.2 METRES
AND THE WHOLE ROOM FELL SILENT

MY VERY FIRST SHIFT WHEN I TOOK UP MY POSITION AS THE OFFICER IN CHARGE OF EMERALD, WAS THE DAY THE VINCE LESTER BRIDGE OVER THE NOGOA RIVER (THE DATUM POINT FROM WHICH THE FLOOD HEIGHT IS MEASURED) WENT UNDER IN THE 2008 FLOODS. WHILST THIS PROVIDED A BIT OF POLICE FOLKLORE, MOST IMPORTANTLY IT GAVE MYSELF, LOCAL POLICE AND OTHER EMERGENCY SERVICES INVALUABLE EXPERIENCE AND THE BASIS TO PROVIDE AN IMPROVED SERVICE IF EVER THIS ALL HAPPENED AGAIN. LITTLE DID I REALISE AT THAT TIME THAT WE WOULD PUT ALL OUR TRAINING TO THE TEST AGAIN SO SOON, AND IN SUCH A MAJOR WAY.

The 2010-2011 flood in Emerald, along with all the other disasters that occurred throughout Queensland, would without doubt be the greatest challenge we have confronted in recent history. Our local emergency services were at the forefront of the response to the disaster and the level of commitment and support demonstrated by all involved was extraordinary, including the wonderful support from a large contingent of personnel who volunteered to travel to Emerald to assist local police and the community members in this devastating time.

My role was that of Incident Coordination for the Queensland Police Service response in the Local Disaster Incident Coordination Centre, where I was able to observe the outstanding efforts put in by all the members of the Local Disaster Management Group. One outstanding recollection is of the morning briefing on the 30th. Each morning at 6am we would have a teleconference where the Bureau of Meteorology would provide river height readings which would allow us to estimate the expected height of water at the Vince Lester Bridge. This time the estimate was 16.2 metres -and the whole room fell silent. Only one unprintable word was spoken. We all knew this meant dire consequences for the town and "Map 2" predicting the extent of anticipated flooding had to be drawn up and made public as soon as possible.

The following days were a blur of activity. The sight of the Incident team catching a few hours' sleep on the floor of the council chambers, someone's wife coming in to help keep her husband awake to ensure his calculations of flood heights were correct, our mayor sleeping in his office as he refused to leave his community in such a dire time, will always stay with me.

I cannot be too proud of the efforts and planning of the local police throughout the entire event. With the assistance of a boat donated by SunWater, we were able to maintain a 24/7 flood boat patrol from the commencement of the flood until it was over. This boat was manned by local police with the assistance of water police flown in from Brisbane. Additional police were flown in from Mackay, Townsville and Rockhampton to boost local police numbers which also greatly assisted in the prevention of any looting throughout this major event.

A temporary police station was also set up at the Airport to provide a police response on the eastern side of the river and we even had an officer volunteer to stay on this "South Island" even though his own house was inundated and his family evacuated. A number of local police had to leave their own homes but continued to work, committed to their community.

Overall the community response was extremely positive. I am proud of the feedback I have received commending policing activity. The recollections of how people assisted each other, the volunteers who came from all over Queensland, the resilience of the community and the work ethics of my own police has made my time here in Emerald the highlight of my career.

Senior Sergeant
Graeme Reeves

FAIRBAIRN DAM IS THE NAME OF THE SPILLWAY AT LAKE MARABOON ON THE NOGOA RIVER, JUST SOUTH OF EMERALD. ITS CONSTRUCTION WAS COMPLETED IN 1972 PROVIDING A STORAGE CAPACITY OF 1,301,000 MEGALITRES, WHICH IS SAID TO BE THREE TIMES THE SIZE OF SYDNEY HARBOUR. THE CATCHMENT AREA COVERS 16,317 KM^2. THE INCREASED AVAILABILITY OF IRRIGATION SINCE THE CONSTRUCTION OF THE DAM HAS ENABLED AGRICULTURAL INDUSTRIES TO EXPAND GREATLY, AND 25% OF QUEENSLAND'S COTTON IS GROWN IN THE AREA. ITS WATER IS ALSO USED FOR COAL WASHING, AND EMERALD'S TOWN WATER SUPPLY IS DRAWN FROM THE DAM.

Holiday makers are well provided for with a variety of cabins and camping facilities, picnic tables and both electric and wood barbecues. The lake, well stocked with eight different kinds of fish, is most famous for the red claw crayfish.

On December 31st 2010, Fairbairn Dam reached a record 176% capacity, with water flowing 5.58m above the spillway. This was more than one metre above the previous record in January 2008.

The earthfill dam is designed to discharge floodwater safely through the purpose-built spillways, and staff from SunWater, which owns and manages the dam, monitored the record inflows 24 hours a day, using the data to manage the dam in accordance with the operating guidelines. At the peak of the flood, water was being discharged from the dam at the rate of 370,650 megalitres per day - more than 4 million litres per second.

FAIRBAIRN DAM

Murray Herwin

Judy McDonald

Jodi Harrold

James Laws

Tracey Dolzan

ROCKHAMPTON
BESIEGED BY THE FITZROY RIVER

A LIFE-SIZE BULL STATUE WELCOMES VISITORS AT THE ENTRANCE TO THE CITY OF ROCKHAMPTON, TO INFORM THEM THAT THEY ARE ENTERING THE 'BEEF CAPITAL OF AUSTRALIA', AND FIVE MORE STATUES ARE SITUATED ELSEWHERE TO MAKE SURE THEY DON'T FORGET IT. THE CITY OF 75 000 LIES JUST NORTH OF THE TROPIC OF CAPRICORN ON THE BANKS OF THE FITZROY RIVER. IT WAS FIRST SETTLED IN THE 1850'S AND GREW RAPIDLY AS HOPEFUL PROSPECTORS CAME SEEKING GOLD, WHICH WAS EVENTUALLY FOUND IN REASONABLE QUANTITY AT NEARBY MT MORGAN, IN 1886. OTHER MINERALS AND COAL WERE ALSO FOUND IN THE DISTRICT, BUT THE HIGH QUALITY CATTLE COUNTRY IN THE CITY'S HINTERLAND HAS MADE BEEF PRODUCTION AND PROCESSING AN IMPORTANT INDUSTRY FOR ROCKHAMPTON, GIVING THE CITY ITS TITLE.

Heritage from early days is well preserved in the central city area in grand sandstone buildings, and in the fine tropical Botanic Gardens, established over 130 years ago, which house the Rockhampton Zoo. The limestone Capricorn Caves are a spectacular tourist attraction just 23 kilometres north of the city, and thousands of tiny bats which live in them can be witnessed flying from the caves at dusk.

The Fitzroy River and its many tributaries drain a large part of eastern Queensland, and when heavy rains fall over the vast catchment, which covers 140,000 square kilometres, Rockhampton can experience severe flooding.

ROCKHAMPTON

MACKAY 335KM

Bruce Highway

ROCKHAMPTON

Fitzroy River

BRISBANE 649KM

Photo supplied by QLD Police

'BEEF CITY' WAS SWAMPED WITH BROWN GRAVY

MAJOR FLOODING HAS AFFECTED ROCKHAMPTON AT LEAST NINE TIMES SINCE 1860, AND THERE HAVE ALSO BEEN ANOTHER TWENTY EPISODES CLASSED AS MODERATE. FOLLOWING THE HEAVY RAINS OVER MUCH OF QUEENSLAND IN DECEMBER 2010 AND JANUARY 2011, THE FITZROY RIVER BEGAN TO RISE SLOWLY, EVENTUALLY REACHING A PEAK OF 9.2 METRES AT ROCKHAMPTON, THE HIGHEST FLOOD SINCE 1954.

After plunging the communities of Emerald and Theodore into mud-polluted chaos, the waters from the swollen Nogoa and Dawson Rivers entered the Fitzroy and surged relentlessly on towards Rockhampton. Having time to prepare was some advantage to the authorities and residents, as was the benefit of past experience, but the inescapable, stealthy invasion still caused 500 home owners to face evacuation, and 600 properties were left without power. Helicopters, barges and flood boats became the only means of transport as the railways flooded, the Capricorn (inland) and Bruce (coastal) Highways were cut, and the airport was forced to close as water engulfed the runways and the terminal. Supplies of food, pharmaceuticals and other essentials ran short and many people were unable to reach their places of employment. At least 3,000 properties were affected to some degree as large areas of the city were inundated by the muddy, debris-strewn sea.

The support of the defence forces, police and emergency organisations was invaluable during the two weeks of the city's isolation. As they have done before, the courageous people of Rockhampton faced the enormous challenges squarely and set about retrieving and restoring their flood ravaged properties, helping the city back onto its feet, ready to march on.

47

FLOOD

ROCKHAMPTON

- **December 11th 2010**
  Fitzroy River at 7.0m. Sandbagging begins.

- Warning of up to ten days' ahead of floods.

- **December 29th 2010**
  Fitzroy River at 7.8m and rising.

- **December 30th 2010**
  Threat of flooding causes panic-buying.
  Shops stripped of fresh produce.

- **January 1st 2011**
  Rockhampton airport closed.
  Railway flooded.
  Capricorn and Bruce Highways cut off.
  City isolated.
  2,000 residents in evacuation centres.

- **January 4th 2011**
  Helicopters begin delivering supplies.

- **January 5th 2011**
- River peaks at 9.2m.

- Worst flood since 1954.

FACTS

- **January 8th 2011**
  Floodwaters slowly begin to recede.

- **January 9th 2011**
  158 residents remain in evacuation centre.
  400 homes and 150 businesses still affected.

- **January 17th 2011**
  Floodwaters low enough for most residents to begin clean-up.

- More than 300 extra police and 1,000 SES volunteers brought in.

- 500 homes evacuated.

- 1,200 people self-evacuated.

- Evacuation centres cared for 36 dogs, 41 cats and 7 birds.

- The airport closed 23 days.

- 600 properties without power

FITZROY HOTEL

Rockhampton

GREAT RIVER VIEWS AT
THE FITZROY FLOAT-EL

AT 100 YEARS OLD, THE FITZROY HOTEL IS POSSIBLY ROCKY'S FIRST PUB, BUILT IN A PAST ERA TO SERVICE THE BULLOCK DRAYS THAT USED THE BUSY DEPOT ON THE HISTORIC SETTLEMENT OF DEPOT HILL.

Tony Higgins took over the hotel in November last year. Only a month later, he received notification of impending flooding. The power was cut, and residents were evacuated. Tony stayed behind to keep an eye on things while everyone was away. Tony says "It's a good community here at Depot Hill, very much a family area. They all jumped in and lent each other a hand in the week before the flood, helping the elderly get their furniture up high, doing all sorts of necessary things.

"It was very different from Toowoomba. They only had 30 seconds notice but we knew it was coming. It was a little surreal, because it was a clear sunny day, and we just had to sit and watch as the property slowly submerged. The water reached 9m high, just lapping the veranda, so we renamed the hotel the 'The Fitzroy Float-el'. We had a sign out the front advertising great river views. A basketball came floating past so we lashed it up to the fence on a pool cue and called it 'Wilson'. A bit of Aussie humour - we tried to put a bit of a positive spin on things, there was no point in getting down about it.

"The road and the airport were cut either side. The isolation was hard to deal with; we were all getting a bit of 'cabin fever'. So we opened up and became a bit of a Town Hall, albeit without power, for three weeks. The emergency services operated from here, we left the doors open for the water police or the S.E.S. to come in and utilise any of the facilities they needed to. At one stage I had a fellow ring me up from town, saying, 'I noticed you were a bit short of XXXX cans yesterday, would you like me to bring some out?' So he brought out ice, and a couple of cartons of XXXX cans, and I paid him his cost price. Then he proceeded to buy them back at full price over the bar! We used an honour system because there was no electricity

to run the till. We just had the drawer open, it was self serve. The customers knew the cost, there was a flat price for everything and every person paid.

"I saw some amazing community acts here. People were wading or taking their boats across flooded streets in a strong current to help someone get their beloved animal from where it was trapped. The water police were up to their necks in snake infested water - there were snakes everywhere. They worked hard in pouring rain and freezing cold. In the middle of the night, there they were out there doing their job - there was zero looting or crime.

"Senior Constable Grant Kerlin was doing a night shift with another constable when he noticed a dog battling in the current. Knowing he couldn't survive, they pulled the dog into the boat and let him out on dry land. Immediately, he jumped in again and started swimming. They hauled him into the boat a second time, deciding then and there to nickname him 'Boofhead'. They brought him into the hotel, where his owner is a regular. Much to their surprise they discovered his name really was Boofhead! Days later, Boofhead was still lying here on the veranda floor, fast becoming a local celebrity.

"When the water went down we had warm weather, making the mud, sludge, smell and mosquitoes almost unbearable. Then suddenly we had heavy rain and a flash flood, about 5 days later, which cleaned 80% of it away. That was heaven sent. You could see the relief on the faces of the S.E.S. and the contractors who were trying to scrub the streets; all of a sudden it was just gone. The roads ran black for a day.

"The river bed has changed over the last 20 years, and now it floods in different areas from where it has previously. The floods caused great devastation around here; some houses are irreparable. I went right around the whole area in a boat and had a look; it was very sobering. It has been a year of tremendous upheaval in Queensland, and it will be a long time before the affected towns recover.

"At the hotel we had no insurance, and we get no grants or anything, so it is just a straight loss. Many of our local businesses will be struggling for years while their trade rebuilds, but I'm certainly not going to whinge. We'll survive."

Photo supplied by QLD Police

THE ISOLATION WAS
HARD TO DEAL WITH

The legendary Boofhead

51

THE WATER STAYED UP FOR ABOUT
10 DAYS

GRANT AND MABEL WOOLER
Rockhampton

I WAS BORN HERE; MY FATHER BUILT THIS HOUSE AFTER HE CAME HOME FROM THE WAR. MY 8 SIBLINGS AND I GREW UP IN BOATS AND SOME EXTENDED FAMILY MEMBERS BECAME PROFESSIONAL FISHERMEN. WE HAVE ALWAYS ACCEPTED THAT FLOODS ARE A PART OF NATURE, THEY COME AND THEY GO. WE GET OVER A WEEK'S NOTICE HERE BEFORE THE FLOODING COMES DOWN THE RIVER FROM EMERALD AND MACKAY, AND WE KNOW THAT WHATEVER THEY GET AT RIVERSLEIGH, WE'LL GET ABOUT A THIRD AS MUCH. SO WE ALWAYS KNOW WHAT WE'RE IN FOR.

The water peaked at 9.2m on 5th of January. It's life, we choose to live here, and we help each other. It was just a big inconvenience, not like the poor beggars down in South Queensland who were devastated. We had plenty of time to lift everything up out of the way.

We all ate at a neighbourhood BBQ in the middle of the street - everywhere else was flooded, and there was no traffic. The water stayed up for about ten days, so instead of the car, I used the tinnie to get what we needed, a loaf of bread, a bag of ice or whatever. My wife came with me, there was no danger. All the policemen here did a terrific job and the water police were absolutely tremendous.

Scores of snakes floating down the river - browns, carpets and green tree snakes. I'd sit on the front steps of an afternoon and watch them coming - half a dozen every ten minutes - all trying to get out of the water. I'd give them a shove with a stick if they came too near the house. After the floods had begun to recede, I delivered some concrete to a building site, and there was a snake in every hole they had dug the day before where they were going to put the posts. Frogs had made themselves at home in them, and the snakes went in after a tasty frog or two, and then discovered the sides of the hole were too steep to allow escape!

Coal Mine swamped

Flooded farmland

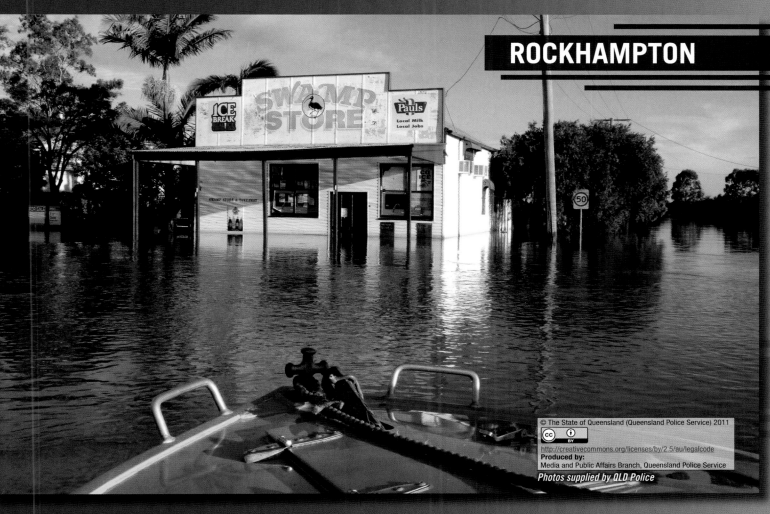

ROCKHAMPTON

BUNDABERG
WAS ISOLATED FOR THREE WEEKS

BUNDABERG, ON THE BURNETT RIVER, IS AN ATTRACTIVE, PROGRESSIVE, SUB-TROPICAL CITY, HAVING A POPULATION OF AROUND 61,000. NUMEROUS SUGAR CANE FARMS SURROUND THE CITY, FROM WHICH ONE-FIFTH OF QUEENSLAND'S SUGAR IS PRODUCED, AND BUNDABERG IS RENOWNED UNIVERSALLY FOR ITS BUNDABERG RUM.

Other agricultural and manufacturing industries prosper in the area and tourism is expanding rapidly, because of the proximity of the Great Barrier Reef and the annual visits of whales. Tourists also gather annually between November and March to observe the intriguing phenomena of baby sea turtles hatching on the sandy beaches, while aviation enthusiasts visit the many memorials to Bundaberg-born Bert Hinkler, the pioneer aviator who, in 1928, won international fame in his record-breaking flight from England to Australia.

Bundaberg enjoys the most equable climate of any Australian city, being refreshed by cool sea breezes in summer and having very mild winters. During the year 2010, above average rainfalls were recorded, culminating in the city's wettest December in history

BUNDABERG

Fred Haigh Dam

Bruce Highway

Gin Gin

Burnett River

BUNDABERG

BRISBANE 354KM

Paradise Dam

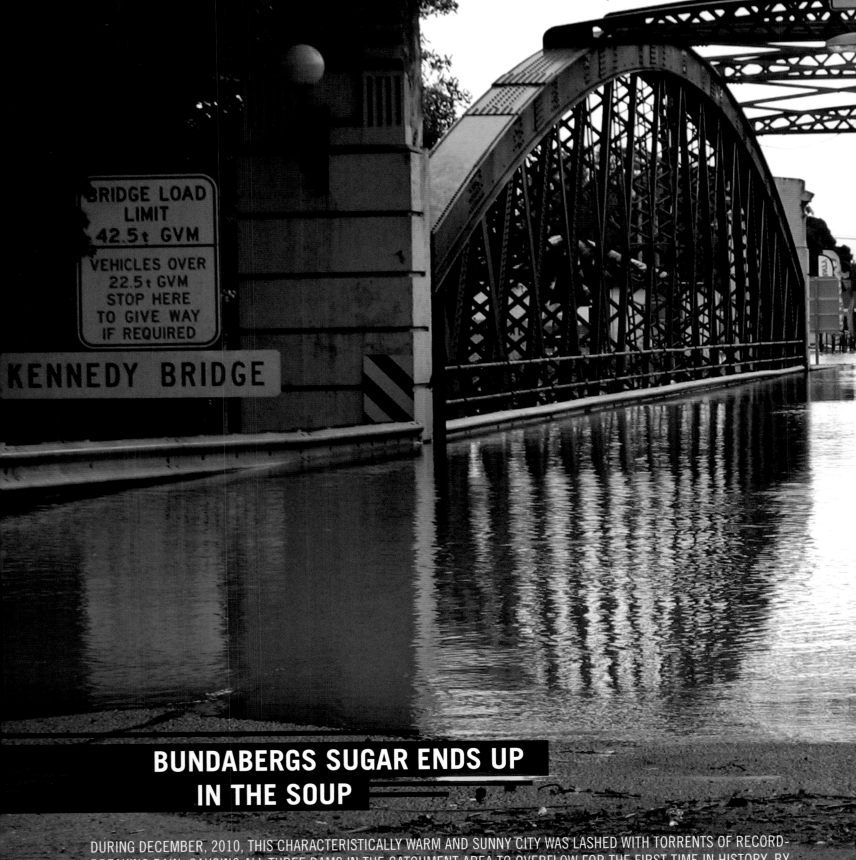

BUNDABERGS SUGAR ENDS UP IN THE SOUP

DURING DECEMBER, 2010, THIS CHARACTERISTICALLY WARM AND SUNNY CITY WAS LASHED WITH TORRENTS OF RECORD-BREAKING RAIN, CAUSING ALL THREE DAMS IN THE CATCHMENT AREA TO OVERFLOW FOR THE FIRST TIME IN HISTORY. BY DECEMBER 29TH, A RECORD 573MM OF RAIN HAD FALLEN AND THE BURNETT RIVER HAD PEAKED AT 7.95 METRES, POURING A MURKY BROWN TIDE OVER BUNDABERG'S FLAT TERRAIN AND SPLITTING THE CITY IN TWO. NUMEROUS PROPERTIES WERE INUNDATED AND MANY TRAUMATISED PEOPLE WERE FORCED TO EVACUATE THE AREA.

The New Year came, bringing with it further rain and flooding. The river peaked again at 5.76 metres on January 12th 2011. By this time the residents, who had been isolated for up to three weeks, were running out of basic necessities, and faced the threat of illness from mosquito-borne diseases and contaminated water. Swirling floodwaters gathered up many personal possessions and other debris of varying descriptions, distributing the battered remnants further downstream, or carrying them out to sea.

BRIDGE LOAD
LIMIT
42.5 t GVM

VEHICLES OVER
22.5 t GVM
STOP HERE
TO GIVE WAY
IF REQUIRED

Although the sugar cane crops survived fairly well, other agricultural crops sustained greater damage and, due to transport disruption, dairy farmers had to dispose of large quantities of milk.

In spite of the losses sustained and the mammoth task of cleaning up, the community spirit is strong, and whilst there are many stories of grief, loss, hardship and tragedy, there are many others of kindness, courage and bravery that will strengthen the people as they meet the challenges of rebuilding their lives.

FLOOD

BUNDABERG

- **February-November 2010**
  Substantial rainfall totalling 1219mm.

- **December 2010**
  Record 573mm rain for the month.
  Some flash-flooding experienced.
  Dams filled and catchments saturated.

- **December 22nd 2010**
  Residents warned to prepare for the 'big wet'.

- **December 23rd 2010**
  High tidal peak of 3.27m.

- **December 23rd-28th 2010**
  Heavy rain continues.

- **December 29th 2010**
  Burnett River peaks at 7.95m.
  Evacuation centres open.
  Sandbags available.
  300 homes and up to 200 businesses affected.
  Bruce Highway closed.
  Many rescues from raging floodwaters.
  Bundaberg Port closed.
  Yachts and river craft torn from moorings.

FACTS

- **January 2nd 2011**
  Cleaning up.
  Residents returning home.

- **January 13th 2011**
  Further rain pushes river back up to 5.76m.
  Many premises inundated for a second time.

- Silt and flood debris prevent marine businesses from operating.

- 100,000 tonnes of raw sugar held in bulk terminal as port facilities closed due to silting.

- 1,000 tonnes of fresh produce has been stranded in the region but not available to depleted local stores because of commercial agreements with grocery chains.

- Some supplies delivered by helicopter.

- Many homes without power.

- Some communities isolated for up to 3 weeks.

- Roads and rail network badly damaged.

NEIL CULLEN

Bundaberg

THE GRAVITY OF THE SITUATION
DAWNS

Bundaberg, Christmas Eve, 2010

Don't get me wrong, I'm not a Scrooge in any sense of the word, but being 'elderly', as Caroline recently tagged me, I have anticipated Christmas with something akin to horror for many years - a lot of overrated fuss for anyone who isn't a child or a retailer. This year isn't your average Christmas though - the weather in SE Qld at the moment is exceptionally ordinary - very wet and windy, as anyone will testify after making it from Brisbane to Bundaberg on a 10m catamaran.

After being away for the past few months, it's time to go back and cuddle the grandkids. We leave our home on a mooring and start heading south to Brisbane. Catching up with friends and family is great, but I am still dreading Christmas lunch. Hopefully a cyclone will save me from that fate. Careful what you wish for Neil!

The phone rings on the 23rd, the Burnett River is rising and we need to return. I take the captain's role, and insist that Caroline stays put and has Christmas with the kids. I arrive in Bundaberg, Dec 24th, at 22:00 hrs in the pouring rain. After much searching, I eventually find a motel.

Merry Christmas everybody! The river flow is getting stronger, and the rain keeps coming down. I help the guys at Midtown Marina with sandbagging; high tide is due at 12:00. The river reaches 4m, and the sand bags are just above the water on the shop. We head out to our boat. We have a broken diamond stay and bow sprit, and a nasty slice in the cockpit on the port side, caused when the boat in front of us broke its mooring earlier.

The gravity of the situation dawns when a wharf with street lights and a fish cleaning station on it slips past just missing the boat, closely followed by a stream of debris. Numerous gas cylinders and tanks follow, things start to get tangled as they roll by; there is a snarl of boats just off my port bow. It's a long night with little shut eye to be had, thank heavens for my daughter's Christmas present - homemade bickies.

13:30, it's Boxing Day and I am tied off to 2 rickety piers at the abandoned wharf. The wind swings NW with the change of tide, pushing the boat onto the piers and punching a hole through the inside starboard hull- fortunately above the waterline. I deploy the sea anchor for the first time ever - it's big enough to pull the Titanic sideways. Finally, some stability. It is 03:00hrs. I have the first decent sleep since the 24th.

December 28th. I wake to find only one rope holding me instead of two. It's still coming down, and the water's still rising. Mother Nature is a strong and dangerous partner. I try to manoeuvre the boat closer to the mangroves and tie another line to the trees. I get another stem line in and inch carefully out of the main flow. I could do with eating something other than biscuits, but the river is now over six metres and still rising. A colourbond shed, massive islands of hyacinth and other debris are continually floating past.

It is December 29th and I'm feeling pretty safe tucked up out of the flow, until 2 yachts come downstream unattended. A third is ensnared after being hit by a 40,000L fuel tank, and they're heading my way. I cut the line to get out of the way. The third yacht bounces out of the tangle and hits my starboard hull, snaps a 1 and 1/2" warp and heads seaward. In the meantime I swing to my port stem line, and find myself in front of Spinnaker's restaurant. In robot survival mode I swim a line over to their veranda.

The boat risks ending up on the top deck of the restaurant if the river keeps rising, so with the assistance of Nigel and more ropes, we slowly drag it back further out of the flow, and into the restaurant car park.

Relief floods through me - life is good again. I enjoy celebrity status for two days, there are many sightseers taking snaps of the flood. I suppose it is not often you see a catamaran moored in a street.

December 30th, the river has finally peaked at 7.9 metres. Caroline arrives, completely amazed by what she sees. We are invited to a party for the restaurant – there's not much else we can do until the water starts to drop.

On New Year's Day we creep back to the river as the level drops. We spend the day helping get the mud out of the restaurant. It's great to be working with so many people, all just helping out. The world is returning to normal.

January 1st, the odd remaining boat is moving up and down the river, but their skippers are all shell shocked, moving on auto pilot. Caroline notices I jump at every bang or jerk of the boat. Nevertheless, we make our way slowly down the river to get the repairs started. The river is still running at about 4.5 metres, but the birds have returned today. We take photos of the less fortunate boats on the way to Burnett Heads. We can finally relax. Then there is a thump and grind; we have hit something in the channel, possibly a sunken boat! It rips a hole in our port hull, tearing off the keel, and water is pouring in.

There are not many boats in the river and it's eerily quiet, but knowing the Bundaberg Sailing Club is only about a mile away we push on. I'm gunning the motor, and Caroline is bailing and praying, but not panicking. We are very lucky – we manage to beach the boat next to the pontoon.

Fortunately, the first person who comes to our aid is Reg, the main stay of the sailing club, closely followed by Alan, a retired shipwright. He eventually prises the bailing bucket from Caroline's hands and calmly assesses the damage. He works tirelessly helping to repair the boat. He is a man with a big heart, and more than enough knowledge to fill several books.

Over the months it takes to repair the boat we meet some lovely people, making our stay an enjoyable one.

We are now finally back on the water and loving it.

Damage to Catamaran

IT WAS JUST
INSURMOUNTABLE

THE SPINNAKER RESTAURANT HAS BEEN AN INTEGRAL PART OF BUNDABERG'S LANDSCAPE FOR THE LAST 30 YEARS. RECENTLY RENOVATED BY NEW OWNERS BRETT AND TALLUS JENSEN IN MARCH 2010, BUSINESS WAS TRAVELLING VERY WELL, PATRONAGE HAD RISEN AND THE SPINNAKER'S POPULARITY WAS SWELLING.

"We'd been working 70 hours a week and so I was looking forward to the time off. My wife was very nervous about possible flooding, so I rang the SES at lunchtime on Christmas Eve and they delivered some sandbags. Some of my regular patrons were down here, and they thought that I was crazy getting sandbags in, thinking, surely things weren't going to be that bad."

On the 27th, the Gayndah area got 200mm of rain, which surged down the Burnett River and hit Bundaberg the following day. "We were out on the deck watching the waters come in, when it began to bubble through the deck, 5.8m above standard high tide level. We had some fire-fighter pumps to pump the water back out of the building, but we soon realised we were fighting a losing battle. I was utterly overwhelmed, just watching everything that we'd worked so hard for get washed down the river.

"The following morning the water had risen even higher, and we were feeling severely depressed. I decided we'd have a beer. Myself, my brother and one of our regular customers who was here giving us a hand thought, 'Yep, we only get to do this once in a lifetime!' So we stood in the bar amongst the water, and we shared a hot beer, because there was no power to the building." The water continued to rise to about 6 feet inside.

A petrol tank from the marina broke loose, cascaded down the river and crashed into some unmanned yachts, connecting with Neil's yacht moored at the front of the Spinnaker (see page 60). "That sent him hurtling over, and he collided with our fence on the riverside of our business. He grabbed a rope and dived over the fence to try to swim into our building. You could see the terror in his eyes, he thought he was gone. The rope was tied around his leg and he almost got washed down the river with his boat. My brother leapt in and grabbed him by the jumper, and pulled him up. We secured his yacht off on the deck and as the water came higher we moved it around the side of the building into a safer area, and then tied it off in the car park.

"First thing New Year's morning we walked into the restaurant - there was just devastation, it was unbelievable what the water had done; there was 4 inches of mud throughout the entire building. Everything, the walls, all destroyed. It was just insurmountable; we couldn't possibly see how we were going to be able to clean it up or recover from it. I contacted a friend to let him know we were coming to pick up his water blaster and generator, and he said 'Turn around and come back, because we're down here already.' When we arrived back, there would've been 30 people here. Everyone just went straight to work - it was incredible to watch. What they achieved in that one day was absolutely extraordinary.

"We were bewildered; we just didn't know what we were going to do. But our spirits were lifted by the people who had volunteered to come down, because they were basically just a bunch of lunatics. They were joking and laughing and having a go at each other as Australians do, and it just went on all day and we couldn't help but chuckle. It was the best thing at a hard time like that. It was also very heartwarming to see a number of businesses who had come together to support us. We had the CWA and Subway bringing in lunch; it was phenomenal. Craft Rental supplied us with free equipment, and Bundaberg Crane Hire put our cold room back in place, no charge.

"But it's been a fair battle, it's taken us until the end of May to get back into full swing, at substantial financial cost —not just financial but loss of sleep, lots of disagreements between myself and my wife —highs and lows, but we're finally now starting to climb out of it. A disaster brings the best out of the good people; it brings the worst out of the bad people. We were looted — we had about two and a half thousand dollars' worth of liquor stolen while we were flooded, but the charity and support we've received has been astronomical. We'll come out the other side and build ourselves a very strong business again.

"It's been an amazing experience. Sometime in the future, when we're once again a profitable entity, I think we'll be able to look back on it, and in some strange way we'll have a lot of good memories from the flood."

WATCHING EVERYTHING THAT WE'D WORKED SO HARD FOR
GET WASHED DOWN THE RIVER

MIDTOWN MARINAS
Bundaberg
IT'S ALL BEEN WASTED

RAY FOLEY KNOWS THE RIVER LIKE AN OLD FRIEND. HE WAS BORN THERE, FISHED THERE AND RAN CHARTER BOATS THERE FOR MANY YEARS. "WE KICKED OFF HERE IN '83 WITH THE MIDTOWN MARINA BUSINESS, AND THERE WAS A FAIRLY BIG FRESH THEN, AS WE PUT OUR FUEL BARGE IN THE RIVER. WE HAVE HAD LOTS OF EXPERIENCE WITH FLOODS, BUT NOTHING AND NOBODY EVER EXPECTED IT TO GET AS ASTRONOMICALLY HIGH AS IT DID."

"We were flat out relocating boats for 1 ½ weeks before the flood, because there were 5 tonne islands of hyacinth (floating water weed) tearing down the river, ripping boats from their moorings and creating all kinds of havoc. We were already rescuing people that had been swept downriver." "Initially we moved boats from the middle of the river into quieter waters. But the flow intensified swiftly, and soon there were no quiet waters to be found anywhere; the floods were surging through at 20 knots, extraordinarily rapid. Down at the Sugar Ferry they calculated it at 23 knots."

"We got most of our stock out, working in knee deep water. All our Laundromat washers and dryers came out in a boat, in the midst of a rising flood, it was incredibly difficult. The water got up to 7.95m, ceiling height of the second floor."

"The worst thing was that it was Christmas and we had a lot of boat owners away on holidays. One bloke returned from Paris within 2 days, and yet there were people in Bundaberg who wouldn't come down and look after their boat. When the flood peak came we were powerless, there were 120 boats here that just took the full punishment of the flood."

"I had a person in a yacht chasing my fuel barge; they rang up one morning and told me it had vanished. It still had about 35 tonne of fuel on board, and would've weighed probably 50 tonne. I had to get into an aeroplane to locate it. It had gone up over the top of a bank and into a cane paddock. Because it was designed as a floating vessel, built under a USL Shipping Code, there was no damage. We used an excavator to drag it 1km, and then bundled it onto a low loader and hauled it back into town."

"After the flood we had a lot of people rally around, amazingly, one couple in their 80s were in here for days washing mud off; they were wonderful. We had a few businesses in town give us fixtures and fittings and some of our suppliers came up from Brisbane to help us. Wattyl Paints donated all the paint for the outside of the building, which was a fairly major saving for us. The spirit of generosity has really shone all over Queensland during the flood aftermath."

"We have 1/3 of the marina up and going, we are working on the next 1/3 - but that is going to be horribly expensive, and the last 1/3 is just absolutely not happening. There are some steel piles at the bottom of the river, and it would cost a million dollars to get them back. To buy another lot in would probably be $2 million. Our seafood unloading facility got washed away too."

"We got $25 000 from the Government and we're going to try for another loan if we can. But my resources are limited; my entire super fund was in that building. About 2 years ago we put it up, all new fixtures; we spent a lot of money prettying the place up, it's all been wasted."
"But we'll start again."

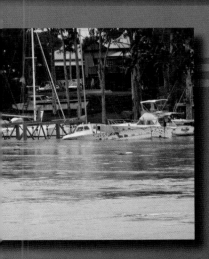

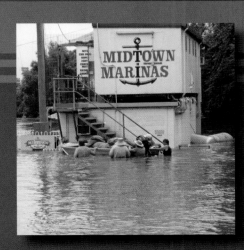

Maryborough Street

Burnett Rail Bridge

BUNDABERG

Flood water meets the ocean

Goodwood Road

...eryl McDowells' house - See page 68

Last minute sandbagging

"Bailing-out"

...erial view of Bundaberg

...vacuating

Bundaberg Rum Distillery in background

Bundaberg

IT CAME UP SO FAST WE HAD
NO WARNING

WHEN BUNDABERG RESIDENT CHERYL MCDOWELL MADE THE FINAL PAYMENT ON HER HOUSE ON 19TH DECEMBER, 2010, IT WAS A PROUD AND HAPPY MOMENT. BARELY A WEEK LATER, HER LOVELY HOME OF 26 YEARS WAS A SPOILED RUIN.

"The flood was level with the drain on Christmas Day, on Boxing Day it entered the yard. By 2 o'clock in the afternoon it was through the windows, a good 2.5 metres. It stayed there for 3 days. We had king tides on top of that, so it just didn't go down. The rubbish bins were tied on to the fence, things were just floating around."

"It came up so fast, we had no warnings, and no assistance. We couldn't get into the house because the carpet lifted up and got stuck behind the door, and all the house contents were floating around. We put on a new door because the other door was buckled and there were a lot of looters around."

"As soon as I came in and saw the place, I walked straight back out again. I was just distraught. I said to Jimmy and my kids, 'I don't want anything to do with it.' The Council dropped some bags off and told us to fill them up. All my possessions, everything I owned went into those bags, and a garbage truck just took them away. It was agonising. I've got no

kitchen; I've lost cupboards and everything. I was living in a camper, washing out of a bucket, until we went to the scrap yard and found a piece of laminex and an old double sink."

"A lot of people came around and were very helpful. One family came and the kids decided not to spend their pocket money on a trip they had planned, and they gave it to us as a donation. The CWA ladies came here every day with meals until we had the electricity put back on. At the moment we are the only ones living on this entire block. We are just going one day at a time. We have our lives, so that's the main thing."

Courtesy of Bundaberg News Mail, Photographer Mike Knott

Bundaberg

THE WATER JUST ROSE
INEXORABLY

BUNDABERG CHAINSAW AND LAWNMOWER SERVICE HAS BEEN OPERATING FOR THIRTY YEARS, AND IN THAT TIME THEY HAVE SEEN A BIT OF WATER THROUGH THE SHOP EVERY NOW AND AGAIN. WHAT REALLY SHOCKED THEM WITH THIS FLOOD WAS THE SHEER VOLUME AND HEIGHT OF THE WATER. THE FLOODING WASN'T FORECAST TO BE SO EXTENSIVE, IT SHOULDN'T HAVE REACHED THE STOCK IN THE WAREHOUSE.... BUT IT DID. THE WATER JUST ROSE INEXORABLY, TAKING THEM INTO UNPRECEDENTED TERRITORY.

"The water initially entered the shop on 24th December. We were still trading as the water was coming up, but by lunch time we realised we just had to pull up stumps and get the stock lifted. It was coming in the back door as we were lifting it," Keith Iseppi states.

"Our front door is 4 metres above high tide, and we ended up with 3.85m through the building. So that's 7.85m above high tide rise. It was huge, so much water! That caught us out the most, because we shifted out all the stock that we could, and lifted everything, but with the height that it got to - there was a lot of damage,

especially in the workshop. It just kept coming up."

"About the 2nd January we started cleaning. We had water in the shop for 7 to 8 days, it finally went down and came back up a couple of days later. We got the second river flood on 12th January, and it peaked again on the 14th January, with just over 2.5 m in the shop."

"We shifted to another premises to sit out the wet season, because with the ground being so saturated, it was just going to take nothing to get water in here again. We couldn't trade for 3 weeks, but long term we've actually had a pretty good season, because of the amount of grass growth that there has been, we'd rather have that than a drought."

"We moved back in at the end of March, after four months of disrupted trading. There are businesses close to us here that haven't reopened their doors, and aren't going to. We've been very lucky to get insurance. We're extremely thankful for that."

Breaking in to second floor for last minute removals

SUPPLIES DROPPED INTO
BUNDABERG

BY JANUARY 12TH, AS THE RIVER REACHED ITS SECOND PEAK, THE CITY OF BUNDABERG HAD BEEN ISOLATED BY FLOODWATERS FOR UP TO THREE WEEKS AND WAS RUNNING CRITICALLY SHORT OF SUPPLIES. OVER THREE DAYS RAAF C-130 HERCULES AIRCRAFT MADE SEVERAL DROPS OF FOOD AND ESSENTIALS INTO BUNDABERG AIRPORT, INCLUDING SUPPLIES OF BAKER'S FLOUR, UHT MILK, BOTTLED WATER, BREAKFAST CEREAL, TOILETRIES AND PET FOOD.

Delegates from the major grocery stores organised the distribution, using local transport operators to convey the supplies to Woolworths, Coles and Bi-Lo, where rationing was employed in selling to the residents.

A ground crew team with a forklift came with the first drop, and remained in Bundaberg over the three days, returning with the last flight.

PARADISE DAM

PARADISE DAM IS SITUATED ON THE BURNETT RIVER APPROXIMATELY 80 KILOMETRES SOUTH-WEST OF BUNDABERG AND PROVIDES ASSISTANCE FOR THE SOCIAL AND ECONOMIC GROWTH OF THE REGION. THE FOUR-YEAR CONSTRUCTION PERIOD WAS COMPLETED IN NOVEMBER 2005. OVER 500 PEOPLE HAD BEEN EMPLOYED ON THE PROJECT, AND HUNDREDS OF REGIONAL BUSINESSES HAD BEEN INVOLVED IN THE SUPPLY OF GOODS AND SERVICES.

The roller-compacted concrete dam covers an area of 2,995 hectares when full and has a storage capacity of 300,000 megalitres, which was reached for the first time in February, 2010. Continuous heavy rain in December, 2010 led to controlled releases through the flood gates as well as significant overflowing at the purpose-built spillway and by December 20th the dam was overflowing for the second time in two weeks and for the third time that year.

On Wednesday 29th December, 2010, at the peak of the overflow, the dam was at 180% of capacity, reaching a height of 5.96 metres above the spillway and discharging the equivalent of 793,000 megalitres per day. This is nearly half the volume of Wivenhoe full capacity every 24 hours.

THE MARY RIVER STEALS A MARCH ON
MARYBOROUGH

THE DEEP NATURAL HARBOUR AT THE MOUTH OF THE MARY RIVER AND THE RICH ALLUVIAL SOIL ATTRACTED EUROPEAN SETTLERS TO THIS REGION IN 1842. BY 1847 THE TOWN OF MARYBOROUGH HAD BECOME ESTABLISHED AS A BUSY RIVER PORT, HANDLING TIMBER, WOOL, COTTON AND SUGAR. ENGINEERING BECAME AN IMPORTANT INDUSTRY IN THE TOWN, ASSOCIATED WITH SHIPPING AND THE DEVELOPING RAILWAYS.

Being one of Queensland's oldest cities, Maryborough's cultural heritage is strikingly evident in its colonial and Queensland architecture. The city is reputed by some to have the best collection of 'old Queenslander' style homes in the state.

A superb riverside oasis of leafy parks and gardens has been established since the city's early days and the original wharf district is now a well presented heritage precinct known as Portside. Stately colonial buildings now house museums and art galleries or have been cleverly transformed into pubs and stylish restaurants. The National Trust has also preserved a corner-store typical of the 1890's.

At the low elevation of 11 metres above sea level, many of Maryborough's 26,000 residents are familiar with flooding. Water coming from the upper catchment areas coinciding with a tidal flow can quickly change the river into a serious threat, but there are usually two to three days' warning.

It was a different story, however, in January, 2011.

MARYBOROUGH
AND HERVEY BAY

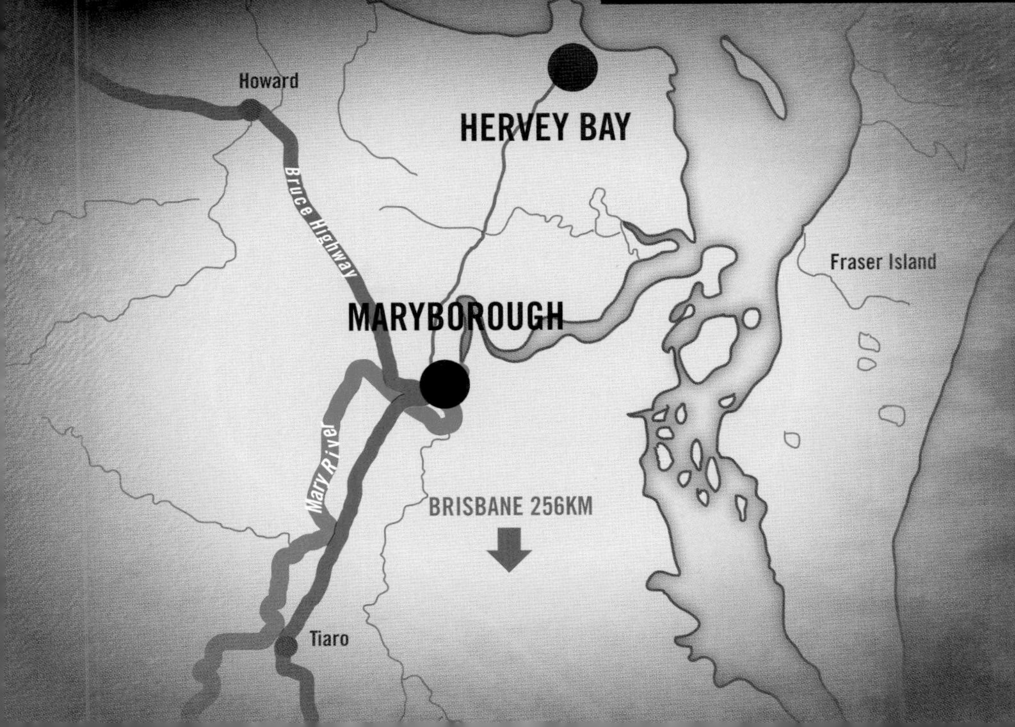

Howard

HERVEY BAY

Bruce Highway

MARYBOROUGH

Fraser Island

Mary River

BRISBANE 256KM

Tiaro

ON THE 7TH JANUARY THE CATCHMENT AREAS OF THE MARY RIVER
RECEIVED RECORD-BREAKING TORRENTIAL RAIN IN AN INCREDIBLY
SHORT SPACE OF TIME. WITH NOWHERE TO GO BUT UP, THE WATERS
OF THE MARY RIVER ROSE RAPIDLY AND THE SHOCKED LOCALS FOUND
THEMSELVES FACED WITH AN UNCONTROLLABLE FLOOD SURGE AND
NO TIME TO PREPARE FOR IT. IT IS INTERESTING TO NOTE, HOWEVER,
THAT FOLLOWING A FLOODING EPISODE EARLY IN MARYBOROUGH'S
HISTORY, THE MAIN TOWN SITE WAS RELOCATED TO HIGHER GROUND,
WHICH CONTINUES TO KEEP MOST PROPERTIES SAFE.

The eastern suburb of Granville, which had been re-built after the 1893
flood, was completely isolated, stranding its 3,500 residents, while the
murky brown torrent invaded all low lying areas, inundating homes and
businesses, overflowing the bridges and undermining roads.

The deluge wrought havoc amongst the heritage listed areas in the city's
CBD, as well as encroaching upon vast areas of farmland and property,
causing widespread damage, destruction and loss of livestock. Those
who were able fled with the little they could salvage to safer areas and
a caravan park owner raced frantically against time whilst tackling
with incredible courage the daunting task of relocating cabins and
caravans to higher ground.

An evacuation centre was established in Granville's Community Hall where
volunteers cared for the needs of stranded travellers and attended to
medical emergencies. Helicopters and SES Boats busily ferried emergency
personnel and vital stores across the river to the trapped residents.

The grim situation was further compounded when the heavy flooding
forced the closure of the Bruce Highway, cutting the city's vital supply
routes from the north and south for more than a week. Nerve-strained
residents had to rely on tickets and their honesty as Supermarket shelves
rapidly depleted, and many business operations were forced to close
as deliveries stopped.

As the waters slowly receded, traumatised people braced themselves for
the heartbreaking task of removing the mud-laden debris, assessing their
losses and cleaning up and repairing what was left of their property. To
their great dismay, further heavy downpours upstream caused Gympie
to flood and the relentless muddy tide surged back into Maryborough
with increasing height and bearing fresh deposits of debris and silt,
tearing again at the road surfaces and further jeopardising transport
and livelihoods.

Recovery will be a long and expensive process but the people of
Maryborough have the courage and determination that it takes to square
their shoulders and move forward bravely. Having a well-thought-out
flood-plan is an essential part of living near the Mary River — but just
occasionally there is not sufficient time to activate it!

FLOOD

MARYBOROUGH
AND HERVEY BAY

- **Jan 7th 2011**
  More than 300mm of rain recorded in previous 24 hours.
  Residents in low-lying areas warned to self-evacuate.
  Mary River rising at 100mm an hour, breaks its banks.
  Some road closures and power disruptions.
  Bruce Highway closed at Gympie.

- **Jan 8th 2011**
  Temporary levee installed in CBD to protect businesses and houses.
  Emergency centre set up at isolated suburb of Granville.
  Hervey Bay Flood Boat commissioned to ferry supplies to Granville's 3,500 isolated residents.

- **Jan 9th 2011**
  Mary River peaks at 8.2m, inundating some homes and businesses.
  Basic supplies air-lifted by helicopter to Granville.
  Sandbags made available to residents.

- **Jan 11th 2011**
  Repairs and clean-up attempts hampered by further rain. Floodwater rises again.

FACTS

ROAD CLOSED

- **Jan 12th 2011**

  River peaks at 7.95m at 9.00pm. Major supermarkets still depleted of staple supplies. Temporary fuel shortage.

- **Jan 13th 2011**

  River down to 7.7m at 8.00am and falling at 100mm an hour.

  SES Flood boats have made 520 trips to Granville in 48 hours ferrying people and essential supplies.

  100 patients have been attended to at the temporary clinic.

  Food supplies resume.

  Repairs assessed.

  Clean-up begins.

- **Jan 14th 2011**

  Boat ferrying discontinued due to hazards as a result of lower water levels.

  Granville bridge re-opened by 5.00pm with one-lane access due to damaged edges.

- **Jan 18th 2011**

  Costs assessed by Fraser Coast Regional Council at $8 million so far.

A WALL OF
WATER

PERCHED RIGHT ON THE BANKS OF THE MARY RIVER, THE TRENDY LITTLE EATERY, MUDDY WATERS CAFÉ, COULDN'T BE MORE APPROPRIATELY NAMED. THE CAFÉ, WHICH DREW INSPIRATION FOR ITS TITLE FROM THE USUALLY TRANQUIL WATERWAY THAT PROVIDES A PEACEFUL BACKDROP TO ITS CASUAL FLOW OF DINERS, UNWITTINGLY PLAYED HOST TO ITS NAMESAKE ON THE GRANDEST SCALE. WITHOUT THE POMP AND CEREMONY USUALLY SURROUNDING THE ARRIVAL OF AN HONOURED GUEST, THE MARY RIVER SWIRLED, UNINVITED, THROUGH THE DOORS OF THE CAFÉ AND PROCEEDED TO EFFORTLESSLY CLAIM THE ENTIRE ENTITY IN A MATTER OF A FEW SHORT HOURS, TAKING THE PROPRIETORS COMPLETELY BY SURPRISE.

Michael and Mia, relatively new to the area, had owned the business for a mere 16 months. Flooding was always going to be part of the game due to their location, but they had never envisaged themselves dealing with much beyond the few feet of water that had made its way in on a number of occasions already.

"We knew on the Friday morning that Miva, upstream, had 200mm of rain. We went up and saw the landlord, he has been here for 20 years so has a pretty good understanding of how the river works." It was indicated that there was a wall of water coming down the river. "When you think of a wall of water you think of a tsunami type thing". Unable to grasp the reality of such an 'impossible' event, they continued to prepare for lunch and dinner.

At around 8.00pm that evening the landlord warned with agitation that the water was rising pretty fast. At 8.15 trading ceased and so began the frantic race to save something, anything they could. "It just came up too quickly, it came up a metre in an hour and kept rising that quick."

"We got three fridges out and chocked up another and by that time the water was waist high." There were no lights, and their race against the River was becoming futile. "All the plates and things were…we didn't have time to get them out… and none of the equipment."

At 2.30am, exhausted, emotionally drained and with the water now head height, they gave in. Their daughters (Chloe, 9 and Graci, 4) had sought refuge in the relative safety of the mezzanine and had to be lifted high as they waded out.

On Saturday they ventured back to the Café in a boat to attempt a precarious salvage operation of the few items they had managed to take up to the mezzanine the night before. There was no room for error and a few tense moments ensued as the coffee machine was eased out through a small window onto the awning and across into the rocking boat drawn alongside it. "Inside, the fridge that we had chocked up on bricks was floating around bashing into walls." The windows at the front of Bill's shop next door started smashing from the pressure of the water, adding to the trauma. "When you're in that little area up there and you hear a smash…" Michael slowly shakes his head at the recollection and with eyes closed, finishes the sentence with a shiver.

Muddy waters rose to the ceiling of their Café, where for 7 days they wrought havoc. The utter filth, chaos, destruction and loss that met them when the water subsided was devastating. "We were here every day for three months, cleaning up. There's only so many times you can clean a floor. We must have cleaned it 50 times. You can see the chairs, there's still silt on them. You can clean them as many times as you like but when you rub you hand along there, there's still silt."

THEIR RACE AGAINST THE RIVER WAS BECOMING FUTILE

MARY RIVER MARINA

MUDDY WATERS

Mud covered kitchen

Complete chaos

Maryborough

WE DIDN'T
SURRENDER

BILL BROWN'S STORY, OWNER OF MARY RIVER MARINE SUPPLIES - MARYBOROUGH. FRIDAY THE 7TH JANUARY FOUND BILL BROWN IN A VERY DIRE PREDICAMENT! HIS SHOP, IN NORMAL CIRCUMSTANCES, COULDN'T BE SITUATED IN A BETTER SPOT FOR BUSINESS, THOUGH HIS POSITION ON THE BANKS OF THE MARY RIVER MEANT HE WOULD NOT BE COVERED BY INSURANCE. SEVERAL DAYS EARLIER, ONE METRE OF WATER HAD GONE THROUGH THE SHOP, BUT NO ONE COULD HAVE FORESEEN WHAT LAY AHEAD. IN GENERAL FLOOD CONDITIONS, THE MIGHTY MARY GIVES RESIDENTS AND BUSINESS OWNERS A DAY AND A HALF TO PREPARE AND EVACUATE, BEFORE BREAKING HER BANKS. THIS WAS SOMETHING ELSE.

It was raining torrentially. Bill felt edgy, so he moved a few things upstairs. He left the shop at 4:30pm but continued to monitor the river levels through the evening. Even though they showed no cause for alarm, intuition prompted him to check the premises. "To my horror, the water was lapping the boardwalk right outside the shop."

Bill's family frantically started to move equipment out. The river was rising 1 ½ metres every half hour! While fridges and freezers were loaded onto a ute and taken elsewhere, the water rose to knee deep. Wading through the shop, they desperately tried to salvage what they could. "Cold, wet and miserable, we didn't surrender until 2am when it had reached our necks", Bill recounts. "We were stranded on the mezzanine for the night."

At first light, they continued in earnest. The force of the water had burst the glass doors of the shop front and the stock was being swept out into the current. By clinging to rafters and using nets they managed to haul in some of their floating wares. "We used one of the dinghies in an attempt to try and save the stock that was drifting around, but we had to be careful not to be sucked out ourselves."

AT FIRST I WAS ANGRY, AND THEN I CRIED LIKE A BABY
"Finally we were no match for the raging torrent. Tired, weary and exhausted, we had to give up. At first I was angry, and then I cried like a baby." The water rose nearly to the roof, so even the things that had been put up on the mezzanine in the hope of saving them, were washed away.

The building was under water for eight days and what emerged was utter devastation. In true Aussie spirit, Mary River Marine Supplies was reopened for trade a month later. "If I hadn't gone and checked on the place, I would have lost everything," he concedes.

WHAT EMERGED WAS UTTER
DEVASTATION

OVER 700 CROSSINGS

THE STATE EMERGENCY SERVICES WERE A GREAT SUPPORT TO MARYBOROUGH'S FLOOD-STRICKEN COMMUNITY. WITH THE ASSISTANCE OF APPROXIMATELY THIRTY HARD-WORKING VOLUNTEERS, THEY ORGANISED THE FILLING AND DISTRIBUTION OF SANDBAGS, AND PROVIDED BEDDING AND FOOD FOR PEOPLE STRANDED IN GRANVILLE AND OTHER AREAS.

Four boats manned with crews from Maryborough, Childers, Hervey Bay and Howard made more than 700 river crossings, ferrying supplies, equipment and emergency personnel across the river and evacuating those requiring medical attention.

As people began to return to their properties, the SES volunteers continued to offer assistance in delivering clean-up packs and helping with cleaning and the removal of debris.

FERRY STREET - LAMINGTON BRIDGE

BBQ SHELTER IN QUEENS PARK

INTERSECTION AT LENNOX AND SUSSEX STREETS IN CBD

PORTSIDE BBQ AREA

Maryborough train crossing

Flooded Cane Fields

Lamington Bridge concealed

MARYBOROUGH

Fort Street - Maryborough

Mary River widens engulfing properties

Salvaging belongings from two storey building

Teddington Weir - Maryborough

WALLACE MOTEL AND CARAVAN PARK

Maryborough

GET UP, PACK UP, THE FLOOD IS COMING
HURRY!

IT WAS FRIDAY 7TH JANUARY AND THE ANGRY SKIES WERE EMPTYING RELENTLESSLY ON THE ALREADY SATURATED GROUNDS AT WALLACE MOTEL AND CARAVAN PARK OF MARYBOROUGH. PURCHASING THE PROPERTY HAD BEEN A CALCULATED RISK FOR OWNER, JOHN KENNEDY, WHO KNEW WHEN HE BOUGHT THE PROPERTY 5½ YEARS AGO THAT IT WAS FLOOD-PRONE. ACCORDINGLY, HE HAD GONE OVER EVERY DETAIL OF THE FLOOD PLAN METICULOUSLY TO ENSURE ALL WOULD BE SAFE AND SECURE IN THE CASE OF SUCH AN EVENT. LITTLE DID HE KNOW JUST HOW USELESS HIS FLOOD PLAN WOULD PROVE TO BE IN THE PANIC AND CHAOS OF SUCH A PROLONGED AND INTENSE DELUGE.

That evening the steady downpour continued unabated. Feeling rather less than confident, John checked all the scientific indicators. Readings were negligible, so despite misgivings he retired to bed. After all, he had been assured of at least 2-3 days warning.

Something awoke him at 2:30 am. Uneasily, he checked the readings again. They had risen substantially, and frighteningly, were continuing to do so. Grabbing a torch, he tore to the back of the park. The ever increasing surge of water spilling over the edge of the embankment sent his mouth dry. He knew then that they were all in critical danger.

"Get up, pack up, the flood is coming, hurry" shouted John hoarsely, over and over, whilst drumming repeatedly on people's caravans and portable houses. Shaken and surprised faces appeared in windows and doorways as, pyjama-clad, they took in the sight first of John, drenched and anxious and then the dark outline of the encroaching water surrounding their circle of dwellings. Their reaction was instant. John laughs about it now. "I only needed to say things once!" Of imperative concern was the evacuation of the guests – over 200 - that they had residing there at the time. This included approximately 50 cabins and caravans that would have to be relocated. Not only were many lives at stake but also John's livelihood. Attempting to follow the flood plan, he raced out to his father's property to borrow his tractor. By the time he got back the water had begun to submerge the caravans in the lower part of the park.

They began evacuating the cabins immediately; parking them on nearby streets, but unfortunately the water was rising too rapidly. Each time they moved one, they would return to see the water already over the concrete pad that it had been on. John says "It was lapping at our feet all day long, we were wading through it, but we never gave up fighting it until 11:30pm that night."

The park was under water for days. As soon as the floodwater dissipated, the Rural Fire Brigade stepped in to help with the massive cleanup operation, hosing the park down and moving everything back in. They didn't get too far. Adding insult to injury, more torrential rain was to follow, flooding Gympie upstream and swelling the already engorged river further. As it rushed inevitably on toward Maryborough, the dirty swirling water inundated everything once again. John remarked "the second time was a lot muddier!"

The park lost many thousands of dollars in assets, but of deeper concern were losses they sustained from missed business in the following months. With no income source, they are currently facing challenges in paying day-to-day bills, whilst building up funds to pay for the substantial repairs needed to put them back on their feet.

THE FOLLOWING DAY...

"We were out evaluating flood damage and I suggested to a co-worker that we wade into the flowing water and attempt to lay a fence flat. It was under a lot of pressure and we didn't want it to collapse. We discussed the threat of snakes and it became quite clear he was terrified of them. He was adamant, 'I REALLY don't like snakes'.

"I don't mind them, so we agreed that he would stand guard in the water, keeping a watch out for the sneaky reptiles, while I negotiated the partially submerged gardens where the fence was. He liked that idea. I was gingerly climbing through branches and undergrowth, acutely aware there were going to be snakes around, and I could encounter a dangerous one at close range, and at any moment. I was quite on edge, as you can probably picture, and the next thing he starts yelling,

'SNAKE, SNAKE!'

"I froze instantly, 'Where'?

'My leg, it's scraping my leg!!', he croaked.

"I haven't laughed so hard in ages."

HE KNEW THEN THAT THEY WERE
ALL IN CRITICAL DANGER

LAMINGTON BRIDGE
MARYBOROUGH

THE FIRST BRIDGE, BUILT IN 1876 TO LINK CENTRAL MARYBOROUGH WITH TINANA ON THE SOUTH SIDE OF THE MARY RIVER, WAS SWEPT AWAY IN THE FLOOD OF 1893. THIS WAS REPLACED WITH THE LAMINGTON BRIDGE IN 1896.

The original railings of the bridge were constructed so that they could be removed in the event of flood to reduce obstruction. These railings are now heritage listed. The footbridge added within the last decade has railings that can be folded down flat when flood warnings are received. On December 29th, 2010, following a flood warning, the rails were all pulled down but no flood eventuating, they were reinstalled a few days later. Then, on Friday January 7th, the Mary River rose so quickly that the attempt to remove the railings had to be aborted and some of the old heritage listed railings were severely damaged, requiring replacement.

With footpath railings folded and old bridge railings removed

FLOODING ISOLATES
HERVEY BAY

HERVEY BAY IS A MUCH FREQUENTED URBAN SEASIDE AREA OF THE FRASER COAST WHERE, ALL YEAR ROUND, TOURISTS ACCOUNT FOR A SIGNIFICANT PORTION OF THE POPULATION.

Heavy rainfall and thunderstorms through the 6th and 7th of January, 2011, impacted heavily over the Wide Bay district and the resulting floods and road damage caused Hervey Bay to be isolated for two or three days. The highway to the south was cut at Gympie, blocking supplies and supermarkets were quickly stripped of fresh produce and essential items by anxious shoppers. Commuters to Maryborough had to wait for low tides and then travel via Torbanlea and the Bruce Highway, but flooding within the urban environs of Hervey Bay was of little consequence.

NO SUN FOR
GYMPIE AND THE SUNSHINE COAST

THE DISCOVERY OF GOLD IN 1867 ESTABLISHED A FIRM PLACE FOR GYMPIE IN QUEENSLAND'S HISTORY AS IT IS REPORTED TO HAVE SAVED THE STATE FROM BANKRUPTCY. THE RANDOM POSITIONING OF THE EARLY BUILDINGS ON THE GOLD-FIELDS LED TO THE PRESENT HAPHAZARD ARRANGEMENT OF THE TOWNSHIP'S OLDER STREETS. DURING THE RAPID GROWTH THAT FOLLOWED, GRAND BUILDINGS WERE ERECTED IN THE MAIN STREET WHICH WAS SOON FOUND TO BE PRONE TO FLOODING FROM THE MARY RIVER, WHICH FLOWS THROUGH THE TOWN.

Gympie is now a rich dairying and agricultural area as well as an important distribution centre for wholesale and retail industries, having road and rail links with Brisbane. Its favourable sub-tropical climate and proximity to the Sunshine Coast makes it attractive to tourists, who may enjoy a historical steam-train tour of the Mary Valley on the 'Valley Rattler', or visit the beautiful beaches along the coastal strip between Bribie Island and Noosa. Overall there are in excess of 220,000 residents in this region, approximately 17,600 of whom reside in Gympie.

GYMPIE
AND SUNSHINE COAST

GYMPIE

Bruce Highway

Mary River

Noosaville

BRISBANE 160KM

SUNSHINE
COAST

Nambour

Buderim

Mooloolaba

89

THE RESIDENTS OF GYMPIE HAVE BECOME FAMILIAR WITH THE FLOODING HABITS OF THE MARY RIVER AND WATCH CERTAIN REFERENCE POINTS TO ESTIMATE THE TIMING AND INTENSITY OF THE COMING FLOOD. THERE IS USUALLY ADEQUATE WARNING OF FLOODING, BUT EVACUATING THE SHOPS IN THE MAIN STREET IS NO SMALL TASK AND IF THE PROPRIETORS HAVE DESIGNED A PRACTICAL FLOOD PLAN, THEY CAN AFFORD TO ADOPT A WAIT-AND-SEE APPROACH. UNFORTUNATELY, IN JANUARY, 2011, NOT ALL WERE AT HOME AS IT WAS DURING THE HOLIDAY PERIOD; NEITHER COULD THEY REACH HOME ON ACCOUNT OF THE INUNDATED ROADS.

Following torrential downpours over Gympie and the Sunshine Coast from January 8th, the river peaked at 19.24m at 3.00am on January 11th, isolating Gympie as the Bruce Highway flooded. On the Sunshine Coast, floodwaters and landslides damaged many of the roads and Bribie Island was cut off.

LIGHT POLES ASSIST
NAVIGATION

The city of Gympie was divided by the Mary River, stranding an island of residents and visitors on the south side and leaving two corner stores as the sole source of food. Chemist supplies were brought over by boat and dispensed from an ambulance parked on the south side and at one point police actually had to intervene when a brawl broke out over a loaf of bread! SES boats made numerous river crossings, using the tall light posts on the Kidd Bridge as a guide.

Flooding is an expensive business, to say the least, and millions of dollars are needed to repair damaged infrastructure and dozens of roads. The enormous monetary cost to individuals in damage and lost business can usually be met over time, but people may struggle with the emotional costs for a lifetime.

FLOOD

GYMPIE AND SUNSHINE COAST

- **January 6-7th 2011**
  Heavy rain in Mary River catchment.
  Gympie drenched.
  Warning issued for localised flash flooding.
  Borumba Dam runs over.

- **January 8th 2011**
  300mm rain fell in 24 hours.
  Mary River overflows.
  Kidd Bridge flooded.
  20 businesses flooded but no homes yet.
  Main street businesses prepare to evacuate.
  Sunshine Coast hinterland deluged, with 321mm in Maleny, 279mm in Landsborough.
  Mary River rising.
  Main Street shops, businesses and some residents evacuate.
  Goomeri, Kilkivan and Woolooga flooded.

- **January 9th 2011**
  Evacuations of businesses begin.
  Flood response meetings held.

FACTS

- **January 10th 2011**
  Community effort to help flooded businesses.
  Help from food, crane and transport businesses.

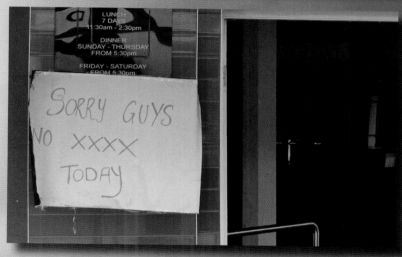

- **January 11th 2011**
  Landslips and road damage on Sunshine Coast.
  Bribie Island isolated.
  One home slipped 5 metres.
  40 metre section of road shoulder slipped about a metre.
  Mary River peaked in Gympie at 19.24m.
  50 homes self-evacuated.
  80 businesses inundated.
  Water enters some pump stations, manholes overflow, forcing sewage into drains.
  Power cuts to more than 900 homes across the region.
  More than 80 council roads and more than 40 state roads cut or closed.

- **January 12th 2011**
  Clean-up begins.

TELSTRA SHOP

Gympie

NO STRANGER TO
INUNDATION

SHOULD WE GO??.....AND WHEN?? A BIG DECISION TO MAKE, AND THE REST OF TOWN IS WAITING ON OUR MOVE TO MAKE UP THEIR MINDS AS TO WHAT THEY DO!!

The Telstra shop building, owned by the Madill family for over 60 years, is one of the first buildings to go under water in a flood. No stranger to inundation, the shop is purpose built to withstand a flood with minimal loss. The building is constructed using concrete and other washable surfaces, and the walls and cabinetry are demountable. Waterproof data cables and strategically placed wiring make the premises as flood proof as possible. Despite their meticulous attention to detail, nothing could stop the water, and in their own words "you can never be emotionally prepared."

When the rain sets in, the Madills and licensee Paul Atkinson carefully study all the signs – flood heights, river levels south at Kenilworth and Cooran, Mary River height at Gympie and all the predictions. Then, they have to make a well-informed but stressful decision; in their words "you are committing to close down your business, committing to losing trade – we have 27 employees and if we're not trading, it's difficult to pay bills and wages". Nobody wants to evacuate their business for what could turn out to be nothing but a false alarm! However, this time, the decision

was so right......this was a big one and by the time the Mary River had filled their shop to the ceiling, it was empty. Air conditioners, cabinetry, doors and ceilings were gone and electrical wire ends were all covered with balloons! So much hard, draining work, but it saved them hundreds of thousands of dollars in damage. The building sat under water for several days and when the floodwater slowly receded, a horrible covering of thick mud and oil from the many car service shops around greeted them. Without waiting for the waters to fully recede, family and friends got into boats and started to scrub walls with chemicals to remove the filth. When the water finally departed, the Council was well prepared and immediately began hosing and cleaning, along with Emergency Service crews. The Fire Brigade came and hosed out the shop completely, followed by the Madill's army of family, employees, friends and volunteers, who scrubbed the whole interior with chemicals again – a massive task. To keep them sustained, other friends and locals supplied eskies and platters of food and drinks – the support from so many people was fantastic.

On the whole, Gympie is fortunate that they can prepare, and the community spirit is very much alive in getting businesses back up and running as soon as possible!

During

After

Gympie Main Street - Mary Street

Water logged playground

Mud line in trees shows height of flooding

A BEWILDERED CHILD PEERS INTO AN EMPTY TOYWORLD STORE, THE SIGHT SO DISCONCERTING FOR THE YOUNGSTER, WHOSE WORLD HAS TURNED UPSIDE DOWN IN THE MAYHEM OF INUNDATION.

The proprietors of this Toyworld store kept a step ahead of the forces of nature, emptying their store of stock before floodwaters engulfed the premises. Seventy-nine pallets laden with toys were trucked out of harms way, carefully wrapped in plastic to prevent damage to packaging.

Gympie businesses flooded

Mary Street

Ferrying supplies to stranded resident

LANDSLIDES ON THE SUNSHINE COAST

DURING THE HUGE WET, THE MASSIVE RAINFALL SATURATED THE GROUND SO MUCH, THAT LANDSLIDES WERE CAUSED ON THE STEEP HILLSIDES OF THE SUNSHINE COAST WHICH FAILED TO LIVE UP TO ITS NAME - MUCH TO THE DISAPPOINTMENT OF TOURISTS, AND THE TERROR OF MANY OF ITS INHABITANTS.

Two pole homes, built with level frontage to the road on the steep north side of Buderim, shuddered and slipped down the hill as the sodden earth parted at the roadside. It was a terrifying experience for the owners, who fortunately were quickly evacuated as parts of their houses tilted dangerously downhill, into their own steep backyards. Trees also slipped, lying at angles of 45 degrees with their roots exposed. Surrounding neighbours understandably became extremely worried that their homes would be next, and the road was cordoned off but fortunately the houses remained in place. It was a sorry sight to see once lovely homes offering such gorgeous views of the coast, hanging

precariously, a ruined tangle of splintered timber. Both houses were later demolished as they continued to collapse downhill, damaged beyond repair.

The hillside also slipped away on the side of the Blackall Range near Montville, and the road had to be closed for many months for repairs. Many homes in the area had retaining walls collapse with the huge pressure of sodden soil behind them. Fortunately no lives were lost, but it was a near miss for many who only just managed to jump away from landslips. They felt the ground under them shudder. Then before their eyes saw the earth part above the retaining wall, where they had been standing, and crash down and demolish the wall. One boy was really lucky - his sandal fell off and was buried just where he had been standing. A car that had been parked below the wall had only just been removed before the wall went.

FOLLOWING THE HEAVY RAINS IN DECEMBER, 2010 AND EARLY JANUARY, 2011, FLASH FLOODING WAS EXPERIENCED IN MANY DISTRICTS O THE SUNSHINE COAST. QUICKLY RISING RIVERS AND CREEKS BLOCKED ROADS IN SOME PARTS SUCH AS NAMBOUR, WOOMBYE, PALMWOOD AND MAROOCHYDORE, AND SEVERAL AREAS BECAME ISOLATED. DURING THE SECOND WEEK IN JANUARY, NAMBOUR RECEIVED 597M OF RAIN AND THE CREEKS ROSE TO 7 METRES. HOMES BUILT ON THE HILLSIDES WERE NOT AFFECTED, BUT SOME LOW-LYING HOUSE AND SHOPS WERE INUNDATED, INCLUDING THE GROUND LEVEL CARPARKS OF COLES AND WOOLWORTHS STORES IN NAMBOUR.

Flooding of roads caused temporary disruptions as people were unable to get to work, but water levels fell quickly as the murky brow deluge rushed on to the coast, littering the beaches with debris and polluting the surf. Wappa Dam swelled to a spectacular thunderin torrent, whilst on the plateau at Buderim, two houses slid down hill in the deluge, suffering severe structural damage.

Food supplies ran critically short for more than a week as the highway to the north and south was cut a number of times. Queue at supermarkets and corner stores grew as people panicked, and later shoppers found choices restricted to less popular items. Mi supplies were limited while dairy farms were isolated, but once the roads were clear, there was quite a line-up of milk trucks hoping dispose of their over-supply. As floodwaters receded and produce was replenished in the stores, food was sent to other flood-affect areas, and although roads were still damaged, many took advantage of the railways to offer help in other flood-ravaged cities such Brisbane and Gympie.

Wappa Dam spilling over

SUNSHINE COAST

Flood waters on the Sunshine Coast

Nambour Main Street

Undercover car park - Nambour

Flooding in Nambour area

CABOOLTURE
WAS NOT SPARED!

A PLEASANT, RELAXED LIFESTYLE AND RELATIVELY INEXPENSIVE REAL ESTATE MAKES CABOOLTURE, IN THE MORETON BAY REGIONAL COUNCIL'S DISTRICT, A VERY ATTRACTIVE PLACE TO LIVE AND THE POPULATION, CURRENTLY WELL OVER 130,000, INCREASES BY SEVERAL THOUSAND PEOPLE EVERY YEAR. ALTHOUGH IT IS STILL CONSIDERED TO BE SIGNIFICANTLY AGRICULTURAL, IT IS BECOMING INCREASINGLY URBANISED, WITH MUCH LAND BEING CLEARED FOR NEW DEVELOPMENTS.

Unfortunately the spreading development and clearing of land impacts on the dispersal of storm water and causes the many creeks in this area to rise more quickly, making Caboolture and its surrounding districts prone to flash-flooding.

CABOOLTURE

Beerburrum State Forest

Bribie Island

CABOOLTURE

Morayfield

NAMBOUR 51KM

Burpengary

BRISBANE 48KM

Moreton Bay

Bruce Highway

Lake Kurwongbah

North Pine Dam
(Lake Samsonvale)

Strathpine

CHAOS IN THE CREEKS

SEVERAL SMALL CREEKS TRAVERSE CABOOLTURE AND THE SURROUNDING AREAS OF MORAYFIELD AND BURPENGARY, BEFORE JOINING EITHER THE CABOOLTURE RIVER, WHICH FLOWS THROUGH THE TOWNSHIP, OR BURPENGARY CREEK. MORE RIVULETS FORM IN THE MANY GULLIES OF THE HILLY LANDSCAPE DURING PERIODS OF RAIN.

The extreme wet weather event that affected most of Queensland in early January, 2011 poured torrents into the Caboolture River catchment area as well. By Tuesday 12th January all the creeks were swelling rapidly and residents were urgently warned to evacuate to higher ground. A major thoroughfare, Morayfield Road, was cut by the Caboolture River which reached 11 metres by 2.00pm. Many low-lying properties were engulfed, roads and bridges were extensively damaged, the Caboolture Hospital became isolated for a short time and the Bruce Highway was cut in both directions.

Many homes, rural properties and businesses suffered in varying degrees from this sudden inundation, either from the destructive invasion of floodwater or from isolation. Transport and trade came to a standstill and supplies were delayed. Sewage escaping from blown manhole covers joined the waterways, rendering them unfit for swimming. Attractive parkland, often the chosen venue for wedding celebrations, was horribly decimated as the turbulent streams charged through it.

Although significant damage was done, Caboolture's flood experience in January, 2011 was not on the same scale as some of the other regional communities. However, once again the various emergency services showed their proficiency in handling these crises, from warnings to assistance, rescues and evacuations. They were on hand to cope with fallen power lines and close off roads where submerged rocks and potholes presented an unseen hazard to unwary and sometimes impatient motorists.

The support and kindness of those manning the evacuation centres gave fresh courage to many victims of trauma and helped to revive their sanity-preserving sense of humour. Kindness is always a feature that comes to the fore in these disasters and this was certainly evident in the overwhelming donations and voluntary offers of help that were immediately received.

The resilience of the local people has led to rapid progress in clean-up and restoration, though numerous potholes continue to yawn in the long queue for Council attention!

DAMAGED ROADS AND
MOUNTAINS OF DEBRIS

FLOOD

CABOOLTURE

- **Jan 8th-9th 2011**
  Heavy rain persists through week-end.

- **Jan 10th 2011**
  Rain continues

- **Jan 11th 2011**
  400mm rain falls during a 10-hour period.

  Creeks rising.

  Just before midday whole of Caboolture and surrounds issued with orders to evacuate to higher ground immediately.

- 2.00pm. Morayfield Road cut as Caboolture River reaches 11 metres.

- Caboolture completely isolated.

FACTS

- Bruce Highway cut in both directions.

- Caboolture Hospital isolated for a short time.

- Water enters about 300 homes and some businesses.

- Waterways affected — Caboolture River, Burpengary Creek, Sideling Creek, King John Creek, Lagoon Creek, Wararba Creek, and Sheep Station Creek.

- Creeks rose quickly and went down quickly.

- 640 requests for assistance and 708 rescues in the Moreton Bay area at the height of the crisis.

THE SKIES OPENED WITH A **VENGEANCE**

CARTMILL RIDING SCHOOL IS A VOLUNTEER-BASED ESTABLISHMENT WHICH PROVIDES HOPE AND ENCOURAGEMENT TO MANY ADULTS AND CHILDREN WITH SPECIAL NEEDS, HELPING THEM TO REALISE THEIR DREAMS AND ASPIRATIONS. IN THE TWENTY YEARS CARTMILL HAVE BEEN OPERATING, FLOOD HAS SWEPT THROUGH THE PROPERTY ONLY TWICE; BOTH IN RECENT TIMES AND WITH DEVASTATING FORCE. THE FIRST FLOOD, IN OCTOBER, 2009, SWEPT A MOST LOVED AND TREASURED HORSE 'SCORE' TO HIS DEATH. ANOTHER FAVOURITE, 'MANNY', WAS LEFT SWIMMING FOR HIS LIFE IN WATER COVERING THE GRANDSTAND, AND WHEN THE WATER LEVEL DROPPED HE SUSTAINED HORRIBLE INJURIES FROM THE SEATING.

Fifteen months later, in January, 2011, after several months of relentless rain, the skies opened with a vengeance once more. Fortunately this time the horses were off the property for a spell.

Riding instructor Jane Sayer, recalls "We heard that the flood was coming, and got in touch with the two most handy blokes to come down. We thought our computers would have been alright because we got them up high. The guys came in to have a look, then saw the water pouring in, so they rushed out again. They had left their car at the gate, but by the time they got there, the water was over its roof."

The water couldn't go anywhere as a large drain tunnel had blocked and created a dam. More surged down from the creek, picking up speed and power, crashing against the building and rolling back in waves. Heavy objects and tables were repeatedly picked up and hurled into corners, smashing their way destructively through the office. The water pressure was incredible, and when it flowed back again it brought the sewage with it to mingle with the mud, creating a putrefying mess. Eventually, it settled level with the train line, 400mm higher than the previous flood.

Two of the heavy outdoor picnic tables, chairs, massive truck tyres and other equipment were found floating down stream kilometres away. A horse float, a recently purchased tractor, and the school's bird cage were gobbled up by the water. A 30 tonne water tank was lifted and swept from the school by a 9 foot wall of water and ended up in the back paddock. "Everything was filled with mud and sludge. We couldn't face the reality; there was no way of dealing with it." The pain of recollection is evident, "it was just too much, so we actually left the

building shut up for the next two weeks, and the water just sat in there. You can imagine what it was like - havoc, chaotic!"

"The water had come into our store and every saddle, and bridle and indeed everything was full of mud and sludge. The power of the water had pushed everything — gear, mud and sludge — into a corner, and jammed it all together. Most of the equipment was damaged beyond repair. Some of the saddles have been recovered, however, we had to hose them down, and dry them out whilst constantly wiping them clean."

"People don't realise, what a flood can do unless they have gone through it. That's why we were really sympathetic with the people in Brisbane, because we knew what they were going through. And what destruction a flood causes! A fire is worse of course, because it's more dangerous, but at least with a fire everything is destroyed, and that's it. The trouble with a flood is that you can pull out all your photos and you can see them, and you pull out all your history and your things out of the mess it leaves behind, and you then have to make the decision whether to throw them away."

One of the volunteers at Cartmill is a cabinetmaker, and with his boss he is working gradually towards replacing the smashed furniture. Some of the young people- the majority of whom have support needs - have done an amazing job of re-establishing the gardens. They were awarded a $40 000.00 grant from the Government after an official inspector visited them and was shocked by the damage. The rebuilding process has been facilitated by volunteer labour and love, and the staff have been able to return - to provide support and build confidence for our special people.

EVERYTHING WAS FILLED WITH
MUD AND SLUDGE

Walkers Road -Morayfield

Station Road - Burpengary

Station Road - Burpengary

CABOOLTURE

Police assistance – Caboolture Floods

Traffic lights on flash at Burpengary

Burpengary Creek

SES negotiate floodwaters

NEVILLE AND CATHERINE
WESTON
Caboolture

THE RIVER WAS ALIVE WITH SWIRLING
DEBRIS

MRS. WESTON IS SPONTANEOUS IN HER RESPONSE TO OUR QUESTIONS ON HER FLOOD EXPERIENCE.

"I think the more important people of this story are the people who didn't know us, that came down the street and helped us. They're the people who should feature in the book," she insists. Overwhelmed by the care and generosity of complete strangers, she is eager to see them recognised for their selfless efforts and reluctant to take the spotlight herself.

The three-storey home of elderly couple Neville and Catherine Weston sits high on the banks of the Caboolture River, seemingly far beyond the reach of the water which flows calmly past below. On 11th January, Mr. Weston awoke to torrential rain. It had been pouring continuously through the night and the river was alive with swirling debris. The deluge continued in earnest and around mid-morning a neighbour delivered the ominous warning; they had less than an hour before their home would be swamped by a 'wall of water'.

This was to be the only notice they would get. "We were unfortunate in that we were never given notification that there was water coming until it was here. Someone was warning people, but they must've forgotten this house existed." Convinced their losses would have been less had they received this information earlier, she laments "We shouldn't have lost anything, we should've been told".

The Weston's began the frantic task of moving the goods they had in their basement to higher ground. Complete strangers turned up to offer a hand. "Don't ask me where they came from, they just arrived," Mrs Weston marvelled. "They were wonderful".

Some of their possessions were loaded into a boat and taken to higher ground; the helpers took some items with them and stored them in their own homes. "We have no idea where the things were taken, but every item was returned afterwards," she said.

With so little time to act, not everything was spared. The water rose 7 feet in an hour and became too deep to wade through. A very wet couple were standing outside their home as evening approached and some kind strangers, out sight-seeing, noticed the "two drowned rats," so they took the Westons home. "They were wonderful."

Another stranger spent the night out the front of their house as there had been reports of looting in the area. Neville laments the loss of tools and other equipment to the flood waters; however he is acutely aware of how much worse off they could have been had the water not stopped just inches short of their living quarters.

The Westons credit the local council's strict building codes for preventing undue damage to the house, vowing to never whinge about council regulations again. The whole house is flood-proof, resulting in minimal damage and facilitating a quick return to normality.

"HERE TO HELP"

Unfortunately, Neville and Catherine were safeguarding the personal effects of a friend who was in the throes of moving house. All her worldly goods were stored in the Westons' shed and in their entirety, were saturated. "It was everything she had. I was out there looking at this dreadful mess, having a bit of a weep, and a lady came off the street and said 'My mother and I are here to help!' She took several bags of stuff home and brought it back washed. I thought that was lovely."

MOORE ROAD - KURWONGBAH

MORAYFIELD - SKATEPARK

STATION ROAD - BURPENGARY

VORES ROAD - KURWONGBAH

NORTH PINE DAM
ON LAKE SAMSONVALE

NORTH PINE DAM ON LAKE SAMSONVALE, WHICH SUPPLIES CABOOLTURE, WAS CONSTRUCTED IN THE EARLY 1970'S TO HOLD DRINKING WATER BUT NOT WITH ANY CAPACITY FOR FLOOD MITIGATION. IT IS CONSIDERED TO BE FULL AT 39.63M. ON JANUARY 11TH THE WATER REACHED 41.11M, ONLY TWO METRES SHORT OF OVERTOPPING THE WALL, WHICH IN TURN COULD RISK THE COLLAPSE OF THE EARTHEN EMBANKMENTS ABUTTING THE CONCRETE WALL. SHOULD THIS HAVE HAPPENED, MORE THAN 10,000 LIVES WOULD HAVE BEEN ENDANGERED IN THE SUBURBS OF STRATHPINE, PETRIE, LAWNTON, KALLANGUR AND MURRUMBA DOWNS.

FOLLOWING THE CONDAMINE INTO THE
SOUTH-WEST

MYALL CREEK, A TRIBUTARY OF THE CONDAMINE RIVER, RUNS THROUGH THE HEART OF DALBY IN A RICH AGRICULTURAL AREA OF THE DARLING DOWNS. HERE THE FERTILE BLACK VOLCANIC SOIL PLAINS SUPPORT THE PRODUCTION OF WHEAT, COTTON, SORGHUM, AND OTHER CROPS AND DALBY'S AGRICULTURAL COLLEGE OFFERS COURSES RELATING TO RURAL SKILLS. PRESERVED COLONIAL BUILDINGS AND OTHER REMINDERS OF DALBY'S PIONEER HERITAGE, INCLUDING OLD MACHINERY, ARE PROUDLY DISPLAYED IN THE PIONEER PARK. THIRTEEN BORES LOCATED ALONG THE CONDAMINE RIVER SUPPLY WATER TO THE TOWN WHERE FEWER THAN 10,000 PEOPLE RESIDE.

The town of Chinchilla, population around 4,000, is situated on the banks of Charleys Creek which also flows into the Condamine River. The town's water supply is drawn from the Chinchilla Weir which was constructed in 1974 on the Condamine River. The Melon Festival, held every two years, celebrates Chinchilla's nationally accepted fame as the 'Melon Capital', as 25% of Australia's watermelons are grown here. Chinchilla can be considered as a future energy source, having large coal resources, with two major power stations now operating nearby.

On the Condamine River, the tiny township of Condamine is home to a little over 100 people. One of its claims to fame is the invention of the Condamine or Bullfrog Bell, which stockmen hung from the necks of their bullocks to keep track of their location when grazing. The town boasts excellent fishing and enthusiastically supports the game of rugby.

The waters of the Condamine empty into the Balonne River which is joined by the Maranoa River at Lake Kajarabie, where the Beardmore Dam was constructed just upstream from St George, a town of around 3,000 inhabitants. This increase in irrigation supply has helped the cotton industry and other farming ventures thrive. Its situation amongst numerous river systems makes St George prone to flooding and has led to the construction of levee banks to protect homes, crops and properties.

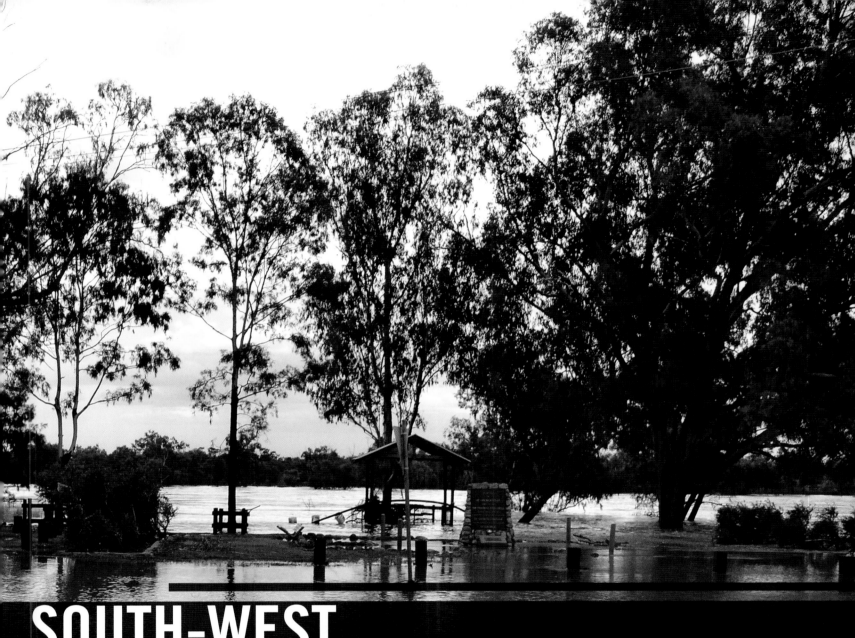

SOUTH-WEST
CHINCHILLA, CONDAMINE, DALBY AND ST GEORGE

Roma

Warrego Highway

Miles

CHINCHILLA

Carnarvon Highway

Conda mine River

Balonne River

Surat

CONDAMINE

DALBY

Leichhardt Highway

Maranoa River

BRISBANE 335KM

Moonie

Beardmore Dam

Moonie Highway

ST GEORGE

THESE TOWNS FACED FLOODING
MORE THAN ONCE

DURING DECEMBER 2010-JANUARY 2011, DALBY EXPERIENCED ITS WORST FLOODING SINCE 1981 AND WAS INUNDATED SEVERAL TIMES AS MYALL CREEK DIVIDED THE TOWN. FAILURE OF THE WATER PURIFICATION SYSTEM RESULTED IN HARSH WATER RESTRICTIONS AND A NUMBER OF PEOPLE WERE EVACUATED. CROPS WERE LOST AND SHOPS, BUSINESSES AND HOMES IN TOWN WERE SEVERELY AFFECTED.

Charleys Creek caused havoc in Chinchilla, which was inundated twice and cut off from Miles and Dalby as the Warrego Highway near town was only open to boats! Several evacuations took place as houses were swamped and a boil-water alert was issued when the Water treatment plant was submerged. Farmers suffered substantial losses through being unable to harvest their mature crops of watermelons or reach the markets.

The entire population of Condamine was evacuated by helicopter twice in ten days as flood waters threatened to engulf the town! Having returned to clean-up their mud-laden homes, they found the later flood extremely disheartening, but were greatly cheered on their second home-coming by a visit from the Governor-General.

St George's levee banks were effective to a large extent, considering that water came from the Maranoa River as well as from the Darling Downs. Very few homes were affected when the Balonne peaked twice during January 2011, however, there were some properties that were actually disadvantaged by the position of the levee banks and became victims of the diverted water.

Condamines entire population awaiting evacuation

FLOOD

DALBY

- **Dec 28th 2010** - Dalby's first major flood peak of 3.5m Myall Creek splits the town.
- **Dec 30th 2010** – 115 residents leave their homes.
- **Jan 2nd 2011** – 160 evacuated.
- Myall Creek's highest peak was 3.8m.
- Flooded 5 times in 3 weeks
- 228 houses completely inundated with water.
- 68 rural homesteads, 92 houses and 30 businesses inundated twice.
- 7,023km of the road network has been damaged.
- Residents endured Level 6 water restrictions due to water purification system being contaminated by flood waters.
- 8 trucks delivered 112, 500L of water. At one stage there was only enough drinking water to last for 24 hours.
- Worst flood since 1981
- Cost to agricultural sector - $400 million
- Delivery trucks stranded for a week

FACTS

ST GEORGE

- **Jan 6th 2011** - Balonne River at 12.78m and rising
- **Jan 7th 2011** - 50 homes affected 35 people evacuated (mostly to Brisbane)
- **Jan 7th 2011** - Isolated by road
- **Jan 9th 2011** - 1st peak — Balonne River 13.2m — 7 houses inundated.
- **Jan 12th 2011** - Highway closed between St George and Surat.
- **Jan 23rd 2011** - 15 Evacuated, 25 homes affected
- St George had 5 days' warning of flood.
- Authorities remained on high alert as rain continued to fall in the catchment area of the Balonne River.
- Properties and small townships like Dirranbandi to the south were cut off for a month.
- Supplies distributed by air, boat and some accessible roads.
- Warnings re: animal diseases —different types caused by insect bites, bacterial spores, contaminated water.
- Danger of water contamination from run-off from mine pumping, chemicals and fertilizer.
- Levee banks effectively reduce flooding

FLOOD

CHINCHILLA

- **Dec 18th- 20th 2010** Heavy rain begins, some flooding in town
- **Dec 23rd 2010** Flood alert – Charley's Creek bridge under water.
- **Dec 26th 2010** Chinchilla cut off from Miles and Dalby. Businesses and homes inundated.
- **Dec 27th 2010** 6.30am - Charley's Ck at 6.4m. Evacuation Centre set up.
- Residents advised to prepare for severe flooding. Considerable road damage.
- Power cuts. Boats using the Warrego Highway.
- 9.00pm - Charley's Ck at 7.0m and still rising. 58 people evacuated. 93 homes affected.
- **Dec 28th 2010** 6.00am – Charley's Ck at 7.25m, Highest flood peak since 1981.
- Power cut off from 30 homes. Main sewerage plants still operational.
- **Dec 29th 2010** Charley's Ck receded to 6.74m. Roads still closed. Further evacuations by air.
- **Jan 1st 2011** Water level 6.07m.
- **Jan 2nd and 3rd 2011** Major clean-up organised.

- **Jan 5th 2011** Some residents return home. Water restrictions in place.
- **Jan 10th 2011** Heavy rain in a 4 hour period during the afternoon. Water rises 5.5m overnight.
- **Jan 12th 2011** Charley's Ck peaks at 7.45m. Second flood peak in 10 days.
- Chinchilla Water Treatment Plant inundated. Residents advised to boil water. Roads closed. Fuel supplies permitted for emergency operations only.
- **Jan 13th 2011** 240 homes without power.
- **Jan 14th 2011** 2.00am – Charley's Ck at 6.04m and receding. Boil water alert remains in place due to presence of e-coli. Cleaning up begins again.
- **Jan 19th 2011** Water supply given the all clear.
- Chinchilla suffered 4 flood surges in Dec-Jan period. 71 businesses and 50 houses inundated twice.

FACTS

CONDAMINE

- **Dec 29th 2010** Extensive rainfall affecting Western Downs. Condamine River rising. River at Condamine township reaches record height of 13.2m. Water 3.1m over the bridge.
- **Dec 30th 2010** Record breaking flooding in Condamine River. Current level at 14.25m and rising.
  Water is 4m over the bridge. Mayor gives 45 minutes notice to residents to evacuate.
  Entire population of 131 evacuated for first time ever by Black Hawk helicopter.
  Evacuation Centre set up at Dalby Showgrounds.
  Police and Emergency Services personnel remain on guard in town.

- **Dec 31st 2010** Condamine submerged. Evacuation complete.
- **Jan 3rd 2011** Condamine River peaks at 15.2m.
- **Jan 6th 2011** Residents begin returning home. Volunteers and recovery teams commence extensive clean-up operations.
- **Jan 12th 2011** Further flooding — river at 14m and rising. Town evacuated again.
  Residents advised to boil water until further notice.
- **Jan 13th 2011** Condamine River peaks at 14.2m at 9.00pm.

- **Jan 14th 2011** Condamine Water Treatment Plant shut down due to flooding.
- **Jan 16th 2011** Town of Condamine submerged for the second time. River at 14.65m. Condamine River 400m wide. Every road into Condamine cut by floodwater. Losses of livestock.
- Later in the month: Residents begin to return. Town covered in mud and slime.
  Huge clean-up begins again. Water restrictions at level 6.
  Residents encouraged by visit from Governor-General.
- **Feb 25th 2011** Water restrictions ease for Condamine.

THIS ONE'S GONNA BE
BAD

'THE FRIDGES WERE POPPING UP LIKE SUBMARINES', SAYS IAN BRASSETT, FRANCHISEE OF HARVEY NORMAN, DALBY, WHOSE BUSINESS CAME UNDER REPEATED ATTACK AS FLOODWATERS ENCROACHED ON HIS PREMISES ON THREE SEPARATE OCCASIONS, OVER THE SPACE OF A FEW SHORT WEEKS.

Water came perilously close to breaching the sandbag barrier that protected both the warehouse and store, on the 23rd December, but receded again without too much ado, and both premises survived unscathed. Ian focused his attention on the end of season trading that retailers so look forward to; in fact, Boxing Day was the best day of sales ever recorded in the eleven year history of Harvey Norman, Dalby.

As the rain fell in torrents on the evening of the 26th December, Ian was hoping against hope that the water wouldn't rise again. But, despite predictions from all the official sources indicating a lower flood level, his store was swamped by 900mm of water. The water was rising quickly and was putting huge pressure on the glass entrance doors. A trickle was meandering its way across the entry mat and as the water continued to rise, the doors threatened to give way. The agonising decision was made to open them, at which water up to waist height rushed in. "We had put all our small goods on top of the white goods in an effort to save them, so when the fridges popped up and fell over, everything went." Ian was caught off-guard; "It's surprising how fast it happens and the damage it causes", he remarks wistfully. "It was quite scary. It was pitch black inside the shop, pitch black!" He still seems haunted by the scene. "Stock was crashing around. We were walking round and bumping into things – 'What's that?' Next thing there's a fridge floating past, or a stereo, or a toaster. Help! Is that a crocodile?" The prospect of snakes in the water was terrifying. "I was thinking about snakes, we have so many of them here, I am so paranoid about them. Things always look better in the daylight", he adds.

The episode was devastating; much of his stock was out on the floor and too difficult to save with such little warning. As the water receded, the drudgery of the clean-up began. It was necessary to find a new storage facility for the unaffected stock - around 20%. Carpets in the store were removed and preparations began for the renovation and reinstatement of the business.

Ian cleaned up the warehouse and set up temporary trading quarters further down the road. The following Sunday evening, around 8pm, Ian took a call from the Southerlys, neighbours of the warehouse. "Mate, you'd better get down here, this one's gonna be bad!" the words rang in Ian's ears as he headed for the store in the torrential rain. They worked frantically with the forklift, getting as much stock as possible to safety. Then it was the waiting game again as the water continued to rise, this time to even higher levels.

Harvey Norman was the hardest hit business in town, with stock loss alone amounting to $1.8 million. To compound problems, the disaster occurred during the biggest retail trading season of the year in; loss of sales was huge. Ian considers himself fortunate in the light of the losses of the Harvey Norman store at Oxley, Brisbane, which amounted to $9 million in electrical goods alone. He speaks appreciatively of the local Fire Service and the many other volunteers who lined up to help in the clean-up effort. Four weeks later, as he serves at the counter of his recently opened renovated store, and the loyal customers stream in, Ian has a message to spread, "Support your local Community".

MAYOR
DONNA STEWART

St George

WE WERE IN
UNCHARTED TERRITORY

"WE WERE FLOODED THREE TIMES IN THE LAST 12 MONTHS, FIRSTLY IN A RECORD FLOOD IN 2010, THEN IN JANUARY 2011 AND AGAIN IN FEBRUARY. THE INITIAL FLOODING CAME AT THE END OF A PROLONGED 10 YEAR DROUGHT, SO WE WERE IN UNCHARTED TERRITORY AND COMPLETELY UNPREPARED."

"The first flood provided experience used in the 2011 floods and immediately the community responded, swinging into action"

"Many homes in St George and beyond were affected by the widespread flooding. Insurance companies refused claims because the flooding was from a river, not from storm water. The little town of Bollon - west of here — was completely inundated twice within a week. The Wallam and the Mungallala Creeks actually swelled into one for the first time in living memory. To the east we had the Moonie River, which was incredibly engorged, and up at Thallon there was a lot of damage to the Council road network - about eighty million dollars worth of repairs Shire wide."

"The Beardmore Dam, which sits up above St George, had over 9000 gigalitres go through during the flood – a massive volume of water. The water did a lot of damage to the rural infrastructure and the farming community. It blew the walls clean out of the dams."

But not all is gloom and doom for the sunburnt communities of outback rural Queensland, possibly the only area to reap much-needed benefits from the disaster. Emerging from years of hardship and drought, crops begin to flourish as water abounds from overflowing water tanks. Former ghost town, Dirranbandi, is active and thriving; every house in town is now occupied. The big farming irrigation crops are booming, and a record 600,000 bale cotton crop valued at 1/2 a billion dollars is stimulating the economy to better than it's ever been.

ST GEORGE MAYOR -DONNA STEWART

DALBY

WARREGO HWY

A2

Chinchilla	80
Miles	127
Roma	268
Morven	445
Charleville	535

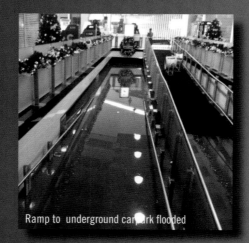

Ramp to underground carpark flooded

ES workers

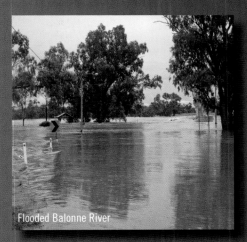
Flooded Balonne River

Fishing for carp from the flooded Balonne River

ST GEORGE

Aerial view of St George

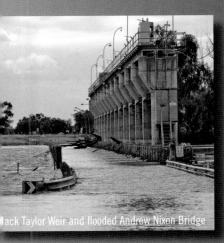
Jack Taylor Weir and flooded Andrew Nixon Bridge

Earth Levee Banks built to protect homes and business

ROGER BOSHAMMER
Chinchilla

IT'S GOING TO GET YOU
ONE DAY

ROGER BOSHAMMER PHILOSOPHICALLY DISMISSES THE TRAUMA OF THE PAST FEW WEEKS WITH A WAVE OF HIS BIG, BURLY HAND. "IF YOU LIVE ON A FLOOD PLAIN, YOU LIVE BY IT AND IT IS GOING TO GET YOU ONE DAY".

And get them, it did! Glenoch Farms Pty Ltd suffered three separate inundations between the 20th of December and the 10th of January. A huge melon crop, in its prime and ready to pick, was completely lost. "The first two floods drowned and killed them and the third washed them away", Roger states matter-of-factly. "The crop was worth a lot, but you've got to look forward. That's why I try not to count what we did lose". Ironically, when the crop was first planted there wasn't enough water to irrigate it with. "Drought costs money, so does flood. It's just part of everyday", he adds. We admire him for his unruffled approach. The farm's losses would have exceeded $1million, we mentally estimate. Roger is uninsured for flood.

The farm covers around 5000 acres, split over four different locations, and supports 500 head of cattle. With their precious bloodlines to protect, Roger had shifted a mob of cattle down to his Canaga property just prior to the first flood. However, the remaining stock had to be closely monitored as the water rose over the property. "We went to check on the bulls and there were about 50 standing on a contour bank, clamouring to stay on top. We had to cut fences, and then swam them out, chasing them with the boat." Fortunately no livestock were lost.

Overseeing a property inundated by floodwaters is no walk in the park. Roger describes one of the many episodes that didn't run according to plan. "We shifted cattle just before Christmas. They were in water halfway up their ribs and we had to walk around in prickles to shift them out." Kilometres from home - their means of transport a boat - they ran into trouble. "We got wire around the propeller. We didn't have any tools other than a pair of pliers and we were in the current, with no oars." Reliant on the anchor, they threw it out into the trees and pulled themselves out of the current and into the shallows. Forced to walk, dragging the boat with them, they traversed through water up to Roger's head in depth, with his teenage daughter having to swim part of the way. By then the darkness of night had closed in. "We got out onto the road, where the water was shallower, and using our phones as lights we untangled the propeller and got the wire out." It was too dark to continue home via the creek. Forced to walk the remaining three and a half kilometres, and in bare feet, they followed the road, which was covered in floodwater all but for the last half kilometre. "My feet were sore for weeks after that. Walking on the bitumen was bad enough, but the water had washed gravel onto the road and we were walking on stones the whole way."

Roger informs us rather nonchalantly "I had come home from hospital the week before after having a kidney out. I told the surgeon he would have been very impressed with how his work withstood the rigors it was put under." No doubt, Roger! We muse over his stoicism.

DOUBLE WHAMMY

GERARD BELLGROVE, OF AINSWORTH MOTORS, CHINCHILLA, IS NO STRANGER TO THINGS THAT CREEP UP ON YOU IN THE NIGHT. WHEN WATER FROM CHARLEYS CREEK STARTED TO CREEP UP IN THE WEEK LEADING UP TO CHRISTMAS DAY 2010, GERARD KNEW WHAT HAD TO BE DONE TO SAVE HIS BUSINESS ASSETS AND STOCK FROM ANOTHER INEVITABLE SOAKING. SEEING THE "WRITING ON THE WALL" AND KNOWING THAT STAFF WOULD BE SCARCE OVER THE COMING CHRISTMAS BREAK, HE ACTED PROMPTLY TO MOVE WHAT HE COULD TO HIGHER GROUND.

Veterans of 4 previous floods, after 35 years in business, Ainsworth Motors have things down to a fine art. Their desks are designed to come apart for hasty removal, and they know when to act on a flood warning. Vital computer equipment, spare parts, machinery, tools and stock all had to be hauled out to minimise financial loss, in what proved to be a 'double whammy' event. The clean-up effort following the first flood took 10 days, but the second time round it only took 4. Staff members waded into the building with pressure cleaners on trolleys, and began hosing the walls down while they were still wet. Once the surfaces dry, the grime is almost impossible to remove.

The second flood came up extremely fast. The 9 hours it took from alert to inundation was a race against time, but a race that they would eventually win. Gerard issued a plea for help on facebook, and within half an hour they had 30 or 40 people there, helping to clear out cars, tools and other equipment.

Gerard suddenly realised that computer equipment vital to the ongoing success of his business might need to be moved even higher than initially thought. Armed with no more than a small boat and a clear determination to succeed, he jumped in to the swollen waters and swam against the strong current to a doorway of the building, swimming inside to try and save the gear. There, immersed in water almost to his chin, he tried in vain to find a way to put the equipment higher up, eventually having to surrender to the possibility that it could become the next victim destined for a watery grave. Fortune would have it that the water didn't rise quite that far, so the equipment was saved, but what stands out here is the sheer will to survive – come what may!!!

A "perch with a view" became a reality in Chinchilla, when Gerard and 3 mates sat on the awning of the building, drinking beer and watching the boats traversing back and forth through the main street – not your everyday experience!!!
The business was closed for about a month, and Gerard estimates that nearly

$200 000 was lost in tools, loss of trade and repairing damage to the premises. Ainsworth Motors have no flood cover, relying on drive and determination to get back up and going. Prolonging the painstaking process of regaining momentum was the absence of a staff member, who suffered a partial foot amputation after a simple cut to the toe, sustained in the event, progressed to infection.

Community groups such as the local Apex club provided much needed support and helped enormously with all those affected in the town. Managers from other established and unaffected businesses in the area, such as Origin Energy, CS Energy and Queensland Gas, offered their staff at their own business's expense, to help in the cleanup and recovery efforts.

Given that preparation and warning time for these floodwaters involved only hours in comparison to days for some larger coastal areas affected by similar flooding, the virtues of careful planning and swift action became very evident in the small town called Chinchilla.

A CLEAR DETERMINATION TO SUCCEED

Warrego Highway between Chinchilla and Dalby

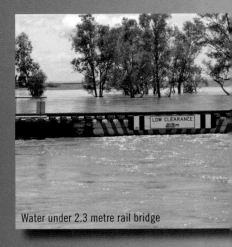
Water under 2.3 metre rail bridge

CHINCHILLA

Warrego Highway - Chinchilla

CONDAMINE

Condamine residents await evacuation

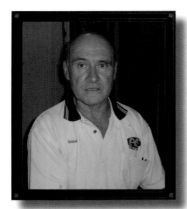

CONDAMINE HOTEL
Condamine

EVEN THE UNPRECEDENTED WAS
POSSIBLE

THE TINY TOWNSHIP OF CONDAMINE BOASTS A POPULACE OF AROUND 150 RESIDENTS; HOWEVER, ITS PROXIMITY TO THE MINES ENSURES IT PROVIDES SERVICES TO A MUCH LARGER COMMUNITY. THE CONDAMINE HOTEL RUNS MANY RECENTLY BUILT MOTEL UNITS, MAINLY UTILISED BY STAFF, COOKS, BACKPACKERS AND CONTRACTORS. FOR 8 MONTHS OF LAST YEAR THE UNITS WERE BOOKED OUT SOLID. ON AN AVERAGE NIGHT, THE HOTEL PREPARES 80-90 MEALS FOR THOSE OF THE 600 OR SO MEN WORKING IN THE NEARBY MINES, THAT COME INTO TOWN.

Back in the 1800's the entire town of Condamine was shifted to higher grounds to avoid flooding. Local knowledge suggests the first time the pub was flooded was in 1896, before relocation. Since then, there have been numerous flash floods, but the Condamine Hotel has remained untouched. Just prior to the recent flooding, locals all seemed to have the same message for owner Shane Hickey, 'It won't come in here, because it never ever has before.'

So when the police came in and told him to stop pouring beers and leave, or he'd be fined and dragged out, Shane initially thought it was the wrong decision. But the sheer volume of water pelting down from the heavens over those few days was astronomical, proving that even the unprecedented was possible.

Shane relates, "Condamine copped it bad; we had two floods. We now have this little bit of unenviable history —we are the second town to ever be completely evacuated in Australia, and the first town to ever be fully evacuated twice in one season. The first time we were flown out in Black Hawk helicopters, the next time we went by boat."

"The first flood reached 15.25m. We never had time to do anything —we had only a couple of hours notice. There was a massive amount of damage, everything was wrecked; walls collapsed, mud and silt everywhere. The second flood reached 14.67m – not quite as high. Next time around there was nothing there, we'd already cleaned up and everything was stripped, all we had to do was re-clean." "A fair few people haven't come back because the first time they lost everything, then they'd begun to replace and rebuild. When they were flooded the second time – that was enough for them. In many cases, insurance will only cover flash flooding and storm water, not slow rising floods."

"For example, Dotty across the road lost all she had, she is only a pensioner and has absolutely nothing left. Dotty was devastated, she said she wouldn't return, but was talked into it because she was given a lot of help. She's now staying in a caravan whilst her house is repaired."

"It has been great. You know there are some people that have never talked to each other before, but we all communicate a lot more now. Everyone has been brought together, all of a sudden the whole town is gathered, helping each other out, or having a sausage sizzle. That part of it has been fantastic."

BILL POWER
Condamine

DON'T
HESITATE

THE TINY CLOSE-KNIT COMMUNITY OF CONDAMINE, SOUTH OF MILES, NOW LAYS CLAIM TO THE RECORD FOR BEING THE FIRST TOWN AND ONLY AUSTRALIAN TOWN TO BE EVACUATED TWICE IN ONE SEASON. THE FIRST EVACUATION, ON DECEMBER 30, CAME WITH LITTLE NOTICE, WITH THE 130 RESIDENTS GIVEN ONLY 90 MINUTES TO GRAB WHAT THEY COULD AND LEAVE. LOCAL SES CONTROLLER, BILL POWER, SAYS THAT THE LITTLE NOTICE WAS WHAT MADE THE SITUATION SO DIFFICULT. "WE WERE GIVEN VERY LITTLE TIME, VERY LITTLE WARNING OF WHAT FLOOD HEIGHTS WERE GOING TO BE". A VOLUNTARY EVACUATION THAT MORNING HAD SEEN ONLY A HANDFUL OF RESIDENTS LEAVE THE TOWN. IT WASN'T UNTIL THESE EARLY ESCAPEES SAW THE REALITY OF THE DISASTER FROM THE AIR THAT THE PEOPLE OF CONDAMINE REALISED THEIR DIRE SITUATION AND CALLED AN EMERGENCY TOWN MEETING. "THEY RANG PEOPLE BACK HERE AND SAID 'LOOK, THIS IS FRIGHTENING, DON'T HESITATE, GET OUT OF THERE!'". THE ADF SENT IN A BLACK HAWK HELICOPTER TO FLY THE 80 REMAINING RESIDENTS TO DALBY. ONCE THEY GOT UP IN THE AIR, "THERE WERE NO QUALMS ABOUT IT, LET'S GET OUT!"

As the Black Hawk crew ferried residents to safety, Bill stayed behind to keep an eye on the town, with 2 policemen and a skeleton SES crew. They watched with pain as the flood waters swallowed up the town, leaving 60 buildings submerged. Bill describes the scene, "Once the river broke its banks, it really started to make some noise — the roar of the flowing water was scary. I'm not a religious person, but they do have a few denominations out here, and the good Lord must have helped them, because not one of their churches were done in!"

Most homes and businesses were still empty when, just 12 days later, the flood waters started to rise again. The residents voted to evacuate before they were forced to, with the river predicted to rise higher than ever before. The water was starting to creep back in as they left. Glenda Power, Bill's wife, thought that she'd just be hosing out the house again; "we didn't have any furniture or floor coverings left to ruin, as it was already ruined." However, the river rose less than predicted, peaking at 14.67m, preventing a lot of further damage in the town.

132

TRAVELLERS CAN'T PASS
WARWICK

THERE IS A PLEASANT, UNCLUTTERED FEELING ABOUT WARWICK, WITH ITS BROAD STRAIGHT STREETS, ENDURING SANDSTONE BUILDINGS AND THE GENTLY WAVING PALMS IN THE MAIN STREET. THE CONDAMINE RIVER FLOWS THROUGH THE CITY PROVIDING GREAT OPPORTUNITIES FOR PICNICKING, WALKING OR SIMPLY RELAXING ON ITS GRASSY BANKS.

Surrounded by large areas of fertile farmland on the western side of the Great Dividing Range, this city of 15,000 people has all the charm and friendliness of a country town, while possessing also a thriving economy. Scenic places to visit abound in the vicinity, including National Parks, the Leslie Dam, wineries in the Stanthorpe region and waterfalls around Killarney. The historic Glengallan Homestead and the Darling Downs Zoo are not far away and in Warwick itself, the weekly "pig and calf" sale with its accompanying "sundries" auction is always an intriguing event. Known as the 'Rose and Rodeo' capital, Warwick is host to the month-long Rose and Rodeo Festival in October each year.

Because it is situated at the junction of major highways linking Melbourne, Sydney and Brisbane, Warwick can be the centre

WARWICK
AND STANTHORPE

WARWICK

Cunningham Highway

Cunningham Highway

BRISBANE 160KM

Condamine River

New England Highway

TOOWOOMBA 80KM

Lake Leslie

Leslie Dam

STANTHORPE

Quart Pot Creek

HAVOC ON THE HIGHWAYS

THE DELAYS ON THE HIGHWAYS WERE AMONG THE MOST SIGNIFICANT FEATURES OF WARWICK'S TWO FLOODS, FIRSTLY ON DECEMBER 27TH, 2010 AND TWO WEEKS LATER ON JANUARY 11TH, 2011. STRANDED MOTORISTS AND TRUCK DRIVERS CONTRIBUTED TO THE LARGE NUMBERS CARED FOR IN THE EVACUATION CENTRES, AS WELL AS IN LOCAL LODGINGS. MUCH DAMAGE WAS DONE TO THE ROADS AND LARGE SHEETS OF BITUMEN WERE WASHED FROM THE ROADWAY ON THE O.O.MADSEN BRIDGE.

When northbound travellers were at last able to leave the town, the only route open to Brisbane was via Toowoomba, which involved long delays on account of the accumulated traffic volume and the restriction of a damaged bridge on the New England highway to a single lane.

O.O. Madsen Bridge approach during flood

Having a few hours' warning ahead of the second flood helped businesses and homeowners in flood-prone areas to minimise their losses but the additional height of 400mm in the second flood took them by surprise and left them battling with more truckloads of thick mud. In both floods the city was divided by the river and SES boat crews had to make frequent river crossings. Although frustrated by foolhardy swimmers and road-congesting sightseers, they greatly appreciated the excellent support they received from many volunteers who assisted in sandbagging and other chores.

In characteristic style, the Warwick residents have accepted this experience philosophically, just taking the precaution of making a mental note of what to do next time. Even whilst wielding mops and buckets they have no hesitation in affirming that Warwick is a great place to live -they all work together and they wouldn't live anywhere else!

O.O. Madsen Bridge approach before flood

FLOOD

WARWICK
AND STANTHORPE

- **Dec 27th 2010**
  Condamine River peaks at 8.0 metres splitting Warwick.

  Cunningham and New England Highways cut.

  O.O.Madsen Bridge severely damaged.

  SES door-knocking to warn residents.

  Evacuation centres set up on both sides of the river.

  More than 400 people housed at the two evacuation centres, including stranded travellers.

  Red Cross and other charitable organisations took on major roles in providing for the evacuees.

  SES received 47 requests for assistance.

  Two men rescued from a rooftop by helicopter.

  SES boat crews kept busy ferrying food and provisions across the river and rescuing elderly residents.

  Foolish people playing in floodwater as well as sightseers waste SES time.

  Homes, businesses, schools flooded.

- **Dec 28th 2010**
  10km traffic queues and up to 3 hour delays on Warwick – Toowoomba highway.

FACTS

- **Jan 6th 2011**
  Leslie Dam full for first time in 22 years.

  Storage capacity of dam was doubled in 1980 - 1986 by raising abutments by 2.6 metres and fitting 7 steel radial crest gates onto the spillway.

  Each gate is 6.6 metres high, 12.8 metres wide, and weighs 34 tonnes.

  All floodgates opened and water released at 10,440 megalitres per day.

- **Jan 11th 2011**
  Second flood 400mm higher.

  O.O.Madsen Bridge damaged by floods again.

  SES door-knocking every house below the 10 metre level.

  Warwick cut off again with long traffic queues and highway delays.

  Condamine peaked at 8.35m.

  150 homes and approximately 30 businesses inundated.

  A lot of stock and equipment ruined.

  Many crops destroyed – a year's income for farmers.

  Some low-lying areas around Quart Pot Creek at Stanthorpe evacuated also.

KAREN BURRASTON

Warwick

SENSE OF SECURITY
SHATTERED

FOR THE RESIDENTS OF WARWICK, HAVING TWO FLOODS IN TWO WEEKS HAS BEEN VERY HARD, BUT FOR THE CHILDREN INVOLVED, IT HAS BEEN EVEN WORSE. TO HAVE THIS POWERFUL MONSTER INVADE THEIR HOMES AND DESTROY THEIR BELONGINGS, INCLUDING TOYS, GAMES AND MUSICAL INSTRUMENTS, SHATTERS THE SENSE OF SECURITY THAT CHILDREN HAVE IN THEIR HOME.

Karen Burraston sheds tears when she speaks of the traumatic effect that the floods have had on her children. Her nine year-old daughter is still often troubled by flood-related dreams, and each time it rains, they become very agitated asking "Is it going to happen again?"

The Burraston's large residential property is in a flood-prone area of Warwick. As well as the house, there are several large storage sheds and a pool. After water came through the house in 1996, following heavy rain, they decided to raise the house above the water level of the 1974 floods to ensure this didn't happen again, which proved to be a very wise move! The January, 2011 flood came to within 50 cms of the floorboards of the upper floor of their raised home! This spared the contents of the main part of their home; however they still experienced heavy losses.

It was a different story for the bathroom on the lower floor. It was ruined, as were the many household effects stored downstairs. When the flood threatened, they worked hard to put all their possessions up high, on top of cupboards, etc. and were devastated when the waters came much higher than they ever expected. Their furniture began to float, toppling over and dumping their chattels into the murky waters. Many of the children's games were lost this way — which was very hard for them to come to terms with. The Burraston's had also moved the valuable contents of their sheds to higher locations — including a large pool table — but it was not high enough and they lost the lot.

The waters of the second flood also destroyed their large above-ground pool, a huge loss for the children. It was traumatising to watch the structure being torn apart by the debris-strewn current. Their wire fences also suffered extensive damage. There had not been enough time to clear all the debris from them after the first flood, so with the second flood they were totally wrecked. The water couldn't flow through them, so it forced them over, flattening them beyond recovery.

When Karen knew flood was threatening, she packed up all the food she could get from the refrigerator and freezers and took it and the family across the road to a kindly neighbour on higher ground. From there they watched the flood creep up and inundate the properties on the lower side of the street, one by one. They watched as another neighbour evacuated his home, albeit a little late, wading through waist-deep water, towing his wife in a canoe! It was all very depressing. One of their neighbours kindly fed all the flood-affected residents in the street — such generosity! Benevolence like this showed itself time and time again during the disaster. Persons like these can be ranked right up there with the heroes of the flood.

Interval photos showing flood waters rising then falling, and the destruction left behind

IS IT GOING TO HAPPEN AGAIN?

Flood aftermath and overwhelming cleanup operation

STEELE'S BAKERY CAFE
Warwick

THE ONGOING
NIGHTMARE

BRAD AND GAIL STEELE LOST EVERYTHING IN THE FIRST FLOOD IN DECEMBER, 2010. WITHOUT ANY WARNING, THEY WERE UNABLE TO SAVE ANYTHING. THEIR FREEZERS WERE STOCKED TO CAPACITY FOR THE FESTIVE SEASON, AS THEY KNEW THEY WOULDN'T BE ABLE TO GET MORE SUPPLIES OVER THE HOLIDAY PERIOD. THE FLOOD OF DECEMBER 27TH RUINED THEIR ENTIRE STOCK — IT HAD TO BE DISCARDED INTO SKIP BINS OUTSIDE. BECAUSE OF THE VERY HIGH DEMANDS ON AUTHORISED VEHICLES FOR TRANSFERRING INDUSTRIAL WASTE, SOME OF THOSE BINS SAT OUT IN THE SUNSHINE FOR DAYS AND THE REFUSE WAS ACTUALLY "BUBBLING". FOR BRAD AND GAIL, THAT BUBBLING MASS REPRESENTED MONTHS OF HARD WORK JUST LEFT TO ROT. IT WAS DEVASTATING.

Another shattering aspect of the experience for the Steeles was that when they closed the shop for the Christmas break, they had left it immaculately clean; five days later...... they came back to a filthy mess: their cabinets had tipped over and mud was everywhere. Nothing was spared. The mud had managed to seep in between the double glazed panels of the cabinets, writing off $95,000 worth of cabinetry. A couple of thousand dollars' worth of machinery was also lost. People who came to help couldn't believe the devastation.
Gail sums their feelings up when she says, "When you get back home, you think, 'Did I witness that, or was it a nightmare?'"

Thankfully, Brad and Gail had an excellent insurance broker who saw to everything. As the couple had the foresight to take out adequate insurance, they have been covered fully for their losses.

The impact of the inundation is still being felt, months afterwards. Many of Brad and Gail's suppliers in Brisbane have been affected by the floods also, so stock availability is limited. Replacement of plant and equipment has also been hampered for the same reason, so they have been unable to return to full production. Consequently, they have had to put off five of their staff.

Yes, the flood experience was a nightmare, and the nightmare goes on.

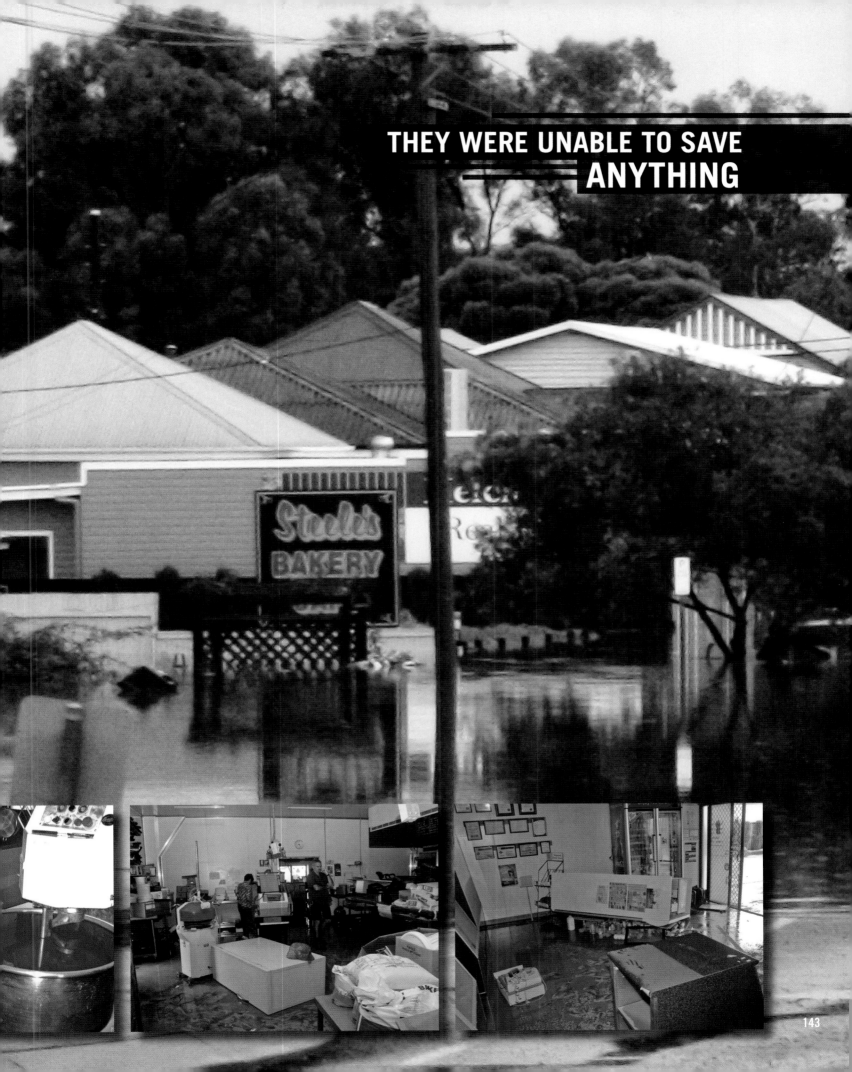

THEY WERE UNABLE TO SAVE
ANYTHING

143

Cnr Albion & Victoria Street - Warwick

Rising flood waters inundate businesses on Albion Street

Fridges from the Service Station swept away

WARWICK

Albion Street

Grafton Street Bridge

Soggy Playground

Victoria Street - McCahon Bridge

Condamine River

Evacuating local Motel

Flooded playing fields at Queens Park

0.0 Madsen Bridge

House on Fitzroy Street

McCahon Bridge - Victoria Street

Flooded Service Station

IT'S JUST COMING

Were you shocked when your premises went under water in the two floods?

Well! I was convinced the flood was coming. The weather had exactly the same 'feel' about it as it did in 1974. The climatic conditions were the same.........
and I thought, "It's coming.........it's just coming!"

So, what did you do as you anticipated this flood?

I rang the electrician and asked him to come and move the air-conditioning units that were beneath the building. We saved a few grand just by getting them out. And then I started packing up and getting everything out of the premises.

It must have been very hard for you to come back after the flood and face the cleanup.........?

Well, yes, it was hard, but I don't look for sympathy – I believe it' s up to you to help yourself......."the Lord helps those who help themselves"..........that's what I was brought up to believe.

How soon did you get the mess cleaned up?

We got cleaned up, the first time, in a day. I got down here at 6am the next day. There was still floodwater around, so I used that water to get all the mud out of the crevices while the mud was still wet. That alluvial mud is what they use to make concrete, when it dries, it sets like concrete. So I got it out before it dried.

Did you make any further preparations for the second flood as a result of what you learned from the first?

We closed the doors, they filtered the water so that not as much mud got in. We taped up all the data points and switches to prevent the mud from getting into them. So we didn't have to replace the data points the second time – it saved us heaps of money.

Did you get much support from the public?

I actually had a phone call from Switzerland! Someone who had been discussing properties with me before Christmas, saw us in the media and phoned to see if we were all right!

I probably had about half a dozen people in here helping with the cleanup.

Your losses must have been very heavy...?

Yes, well, I'm afraid to calculate the total monetary loss. Just over a year ago we totally renovated this building. We put a lot of money into it. We had been back in the premises for just over twelve months when the water came through. All the doors swelled; the water got into the insulation in the walls, so we had to rip all the sheeting off. The kitchen will have to be replaced. A lot of electrical work had to be redone.

Does your insurance cover any of this?

I don't have insurance, but at least I still have the land with the building on it.

So, do you intend to stay here?

What else can I do? It is not financially viable to go anywhere else. I have invested so much in this building.

Can you make any recommendations as a result of your flood experience?

Well, firstly, we can't say that there will not be another flood for fifty years! It's only thirty-five years since the last big one!

I also think that a list of precautions could be prepared for people who are in flood-prone areas. It could be distributed around if there was a flood alert............ ideas like taping up the data points and closing the doors........a flood plan, so people can effectively reduce their losses.

During   After

FLOOD GATES OPENED FOR FIRST TIME IN 22 YEARS AT
LESLIE DAM

LESLIE DAM IS A MASS-CONCRETE STRUCTURE ON SANDY CREEK 13 KM FROM WARWICK, WHICH WAS COMPLETED IN 1965. THE ABUTMENTS WERE LATER RAISED BETWEEN 1980 AND 1986, ALLOWING THE ADDITION OF SEVEN STEEL RADIAL GATES, MORE THAN DOUBLING THE STORAGE CAPACITY WHICH IS NOW 106,200 MEGALITRES. THE CATCHMENT AREA COVERS 603 KM² AND THE OUTFLOW FROM THE DAM ENDS UP IN THE CONDAMINE RIVER. MANY PEOPLE VISIT THE LAKE, CREATED BY THE DAM, TO ENJOY BOATING, SWIMMING AND FISHING. THERE ARE ALSO EXCELLENT CAMPING FACILITIES AND BARBECUE SITES.

During the extreme wet season of 2010 - 2011 the dam filled to overflowing for the first time in 22 years and the gates were opened, releasing up to 10,440 megalitres a day.

Road closed due to flooding

STANTHORPE

Stanthorpe is located in the Darling Downs and Granite Belt regions, about 2 ½ hours southwest of Brisbane. During the extreme wet season of 2010-2011, Quart Pot Creek overflowed as a result of heavy rains. Roads and bridges were cut and some residents were evacuated as flood waters inundated a number of homes.

Raging torrent over road

Flood waters cut bridge

Quart Pot Creek

Park inundated

Evacuation as Quart Pot Creek floods

Flooded residence

Homes inundated

149

WILD MONDAY IN
TOOWOOMBA

TOOWOOMBA, THE GARDEN CITY, IS SITUATED ON TOP OF THE WESTERN SLOPES OF THE GREAT DIVIDING RANGE. IT IS RENOWNED FOR ITS BEAUTIFUL PARKS AND GARDENS, AND THE POPULATION OF ALMOST 100,000 PEOPLE IS SWELLED BY A LARGE NUMBER OF TOURISTS DURING THE ANNUAL CARNIVAL OF FLOWERS. THE BROAD VIEWS TO THE EAST ACROSS THE LOCKYER VALLEY MAY BE OBSERVED FROM PICNIC POINT ON THE ESCARPMENT.

The city's heritage is preserved in many historic buildings, including the Bull's Head Inn, the focal point of the original Drayton settlement, and around fifty other preserved and restored sites. The Cobb and Co museum houses a fine collection of horse drawn vehicles as well as displays of blacksmithing skills, saddlery and other crafts.

The ridges and valleys within Toowoomba have led to the formation of East Creek and West Creek which originate near the southern extents of the city and join to form Gowrie Creek in the northern part of the CBD. Another catchment known as Black Gully is north of the CBD. Although the normal volumes of the creeks are minimal, the sloping terrain leads to a reasonably rapid flow, and a good shower of rain falling on the impervious ground of the built-up catchment areas can increase the size of the streams very quickly.

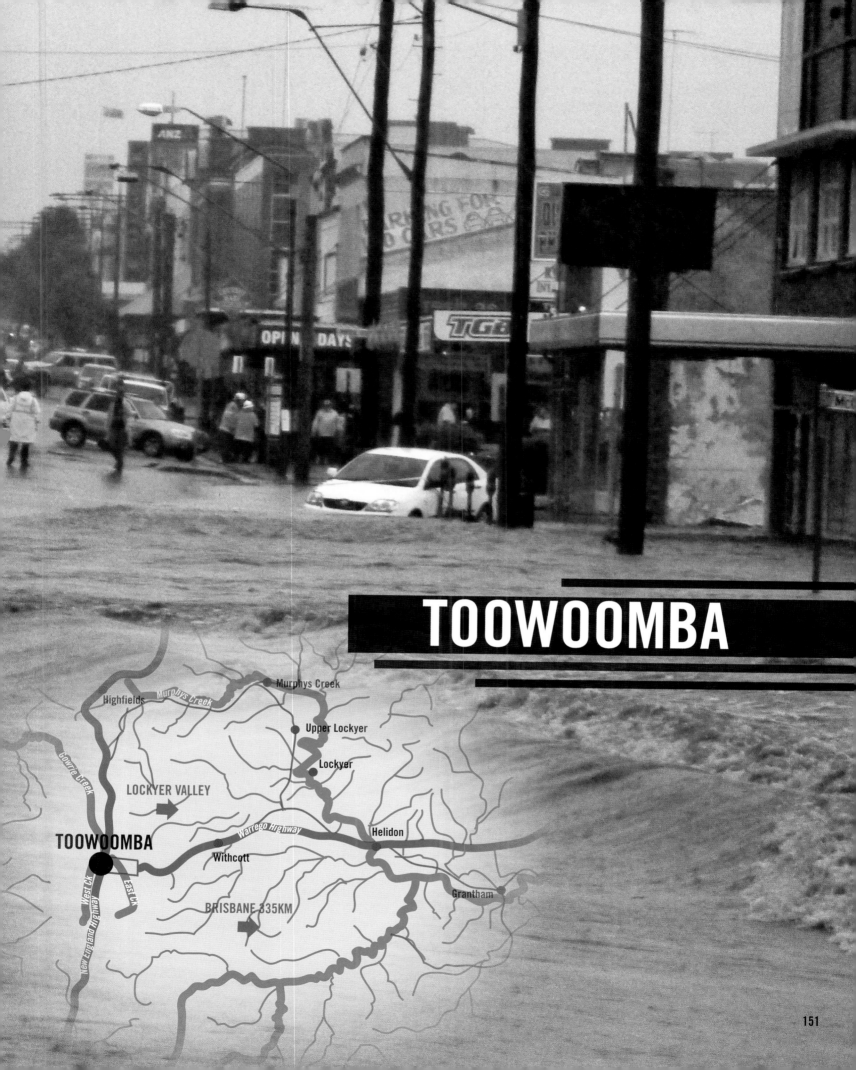

TOOWOOMBA

Highfields
Murphys Creek
Murphys Creek
Upper Lockyer
Lockyer
Gowrie Creek
LOCKYER VALLEY
Warrego Highway
Helidon
TOOWOOMBA
Withcott
West Ck
East Ck
New England Highway
Grantham
BRISBANE 335KM

DEVASTATING DELUGE THUNDERED THROUGH TOWN

IT WOULD NATURALLY BE EXPECTED THAT TOOWOOMBA AT 700 METRES ABOVE SEA-LEVEL WOULD BE IMMUNE FROM FLOODING; BUT BEING IN THE SHALLOW CRATER OF AN ANCIENT VOLCANO, IT IS BOWL-SHAPED AND CONTAINS SWAMPY AREAS FED FROM MOUNTAIN SPRINGS. THE WATERWAYS OF THE CREEKS HAVE BEEN MODIFIED OVER THE YEARS AS DEVELOPMENTS HAVE TAKEN PLACE ALONG THE BANKS, INCREASING SURFACE RUN-OFF AND A TENDENCY TO FLOOD. EXTENSIVE FLOOD MITIGATION WORKS WERE BEGUN IN 1998 AND BY DECEMBER 2010, ABOUT TWO-THIRDS OF THE PROGRAM HAD BEEN COMPLETED.

During December 2010, Toowoomba received more than 300mm of rain, most of which soaked into the dry ground and did little to supplement the city's critically low water reserves. In the first week of January 2011, further rain fell, and although some flooding episodes occurred, the residents were cheered by the rising levels in the dams.

From around 1.00pm on January 10th, however, an intense, slow-moving sequence of thunderstorms poured torrential rain over the Great Dividing Range, Toowoomba receiving up to 160mm in one and a half hours.

Chaos erupted almost instantly. The rushing waters spread beyond the inadequate creek beds and over-topped the bridges, which impeded the water flow as vehicles, vegetation, and other debris of all sizes and varieties piled up against the bridge structures and crumpled railings. Roads became rivers, and a huge wave of brown water charged into the CBD, invading shops and sweeping cars aside. Vehicles parked above the creek banks were gathered up by the torrent and tumbled away downstream. Lounge chairs swirled out of a furniture shop and, as the waters receded, posed as comfortable bus-stops in odd places along the streets, whilst an inner-city dwelling was exposed to public inspection when a wall collapsed. Further wreckage occurred in many suburban properties.

Emergency services responded to numerous calls for help, involving several rescues. Sadly, two lives were lost; a thirteen year old boy, Jordan Rice, and his mother Donna.

By 3.00pm the worst of the flooding was over and the water in town was receding quite rapidly as it surged on westward towards Oakey. Anxiety still remained, however, until people were able to locate or make contact with those who had been stranded in town. Some who had been out of town were unable to return, as landslides and road damage had cut the highways.

A subdued silence was noticeable in the mud-laden CBD on the following day as people took stock of their damages. Once again, the Army and many kind volunteers were active in helping clean-up and restoring the flood-ravaged properties.

Whilst further flood-mitigating strategies have yet to be implemented, it is still a question whether in such an extreme set of circumstances they would have been sufficient. It is certainly to be hoped, however, that such an unusual event never occurs again.

FLOOD

TOOWOOMBA

- **Dec 2010**
  more than 300mm of rain falls in
  Toowoomba. Combined water storage
  in dams below 10%.

- **Jan 2nd-8th 2011**
  160mm rainfall in Toowoomba.

- **Jan 9th 2011**
  Another 84mm rain.

- **Jan 10th 2011**
  9.00am – rain falling.

- **12.00noon**
  Rain increasing.

- **1.00pm**
  Torrential downpours begin with
  thunderstorms.

- **1.30pm – 2.30pm**
  160mm rain falls in one hour.
  Floodwaters peak at 2.00pm in the
  CBD. 2 lives are lost.

FACTS

- 3.00pm
  Rain easing. Vehicles and debris scattered. At least 50 shops and businesses inundated. Bridges, railways and roads have been wrecked.

- 5.00pm
  Water subsided considerably from roads.

- **Jan 11th 2011**
  Some water supply issues remain. Much road damage evident. Authorities patrol CBD area. All dams full and overflowing

- **Jan 12th 2011**
  Parts of the CBD re-open. Volunteers assist with clean-up.

- **Jan 18th 2011**
  Visit from Queensland's Premier, Anna Bligh to inspect the CBD. Repair bill estimated at over $50 million, excluding Federal and State roads.

GEO. COSSARTS SADDLERY
Toowoomba

AN ENORMOUS WAVE OF
WATER

THIS IS ROB MERCER'S STORY. ROB IS PART OWNER OF GEO. COSSARTS SADDLERY, A HANDCRAFT/HOBBY SHOP THAT HAS BEEN A FEATURE OF DOWNTOWN TOOWOOMBA SINCE 1904. DURING THAT TIME, OVER A HUNDRED YEARS, THERE HAVE ONLY BEEN TWO OTHER NOTABLE FLOODS, AND ROB SAYS THAT THEY WERE NOWHERE NEAR THE SCALE OF THE JANUARY 2011 CATACLYSM.

We never thought we could get that much water in Toowoomba - all we had time to do was to react, we didn't have time to think, 'Do I have time to do this? Will this be the problem?' A sudden cloud burst and then an enormous wave of water just rocketed through the whole place. It came with a deafening roar I never want to hear again. Staff acted instinctively. As the water built up against the front doors, an employee gallantly held them shut using all his strength. He was bracing himself on the counter, while the water outside quickly rose to three feet. Other staff, racing against time, hurried around putting things up on benches. The tremendous force against the doors was becoming too great to hold, so we made the awful decision to let go and race upstairs, grabbing the computers off the main counter as we went. As the doors were let go they literally exploded open and water rushed in, shifting everything in its path.

We had almost 5.5 feet of water through the shop. As the murky red-brown torrent poured in, so did the furniture from the shop across the road. It literally pushed our stuff out through the back doors. These doors open inwards but with the enormous water pressure behind them, they exploded and out everything went.

The most terrible thing was not being able to locate Mum and some other staff members. After a frantic 10-15 minutes, not knowing whether they had escaped, I located them sheltering upstairs, still in the shop. I had to wait for the water to go down enough to wade in to look for them. My legs were burnt red raw from being in that horrible, acidic water.

So much went out the door - we lost $150 000 in stock alone. We lost shop furnishings, display cabinets; anything that was five foot five and below, went. Even our antique fridge! The force of the torrent moved our safe three feet- and it's a heavy safe. Two ladies from the shop next to us were swept right into our shop! Very sadly, we lost a well-known employee, Bruce Warhurst from Postmans Ridge. It was his day off. Life will never be the same here.

I opened the shop doors the next morning, looked in and thought 'How am I going to clean this up??' By Tuesday afternoon, it was done! I never knew Toowoomba had it in it. We had strangers saying 'Can I give you a hand?' There was such great community spirit - you hope it never dies. Everyone wanted to help. Some of our model cars were returned to us from 8 km away! Unfortunately, because of the acidic water, they rusted out within two days.

I think I'll always panic about heavy rain now. I am terrified when a storm comes through – How much rain is going to fall? Everyone will feel the effects of this disaster for years to come.

Russell Street in flood 1906
- Source: Local History and Robinson Collections - Toowoomba City Library

Russell Street in flood 2011

DEBRIS STREWN RUSSELL STREET

ROWES FURNITURE
Toowoomba

RECLINERS RODE OUT ON THE
TIDE

STAFF AT ROWES FURNITURE STORE HAD NO TIME TO DO ANYTHING WHEN WATERS SURGED UP RUSSELL STREET IN TOOWOOMBA'S CBD.

The water was first observed by a staff member as it reached Rowes building on the corner of Russell and Victoria Streets, but there was no keeping the swelling tide out of the shop as the electric front doors had jammed open. The foul torrent poured in, firstly through the front doors and then through the back door as well, reaching a height of 170 centimetres in fifteen minutes.

The showroom stock of quality lounges and recliners swirled round chaotically on the muddy tide, smashing the glass windows and flowing out into the flooded street. After leaving the shop, some chairs were carried across the roadway, a few breaking through the front doors of the National Hotel and others entering Cossarts saddlery. As the water subsided, the gutters opposite Rowes were lined with soggy, mud-stained and battered lounge chairs, whilst the showroom they had come from was a very sorry sight, with saturated carpets laden with silt and broken glass, and slimy, brown stains on the walls indicating the height reached by the water.

Despite the wreckage and considerable loss of stock, the showrooms were cleaned and restored, and the business was back in operation five weeks later.

KNIGHTS LAUNDRY

Toowoomba

EVERYTHING
UNSALVAGABLE

KNIGHTS COMMERCIAL LAUNDRY SERVICE HAS BEEN PROVIDING CLEAN LINEN TO THE HOSPITALITY INDUSTRY FOR 114 YEARS, AND IN THAT TIME THE PREMISES HAS NEVER BEEN THREATENED BY FLOODWATERS… UNTIL NOW!

Staff watched helplessly as the water rose to armpit level inside the building, soiling linen and ruining expensive machinery. A technician had to be flown out from Germany at the company's expense, and spent a week working to get their Continuous Batch Washer - capable of washing 50 kilo's of linen in two and a half minutes - operational again.

All their vehicles had to be replaced. Staff waded gingerly into the filthy water to stop them floating away, but silt and water damage rendered them useless.

THE TORRENT SPARED
NOTHING

ALTHOUGH TOOWOOMBA PIE SHOP FRANCHISEE VICTORIA TOWNSEND AND HUSBAND STUART HAD BEEN PROUD OWNERS OF THE NEW STORE "BIG DAD'S" FOR JUST FIVE WEEKS, THE RUTHVEN STREET BUSINESS WAS ALREADY THRIVING. "WE WERE JUST GETTING TO KNOW OUR CUSTOMERS AND WE WERE DOING REALLY WELL. IT WAS A NORMAL DAY, BUT IT CHANGED IN A HEARTBEAT."

ABRUPTLY, THEIR EXCITING NEW VENTURE TURNED NIGHTMARE INSTEAD.

Vicki was cheerfully serving a builder who had left his ute parked under the shop's awning. As he took his change and turned towards the exit, his bewildered eyes met an empty parking spot. "Where's the ute?" he asked. All too rapidly it dawned on him; the water was rising so quickly, the ute had just floated away. The builder tore out of the shop and began providing assistance to others who had also been caught unawares.

Inside the shop were Vicki, her two daughters Belle, 9, Johanna, 7, and an employee, Colleen. Colleen left when the water started coming up, but the family remained behind in a valiant attempt to keep the water out of the shop, or at least save the cabinets. Before too long, Vicki recognised the futility of the battle, and decided they had better leave. As she tried the door, horror flooded through her. The pressure of the surging water was so strong that they couldn't budge the sliding glass doors. They were trapped!

Vicki urgently rang 000, but despite continuous frantic attempts only got the engaged signal. Emergency services were stretched to the limit. Having two of her children with her magnified the trauma; there were three lives at stake here, two of them little. She made a desperate phone call to her father, John Watson. How he eventually managed to make his way through the turbulent water to the scene is a wonder; but for now they were on their own.

Outside, heavy trucks were pulled along like toys in the current and became wedged under bridges. Cars banked up behind them, blocking the flow and adding to the excessive flooding. As they peered, terrified, through the large glass windows, a huge silo at Allied Mills flour mill toppled and collapsed. This was inconceivable! It, too, became jammed on the Jellicoe Street Bridge, further obstructing the massive flow of water. The car park over the road, which overlooks the creek, was full of cars which all floated away, to be randomly strewn across the city.

Vicki describes with horror the sheer sound volume of the terrifying surge of water that tore away her dream; and very nearly their lives too. "There were things falling, glass breaking…all at once" The noise was earsplitting and discordant. "EVERYTHING was loud and frantic. The water was loud, the sirens were loud, the screams were loud."

Stuart arrived after he had been helping people move cars, but he could only look helplessly from outside the toughened glass windows. He and others hammered frantically on the resistant glass in a frenzied attempt to smash their way through. Inside the shop, his family screamed and struggled for their lives as the 3m high torrent swept through, pinning Vicki and her two daughters inside the building. Vicki was trying desperately to keep a hold on her younger daughter when the force of the torrent ripped out a glass pane, releasing her and the girls with it.

Jo was screaming, while Belle attempted to calm her, repeating "It's going to be alright, Jo". Vicki is sure that had she had Joshua there with her too, she wouldn't have been able to manage, and they would have lost one of the children. But suddenly, helping hands were there, reaching out. Stuart grabbed the glass pane so it wouldn't hurt anyone. Vicki threw Johanna to a complete stranger who caught her and waded to higher ground. Belle, a strong swimmer, swam her way to safety.

Across the road, three employees of Downs Group Training were dragged into the water, but managed to avoid being swept away by clinging to the window frame on the shop front for hours in rushing water (See page 162). Finally the water went down and completely exhausted, they were able to let go.

Days later, the Pie Shop emerged from the wall of floodwater that had cut a swathe of destruction through Toowoomba, nothing more than a battered shell. Situated on the banks of East Creek, it was directly in the firing line of the 'tsunami'. The torrent spared nothing. "I've lost absolutely everything but I have my girls, so it doesn't matter," says Vicki, who is desperate to get back behind the counter and start serving her customers again. But first, the whole shop will have to be gutted, and all the Gyprock pulled down. The studs need to be sanitised and dried and then re sheeted. The vinyl will have to be pulled up, and the concrete sanitised and re-covered.

fears. Even the aluminium shop front needs to be pulled apart, sanitised and reassembled. It will be cheaper just to replace the whole shop front. Their landlord's insurance covers the building, but all the trolleys, shelving, pie racks, etc. must be destroyed. Anything with direct food contact is very critical.

The most uplifting thing was the generosity of the people who helped. "The support from the community has been amazing," said Victoria, who received a letter from a couple in Tasmania. They had been reading an article on the floods whilst in a doctor's waiting room, and were moved by her story. Enclosed was a $50 cheque to help them get going again. Vicki's Mum, Mrs. Watson said, "A disaster brings out the good side of people. Friends and strangers asking 'Hey, I feel for you, how can I help?'"

Some came and helped all day; the cleaning up operation was daunting. Mr. Watson said, "On the Thursday, about 3:00, the willing helpers started to drop off. And I'm thinking it's up to me to clean these walls. About 3:15 a big fire truck turns up and they asked "Is there anything we can do to help?" Seven or eight of them cleaned up heaps of silt and dirt outside, and cleaned off the walls inside." Mr. Watson found out later that those crew members were on voluntary service and

should have been off duty. Other people, who had no way of physically helping, contributed what they did have. An old lady came in with her little dog, wanting to amuse the kids.

Somebody brought in a front end loader and a truck for the ruined food and equipment. Details were recorded meticulously for the insurance company, who promptly advised them not to send their records, as they didn't have enough room to store all the proof of damage! But the recovery process from January 10's flash flood will be a long one. Her husband Stuart got a bad foot infection as a result of working in the filthy sludge in the shop, even though he was wearing joggers. His feet swelled up with the infection, and he couldn't wear shoes for quite some time.

Through it all, Vicki is determined to put on her best front, rising to each challenge as it comes. She has been making the most of her enforced break to spend more time with her family, the family that came so close to being lost forever. And she swears she'll bounce back - "the new store will be better than it was before!"

IT'S COMING UP THE
STAIRS!

DOWNS GROUP TRAINING CENTRE OCCUPIES TWO BUILDINGS ON RUTHVEN STREET, EITHER SIDE OF A LANEWAY. THE SECOND BUILDING AND THE CAR PARK ARE ON AN ELEVATED CONCRETE SLAB ABOVE EAST CREEK, WHICH IS USUALLY A MERE TRICKLE OF WATER, ALTHOUGH IT CAN SWELL QUITE RAPIDLY DURING RAIN.

The creeks rose and fell several times during the first week of January 2011. Darren McDonell, the Operations Manager, and his staff watched anxiously for any signs of flooding. Unfortunately, the water rises so rapidly that there is very little warning, and when the creeks broke their banks on the Friday, the lower areas were inundated. Downstairs company records and equipment were soaked, and filthy deposits of mud were left behind after the waters receded.

Darren and his staff set to work to clean the place up again, fervently hoping they'd seen the worst. However, on Sunday, rain was falling again, and Darren made four trips to the premises that afternoon to check on the creeks and take a few extra precautions. He returned to work early on Monday, relieved to find everything safe, and following an uneventful morning, went home for lunch. He'd hardly sat down with his kids when there was a call from the Training Centre.

"Hey, Darren! You'd better get back here quick! The water's on its way up again!" The two children, a fourteen year old girl and her twelve year old brother, jumped into the car with their father. The water had risen considerably and some employees moved their cars to higher ground up the road. Other vehicles, including Darren's, were considered safe enough in the elevated parking area.

The water came up with incredible speed. Darren's son, who had been given charge of the mobile phone to video the action, was soon yelling, "Dad! It's coming in the door!" and then "Dad! It's coming up the stairs!" The three remaining staff and the two children took refuge in the upstairs lunch room, from where they could see through the windows of the second building. The three employees who were over there had been inside the single storey building, but fearing the rapidly rising water, they decided that their only chance of escape was to get outside while they could. They grabbed onto a steel handrail outside the front door as the rushing water swirled around them, threatening to sweep them away.

Darren was concerned for their safety and took down a length of electrical cable, hoping to be able to get them over to the main building, but as he began to open the sliding door, the force of the water pushed it off the track. With the help of another employee, he had almost got it back, when with a mighty crack, the glass shattered and water came rushing in, surging up the stairs.

Not knowing how high the water was going to come was rather nerve-racking and the uneasy group in the lunch room decided that the only option left was to remove the bars from the window and climb out onto the shed roof. When Darren returned from searching for a screwdriver, he was amazed to discover that his daughter had found a hammer and had already broken two of the bars. With a man's pride at stake, he ordered her out of the way and broke the third one himself, making a much more ragged job of it than the girl had, much to his chagrin! He put his children out on the roof with two of the staff, while he and one other remained inside.

Over at the second building things were pretty grim. The window had broken in, so the girl was able to secure a higher grip on the window frame, while the two men continued to cling to the railing. Darren's encouraging shouts from the lunch room window were drowned by the roar of the water, and for an hour and a half they simply hung on, expecting at any moment to be hit by drifting debris and vehicles afloat on the churning torrent. Those on the roof at the main building could see others who had taken refuge on another rooftop nearby, whilst out on the street they watched motorists frozen in indecision as the force of the flood was felt. They watched helplessly as the supposedly safe vehicles in their own car park were rounded up by the relentlessly rising tide and jostled together along with an industrial bin. They could also hear desperate cries for help, which they found later to be coming from a neighbouring property, where three adults and a small child were huddled on top of their vehicle which had washed up beneath an awning.

Behind the building there was chaos as vehicles, furniture, fridges and all manner of debris rushing along in the maelstrom, reached the bridged confluence of East and West Creeks and could go no further. The wrecked bodies of eight cars were later extracted from beneath the bridge, where they had further contributed to the disaster by blocking the path of the water.

Once the rain subsided, the water began to recede visibly, the whole ordeal having lasted little more than an hour and a half. In the main building the water had risen to the second top step and had completely flooded the lower levels. Any precautions staff had taken to elevate equipment and machinery had proved useless, with welders, engine blocks and motors all ruined beyond repair.

Cleaning up took a week and a half. With the overwhelming help of staff and volunteers, many truckloads of sodden wreckage were removed. Darren expects that downstairs will probably be turned into car parking eventually and a general re-allocation of space will be required.

When asked if he thinks it might happen again, he replies with a look of absolute horror, "I sure hope not!"

THE RUSHING WATER SWIRLED AROUND THEM, THREATENING TO
SWEEP THEM AWAY

Maelstrom where two creeks join together

3 drenched staff surface (water level shown on white shirt)

waters at the peak

Staff hanging on to rail at the front of the building

Water in the shed behind main building at its peak

TOOWOOMBA

Swiftwater Rescuers

Stranded people take refuge on 4WD roof

Rescue workers prepare to search flood waters

Car pile-up

Damage to railway line - Dent Street

Flood ravaged Cement Mixer

Griffiths Street Power poles ready to go

Rescue in progress (note: man clinging to tree)

An attempt to save a Knights vehicle

rce of flood water caused this wall in Scholefield Street collapse.

Weale Street Bridge gone!

Water raging across Toowoomba Range road

165

BATTLING THE SAME
CALAMITY

THE COFFEE CLUB - CNR MARGARET AND VICTORIA ST-TOOWOOMBA
THE WEATHER WAS HORRENDOUS. HEAVY RAIN, FOREBODING DARK SKIES, YET IT HADN'T DAMPENED THE SPIRITS OF THE FEW CUSTOMERS WHO HAD BRAVED THE CONDITIONS AND CALLED IN FOR A WARMING COFFEE AND A BITE TO EAT AT THE COFFEE CLUB. HAPPY CUSTOMERS CHATTED AWAY, WITH ONE TABLE SUPPORTING EIGHT ELDERLY LADIES ENJOYING A CATCH UP OVER THE TRADITIONAL 'CUPPA'. STAFF WERE BUSY PREPARING THE FARE FOR WHICH THE ENTITY HAS BECOME SO WELL KNOWN.

Manager, Kate, perturbed by the rapidly rising creek directly across the road, rang her boss, Jon, who was busy managing another store. He advised it best to ride things out for another five minutes before making a decision. Kate kept busy, the customers content and seemingly unconcerned with what was transpiring outside. It all happened very quickly in the end. The swollen creek became a raging torrent and began buffeting their side door. The customers watched in utter disbelief as a motorist in a four wheel drive came around the corner in the blinding rain, driving straight into the rushing current, to be swept out of sight. Kate, still calm, tried to contact Jon again. Battling the same calamity just a few streets away, he did not answer the call.

Kate recalls with a deep breath, "I had to decide myself. It was time to get out." The customers and staff rallied quickly. It was unbelievable what they were witnessing. First there were the elderly ladies to be evacuated - Kate reckons on none of them being under seventy. The staff had to ferry them out through knee deep water and according to Kate, they cooperated perfectly. The emergency evacuation point in Market Plaza carpark was well under water, so in the teaming rain they headed to higher ground at Garden Town Shopping Centre.

The managers were the last to leave, locking the door behind them and wading out. The sight of cars being swept backwards down the creek, and the likelihood there could be people in them, was difficult to deal with. "It was like a horror movie. It was surreal", she recounts. "It was happening so quickly, there was no warning." The creek was rising rapidly and devouring everything before it. Within 10-15 minutes of evacuating the café, the pressure of the rising water burst the front glass, and the torrent roared in. She recoils at the recollection, "The whole place was devastated."

Kate wasn't worried so much about the shop at the time, she was just so thankful her customers were safe. "If the shop had been fuller that day, it could have been a far worse situation." The story, had they left it any longer to evacuate, would be reading very differently.

What Kate witnessed outside was terrifying, "Cars twisted like a piece of tin foil." A huge tank washed past and shattered as it was sucked under the bridge. A walk bridge from further upstream was torn off, and, along with cars which tumbled like toys in the torrent, it followed the same deadly path. She watched helplessly as a young man clung for his life to a tree in the raging current. Horror overcame her, as a vehicle swept towards the tree, hitting it with colossal force. How he managed to hang on remains a mystery. "I couldn't believe what I was seeing! I hope I never see anything like it again. I was in such utter disbelief at what was unfolding. Later on I went into shock…." Her voice lowers and she trembles, "I still find it hard to talk about".

Kate's husband, meanwhile, was safe at home, but his unfortunate workmates were trapped in the ceiling at work, and only escaped by kicking off the roof sheeting, and waiting on the rooftop for rescue.

The torrent subsided to reveal a devastated coffee shop. All 8 freezers, 5 fridges, the cold room, furniture and stock were contaminated and had to be removed. The place was thick with mud and the smell was horrendous - a far cry from the aroma of freshly ground coffee! Some of the staff lost cars; they were amongst the twenty or thirty vehicles that were damaged or swept away at the back of the shop. Kate's distress is obvious when she speaks of having to lay off staff while the premises are refurbished. "We'll rebuild. It will be a better store than what we had. The insurers have been good to us."

"The store was devastated, and a few lost cars…" Kate speaks slowly, her sympathy evident, "but that is minor compared to what some families have lost. It's very sad!"

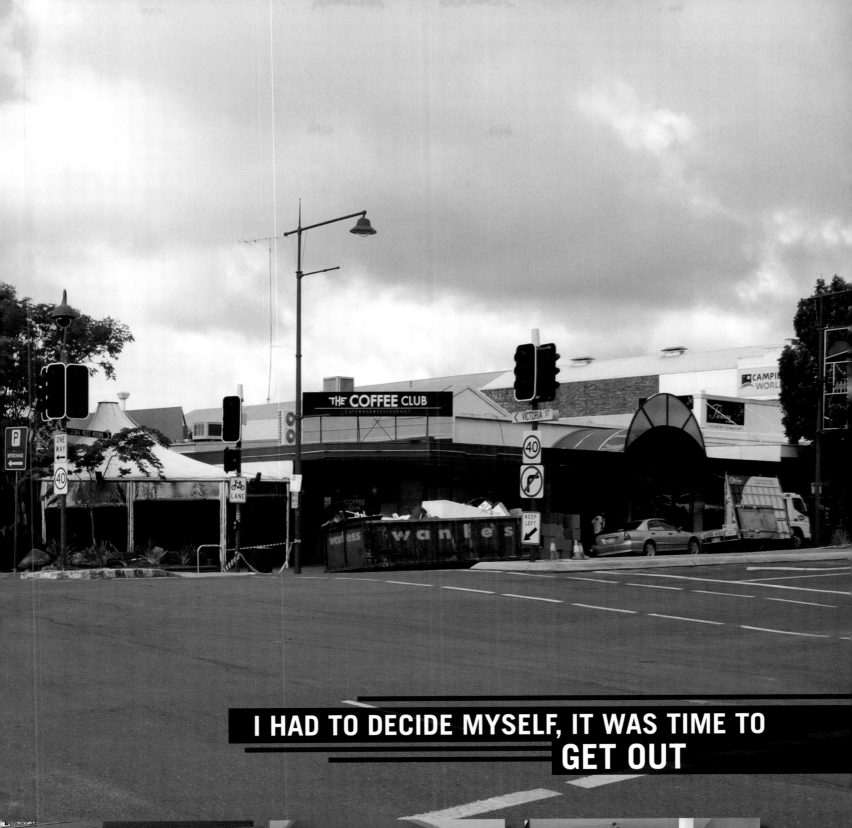

I HAD TO DECIDE MYSELF, IT WAS TIME TO
GET OUT

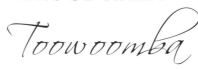

COURAGEOUS MID-STREAM
RESCUE

"I'D LIKE TO THINK THAT SOMEONE WOULD DO IT FOR MY WIFE AND CHILDREN" BRUCE RILEY'S COURAGEOUS MID-STREAM RESCUE IN TOOWOOMBA. BRUCE RILEY IS THE MANAGER OF THE WOW SIGHT AND SOUND STORE IN RUTHVEN ST, TOOWOOMBA. IT IS JUST ONE CITY BLOCK FROM EAST CREEK, ONE OF THE TWO MAIN STREAMS THAT TURNED INTO RAGING TORRENTS IN TOOWOOMBA'S EPIC FLOOD.

In the twenty-nine years that Bruce has worked in that vicinity, he has never seen water from East Creek break over the road, but in January 2011, he saw it happen twice.

Bruce recalls the events of Toowoomba's most infamous day with vivid clarity....

"Water was coming up the street and one of the young fellows from work had a car on the other side of East Creek that he wanted to get, so we went around there in the company van. When we crossed Chalk Drive on the other side of East Creek, there was no water over the road, only under the bridge. By the time we drove around into Chalk Drive and had almost reached the car, water was washing down Neil Street and entering the intersection with Chalk Drive, causing our van to stall. We pushed the van out of the water, and then pushed my worker's car out also, and by the time we had done that, in the space of ten or fifteen minutes, the whole of Chalk Drive was under about a metre and a half of powerfully surging water."

At the same time two lives were being threatened........

"We then realised that there was a car stalled at the intersection, with a lady in it, waving her arm out of the window. With another fellow who had been helping us, Tom, from Comtel, we took off towards the intersection, but finding the water up to our chests and flowing too swiftly, there was nothing we could do. The car then started to float and then stop, several times, travelling about twenty to thirty metres every four or five minutes, until it stopped about halfway down Chalk Drive where the creek had spread out and was not flowing so fast."

The opportunity was now for Bruce, Tom, and others to turn from anxious bystanders to gallant rescuers....

"We nicked some ropes and a sling out of a parked ute. Tom was a super knot tier. With the sling tied around me and two other fellows holding onto it, I waded out into the middle of Chalk Drive, tied the rope to another tree, and waded out to the car. I got the lady out and then the man, who was her husband's cousin, and helped them back to the tree, where they were assisted by one of the others, back along the rope."

"The twenty-two year old lady, who was expecting a baby shortly, was terrified through the whole ordeal. The two of them were lucky to be alive. The car had been facing into the stream, creating a wave that was washing right over it some of the time. Tom took them back to his office and called the ambulance."

The baby was born two weeks later, and Bruce accompanied The Courier-Mail to participate in an interview at their house. It was a satisfying sequel to that dramatic episode.

Bruce's unassuming description of his involvement in this heroic rescue is typical of the selfless spirit that shone in many of Toowoomba's citizens on that day of horror. When asked what motivated him to risk his life for others, he replied simply,

"I'd like to think that someone would do that for my wife and children!"

"WHEN THE GOING GETS TOUGH, THE TOUGH GO SHOPPING."

There's nothing like a little retail therapy to relieve the tension when a city is under siege from the greatest natural disaster it has ever seen.

At the height of the torrent, and with 600mm of water flowing through their store, WOW Sight and Sound had to turn shoppers away who, in spite of the flooded conditions, still wanted to come into the store!

"No, I'm sorry we can't serve you at the moment — we're in a spot of bother."

THE TWO OF THEM WERE
LUCKY TO BE ALIVE

TAKING EVERYTHING IN ITS
PATH

SUDGEN KERR, A FAMILY BUSINESS SELLING INDUSTRIAL ENGINES AND MOWERS, WAS STARTED BY THE CURRENT OWNER'S GRANDFATHER IN 1936. ITS PREMISES LOOKED STRONG ENOUGH TO TAKE AN EARTHQUAKE AND ITS STRENGTH WAS SURELY TESTED ON THE DAY OF TOOWOOMBA'S FLOODS. THE OWNERS PROVED TO BE AS STRONG AS THE BUILDING TO SAVE THE STOCK AND BUSINESS THEIR GRANDFATHER HAD ESTABLISHED.

There were no customers on the day that the rain became torrential and the creeks began to flood, and owner manager Steve Sugden was thankful that the business was not in the direct flow of it. He and his wife could see the creek rising more than they had ever seen before.

His wife went up the road to Myers, saw how rapidly the flood was developing, and rang urgently, "Get the cars out!" - the only warning they had. They quickly moved them to higher ground, and watched trees, logs and all sorts of things being carried down the creek. "Some car owners had no warning including the people next door who lost 4 cars – one virtually brand new. It floated down the creek, got caught under our sign, then got wedged over here near Myers. It was found a week later somewhere down the creek. Our sign was shown on the national news, with another car – a falcon ute - wedged under it, which meant that the water was up to your shoulders. It was flowing fast, sort of swirling, just like a dam or a tank filling up, and cars were being sucked into it from the carpark."

Then a great wall of water - taking everything in its path, converging into a massive "inland tsunami" - went through the centre of town. At one point 300 metres wide, it crept rapidly up to the Sudgen building and began leaking into the building. It came in under the windows, under the door, around the windows, the back door, through any available space. The Sudgens moved all they could to higher ground - onto the front counter, anywhere high - but big things like generators had to be left where they were. The water came 750mm in their lower showroom – with glass all round which held the water out, like an inside-out fish bowl. " When your shopfront looks like you're in a fish bowl - that's trouble" Steve said.

The Sugden's staff were trapped inside unable to force the doors open. "We were stuck in here. We couldn't open any doors because of the pressure of water. But then again, we didn't think of getting out. It started as only ankle deep, then it was knee deep, and then it was over your knees, and then .... It kept going. All we thought about was trying to save what we could… getting stuff up onto shelves and counters, anywhere high, not knowing if it was going to be half an inch, 2 inches or 2 feet deep. It began to leak in under the sliding glass doors out the front, onto the tiles, slowly starting to fill up this whole carpeted area, so we put stock up on the step and we got those big generators and put them up there, but then it filled up to there, and kept going up to the next step. So we kept putting stuff higher. Then it was the workshop, then the computer… everything was going under – what could we do? The four of us were going crazy. We just tried to save what we could of the expensive stock. Bottles of oil and all sorts of

things were floating around. Tubs were floating around, but the mowers didn't, they stayed where they were!" Next time we'll have a winch and a strap and we'll just say…That level was the 2011 flood. Now we're going to make sure we can winch 'em to the ceiling."

"Outside the fishbowl - everything was happening, and only 20 metres away, people were being washed down the street, cars were just bobbing along like corks, debris, whatever! You just couldn't believe what you were seeing!" There was a new steel bridge across the way and while Steve was watching the water rise over it between frantically moving stock, he suddenly yelled "There goes the bridge!" and it just floated away pushed along by the logs, cars and trees floating down the road.

"We saw a lady with kids sitting on the roof of a car. As rescuers tried to reach them, one with a rope tied around his waist, another car came floating by, hit the lady's car, and knocked them into the charging water. Fortunately they were washed toward Grand Central carpark, grabbed a railing and escaped. Later they thanked the men who tried to save them. Didn't get their names. No one knows who they were or where they came from. They were alive and that's the main thing". Steve went on to say, "I couldn't sleep properly for nights. Nightmares of floods! I don't want to ever see that again. When water starts getting above your waist, chest height, forget stock, all you can think about is getting yourself and any others who are in the shop with you to safety."

The business is still in limbo. Much has been lost, including many thousands of dollars worth of mowers and engines ruined or damaged, and thousands of spare parts to be counted and either salvaged or thrown out. "For the last month we've been 7 days a week, and an average of 12 hours a day, trying to restore order. We had to pressure clean our floors, move shelving and everything else to get the mud out. Every shelf, stand and step was coated with thick mud. We had to move 20 engines, every one was bolted down. Every shelf had to come off, and every stand so we could get the mud – and the carpet - out, before the carpet layers could come to replace it. Ten times worse than a stocktake- clean it, sort it, throw it. There's never been a dull moment for about 4 weeks".

"There is still another 6 months of cleaning, you can only get to it when you can, and do a bit more every day - and it's hard when you're burning the candle on both ends and it's lighted in the middle as well".

Many people and family came to offer a hand, "If we had more people here we would have been falling over each other. It was so good!"

"We were sure affected badly, but many were worse off than us. We're still alive with a roof over our heads and a shop we can use. Loyal customers have been coming in and saying, "We want to support you, you have always been here and you have been hit, and we want to buy from you." That is great. And so Sudgen Kerr continues on, with a will to survive and to grow, as strong and old as its foundations.

171

Chalk Drive carpark

Destroyed Truck

Emergency Services at work

TOOWOOMBA

James Street

Margaret Street

South Street

Swiftwater Rescuer

oded Businesses

Gowie Street

Jelico Street

mes Street

woomba City flooded

Van caught under Herries Street bridge

Vehicle pulled from West Creek

WE JUST RAN OUT OF TIME

MURRAY'S ART & FRAMING HAS BEEN SELLING ART SUPPLIES, PICTURE FRAMING, OFFERING ART CLASSES AND RUNNING A GALLERY FOR THE LAST 65 YEARS. IT HAS SURVIVED A FIRE, A RECESSION AND NOW A FLOOD. WHEN ASKED TO SUMMARISE WHAT HE MOST WANTED TO SAY ABOUT THE LATEST GUT-WRENCHING EXPERIENCE OF COMPLETE INUNDATION AND STOCK OBLITERATION, PETER GRANFIELD, THE OWNER OF THE BUSINESS, RESPONDED, "WELL, WE'VE STILL GOT OUR LIVES, STILL GOT OUR SHOP AND WE'VE STILL GOT FAITH IN GOD".

Peter went on to say, "On the Monday, when it started to rain heavily and we could see that a flood was imminent, we tried to get everything of value, like custom artwork waiting to be framed above what we expected the flood level to be. But the water rose so quickly that we just ran out of time, and all our efforts proved to be a waste of energy, because as the water came up the benches we had put the stuff on floated, rolled over and tipped everything into the water."

"The water started coming in through the back door of the workshop, but as the water backed up in Ruthven Street, it came in the front door as well. Part of the problem was that the 3 arch bridge in Ruthven Street had at least 2 cars jammed under it, blocking the flow. To give you some idea of the strength of the water, one of two 44 gallon (200litre) drums we have in our workshop for broken glass floated from the back door, about 15 metres through the workshop and got deposited at the front."

When the clean-up began, we had plenty of offers of help from dedicated volunteers, even despite accidents. "One of the guys helping me fell on a bit of glass which sliced his leg deeply. He was an intensive care nurse, and said 'I'd better go and get some stitches in this, but I'll be back afterwards', and sure enough, he was back."

"We had to throw out 4 skip bins, 2 council tip trucks and about five 2 cubic metre industrial bins of ruined stock. Some of the artwork was worth several thousand dollars, and others were maybe worth 10 dollars, but everything was of high sentimental value. Frustratingly, there was so much that had already been framed, and the customer had been rung and asked to come and collect it, but they hadn't got around to it. Most customers have been understanding. Others would say, 'it's been damaged; I want a discount', and I used to think, 'Thanks, kick me while I'm down, why don't you?'"

Initially, the insurance company refused to pay out as it was a flood and not storm damage they were insuring for but, fortunately, the insurance council of Australia decreed that everything affected in Toowoomba was storm damage. But the Art shop lost all records – everything - including hard drives and computer records, so they now have to construct an estimate for insurance purposes. They are paying their staff out of savings, whilst trading with partial stock and trying to repair damaged items.

The shopfront is still gutted, so what was salvaged and everything else is being kept upstairs until it can be refitted. A nearby shop had its insurance company call in an independent expert, he took swabs of the floor, and determined that it has been contaminated with sewage, so it's got to be desludged, treated, refilled with sand, reswabbed and finally refloored before the problem will be fixed.

"It would have been easy to walk away" Peter said, "but my shop is my superannuation fund, I must rebuild so that I can sell it to fund my retirement, because I'm old enough and ready to retire. But I am restful about it all in the knowledge that 'all things work together for good for those who love God and all that happens is according His plan.'"

INSIDE MURRAY'S ART & FRAMING WORKSHOP

Nobby

CONFUSION WAS
TOTAL

BOB MALONE REALLY BELIEVES THAT NOBBY IS A GREAT PLACE TO LIVE. THE FIRIES, THE SES, THE POLICE, AND EVERYONE KNOWS ONE ANOTHER ON A FIRST NAME BASIS AND IN AN EMERGENCY WE ALL WORK TOGETHER.

On the Monday of the bad flooding, a friend from Toowoomba rang and called for a truck. So we sent one in, and they began screaming out for more. I thought there were probably a few cars - no-one told me how bad it was, and I hadn't seen the news. When we got there, we saw a massive number of vehicles all stacked up on top of one another in a car park. We just grabbed them without asking for signatures or forms. It takes ½ to ¾ hr per car, I reckon there was a hundred, all from the car park in Chalk Drive, and by the time the car park was emptied, it was 1:30am on Tuesday morning. Then we drove around town, picking more up. It just happened so quickly.

There were a huge number of cars jammed under the bridge in Chalk Drive, blocking the flow of water. I got one vehicle out, came back and they said there's another down in under there, and kept going. Until we'd cleared the front ones we couldn't see those further in. There were cars in the pencil pine trees along that car park side in Short Drive. We couldn't see them, they just kept on floating out. Those that ended up in the creek got jammed up against the bridge near Neil Street. Thousands of things were happening all at once. Everybody was making phone calls, the police were rescuing people. Warwick callers wanted to know what's going on, confusion was total. One car was washed off Spring Creek Bridge and still hasn't been found — it just disappeared. There were really big holes on the other side of the bridge, it must have sunk into one. There was a big, yellow Windscreens O'Brien Hi-ace van in Spring Creek which is usually not much of a creek: a policeman walked out with a rope to rescue the driver. Four days later its roof reappeared!

That little creek is usually the pleasantest little thing, always trickling and fed from a spring that starts up on the hill: when it rains the water runs into it, and then flows into the Condamine River. This day it was a raging torrent! The abutments of the railway bridge got eaten away, and all the railway line from Nobby to Clifton too — it is still out, with tracks hanging in mid-air.

I can't imagine how many cars would be in the insurance company car parks at the moment - thousands. Also aircraft - we had to cut the tail off to get one aircraft out - I just pulled it off sideways. It will never fly again. I do aircraft transports for a bloke in Toowoomba; the insurance company told him that they've got to move

them somehow, so he got me to pull the wings off another one. It got washed about 2-3kms down the river.

In a paddock over in Clifton, an old dry well from fifty years ago which had been covered up, was exposed when the stream, ten metres down, started flowing again and it gradually flushed all the silt away. It was in the middle of the paddock and old mate is slashing his sorghum in the paddock and the tractor just went 'flump' straight down in the hole and knocked him unconscious. When he came to, the tractor was still running! Luckily it couldn't go anywhere - the wheels were stuck in the hole and it was too big to go down the well. The sorghum was 2ft high and he wouldn't have seen anything, he was driving along and next minute just dropped out of sight. The well had disappeared forty years ago and everyone had forgotten about it.

All the services are flat strap at the moment - builders, plumbers, electricians the lot; it's a real stimulus to the economy and probably the only ones that don't like it would be the insurance companies. They've so far paid us for probably half the cars we've done and I really can't fault any of them. And if a car's been under water they don't inspect it, they just write it off and make sure that it can never be resold. If they didn't, somebody would surely bodgie it up and sell it to an unsuspecting buyer — who would be buying worthless junk.

LOCKYER VALLEY

GRANTHAM, MURPHYS CREEK, POSTMANS RIDGE, WITHCOTT, HELIDON, LAIDLEY AND FOREST HILL

MURPHYS CREEK

Murphys Creek

UPPER LOCKYER

TOOWOOMBA

LOCKYER VALLEY

POSTMANS RIDGE

Warrego Highway

HELIDON

WITHCOTT

Lockyer Creek

BRISBANE 127KM

GRANTHAM

FOREST HILL

Flagstone Creek

LAIDLEY

THE LOCKYER VALLEY IS THE NAME GIVEN TO THE FERTILE BLACK SOIL PLAINS BELOW THE GREAT DIVIDING RANGE, EAST OF TOOWOOMBA. THE TOWNS OF SPRING BLUFF AND MURPHY'S CREEK ARE LOCATED ABOVE THE VALLEY, WITH WITHCOTT AND POSTMANS RIDGE LOWER IN THE FOOTHILLS. HELIDON, GRANTHAM, FOREST HILL AND LAIDLEY ARE TOWNSHIPS WITHIN THE VALLEY, HELIDON BEING FAMOUS FOR ITS SANDSTONE AND MINERAL SPAS AND GRANTHAM, IN ADDITION TO AGRICULTURE, PRODUCING AND EXPORTING FINE BEEF.

A wide variety of vegetable crops flourish in the valley all year round and the region is referred to as a 'salad bowl'. At any time of year there are back-packers stopping for a short period to earn a few dollars by helping with the harvests. Produce is sent to all major cities and supermarkets, and overseas exports from the area are increasing every year. Fresh produce can also be purchased locally at several roadside markets. Many historic sites in the towns reflect the valley's early European culture, and the beautiful landscaped gardens of the heritage-listed Spring Bluff railway station are a blaze of colour during Toowoomba's annual Carnival of Flowers.

Lockyer Valley is surrounded on three sides by mountainous country and many creeks originating high in the ranges flow through the plains, eventually finding their way into Lockyer Creek, which joins the Brisbane River below the Wivenhoe Dam.

CATASTROPHIC 'TSUNAMI' DESTROYS THE LOCKYER VALLEY

THE LOCKYER CATCHMENT RECEIVED SATURATING RAINS DURING DECEMBER 2010, BUT NO-ONE ANTICIPATED THE DISASTER THAT WAS YET TO BEFALL THE VALLEY'S COMMUNITY OF 37,000 PEOPLE. ON JANUARY 10TH, 2011, THE SAME INTENSE BAND OF THUNDERSTORMS AND HEAVY RAIN THAT DEVASTATED TOOWOOMBA, SHEETED DOWN IN TORRENTS OVER THE STEEP MOUNTAIN ESCARPMENTS AND LOCKYER CATCHMENTS, CAUSING AN UNBELIEVABLE VOLUME OF WATER TO CASCADE DOWN EVERY MOUNTAIN VALLEY AND RAVINE. THE NORMAL WATERCOURSES WERE COMPLETELY OVERWHELMED AS THE WATER GATHERED INTO ONE ALMIGHTY WAVE THAT CRASHED DOWN THE RANGES WITH INCREDIBLE FORCE AND VIOLENCE, UPROOTING AND SPLINTERING TREES, LAYING BARE THE LANDSCAPE AND DEMOLISHING HOMES, SHEDS AND ANYTHING THAT STOOD IN ITS PATH, CARRYING MANY OF ITS BATTERED TROPHIES WITH IT TO USE AS WEAPONS OF DESTRUCTION ELSEWHERE. VEGETABLE CROPS WERE RIPPED FROM THE FARMS AND THE DAMAGE TO LOCAL INFRASTRUCTURE WAS ENORMOUS.

Withcott township was suddenly inundated, any sandbagging precautions that had worked the time before being virtually useless in this deluge. The violent surge of water forced entry into homes and businesses with disastrous results. The town was completely cut off by landslides on the highway above and flooding across the roads below. Much damage was done and some residents had to be rescued from rooftops.

Murphys Creek, Postmans Ridge and Helidon were very severely ravaged as the turbulent deluge tore through, tossing vehicles around like unwanted toys and tearing homes to pieces. Residents had no warning other than the tremendous roar of the approaching torrent, and sadly, some were caught by the floods and lost their lives.

Forest Hill and Laidley experienced extreme flooding also, requiring many evacuations and rooftop rescues, the failing light and poor weather conditions making it extremely difficult and hazardous for the rescue crews.

THE TINY, CLOSE-KNIT TOWN OF GRANTHAM, ON THE JUNCTION OF SANDY AND LOCKYER CREEKS, WAS HIT HARDEST OF ALL, THE TREMENDOUS DEBRIS-LADEN WALL OF WATER THAT HAD HURTLED DOWN THE MOUNTAINS COMBINING WITH THE RUSHING SWOLLEN CREEKS TO FORM A DEADLY TORRENT THAT DEMOLISHED MOST OF THE TOWN, TRAGICALLY TAKING SOME PRECIOUS LIVES WITH IT. MOUNTAINS OF DEBRIS WERE CAUGHT UP IN THE RAILWAY BRIDGE, HUNG UPON FENCES, CAUGHT UP IN TREES OR STREWN OVER THE SURROUNDING FARMS, ALL BEING BOUND TOGETHER AND OVERLAID WITH THICK LAYERS OF FOUL-SMELLING MUD.

Rescue operations were a mammoth task in Grantham, where many from the population of 370 were missing. Army personnel waded through the tangled and matted sludge, painstakingly probing every inch of the countryside several times, pulling apart bundles of mud-bound debris and searching the wreckage of homes and vehicles. Several bodies were found, but sadly, some remain unaccounted for. One of the hardships faced by the residents was not being allowed back into the town for several days to take stock of the damage to their properties.

Hearts were deeply touched by this tragedy, and people responded with overwhelming support and generous donations, from basic personal needs, to offers of machinery to clear debris from roads and properties. The genuine kindness and compassion shown was greatly appreciated by the local survivors, but inquisitive intrusions into their private grief were naturally resented.

No amount of detailed discussion or poring over photographs will ever suffice to reveal the extent of the trauma endured by those townspeople. Even the rescue personnel that arrived on the scene soon afterwards said that they had no idea of what they would be up against, and that nothing reported to them could compare with actually witnessing it for themselves.

The 'inland tsunami' that devastated the Lockyer Valley in January 2011, has undoubtedly gouged out a permanent place in Queensland's memories.

FLOOD

LOCKYER VALLEY

- **December 2010**
  Significant rainfall saturates catchments of Lockyer Valley.

- **January 10th 2011**
  An extreme weather event delivers 160mm rain in 2 hours over Lockyer Valley and surrounding mountain escarpments.

- 8m tidal wave of floodwater and debris descends on Valley towns and countryside, devastating Grantham.

- Water rises at Helidon in 22 minutes

- Some parts of creek bed lowered by up to 2m, scoured to bedrock.

- 5,000 people fled their homes.

- 500 airlifted to safety from Laidley and Forest Hill.

- Lockyer Creek reached 18.92m before the gauge swept away.

- Helidon Creek at 5.2m before gauge swept away.

- Shipping container travelling at 78km/hr.

- Bridges, culverts, roads, railway lines destroyed.

- Efficient Evacuation Centre established at Murphys Creek Tavern.

- Facilities and equipment of Murphys Creek Rural Fire Brigade destroyed.

- Over 120 homes destroyed.

- 855 vehicles displaced.

- 80% of Council roads damaged.

FACTS

- **January 11th 2011 and onwards.**
  50 staff employed at Police Operations Centre

- 663km² searched and 131km of creekline.

- Entire creek line searched three times on foot and twice by helicopter.

- Communications difficulties impede recovery operations.

- 25 companies donated heavy equipment and labour.

- More than 50 driveways cleared of obstructions.

- Stranded pets and animals cared for by Gatton Agricultural College.

- Horse stranded in racing stable treads water for 30 hours.

- Danger from swimming snakes in water.

- 50 families left with nothing.

- Risks from contaminated water.

- Power cut to many properties.

- 3 platoons of soldiers assist with search.

- Photos of properties shown to anxious owners to show extent of damage.

- Preliminary estimates of $176 million for roads and drainage repairs.

- More than 20 lives lost in region.

- **January 18th 2011**
  Grantham residents allowed home.

Withcott

MIRACLE AT
WITHCOTT

WARNINGS CAME THROUGH THAT 'THE BIG ONE' WAS ON ITS WAY. WITHCOTT BUTCHER, MACHIEL 'MIC' HEYNS AND HIS DAUGHTER, RINA, THOUGHT THEY WERE PREPARED, BUT WHEN THE FLOODWATERS FROM THE STORM OF JANUARY 10TH, 2011, INUNDATED THEIR LITTLE TOWN, IT WAS BEYOND ANYTHING THEY COULD HAVE IMAGINED.

Machiel and his family came to Australia from South Africa 3 years ago and bought a motel in Helidon and a butcher's shop in Withcott. His wife, Este', runs the hotel, while Mic looks after the butcher shop, 'Stevemic Meats', with the help of an employee, John. Mic is a tough guy who's been around, an Action Force Commander who has 'seen it all' - and a man with a deep faith, a heart of gold and a smile that lights up the day.

The small shopping precinct at Withcott is located more than 200 metres from Gatton Creek, which runs along the back. Normally the creek is just a tiny, unimportant trickle, but the storm alerts were severe, so Machiel didn't take any chances. With the help of Rina and John, he prepared 40 sandbags and stacked them across the front of the butcher shop and also the vacant shop next door; they knew that if the vacant shop flooded, it would affect them too.

Then it started pouring with rain. Mic says "at first it was quite fun, everybody was excited, taking photos ...when all of a sudden, it happened so quickly, the next moment the joke was over. It was just water everywhere".

Machiel described the next few hours – a little drily – as "nonsense" – a chaotic, adrenalin-filled madness of trying to protect their livelihood from surging floodwaters. As the flood raged through Withcott, it seemed at first that sandbagging the front of the shop had been successful; the water rose - over the handrail in front of the shop, to higher than the windowsill, then even higher.

Then, completely without warning, water burst through the side wall of the shop – from the empty shop next door! Literally within seconds, they were inundated. What the Heyns didn't realise was that the door of the vacant shop had a broken window pane; the flood waters had poured into the shop and dammed up to over two metres high! All that water had to go somewhere and the weakest point was the wall between the shops.

The whole shop was full of water up to a metre deep and Mic, John and Rina were standing right in it! All around them was butchering equipment – saws, fridges, slicers – three phase electrical equipment – all plugged in, all running! The water

was so deep and the current so strong that it lifted a big display fridge right off the floor! For a few heart-stopping seconds, Rina was trapped by the floating fridge, until Mic jumped right over it and freed her.

What they did next is almost unbelievable.
With the water still pouring through the wall between the shops, the two Heyns' went out their back door and waded through the swift, waist-deep flood water to the front of the vacant shop. The only way to save their own shop was to release the 'dam'.

Machiel was about to go in when Rina said "No Dad – you will get wet!" and before he could stop her, she dived down into the murky, filthy flood, through the broken window and into the shop! She managed to break down the back door, which lowered the water level sufficiently to save both shops.

For two more hours, the Heyns' and John stood by the window, watching the devastation unfold. Then, as suddenly as it had begun, the worst was over and the mind-numbing task of cleaning up began. The filthiness of floodwater can only be understood by those who have experienced it – and for the Heyns' it was there in spades-full; load after back-breaking load of sticky black mud that had to be shovelled out and cleaned from every surface. They couldn't get back to the motel at Helidon where Este' was, so for two days straight they worked in their revolting dirty clothes and slept on the benches at night.

Meanwhile, up the hill at Helidon, Este' Heyns experienced her own little drama. The motel was on high ground so it was perfectly safe from the floods and it became an evacuation point. With no power to keep food fresh, Este' simply opened the motel and with the help of some very unexpected 'guests', she cared for sixty bedraggled refugees – some who arrived with nothing and had lost everything. For Machiel and Rina, the drama didn't end with the flood. The next day, a further warning was issued for a storm twice the size of the first! Orders for the entire

township to evacuate were broadcast, but the intrepid South African calculated that the water would rise to about 3 metres and he would be safe on the roof of the shop. So he decided to stay on despite the evacuation order and described the following night as 'the scariest' part of the whole experience.

Thankfully, that second storm bypassed Withcott and the town was spared from further damage. Through all this, Machiel Heyns and his family have emerged with their smiles and their deep faith in God, firmly intact. For the Heyns' witnessed their own miracle and nothing can shake their belief that they were protected from harm – and almost certain death – in a most amazing way.

After the floodwaters drained away, the electrical equipment in Stevemic Meats was still running and undamaged after being totally submerged! But that is not all. How does anyone explain how three people survived being surrounded by three-phase electrical motors that were all connected to the current without being electrocuted? Just dropping a hair-dryer into a bath can kill. So why aren't the Heyns' dead? Machiel just smiles, his English not quite up to the task of explaining his 'miracle at Withcott' – "if that is not the hand of God – there ain't a God!... there is a big God in heaven, mate..."

THERE'S CARS WASHING DOWN
THE STREET

"... SEE THAT MUD UP ON THE EAVES? A WALL OF WATER CAME THROUGH THREE METRES OVER THE ROOF. THAT'S THE BATHROOM; THE SPA GOT WASHED OUT. YOU'RE STANDING IN THE BEDROOM; THAT'S THE LOUNGE ROOM; THAT'S WHAT THE BACK OF THE PLACE LOOKED LIKE. THESE PICTURES WERE TAKEN A COUPLE OF DAYS AFTER THE FLOOD, WHEN WE WERE ALLOWED BACK IN. THAT'S THE SWIMMING POOL ... WITH THE LINING SUCKED OUT. THAT'S THE SIDE OF THE SHED ... WE HAD THE GATES SHUT TO KEEP THE STUFF IN; SO IT JUST SMASHED THE SHED UP ... SEE THE PURLINS UP ON THE ROOF; THEY'RE ALL BENT."

David Collison of Helidon, Lockyer Valley, Queensland, is walking us through his house six weeks after the flash flood tore through the town. The building is gutted - cleared as though preparing for renovations. His story is backed up with over 100 photographs of the sheer devastation. The damage is mind-boggling - in the pictures, a roof gutter hangs crazily down one side; water-soaked furniture lies in heaps; whole rooms are stripped to the wall studs. Mud is splattered over everything.

David's voice is the calm monotone of the rural man, but he cannot conceal the raw emotion he felt about the unprecedented volume of water which passed through his home.

Fortunately, no-one was at the home at the time.

"I found out when Diana [his partner] rang me from Toowoomba and said 'You won't believe this, there's cars washing down the street!' and she said 'Just duck home and make sure everything's all right.' ... so I ducked down the street to get some basic foodstuffs, and by the time I got back out to the highway the coppers had it blocked. So I went back to Gatton, which is right on the creek, and all the people were milling round – 'There's a big wall of water coming' – it was on the news, and everyone is panicking about it. I thought, 'once you get past Withcott ... the ground sort of spreads ... all the way to Brisbane."

"No-one had seen anything like this before – nor is likely to again. Look how high above the highway we are here. There's a long way between here and there, a lot of water between here and there, and it was this high – it's impossible to work it out. It was a once in a lifetime event... We'd had so much rain- about 4 inches (100mm) in a few hours, and then we got this big dump of water on the range – between Toowoomba Central and Withcott. They had five inches in twenty minutes, on ground that's already soaked. So you get this massive fall of water over ten thousand acres, and by the time it gets to the bottom of the range it's that deep, a wall of water five kilometres wide and nothing to stop it."

"The wall of water came alright, it lasted about twenty minutes and once it's gone it's gone. Not like an ocean where one wave follows the other – it was like a dam wall breaking. And if it happened at two or three in the morning when we were all asleep, then there'd be hundreds of us dead, not just the few that were lost. So if it had to happen, then in one sense we're lucky it happened in the middle of the day.

"I've heard stories about people who were told not to drive in places, and they said 'She's right, mate, I've been here for years' – and they're dead. Others (at Grantham) were told 'Get on your roof!' – and they said 'it's flooded here before, we'll go under the house.' Then the house moved a few seconds later."

We ask, perhaps rather callously, how much David has lost. In a matter-of-fact way he estimates around $300,000 for his farming equipment, including his tractor which was washed away - and $500,000 to replace his house and fittings. There were $20,000 worth of strawberry plants in the ground – as well as consumables (fertilizer and so on). Then there's

$100,000 of timber at David's sawmill – mouldy and rotting. "We've gone from 17th of December until now, without any an income. I've run out of money ... and steam. I don't have an overdraft, we're just taking every day one step at a time. I just keep soldiering on – it's what you've got to do – you've got to live."

David is grateful for the help and support they have received – "We've had three people here today we don't even know, offering stuff – mattresses and so on. We've said to them, 'We're insured, we'll get some contents cover.' They said, 'We don't care – whatever money you've got you're going to need it to rebuild because you've got to pay for all this other stuff.'"

"Some people have been pretty thoughtless though, offering worn-out towels and such when you can buy new towels for five dollars. You understand what I'm saying? I'm not being mean, you don't mind second-hand if it's all right.

"Not everybody has helped, just individuals. A lady came today from the Gold Coast. There was a bloke from Highfields and another from Caboolture – he took time off work in that initial period and he was here every day. Another lady who owned a cleaning company - we didn't know her very well at the time - came here after they cleaned up the Myer Centre in Toowoomba, to shovel mud. The lady who's running this clean-up now, her name's Kim – they lost all their crop and everything – and she's organised all these teams. They're here helping everyone else and they need help."

Some people from the Lockyer Valley, after what has happened, are moving out. Is David staying?
"It's never going to happen again. And if it does I'll stay anyway….."

The voice of the survivors.

"We're just soldiering on. We've got a plan ..."

REBECCA SPARKES

Grantham

....AND THAT'S WHEN IT ALL GOT UGLY
REALLY FAST

REBECCA SPARKES RECOUNTS, THROUGH TEARS, THE TRAUMA EXPERIENCED BY
HER FAMILY DURING THE DISASTROUS FLOODING OF GRANTHAM, 10 JANUARY 2011.

We lived at number 38 Railway Street. We'd been there for about ten years. Our house is still there; structurally it is alright, but because of the water damage, it needs repairs. Grantham hadn't flooded once in that time, and then suddenly it's four times in a couple of months! Each time the water came, we'd lift everything; we sort of got used to it! Dads house, up the street at number 28, is closer to the creek, so when the water started rising, we'd lift everything there up, and then we'd have an hour or two before the water got to our place to put everything up as high as we could.

On the 10th of January, I had a call from my husband, who's a truck driver, telling me that water was over the bowsers at Withcott. I thought that was a little strange, but I didn't really worry too much. I rang Dad, to see what he thought about it, and was no sooner off the phone when my boss from the Grantham shop rang to say that a car had been washed off the highway at Helidon. It wasn't long before Dad was on the phone again, "I think we are going to be in trouble!" We quickly moved the cars up the road to where we thought they would be safe. As we were moving the second car, we could already see water on the opposite side of the highway. We raced back home, and my two girls and I went up on the verandah. Dad decided to get his boat so as to be prepared, in case we needed to get out, and that was when it all got ugly, really fast...........

Next thing our friend, Kristy, was washed down the road, and I don't know how, but our front gate broke. The water changed direction and swept her into our place, which was a miracle! By the time she got up on to the verandah with us, the water was already through the house and into the second storey. We kind of pushed a bit of furniture around to try to get up on the roof. My seven-year-old, Karissa, climbed a ladder and got up first, and I passed her up Sophie, our 3 month old baby. When I jumped on the ladder, because it wasn't in good condition, it broke! Kristy climbed up on the furniture – she's quite a bit shorter than me – and I boosted her up on to the roof, then scrambled up myself. And that's where we were stuck for the next four and a half hours! We watched Kristy's shed get flattened; we saw all sorts of bizarre stuff; we were just, like, "This really can't be true!" I reckon I could easily have counted 50 people being swept along. I especially remember two people clinging to each other. They were beside a white ute, squashed between a fence and the ute. They were screaming – I'd say they'd have had broken legs, because, man, it hit hard! The last time I saw them, the car was still against the fence, and they were trapped there. I haven't a clue who they were. I've asked around but nobody's heard anybody talking about it. I was a bit worried when we looked around after we were finally allowed back in. I was thinking, "I hope those people still aren't here........." The ute was still against the fence. They might be lucky survivors somewhere, I don't know.......... We

saw a lot of people going down between our place and the highway. There was so much noise from the rushing water, it wasn't until later we could hear them calling out from trees and that sort of thing. From what we saw, unless they were all lucky enough to survive, I don't know how they can say the death toll is only 22.........

We saw helicopters, the channel 9 chopper first, and then rescue choppers getting around. They gave us a wave, to show they knew we were there, but had to prioritise who needed help first. Eventually we were rescued. I was strapped up first, and they passed me the baby. I was told, "Now, you are holding her for her life!" There is no way to strap babies into the air lift. At a reunion a month or so later, the rescue crewman told me he and the winch operator had had a heated discussion as to the best way to rescue Sophie. The winch operator reckoned you couldn't pick a baby up like that, while the rescuer claimed he had no choice, he had to get her off the roof. It has dawned on me only recently, how big a risk they took; how I was winched into a chopper holding a 3 month old baby, with absolutely nothing to restrain her; just in my arms........We are so grateful they did it though. At the time, even though I realised it was pretty extreme, I thought it was normal procedure! Then Karissa was winched up, and finally Kristy.

Kristy thought her husband had gone. Thinking that Dad probably had drowned as well, we spent those hours on the roof praying for the best. Unbelievably, next person winched into the chopper after us was Kristy's husband! It was another totally bizarre moment! He'd been in the water for four and a half hours, hanging on to a tree. We'd been hoping he was on a roof somewhere............ We were delivered to somebody's place, the other side of the railway line; then taken by four wheel drive into Helidon, where we spent the rest of the night.

It wasn't until 10 or 11 pm that I got a message that Dad was still alive. He was washed off the road in my Prado. He had grabbed two girls in trouble off the back of a Jumbuck ute, put them on the Prado roof, and they were being washed back down past my place when they hit a power pole stay. One girl was swept into a neighbouring property, and Dad managed to grab onto a power pole further along. The other girl was snatched off the roof of the Prado just as it went underneath the rail lines, so all three survived! It was such a relief to finally find out Dad was alive. I was sure he'd be dead, as he can't swim.

It was a very real experience, and every now and again it all comes back. I had to survive, and keep surviving. It's when I'm lying down that I have time to think – it was pretty extreme; I hope it never happens again......no more helicopter rides!

IT WASN'T A FLOOD IT WAS A
DISASTER

GARRY CAMPBELL

Grantham

GRANTHAM RESIDENT GARRY CAMPBELL AND HIS WIFE HAD NO WARNING WHATSOEVER OF THE IMPENDING DISASTER ABOUT TO CHANGE THEIR SMALL TOWN FOREVER. LEAVING WORK AS USUAL ON MONDAY EVENING, THEY WERE SHOCKED TO FIND ALL ROADS HOME WERE COMPLETELY BLOCKED. AFTER PLUNGING THROUGH THREE FEET OF WATER IN THEIR 4WD UTE, THEY MADE IT TO THE RAILWAY LINE. GARRY REALISED THAT WAS AS FAR AS THEY WERE GOING TO GET. STRANDED THERE IN THE MIDST OF A MASSIVE INLAND TSUNAMI, ALL THEY COULD DO WAS WAIT AND WATCH AS THE HORROR UNFOLDED. CARS BEGAN TO FLOAT PAST, TOSSED AROUND LIKE TOYS UNTIL THEY WERE SUCKED UNDER BY THE TREMENDOUS FORCE. "THERE WOULD HAVE BEEN BODIES IN THOSE CARS WE SAW." HE SWALLOWS HARD, PAUSES, THEN CONTINUES.

"We saw one woman on a car, we helped grab her off at the railway line. Then I ran across the railway line to get some more people. Got them off, but we couldn't do anything else. The lady we got off the car, all she was worried about was her Dad and Mum and brother. They must've been in the car and got sucked out."

Garry describes the turbulence of the water "like starting an outboard motor." "A lot of people say we've had a flood. It wasn't a flood, it was a disaster."

On Monday night the clock almost stood still for the hundreds of Grantham residents as they subconsciously struggled to come to terms with what they had seen, heard and suffered. Numbed by shock, Garry paced about helplessly. "I've never walked around so much in all my life. We couldn't do anything." Several times during the course of our conversation he repeats those words of obvious frustration, "We just couldn't do anything."

Garry finally crashed at a mates place at one am Tuesday morning. After a restless few hours of sleep he awoke "just to see it all again." Weary and raw from the heartbreak of what he had witnessed, he decided to try wading through the flood waters to see what was left of his home. What met him had all the hallmarks of a horror movie. "I've never seen so many snakes in all my life." As he waded gingerly into the murky, brown water, these desperate creatures frantically made a beeline for the only refuge point they could see – his body. "One was coming up my chest, trying to find somewhere to camp." Garry quickly ripped it off with his bare hands and "took off", telling the distressed reptile "I ain't campin' with you mate." The snakes "were just coming up out of the water. I saw five within a few feet."

Weeks on, the nightmare remains. "A lot of things go through your mind at night. I've nearly had enough. There's nothing left of the town now. We've been told not to say too much, but what we've seen…" Garry's voice trails off, and with almost a whisper he adds, "Clearing all the stuff away and finding bodies is terrible."

FOREVER
HAUNTED

PHIL BLOOMFIELD

Helidon

"I DON'T EVER WANT TO GO THROUGH IT AGAIN," ARE THE EMPHATIC WORDS OF PHIL BLOOMFIELD.

With no warning the water rose to five metres in five minutes. But there were some astonishing survivals – a man attempting to climb onto his roof found a highly poisonous Brown Snake wound around his arm. Frantically he shook it off, only to feel another wrap ominously around his leg. This time, it was just a brown paper bag! Another couple were facing certain death, unable to escape the rising flood waters. But at the last minute a timber pallet floated in beside them! They were then able to use it to climb onto the roof – saved by an old shipping pallet!!
As the water receded, it left poignant reminders in the debris – a refrigerator stuck on a bridge, full of food and with photos of family on the door.......were these people still alive? As far as the eye could see, the high water mark was littered with white goods that had floated out of homes – an inconceivable sight. One aftermath is a lot of shattered nerves. One crack of thunder or a hint of rain can still keep these devastated communities awake.

4WD washed into a gully - Murphys Creek

A Slab is all that remains of this home

Van beaten up by the torrent and dumped into a
beside Murphys Creek Road

Lilydale Road - Helidon

MURPHYS CREEK, POSTMANS
AND LAIDLEY

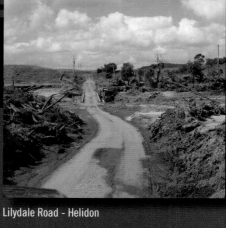
Remains of a Postmans Ridge House

Lockyer Creek - Helidon

SES and Police tape - indicating property has been
searched - Murphys Creek

Substation - Helidon Park

Truck Trailer - Postmans Ridge

194

in the Trees - Postmans Ridge

Damage after water came through Withcott

Rosewood - Laidley Road - Laidley

RIDGE, WITHCOTT, HELIDON

ter over Warrego Highway - Withcott

Matilda Blue Fuel Station - Withcott

Remains of a Shed - Helidon Park

ter rising in Rosewood - Laidley Road - Laidley

Boat - Postmans Ridge

Flooding of Tomato Land - Withcott

LEEROY SHEPPARD

Grantham

OLD MAGIC
MONDAY

SHE WAS A FUNNY OLD DAY, MAGIC MONDAY - THE DAY WE WENT FOR A FLOAT. EARLIER IN THE MORNING YOU COULD HAVE WALKED PEACEFULLY UP OUR STREET, BUT BY 10 O'CLOCK, THE WATER HAD STARTED SCREAMING DOWN THE ROAD AND PAST OUR FRONT DOOR.

One of my mates has seen a few floods. He usually sits out the front of his loading dock, dangling his feet in the water, having a beer, saying, "It's up again, and then it's down again." So I and my better half, Wendy, decided to catch up on some sleep, because we were housebound. We were startled awake by her son yelling, "The water is getting higher!" We looked out in the nick of time to gape in surprise as the car popped out from under the house. It floated away with its headlights facing up towards the sky, around the tree and off into the never-never. Right before our eyes the roof of the shed just gave a little shake, the sides peeled away like banana skins, whilst the back wall exploded, and the contents spewed out from underneath. We couldn't have blinked twice before the whole thing was sucked away, followed by the cladding off the sides of our house. As the water got to the thirteenth step of the house, the amount of junk it brought with it was unbelievable, fence posts, trees: a total log jam. We heard a bit of a bubble as the water welled up through the floor. A stream poured in one corner, and then it did an about turn and rushed back out again. That really was bizarre.

I felt the floor ripple under my feet, then heard a loud bang as the front door snapped in half with the lock still in the bolt, the bottom of it left flapping as the water gushed in. Wendy grabbed the phone to call emergency services. The first time she rang they just hung up. "We are at 7 Anzac Avenue, Grantham, and there is lots of water coming in, we need assist….beep….beep….beep…. So she rang them back. They just told her to calm down. No problem - water is surging through our house, we're clambering in desperation onto a floating lounge whilst attempting to keep our heads above water, I'm gripping the lounge with one hand to stop it going out the back door as it lurches around the room and clinging onto the wall for grim death with my other hand… but yes, we'll calm down!!
I could physically feel the floor of the house getting sucked lower before it burst off its stumps, and we went spinning around and around through the back yard. I watched in a shocked blur as a 5 foot fish tank swung past my head. With an ear splitting crash we finally careened into the next door neighbour's trees. The water was up to my armpits; a total of over 3m depth. Old mate on top of the pub was watching, and I asked "How many times did I spin around?" He said "Man, I lost count." It was like being inside a Frisbee, with no idea of where we were headed.

When we finally stopped spinning, we staggered out towards the tree, then climbed shakily up to the roof to escape the water which was still pumping through the house. Wendy suddenly remembered the dog, so I went back in to look for her, but she'd gone. I did find a little torch belonging to Wendy's grandson, and a floating cupboard full of baby blankets and nappies. I opened it up, you beauty - dry blankets. Those articles of clothes and baby's blankets were pretty much what kept us warm and partially dry while we sat on the roof for 5 1/2 hours.

Our blue Ford filled up with silt, then when it was hit by another floating house, it acted as a handbrake and stopped the house dead in its tracks. I think the car was about a tonne and a half heavier than when it was built. Later on, the scrappers didn't like it; they had to pay extra for all that silt! The tree from out the front was snapped off at the roots with the force of the water, and thrown through our front door. It really was horrific, sitting up there helplessly, just watching events unfold. It was a pitched roof, so we had to sit on the apex, and that really hurt. I tore off a bit of fascia that was down one side and I put that at the bottom of the roof in the trees, just in case we did happen to slip. We were losing daylight, so we knew that if we did make a slip there was no way we were going to be able to get back up in the dark. Lucky the adrenaline negates the fear, we should have been terrified, but somehow we weren't.

As darkness descended, we communicated with others sitting on their roofs during the night with the little torch. It was even slightly humorous. Click, click, click, over to the pub, yep we are all still here on top of our roofs. If it wasn't for that little flash light, nobody would have known we were there. We would have stayed put all night, because we didn't have a clue if it was an inch of water or 7 feet

Cow on Rail Bridge

Original location of Leeroy's house - only stumps remain

deep on the ground - sitting up there frozen in utter darkness, in the rain, wearing nothing but a pair of shorts, a t-shirt and a beanie.

About 10pm Swiftwater Rescue came up Harris Street, and Ray told them to go and get us. The water troupe came over and asked, "Have you got a dog?" We answered "We had a dog mate." They said "There's a dog hanging on to a tree out the front of your house." She had held on to that tree for the entire time we were up there.

No one was prepared for what they saw here, absolutely no one. Swiftwater, they came in blind. Everyone was in instant shock really. I asked those I thought were better prepared for the afternoon's events, "Well, what do we do mate? Do we sit here, or do we keep moving?" And they said "Mate, do we sit here or do we keep moving?" I just wanted to stand still, but my feet were slowly slipping across the top of the bitumen, pulled by the current. So we crossed the main road.

We cruised along bracing hard against the flow, avoiding the creek and the gutters, until we saw someone with a torch in the corner of the railway yard, a point of reference to move to. The water was just as fast here as the main road, only it was knee deep instead of up to the waist. We spent the night at the School, and the Tuesday morning when it went down, we had a look down the road, there were cars, all kinds of rubbish, mud, fish tanks, and a big fat dead cow, man it stunk. I'll tell you what, people in Grantham love fish. If they're not fishing for them, they are keeping them in tanks. Seriously, they were absolutely everywhere. You go out in the paddocks afterwards; there were boats, fishing gear, and fish tanks. I lost two, but I found one, it sliced the bottom of my foot open. And the mud — it just won't budge. There was a dry cake of silt covering everything, it got wet and it won't wash off. It's a peculiar colour - everything around here was that colour for about a week afterwards, 'til the grass tried to break through. All was silent; a cemetery would have had more life in it. It was eerie.

I was in shock for a while, so I occupied my mornings a couple of weeks afterwards by joining a group who cooked an all day barbeque for whoever wanted to eat it. All the time, we could hear the constant churn of water all around us; similar to if you stuck your head in a bucket of water and turned the tap on flat out. I could still hear that noise for a long time afterwards in my head.

They had a special on the Grantham floods on ABC, I thought 'Great, a little review of the flood.' I'm sitting there watching the telly, looking at the dirty brown water, and thinking "That looks like our house and shed.........wait! — That is our place. There's the little red car bobbing up and down, and the water coming through the front door. I can't watch this." Lots of others can't either. It scares you. It's heartbreaking that we lost a lot of great people, some I'd never even met. I'm making sure I meet the rest of their family. I really am so happy that I'm still here. It was definitely different.............Old Magic Monday.

Remains of Leeroy's home

JOHN AND KATHY MAHON
Grantham

LAST SECOND
ESCAPE

JOHN AND KATHY MAHON'S WARM, RELAXED MANNER ALMOST CONCEALS THE HEART-RENDING TRAUMA OF THIS GRANTHAM FAMILY'S NEAR-DEATH EXPERIENCE.

"The day started out ordinary.......but it was a horrific afternoon," John recalls. Minor flooding of local creeks overnight had subsided and as morning dawned in the tiny rural town, the only hint of more to come, was a slight rising of Sandy Creek. By midday, news of 'roads cut' and 'creeks coming up quite high' in the district, was filtering through. But no-one could possibly have imagined the calamity about to engulf their close-knit community!

The Mahon's daughters, Jessie and Andrea, and Andrea's little sons, Liam 5 and Lachlan 3, from nearby Toowoomba, had called in for lunch, but when they made to return home they found the road covered by floodwater, so they returned to their parents' home. John assured them that they'd be safe, 'we're higher than the 1974 flood level!'

John and Kathy called on Kathy's mother, who lived a few blocks away, and tried to coax her to come home with them. But she refused, 'No, I'll be alright here with my dogs. I'm higher than you!' Then Kathy's phone rang................It was their other daughter Rochelle, in Brisbane.

'Mum....I'm watching TV and there's a huge wall of water in Toowoomba!!!! A friend's house at Withcott has been inundated with water!!! It'll be heading your way soon! There'll be a wall of water!!!!! '

'B...but Rochelle....... It's not even raining here!' Kathy replied in stunned disbelief. 'Mum, you're not listening to me! PLEASE LISTEN TO ME!!!' Rochelle started yelling. She read out the warnings for Toowoomba, from the police website. 'Put towels in your toilets; Boil your water - because sewerage is getting into the town water supply; Unlock your doors so you don't get trapped inside!'

'But that's for Toowoomba, Rochelle.' Kathy knew that Toowoomba's water doesn't cross the range.

She was just screaming by then, 'MUM YOU'VE GOTTA LISTEN TO ME!! IT'S SERIOUS!!....YOU'VE GOTTA GET HOME AND GET AS HIGH AS YOU CAN!! And then, she got another urgent call, from nephew, Michael ......

'Auntie, where are you? Can you get home and take Grandma with you? Get as high as you can! There's a wall of water coming..........IT'S HIGHER THAN IT'S EVER BEEN! IT'S OVER THE BRIDGE AT HELIDON!!! This was startling news! Hardly able to comprehend, the stunned couple kissed Kathy's Mum goodbye and raced home to prepare themselves.

Andrea grabbed floatie rings and an inflatable boat from the pool for her little boys. Kathy unlocked all doors as warned - a life-saving decision and John rushed to the shed, but a strange roar startled him.

'I saw a huge lake of mud and debris moving down Lockyer Creek and across the paddock! It was about 4 or 5 feet high and didn't really look like water.' His heart pounding, he slammed the shed door and yelled, 'IT'S COMING!! EVERYONE GET INSIDE!!'

Like a crazy, uncontrollable monster, the huge inland wave hurtled wildly towards the quiet village, destroying all in its path!!!

Seconds later the Mahon's home was inundated by the flood. Then.....with a crashing sound the raging torrent forced its way inside. With water lapping angrily at his ankles, then......higher....it was rising so fast.....John realised he couldn't possibly save his home, but must try to save his family and he ordered everyone into the kitchen. The girls huddled up on the kitchen bench holding the terrified little boys, with their floaties on, while John and Kathy stood on chairs nearby. Still gushing in, the water soon rose to waist level!

Scarcely trusting his own words, John attempted to keep everyone calm.....'Don't panic! It will stop soon! It's not going to get much higher!' But it was not to be. Their ordeal was far from over! As the merciless deluge continued, the whole house shook, with glass breaking, doors ripping open and snapping off halfway up. Then, when the fridges fell over and Andrea's four-wheel-drive floated past the windows, the petrified family thought........'This is it! We're gone!' Barely ten minutes had passed since the warning calls, and now they were staring death in the face.

Clinging desperately to each other, they whispered goodbyes, bravely trying to hold back tears, so they wouldn't upset little Liam and Lachlan. Numb with fear, their heads only just above the filthy water, the family calmly recited the 'Lord's Prayer' together. Believing there was no chance of survival, Jessie and Andrea rang their shocked husbands, to say goodbye. Kathy rang Rachelle..................... 'Could you tell everyone we love them...........we're going to drown! The water's so high in the kitchen now.......and still rising!! We don't know what we're going to do!' 'NO! YOU CAN'T DROWN MUM! I'LL GET HELP'

'How could anyone help us? It's too late now,' they thought. Then, two long minutes later..............she rang back. 'Mum......CHOPPER'S ON ITS WAY!!!!' Maybe they'd survive......

Jessie wisely suggested they attempt to get onto the roof, John agreed it was their only chance of escape. The water was almost to the top of the doorways and the backdoor was buckling in. John opened the door, and the family rushed out as the floodwater surged in, blowing the opposite door right out! Miraculously none of them were washed away.

With superhuman effort, they got the women and the boys onto the roof, but John was left stranded on the pool fence, which had dropped. He just hung onto the house gutter.

'It was so hard clinging there watching 36 years worth of family possessions float by!' John said. When the family Bible drifted by, he valiantly, swam out and retrieved it.

'Leave it, leave it!' warned Kathy, fearing he would drown.
'No...I've gotta get it!' He threw it up onto the roof along with a couple of kids' toys. Adding to the terror, a large brown snake swam towards John. He was sure it would bite him and every time an object touched his legs, he panicked, thinking it was the snake.

Although relieved to be above the brutal floodwaters, the girls were still certain they were going to die. The continually rising swell caused the whole roof to vibrate beneath them and they could hear the cars bumping around in the garage. The scene of sheer devastation surrounding them was difficult to comprehend. Severely traumatised, the poor little boys screamed at times, and Kathy became hysterical when their 6 month old caravan was washed away, crashing into a car as it went. Her dreams of travelling Australia with her husband were destroyed in an instant! It was after an hour of terror that the welcome sound of a helicopter lifted the marooned family's hopes.......... But it was only a News Chopper..... unable to offer assistance!

Finally the EMQ rescue chopper arrived! With tears of relief, they helped the brave little boys, Liam and Lachlan, one at a time, be winched up to safety. The news chopper returned to film the rescue and the downdraft from two helicopters, caused Kathy to lose her grip and start sliding down the roof. Luckily, Jess grabbed her and she was rescued next. When the girls had all been lifted, they then alerted rescuers to an elderly neighbour, Dave, who had been clinging to his gutter in a strong current. So Dave was saved next.

Leaving John behind, the loaded chopper dropped its passengers near a farmhouse, on a nearby hill. "I cried my eyes out with relief!" said John, "we had thought we were gone!"

When the rescuers returned, John signalled he was okay, allowing people in greater danger......some stuck in trees, some stranded in vehicles and many on rooftops to be saved, after over two exhausting hours immersed in the murky water, John was rescued. He can't remember getting into the helicopter. 'I must've blacked out!'

Soaking wet, cold and caked in mud, the Mahon's were reunited at Fullerton's farmhouse to discover -with distress - they were among the 'lucky ones'. Many of their friends and townsfolk were missing — presumed drowned, it broke their hearts. Kathy's mother had been rescued alive but an elderly friend wasn't. They were greatly saddened by what happened to their neighbours, Matthew and Stacey Keep. When the ferocious wall of water struck their newly-built home, the young couple and their baby were swept away. Matthew ended up alive on a house-top a kilometre away, and 21-month-old Jessica was torn from her pregnant mother's arms only seconds before Stacey was rescued by helicopter. Remarkably, their older two children survived the terrifying drama alone in the family home. Their young girl had clung for her life to a couch which floated up to the ceiling like a life-raft. But sadly, the Keep family had lost both 'grandmothers' as well as baby Jessica that fateful afternoon.

After spending the night at the Helidon Community Hall with other survivors, the Mahons awoke to an overwhelming scene of mass destruction. Most of the floodwaters had receded, revealing carnage of unprecedented proportions.

The ruthless deluge had crushed vehicles, flattened homes, uprooted trees, wrecked roads, twisted railway lines, ruined livelihoods, shattered dreams, extinguished lives and broken hearts as it carved its way through a region that would never be the same again!!

John and Kathy may have lost everything but the clothes on their backs but........... they are so thankful God answered their prayers. 'We are so grateful to be alive......... We could get onto the roof......and survive to tell the story!'

KEN AND FRAN ARNDT

Grantham

THIS WATER WAS

ANGRY

IT HAD BEEN RAINING FOR WEEKS. THERE WAS A BIT OF FLOODING ON THE ROAD SO I WAS JUST GOING OUT TO GIVE OUR NEIGHBOUR DANNY A HAND TO GET A ROAD BLOCK IN PLACE. THE PHONE RANG. IT WAS MY DAUGHTER, SCREAMING 'GET OUT OF THERE FAST!' SHE HAD SEEN A SHEET OF WATER MOVING SWIFTLY TOWARDS OUR HOUSE. I AND MY WIFE FRANCES LEFT INSTANTLY IN OUR UTE.

As we headed out, we saw the water coming; the whole flat was already covered. Sandy Creek was impenetrable - swollen to 6 feet. We headed towards higher ground, but got barely ½ km up the road when we were trapped by a deadly 7 metre wall of water. And it wasn't like the Brisbane flood where it rose slowly. This was boiling, madly bubbling water. This water was angry.

It crashed into us with an almighty bang – it was like being hit by a solid brick wall. Our ute was a heavy 6 wheeler, but we were tossed off the road instantaneously like a piece of driftwood. We made a frenzied clutch for the door handles, and our blood ran cold. They were pinned shut by the water, and both our windows wouldn't budge. The pressure prevented us punching a window out. We thought we were gone. It was a terrifying, struggle to get out. We finally got a window half way down and the current sucked us out like a raging beast. Two seconds later and the ute filled up with water and vanished from sight.

We were hurled 50m into the paddock by the powerful current, and managed to grab hold of a leopard tree. We couldn't get any further up than about waist deep because the tree was only small. We were hanging there praying, when I looked over my shoulder and froze! A huge shipping container was floating toward us at high speed! We hastily said a tender goodbye to one another.

But because of the rubbish that had washed up against the leopard trees it suddenly took a left turn. I could have put my hand out and touched it as it went past. For 3 hours we clung to that tree while the rescue helicopter flew overhead. They couldn't see us for the foliage of the tree. Frances was out on a branch waving it to try to attract attention, until she realised the futility of it - all the tree branches were waving in the wind. Then the branch broke, and she tumbled into the water. She couldn't get back up the tree, just managing to clutch on to the trunk.

We hung on there for about 3 hours. We saw a lot go past in that time, cars, feeders, refrigerators and kitchen sinks – you name it. I had to keep changing my position all the time – I was in a sharp fork –I couldn't put my whole foot in there, so I used my toe. When it would start hurting I'd change feet, and put my other big toe in. It was creepy in there – spiders kept crawling all over us, but I was more worried about the brown snakes we'd seen. We saw cars go past half submerged, there could have been somebody in them, but we couldn't see because of the thick leaves. It would have freaked me out too much if I had seen a body, as others did– it was bloodcurdling enough as it was. Thank God, we were spared that experience.

Someone was on the house roof next door – we couldn't see them but we could hear their voices. We called out, and when the helicopter came for the others they pointed out where we were. It was the most difficult place to perform a rescue. Frances, exhausted, really struggled to get the rescue harness on. The crew up in the helicopter couldn't get a visual because of the foliage, and they let too much slack cable go from the helicopter. She and her rescuer went under the water twice. They were taking so long that the helicopter became endangered, and could have slammed into the water, or nearby houses. Thinking they had become entangled, the helicopter pilot had his finger on the button that would cut the cable. Both would have been carried away, strapped together. They could never have survived. Then, with just seconds to spare, they navigated clear of the trees. All the skin was torn off Frances' arm but thank God she was alive. Then it was my turn, I reached the helicopter safely. I tried to move to the side to fit others in– but I couldn't get up off the floor. I just lay motionless, unable to move – I had no power to even get on my hands and knees. I think when it's life and death, the adrenalin kicks in, and when I reached safety I just utterly collapsed.

A SHEET OF WATER WAS MOVING SWIFTLY TOWARDS
THEIR HOUSE

The helicopter took us up to Charles and Betty Fulton's house, up on high ground. They were dropping people there and going off to get more. Charles and Betty were grand - real old country people, both in their 80s, and they took us all inside. Everyone was shivering and they gave us clothes, blankets, cups of coffee and biscuits. The power was off – but luckily they had a gas stove. The chopper ended up saving 28 people.

We didn't know that our neighbour Lenny had gone, or Danny's wife and children. When we first knew the water was coming, we rang Danny, asking for assistance. He rang back and told us 'I can't help you'. He was in the fire truck; I looked in my side mirror and saw it get pulled backwards by the force of the water. We had no way to contact him after that, and it wasn't until I read the paper that I knew the 3 of them had died. We had spent Christmas Day together. At least we have some good memories – and now they're up there without a worry and we're left here battling on.

Lance at the pub was filming on the pub roof; he stopped his recording when a car went past with people in it screaming for help. He also saw a brick house explode with 3 people inside, it just levelled like a dozer had been at it. Wilkinson was headed for his shop when somebody rang and told him that the water was coming, so he and his wife left the shop and just jumped back in the car. He was heading towards high ground when he glanced in his rear vision mirror and saw the wall of water bearing down on him. By the time he got to the top of the hill the water had hit the bank behind him, it was going so rapidly. The speed of a tank floating down the river taken with a radar gun was 80kph. The force of the water was such that a bale of onion bags strapped together with steel was washed from here and ended up on Southport beach.

I've lived in Grantham my whole life – I was born in this area. My great grandfather came out from Prussia in 1788. I have a daughter, a granddaughter and 3 great grandchildren – they are the ninth generation. Many of those who came out from Germany settled in Lockyer Valley. We had good neighbours, but too many will never come back.

We've basically lost everything– we've got nothing left – the whole lot's washed away. The amount I had it insured for was only about a quarter of its real value – we hadn't updated the policy. We had put new red cedar blinds and carpet in about 6 weeks before the flood. We had also put solar power on and never even got to see what the new electricity bill was. We will build again when we get the money, but we right now are playing a waiting game for the insurance. I want to go back. Where I am now is somewhere to live, but it's not home.

Thanks

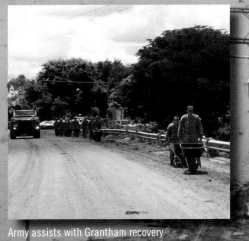
Army assists with Grantham recovery

Flood waters engulf Grantham

LOCKYER VALLEY

Prime Minister Julia Gillard at Grantham

Emergency services assistance

Grantham Hotel

porary Police base in Grantham

Receding water reveals destruction

Cars and debris caught up on rail bridge

oding inundates main street of Grantham

House interior destroyed

House washed onto road

203

PETER AND MARIE VAN STRATTEN

Grantham

THEIR STORY

MARIE: We moved into Grantham in July last year and we really didn't know anybody as such.

PETER: After the first flood we sort of met them all because their rubbish was strewn right through our place!

MARIE: Yeah.... by the time we'd had three floods go through, we got to meet a lot of the residents. It seemed to us, the flood water would virtually stop at our house. Our yard would be inundated, but from there towards the convenience store, it would be dry. I said to Peter one day, "Are we the dam to Grantham, that we collect all the water?" It was amazing; it was sorta like – inbuilt swimming pool!

PETER: It really used to come through our place too; whereas other places would always be slow water, with us it was always fast water.

MARIE: Even the video we took of the Boxing Day flood, you could actually hear how fast the water was going, and that was the first flood. There was Peter up to his knees in the dark trying to save the Guinea Pigs, and the chooks.........And the shed where he had the car, was like.......the water........ even from the first three floods, the water got really high.

PETER: I jacked the front of the car up on car ramps and put the trolley jack up full height, and the water would get just below the exhaust of the car every time, and – you know it alright, it's safe where it is!

MARIE: That's when we knew we were in deep trouble, on the day of the big flood. When the water first started coming up, even though we knew the steps had gone, because we had seen that, I'm lookin' out the back, and literally, our car was sucked out like a vacuum, and thrown up one of the trees! Then next minute the shed, where the car had been, just crumpled up like origami, and it was, like – just spin it –it went into itself, and then was gone. And we had another shed and it was sorta... the two sheds both went; the garden shed went first; it too, just crumpled up like tissue paper. It was the most extraordinary thing to see! You could hear the water, and you could see how fast everythin' was going past, but to actually see what belonged to you just crumbling up like......... You think of your sheds as stable and secure........ The shed the car was in had been there 45 years or something, and it was just 'pop', gone! They talk about fast and furious or somethin', and yeah, it wouldn't even have been three minutes before both sheds were gone; the chicken house was gone because it was attached to the shed, and then very shortly we were gone!

I was suffering from stress disorder after the first three floods, and the first thing I would do every mornin' was check the Bureau of Meteorology site. I'd be lookin' at the creek levels.... So to a certain extent, when I saw the water coming that day I was thinking, "Ok yeah, it's been on the website, so it's alright." We had the pets on the back veranda and I said to Peter, "We'll put the pets in the bathroom, because they will be safer there," thinkin' that it would be like every other time; that the water would come up to a certain level, and then peak, like it had done the last three times........ but the water just kept on comin', didn't it?!

A massive big tree came down in front of our gate during the flood the day before, and obviously with Peter having being diagnosed with Diabetes a couple of weeks before and needin' blood tests , we wanted to get it removed. We rang up the Council and we were standin' out the front waiting, when a Chanel 9 news reporter walked past so we got interviewed! He's goin', "How are you copin' with two floods," and I said "Two floods? We have actually had three!" We talked a bit more and at the end of it as he was walkin' away I said to him, "Oh yeah, we've grown webbed feet and flippers", and I went "quack quack, blub, blub, blub!" And it's going live all over the place! My daughter rings me up about five days afterwards and she goes, "Mum, you're such a crack-up, you're on You Tube as the duck lady!" They actually took it off, because they reckoned it was inappropriate, with all the trouble that happened afterwards.

PETER: The water had gone down enough to get the car out and go to get a blood test.

MARIE: It was still up in places, because I remember saying to Peter, "Don't you dare go anywhere else, go and get your blood test done, and then come home straightaway," because I was freakin' out. Luckily he did come home when he did, because not long after that was when the water hit.

PETER: When I got home from the blood test I went and had a poppy nap.

MARIE: Peter got woken up with a phone call from Wayne Lander, our friend; he said, "There is a wall of water heading your way, get to high ground". Well there was no where we could go, because already we had the water still high from the flood the night before. Next thing I remember screaming, "Peter the front steps have gone!" We were runnin' around the house tryin' to put things up high. Imagine a 13 steps high Queenslander, and already the water and mud was comin' up through the beautiful timber floors......we were ankle deep in water even as we were tryin' to get the electrical stuff up. I ran into the bathroom where we had put all the pets, and the next thing I remember is the water went from ankle deep to....... I was under it! Imagine the guinea pigs cage, the budgie cage and everything all in the bathroom – we didn't have a very big bathroom; I don't know how, but I ended up in the bath for some reason....... I think I must have slipped; that's when I first went under the water. Fortunately I got out of that and thankfully the bathroom door hadn't shut. I was able to grab one of the guinea pigs, she was up on one of the taps, and got out of the bathroom. The next minute I remember Peter yellin' at me, "Grab hold of the dining room table!" On the table we had the drawer where we put all our papers, so we threw them out, and put the guinea pig into the drawer. Chloe, our beautiful dog, is on the table, Peter and I are holding onto the dining room table! We were up to waist high water by then already........ From then on Peter will have to tell you the story, because I don't remember anythin' until we got into the middle of the paddock, and I'm walkin' around in circles, he's holdin' me, and I'm sayin', "Where are we?"

PETER: We get asked, what did it feel like when the house lifted off its stumps; what went through our minds? What went through my mind was........we're in big trouble. About that time, as the house started to lift, we actually rang my bishop up. "Bishop, you had better pray for us, we're in deep trouble!" That's when the phone died.

MARIE: We rang emergency before that, and they put Peter on hold, which was pretty awful.

PETER: When the house went through the trees was the absolute worst, because it was actually ripping itself to bits. When the kitchen came off, you can't imagine the noise.....it was awful. I will remember that noise forever it sounded so bad.......

MARIE: Paul and Linda was tellin' us, we were headin' for them, then, because there was so many different currents of water, we were lifted up and actually went right around their house! As we were goin' past they was saying, "look at their house, thank goodness there is nobody in there," and then we spun around, and they could see us! I remember seeing Paul and Linda's house, I could see them on their veranda, but we couldn't hear them, the noise was so bad..... And they're sort of like, "we can hear you." They could hear me, and that's all Marty could hear when we were going.......

PETER: He could hear you squawking!

MARIE: What do you expect? I was terrified; I literally........I may have faith in God, I may have a good attitude to everything....... but I WAS TERRIFIED.

The house was spinnin'........ I still can't remember it, but people are tellin' us that the house was turnin'; and we found out much later, when we went through the trees we actually had a car comin' with us!

PETER: The car must have been just in front of the house, so when the house stopped on the bore pipe, the blue car just came to a grindin' halt and sunk, creating an eddy there. We couldn't see it from where we were.

MARIE: We didn't even hit electric poles, our whole house went between electric poles and didn't tear them down or anything, and we went over a whole road, and there was another house on the corner....... We weren't like, "Oh, floating down, this is real fun"; the speed, I think Peter clocked it roughly about 60-70 km/h. Yet we didn't pull down any power poles, we didn't smash into their house, and even getting out of the trees we should have died then and we didn't. Missing Linda and Paul's house was such.............we are Latter Day Saints, we believe in God, we believe there is a higher Power anyway, and we were saying our Heavenly Father is definitely looking after us. We should have hit the trees, we should have crumpled when our house came off the stumps, we should have been dead........

It was bad enough screaming and screaming out for help; but when the helicopters kept flying away, that really was the worst, because it was like, "They can't see us, how are we going to get out of here?" So many times we kept on thinkin', "if we could just have got out somewhere, they could see us......."

We could see all this horrible rubbish and debris and stuff going past us at enormous speeds and then the boat..........we could see a boat and at one stage, because the helicopters were always leaving us, I said to Peter, "What if we grabbed one of those pieces of timber and got over to the boat......" That would have been the most stupidest thing to do, but all we could see was the helicopters constantly leavin' us, and that was actually worse than being in the water. At that stage we were still in the dining room, how did we get from the dining room?

PETER: Because the fridge was floating, I thought if we could hang onto the fridge it will give us some flotation to hang onto.

MARIE: We went under almost 10 times.

PETER: When I went out to the fridge I managed to jam the door open. When we got into the current, the water just slammed the fridge straight up against the kitchen ceiling. I sorta could hang onto the timber with one hand, and try to wave at the helicopters with the other hand, trying to attract their attention; I had to pick my pants up at the same time, and later on I had a dog on my shoulder too!

MARIE: He got really tired hanging onto the fridge and a timber beam.......We were thinkin', because the dining room was still intact, maybe if we got the dining room table and held onto that.......

We thought we had lost Chloe, because she was on the other side of the fridge. At first she was whimpering, and then we couldn't hear her anymore. We thought, "That's it, she's gone." It's funny, because I was so angry at the helicopters for not rescuing us earlier, and yet, if they had rescued us the first time we saw them, we would have definitely lost Chloe. We honestly thought she was dead; she's drowned, she is history. Thankfully, as Peter was going around the fridge to get the dining room table, he saw her floating up on the couch, so even that is another miracle as well.

We were in the water and we just had to wait; there was nothing we could do....... we couldn't go anywhere. The water was not nice gentle waves...... I remember at one stage the water was going so fast, I got hit on the head by debris floatin' past; I got all these scratches and bruises.

PETER: We were impaling ourselves on nails and things; we didn't feel a thing!

MARIE: Talk about getting a major head ache! Because I was so worried about Peter, with his diabetes, and being on Warfarin for the blood clots floatin' around in his body, it didn't even occur to me for about three days that I was actually injured as well. My wrist was broken from slipping after the second flood, and it re-broke; when Peter went under at one stage and his arm came up, I thought, "He's in trouble here," and I remember grabbing his arm and hearing a crack in my wrist. I had re-broken it in the same place, even though it was in plaster. I remember thinking the hospital would be cranky about my plaster gettin' wet!

This is how your brain works – we were lookin' around and surveying the damage, and I said to Peter, "I wonder how we are going to pay the rent this week, what's going to be our address?" We had to have a sense of humour or we would have crashed. The water was so powerful that I lost my shorts, and I remember the force of the water being so strong, Peter was actually losing his grip on me. Instead of sitting on his knee like I had been, I was straight out in the water – I have only just remembered this – and I thought it was so easy to have been ripped away, and then the next day we would have been a statistic, like everybody else.

PETER: The most eerie thing was that just before we got picked up by the helicopter, the smoke alarms went off. A weird old sound that was!

MARIE: That was in the house; I mean we were dealin' with all the sound of the water which we will never forget, but then just as they were rescuin' us, the smoke alarms went off, "ooaaooaaooaa!"

They weren't going to save us, Marty was telling me yesterday. They figured because we were in our house, we were safe. Obviously the helicopters didn't realise that we had changed address! Apparently, because they had run out of petrol and it was getting dark, and starting to rain again, they were going to turn back, but because the people of Grantham told them where we were, they said they would give it one more try. We were the last ones.

It is very sobering to hear how close we came to not being here. There is no way we would have survived that night. The water got so cold; by the time they picked us up we were already in hyperthermia. Peter was a real mess, he was that awful horrible grey purpley colour. At one stage I actually thought I was going to lose him. There is no way of knowing if we would have been alive the next morning; the water took forever to go down.

PETER: Just before we got picked up the water pressure sort of eased off a bit; not going down, but eased off.

MARIE: We weren't just sitting there with the waters lapping gently against us; it was coming at us with force. I said to Peter at one stage, "Does it work like a tidal thing?" It would be manageable, and then all of a sudden it was like another wave would come through, and with it would be all this debris and garbage. We were stuck in a corner Peter was up to his neck, literally, and he was holding me on his knees because I can't swim, so I was a little bit higher, but it was awful. All the rubbish that was in the water, it was floating around his neck. We weren't just sitting there saying, "Isn't this fun?" We would see things floating past; at one stage, we're still not 100% sure, but it looked like a body to me............

PETER: It could have been a body; it could have been a rag. We chose to believe it was a bundle of rags.

MARIE: But it was a very big bundle of rags, if it was. That was awful.
When the helicopter finally came, we knew he had seen us because of the way he came down and we were waving and everything. Then he went away, and that was it; Peter started to cry, I started to cry; I even wondered about my faith in the Heavenly Father, there's a limit.............Peter and I watched it go away; we were cold and we told each other we love you; we said goodbye, thanks for the memories; we thought we were gone. In less than 20 minutes they came back.......and, thankfully, we were saved. Peter was hanging on; I was sort of like.......braced; broken wrist, holding onto the door with my legs up in the doorway. He goes to the helicopter man, "You take my missus first." The helicopter was so close to the house it was actually throwing the corrugated roof iron everywhere. They had to gain height to stop it being so dangerous. When they were lifting me, I went back under the water again, and I'm thinking, "I'm going to drown before they save me", because it was horrible, absolutely awful. They got me up in the helicopter and then finally Peter and Chloe came up.

PETER: To me the biggest relief was seeing her go through the door of the helicopter.

MARIE: It's pretty surreal when you look at the pictures, and think that's our house, that's where we lived; people don't believe that we survived. When they got us to the school, the evacuation point, I wouldn't get out of the helicopter. They kept on saying, "You will be right"; and I'm saying, "I'm not getting out, I'm not getting out!" They literally had to carry me, and lift me over the fence as well! I said, "I'm not touching the grass, it's all wet!" We were in the school overnight in the Principal's office. It was lovely to be safe. At one stage because I had swallowed so much water, I wanted to throw up; I was feeling really sick and they tried to get me to the ladies' toilets downstairs. I had to face this black.......obviously the lights weren't on yet, and it was wet. I'm standing on top of the stairs, Peter was at the bottom of the stairs with Chloe, "Look here's Chloe"; they had at least two people on either side of me trying to get me down stairs! Even the next morning, the medic had to actually push me across to the helicopter, because I wouldn't go on the wet grass. I had a phobia for wet grass for a long time. It was terrible; the water just freaked me out. After the first three floods I was virtually post-traumatically stressed, so you can imagine by the time they were tryin' to evacuate us into Helidon, they weren't getting me out of that helicopter for nobody!

We were in Helidon for 4 or 5 hours, and then they sent us to Gatton by bus. Obviously the water was still up along the roads. We were at Gatton four days; Peter and I were sittin' in the hospital trying to recover. They put us into a lounge room, we were on a fold out couch – we had a lovely room, it was like a motel; Peter said it was the Gatton Hilton because it was so nice what they did for us!
We heard horror stories about Gatton because it was blocked off with the floods and landslides. They had no food; all the shops sold out and they couldn't get any more in.

PETER: The worst part of it was that they were running out of water – they had no safe water to drink – there was only bottled water and not much of that left.

MARIE: Peter couldn't sleep – for about 4 days he wouldn't close his eyes..........

PETER: Every time I closed my eyes that wall of water would start heading for us again.

MARIE: I finally went down to the nurses and said, "You have to give Peter something, because he is not sleepin'." They ended up giving him sleeping pills. It's the sound........even in the hospital, I could still hear the water and Peter kept on saying to me, "It's alright, it is the air-conditioning!"

About 2 o'clock in the morning, I gave the poor old nurse such a fright – I gave myself a fright! I'm at the edge of the bed and she said, "What's the matter, Marie?" I said, "I need to go to the toilet," and she said "Well that's ok, let's go!" I screamed, "I can't, the water is coming!" I COULD SEE THE MUDDY WATER. It was so real. This was inside the hospital, nowhere near a doorway or anything. I could literally see the water and mud, and I wouldn't put my feet on the floor. She kept saying, "You're in the hospital, you are safe now." I'm looking at it, saying "Are you mad? Can't you see the water.......!"

PETER: She was standing on the bed, middle of the night, and reckoned that the mud is comin' down the hallway!

MARIE: It was so real. I could see the water and the mud.
It is actually worse afterwards........ By the time we were rescued, everything was happening. The very next day, Ipswich was under. We had moved from Ipswich to Grantham, so all our friends and church members were there. Then Goodna went under – we'd lived in Goodna. Cairns, where my family is, went through the cyclone, then we had Perth going through all those bush fires, then it was Japan and Christchurch............ I hope people realise that, as horrible as it was, people survive and they can be happy again. At the hospital people would say, "Are you going to go back to Grantham?", and I'm like, "Nope, I'm never going back there; I am not going to see anybody there, I don't want to see where we were!" About three weeks afterwards, we had to go back to fill out the paperwork, and Peter said, "You are going to have to come because you have to sign the papers." Because I had to go, I'm now a lot better. I still can't go past our block without..........We had a really happy time there. We have been married almost 16 years when we moved to Grantham, and it was the first time in our married life that we had been on our own. We had this massive, lovely big block of land; room for the dogs, room for the chooks, room for the guinea pigs, room for the kids; it was like heaven on earth, seriously, and then......... it's all gone.

We had a brilliant counsellor, and she said what Peter and I needed to do was go was to go back to the block, and sit in the middle. It was really awful, but we wandered around, we weren't looking for anything because I refused to have anything from there. I can't stand the smell, it's still there........ that's the hardest things to get rid of – the sounds, and the smell.

I hope our story will help people. Personally I think Grantham represents the fact that you can totally and completely lose everything, but the community spirit is still very strong. There may only be 320 people, but it is a really nice place. At the last Residents' Meeting, the Council showed plans for the next two years, and it's very exciting. It's like Phoenix rising out of the ashes. They are offering a land swap – moving people up to higher ground. Not that we will ever go back......... Peter reckons he would, but I love being here. I love the five exits! It's the first thing I looked at. And the roads, I've made sure there is access to the roads, because that was the worst part – when the water came down and we were stranded.

IF YOU'RE IN THE WATER, YOU'RE
GONE

MARTY WARBURTON HAS RUN THE PETROL STATION IN THE CENTRE OF GRANTHAM FOR 18 YEARS AND HAS SEEN SEVERAL FLOODS COME AND GO. THE FEROCITY AND SPEED OF WHAT OVERCAME HIS TINY TOWN ON THAT FATEFUL JANUARY DAY COULD BE LIKENED TO NO OTHER EVENT MARTY HAD WITNESSED...

On Sunday, Marty was conscious that the River catchments were rising, so set about doing the normal precautionary procedures. Anything in the shop below two and a half feet gets lifted up higher, the freezers get lifted up on milk crates etc. "We had that all down pat pretty well," he says.

When the water rose rapidly to the counter in his service station, Marty realized there was nothing 'normal' about this flood. "I'd gone back into the Service Station to lock it up; grab my personal stuff, licence, wallet and all that sort of thing, and by the time I had walked in off the street it was waist deep." The sound of the water pouring in through the personal access door is firmly cemented in Marty's memory; he likens it to a huge funnel. As he describes the harrowing sounds of the stock and shelving crashing around in the mayhem and then the clamour of the front office window caving in, the trauma of the situation is well etched in the furrows of his face. "I could tell by the feel of the water – it just felt wrong!" The next Marty knew, the huge wall of water blacked out all daylight in the shop, and in an instant he was treading water where only hours before he'd been serving customers. "I could feel the peak of my hat hitting the ceiling - that was my first taste of 'I'm going to meet my Maker,'" Marty shudders as he recalls. Gripped by panic, he knew he just had to get out of there. "So I took a breath and duck dived under the water through the door. As my torso came out the door, the current spun me around, it smashed my head into the door jamb and took me – somehow, I don't know how – but I was able to grab the baton that comes off the front of the building that holds the awning up. It took a few prayers, and I managed to grab hold of it with both hands, shimmy myself to a point where it came down and pull myself up onto the roof."

Marty attributes his survival to his trusty Drizabone coat. "It was a full length Drizabone, it acted like a wetsuit skid. If I didn't have it on the pockets of my jeans would've filled up like balloons, the water was flowing that quick. I still wake up in the middle of the night in a cold sweat thinking 'I can't do this, I can't hold on.'"

From his position on the roof of the Service Station, Marty struggled to comprehend all that surrounded him. As far as the eye could see was a raging torrent, with all manner debris rolling and tossing in the churning waters. Anything that had a bit of size about it, whatever it hit, it plowed straight over the top of it. Tree trunks three feet wide with the root balls still on them, and six or seven feet in height were carried like twigs, as were cars, boats, water tanks, containers...even a 20,000 gallon rainwater tank. "I saw people in the water. Out of the corner of my eye I thought they were trying to swim. I leant down to give a hand to someone who was swept past, only to realise they were dead! After the first two attempts I realized that if you're in the water, you're gone. The second attempt was the tell tale for me. I grabbed a hand – and it was not a good sight! A couple of cars floated past, just six or seven metres away. The first one had two people sitting on the roof and all you could see was the roof turret and two people sitting on top – just screaming, sheer terror and close enough that you could see it in their eyes....then the same thing again – I couldn't do anything for them, I felt so useless. About 10 metres past the Servo driveway, the car disappeared... they disappeared and I didn't see them again. Not long after another one came past; a well-dressed gentleman, probably going to a function or business meeting; same thing- you could taste the terror! It must have been something across the road there; it got to the same spot and went down. That's when I realized you know - I'm not able to help anyone!"

Leaning back on the skillion roof up against the awning, Marty was shocked to realize there were power lines just above him. Moving himself onto the pitched roof of the showroom and office, his attention was caught by the house diagonally across the road.

"It looked like someone had picked it off the stumps and spun it around...then it took off in the direction of the paddock. It narrowly missed several other houses, pushed out around a clump of trees and was swept away, eventually coming to rest in Shultz' paddock. Even though there was the terrible noise of the water, and things were banging and clanging together, clear as day you could hear the people screaming - just sheer terror, the people screaming in that house." (See page 204)

Photo taken by Marty from Petrol Station roof during flood

I COULD TELL BY THE FEEL OF THE WATER – IT JUST FELT WRONG!

Highly traumatised by all he had seen and experienced, and with darkness descending on the horrifying scene, Marty resolved he'd have to wait until the SES came and rescued him. The next seven hours were spent in survival mode. Linda, in the house opposite, and Marty yelled over the roar of the water several times in the darkness, checking that each other were safe. With all power cut, Linda lit a candle and stood with it at the window, while Marty improvised with his cigarette lighter, flashing her with the little flame every now and again. The sight of another human was so reassuring. "I'd flash her with the cigarette lighter every 30 seconds or so, and she was there the whole time with her candle in the window. I'd spent all Saturday and Sunday night without any sleep. Constantly flashing the lighter was enough to help keep me awake on the roof and it didn't take long to wear a hole in my thumb. The pain from that kept me awake, though

I did dose off at one stage, and woke to Linda's yelling. I knew if I fell asleep on the roof I was gone."

The rain continued, followed by lightning. By now Marty's nerves were in shreds, and the peril of being zapped off the roof was more than he could handle. "I decided I'd get down. The water was still up, but I had no way of knowing how deep, I just had to get off that roof." Marty shimmied to the end of the roof and dropped into the water. "I don't remember anything after that, until I got two doors back up to the house behind the shop. I remember standing on the verandah, the sliding doors opened up, and Wayne stuck his head out looking like he'd just seen a ghost. He grabbed me and pulled me inside just as the verandah was swept away, as the stumps under it had been taken out by the current."

Photos of in, and around, Marty's garage

Mal Dionysius & Ken Harm

WATCHING A TRAGEDY
UNFOLD

KEN HARM RECALLS STANDING AT HIS FRONT WINDOW, WATCHING IN DISBELIEF AS THE EVENTS OF THAT TRAGIC MONDAY UNFOLDED BEFORE HIM. "NORMALLY WHEN THE CREEK RISES, IT RISES STEADILY. THIS CAME NO WARNING, WHATEVER! WHAT WE SAW DOWN THERE, I NEVER WANT TO SEE ANYTHING LIKE IT AGAIN…" KEN PAUSES, THE AGONY OF WHAT HE SAW OBVIOUSLY WEIGHING IN ON HIM. HESITATINGLY, HE CONTINUES, "IT TEARS AT YOUR HEART STRINGS. IT IS ONE-THING TO HEAR ABOUT IT, BUT WHEN ITS PEOPLE YOU KNOW SAYING IT………"

Mal Dionysius and his two boys were standing on the railway line, watching the water come up. His observations were equally disturbing. "Within about five minutes it had risen so much I said to the kids, 'Let's move to the other side of the road where we'll be a bit safer.' We did and there was a fence to negotiate. I sent my son home for a shifter to undo the hinges to the gate (there is a $3000.00 fine for cutting locks or a chain so I undid them instead). We threw the gate down and within 15 minutes it was under water. A car come down the road with the water and we watched it slam into the railway line. Someone said, 'We told him to shift his car, he wouldn't listen.'

Within 2 minutes there were 10 or 15 cars coming down, some towing boats behind them, straight into the railway line. There were people standing up on the platform taking photos and I looked up and I saw the water go straight over the railway line. I yelled, 'Get out of there!'

They gaped at me stupidly, 'Why?'

I screamed, 'LOOK!' They just took off running; the water was coming down, like a big wave at the beach. The next thing I looked up and here's this house coming down the road, completely intact, not a mark on it. It took out a pump shed on the way. 'Where did that come from?' I stammered. It just came down the road, unbelievable!

SAVED BY A ROOF-RACK

We took-off up the hill then, kept on running, trying to get away. The railway line is the highest point on the lower side of Grantham. As the last people were running off the bridge, the water was rising over the railway line and all these survivors were trying to get across the water. One woman had two kids, one under each arm. My mate and his brother couldn't stand there and watch it. 'We've gotta go and help her', they agreed with a hasty nod and raced down there as quick as they could and somehow, without getting drowned, each grabbing one of the kids they managed to save them. One car that had been washed down had someone hanging onto its roof racks; it slammed into the bridge, and the occupant managed to jump over the railway line and reach safety; I never found out whether it was male or female, or who it was!

There was a couple on their way home from Brisbane where they had just bought their car an hour and a half earlier and had been diverted this way as the Gatton bypass was closed. They met this wall of water heading right for them. They jammed the car into reverse and would've been doing 40 to 50Kph, flat out in reverse – when water caught them, flipped the car over and slammed them against one of the houses. They scrambled up onto the roof of the house but it too, began to go under but they managed to jump onto the roof of a car floating past and were swept to the railway line where they managed to jump off.

TWO CHANCES OF SURVIVAL, NONE AND NONE.

Mal continues his story: I just stood here watching helplessly as everything washed by. The debris in the water was amazing; gas bottles, shipping containers, Styrofoam boxes, millions of water tanks, a seriously amazing amount of tanks; didn't know there were so many people living out here. A shed just took off, then the house across the road next to the pub. Some blokes were sitting on the roof of the pub and they just watched it shift off its stumps. It shifted about five metres then it just caved in, 'boof' and the roof fell down. There were three people in there at the time. They've found one body over the railway line in Philps Road, the other one down at Harms Farm and they haven't found the third one. The guy on the pub roof knew they were inside the house. They had two chances, none and none. I rang up the bloke about 9:45 that night and I said 'Are you still alive?'

He was still coming to grips with it. 'Yeah', he said 'I'm sitting up on the pub roof and I saw three people die. You don't want to know.'

IN A TIME OF CRISIS YOU CAN ALWAYS COUNT ON ...... THE HEALTH INSPECTOR.
IN FIRE, TEMPEST AND FLOOD THE HEALTH INSPECTOR ALWAYS GETS THROUGH.

On the Thursday immediately after the flood Mal found a rather officious health inspector in the cold room at the evacuation centre. "What are you doing in here?" questioned Mal.

"I'm just checking your meat. You're lucky it's 1 degree below the recommended temperature," he grunted.

This same inspector turned up again at 6am the following Sunday. Fortunately there had been a major clean-up of the cooking and dining area on the Saturday night!

One of the local volunteers was busy changing bin liners when she was approached.
"I'm the health inspector, how many people did you cook for last night?"
"About 75,"she replied hesitantly.
"Any of them sick?"
"What's it to you?" she retorted.
"Have you ever heard of cross-contamination?"
"I used to work in the shop down here mate. I've got my catering certificate; you can go and get …."

A "FLOOD" OF FOOD

Faced with the prospect of no power in Grantham for several days, many residents decided to donate the contents of their freezers to the community diner that had been set up at the school.

Mal recounts…. "The barbie - it never stopped! She just kept goin' and goin'. We had sausages, mince, steak, kidney - you name it. T-bone for lunch, t-bone for

dinner; someone had three huge snapper in their freezer, beautiful!" One of the residents commented that they had eaten more meat in three days than in the past twelve months. A breakfast of scrambled eggs for the stricken residents consumed four dozen eggs alone, along with a huge quantity of bacon! The dining area became a hub of comfort in the dark days that followed that fearful onslaught of water.

"SILTED UP" TAKES ON A NEW MEANING

Floods have been depositing silt in the rich river flats of the Lockyer Valley for millennia, which has become affectionately known as the 'salad bowl' of Queensland. However, it is not so appreciated when its inside cars and houses!

It took a two tonne crane and an excavator to load one vehicle, full of silt, onto a truck, and off it went to the scrap metal merchant where the truck driver was somewhat hesitantly received.

"We're not paying for the mud," announced the Scrap Metal Merchant, authoritatively.
"Well, you get it out and pay us for the rest of it," responded the driver.
That particular Ford Falcon weighed in at two tonnes!

The tremendous force of the water shifted several houses off their stumps. One of these was filled to the window sills with silt. The house had been condemned under a demolition order and the owner, overwhelmed by the magnitude and futility of a salvage operation for his personal effects declared, "Whatever's in there can stay in there!" His overzealous brother had always coveted a particular set of barstools. Picking his way through the house - up to his pants in slop - he located them, dragged them out and cleaned them up. "Beewdiful! Nice,big, Kenworth bar stools, all clean and shiny!"

211

Thanks

Army

Car and debris

LOCKYER VALLEY

Premier Anna Bligh at Grantham

Shop removed off stumps

House totally moved by force of water

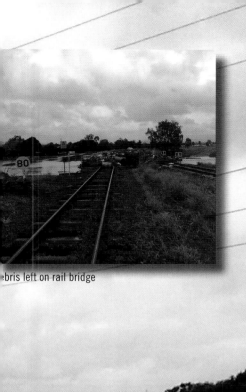
bris left on rail bridge

Concrete slabs are all that remains of some homes

Force of water caused untold damage

ouse dislodged

Properties filled with mud and debris

Walls completely washed away

213

THE WATER LEVEL HAD RISEN
AGAIN

"DANNY, OLD KEN NEXT DOOR WANTS TO SEE YOU", THE URGENCY IN HIS WIFE'S VOICE AROUSED DANNY MCGUIRE FROM A WELL EARNED CATNAP THAT FATEFUL MONDAY. AN OFFICER OF GRANTHAM RURAL FIRE SERVICE, DANNY WAS EXHAUSTED, HAVING ATTENDED QUITE A FEW INCIDENTS OVER THE PREVIOUS WEEKEND. IN FACT, WHILE HE WAS ATTENDING A MEDICAL EMERGENCY ON SUNDAY NIGHT, HIS WIFE LLYNC WAS DUTIFULLY MANNING THE FIRE TRUCK AT A ROADBLOCK ON THE WESTERN SIDE OF TOWN. THE SAFETY BARRIERS, WHICH HAD BEEN PREVENTING MOTORISTS FROM INADVERTENTLY DRIVING INTO A FLOODED SECTION OF THE ROAD, HAD BEEN DAMAGED BY A DRIVER WHO DELIBERATELY DROVE INTO THE FLOOD WATERS. TO MAINTAIN SAFETY FOR THE ROAD USERS, DANNY HAD DESPATCHED LLYNC AND THE FIRE TRUCK TO ACT AS THE SAFETY BARRIER.

As Danny headed across his yard to old Ken's, he noticed that the water level had risen again. With all the rain during the past week, the water level in the lower part of their yard had risen and ebbed countless times, and the current level was no cause for alarm. It was Ken's frantic gesticulating in the direction of the creek that caught Danny's attention. When he turned in the direction of Ken's pointing, he saw it..................................in the distance, a house and trees were riding a huge wave of water down the creek towards them. As they turned to each other in horror, each uttered in unison "we're out of here" and raced for their vehicles, frantically bellowing for their wives and families to hurry up. Danny paused in the Fire Truck at the front gate as Llync, 31, Gary, 12, Zac , 7 and Jossy, 5 flung themselves into the cabin.

In Danny's haste to get to the gate, he'd run over a 44 gallon drum, which had become caught under the body, just behind the front wheel. Llync dutifully notified Danny of the problem as she slammed the door. Danny dismissed her concern, intent on getting out that gate and up the road. When he looked up, the wave of water was bearing down on them. Before they even reached the bitumen of the road, the wave smashed over the truck and Danny could feel them being spun

around like seaweed in the surf. The cabin of the truck was rapidly filling with water in the swirling mayhem that ensued, and as they brushed past a tree, Danny's instinct took over and he thrust Zac out of his open window into the safety of the branches, above the raging torrent. Danny had fondly watched Zac climb trees many times and knew that he would be able to climb higher, should the water continue to rise.

How could anyone in their right mind ever think the water would rise further? This was a road in a quiet little town, not part of a river system!! As Danny turned back to grab Jossy , he was sucked out the window into the churning torrent. Carried along by the angry tide, he remembered hearing Llync screaming that her window wouldn't go down. With a frantic feeling of helplessness for his trapped family, Danny lunged with all his might at the last gum tree still standing in his street, hauling his wet and weary body against the trunk. Still incapacitated from a previous foot injury, he was unable to climb higher up the tree, so positioned himself as securely as he could, as the water rushed around him. As the cold reality of losing his wife and 2 children overcame him, he turned his attention to Zac, calculating he was in a tree about 150m away.

At this point, EMQ pilot Mark Kempton was refuelling the rescue helicopter at Archerfield Airport on Brisbane's outskirts, 90km to the east. The radio crackled to life, "Grantham five one, one three four six Gatton-Helidon Road. 2 adults, 3 children in fire truck, send chopper". From the many times Mark had worked with Danny, he immediately recognised the call sign and made a mental note that the location would be the first point he would head for when he returned to the air. "Are you O.K, Zac?" Danny hollered, struggling to make himself heard above the roaring water. Great relief swept over him as Zac replied.....all he had left of his happy family of five. After scanning the foaming water, Danny realised that the wreckage of the Fire Truck was located between them, and that it was quite possible that Zac could actually see through the windscreen into the cabin of the

214

THE WAVE OF WATER WAS BEARING
DOWN ON THEM

truck. Despite their predicament, he was relieved when the cloak of darkness began to set in, removing the possibility of Zac seeing anything of his lost family. As darkness closed around them, Zac became agitated and Danny increased the regularity of his calls. Zac's response provided some consolation in the distress which was consuming his thoughts.

After six long, lonely hours, Danny and Zac were rescued by locals. Before they left Grantham, in keeping with his true devotion to his work, Danny assisted in the rescue of 3 adults, 2 children and a number of cats and dogs from the roof of a nearby house, using a ladder from a truck in his yard. Danny and Zac were taken to Helidon where one of Danny's Careflight colleagues checked Zac over for injuries. In an effort to preserve them from undue media attention, they both were taken to Toowoomba for 5½ weeks.

Danny's return to Grantham brought mixed feelings. The place had morphed into an eerie place of habitation, with a large contingent of officials still working to organise and coordinate initial rebuilding efforts. With his zest for community involvement, Danny was soon added to local committees which are a vital part of getting Grantham back on its' feet. Much is still to be worked out, with broken hearts needing time to heal and understanding and compassion needing to be displayed by all involved in the decision making processes.

The McGuire family will never be the same again. Grantham will never be the same again.

WE STARED INTO THE
DARKNESS

THE PHONE CALL ENDED AS ABRUPTLY AS IT HAD BEGUN "....JUST GET THE HELL OUTTA THERE", HE HOLLERED. WHIPPED INTO ACTION, A COMBINATION OF FRENZY AND FEAR TOOK OVER. WHAT WAS THIS? IN NO TIME AT ALL, WE GRABBED OUR RIGS AND LOG BOOKS, HUSTLED A NEIGHBOUR AND HIS DOG INTO THE VAN AND EVACUATED. NEGOTIATING THE HIGHWAY AT BREAK NECK SPEED, IN THE DRIVING RAIN AND DEAD OF NIGHT IS NO ORDINARY FEAT. NERVOUSLY CHECKING OUR MIRRORS, WE SPED ON IN A DESPERATE ATTEMPT TO OUTRUN THE TURBULENT MASS OF WATER THAT HAD SWEPT IN UNDER THE COVER OF A PITCH BLACK NIGHT.

Further up the highway, shaken, but feeling an uneasy relief at reaching higher ground, we stopped. A group of similarly dazed souls who had, like us, just managed to escape a monster's clutches, began to gather. Helpless, homeless and silently wondering what to do or where to go, we stared into the darkness. The drama had unfolded so quickly, but where had the water come from? Who out there didn't get away?

CALM BEFORE THE STORM
Our drop zone is located right in the heart of the Lockyer Valley, a tranquil country retreat remote from the hectic pace of nearby cities Ipswich, Toowoomba and Brisbane. Traveller's on the Warrego Highway often slow down to observe the kaleidoscope of colours descending gracefully from literally out of the blue.

SATURATION
The ground was already sodden from weeks of torrential rain. Laidley Creek, which flows around the eastern end of our property, had broken its banks and crept up our airstrip, only to retreat and rise, again and again.

We live in Australia. We know the endless cycle of flood and drought, so we were apprehensive. Still the rain poured down. Alarm bells began to ring. We began preparing for what we knew – the '74 flood level. A tsunami didn't enter our imaginations, simply because tsunamis didn't occur inland – at least here-to-fore. We moved things to higher ground and began furiously sandbagging in the unrelenting rain, topping up the levee banks in the lower areas around the house. We plugged up the driveway entrance, smugly comfortable this would hold the water back and we would ride this one through.

On Monday, 10th January, the torrential rain did not abate. Our C182 had become trapped on the tarmac, so we pushed her to higher ground and choked her wheels. She would be completely submerged within a few short hours. How oblivious we were!

We locked the fuel shed – at least the contents would be securely contained – carried Club House and Skydiving equipment upstairs to a safer level and got back to our sandbagging.

As the day progressed to evening the noise level of the critters – frogs, toads and crickets – rose alarmingly. Little did we realise they were sending us an urgent message of imminent danger. Their instincts were keener than ours and they were ringing alarm bells with all stops out.

At 9:45pm the phone rang. A neighbour screamed down the line that a giant wall of water was bearing down on us from the western end of the Valley..."just get the hell outta there," he hollered.

AFTERMATH
On that fateful night 8 feet (244 centimetres) of toxic, contaminated, filthy water engulfed our property and filled our Club House. Parachute equipment, student's gear and helmets, radios, aircraft equipment, personal belongings, bedding, kitchen and bar facilities, our office and an aeroplane were completely destroyed.

We were accommodated for the next four nights at a stranger's house. Six of us, along with two dogs, found refuge in this empty abode. The owners, fortunate to be so far removed from the trauma, were away on holidays and had agreed to open their home for the flood affected.

CLEAN-UP
Where to begin...? Filthy, toxic sludge thickly coated everything in sight. The task ahead was daunting, overwhelming at times. Volunteers arrived from far and wide – the joy of giving was just as important as receiving. Our clients - skydivers from Brisbane - pitched in to help, as did volunteers from Toowoomba, a plumber from Victoria, units from Amberley Air Force Base, the Army, SES, Fire and Rescue personnel... the list is humbling.

Several weeks on, the Drop Zone is looking more respectable. The grass is green again and the pulse is becoming normal. We are anxious to restore the Club House to its former glory, complete with its lively stream of adventure seekers. For nothing beats the adrenalin rush of a freefall from the blue skies over our beautiful Lockyer Valley.

WE BEGAN PREPARING FOR
WHAT WE KNEW

217

RIPCORD SKYDIVERS
Lockyer Valley

AUSTRALIA DAY
2011

The 26th January, 2011 was as monumental to the residents of the Lockyer Valley as was this same date to our whole nation some 110 years earlier. Dropping silently from the heavens, parachute billowing above and the red, white and blue of our honoured flag unfurling below, was our ultimate moment of triumph. Together we had survived and together we were recovering. Australia was still the land of promise, epitomised by the good old Aussie mateship that has endured for generations. Just as disaster came from the heavens, skydivers descended from the heavens to pay respects to the victims of the Lockyer Valley Floods.

Ollie, Kat, Casey, Harry Plint, Damien and Monique

SO MANY UNFULFILLED PROMISES

WORKING FROM 'THE DINING ROOM' - AN OPEN CARPORT ON DAVE COLLISON'S RUINED FARM IN HELIDON, ARE TWO INCREDIBLY DEVOTED AND UNSELFISH WOMEN, THE HUMAN FACE OF THE POST-DISASTER RECOVERY EFFORT IN THE LOCKYER VALLEY.

Arriving on January 18th, 2011 — 8 days after the "inland tsunami" practically destroyed everything in its path, Ollie Mans — going on 60 — and her daughter Monique (27) have been organising flood relief in the form of donated food, clothing and other essentials to the stricken community, helping to rebuild devastated lives. How they got there is quite a story. They had been helping out in their home town — Brisbane - when PM Julia Gillard, observing their selfless energy, asked them if they would be prepared to help out at Grantham. They were, so she arranged a clearance for them, and they arrived at the cordoned-off township on the same day as the Army.

Expecting to be providing for 130 people, they quickly discovered that the number was closer to 700! After working for some time from Marty's Service Station, they moved to Dave's farm and set up operations there. How they got there is a story, too. Monique found Dave lying on a mattress in his shed, and realised that his condition (he has recently been given a stent in his coronary artery after 4 stress-related heart attacks) was serious — and she finally managed to get him to accept her help. After that, he insisted that they make their headquarters in his shed. The major part of their activities includes the distribution of food and other necessities provided, initially, by Radio B1.05FM, The Courier-Mail, a Sunshine Coast newspaper and other donors, but now it comes regularly every Thursday from a church on the Gold Coast. The latest (at the time of our visit) was $5000.00 worth of food and other goods.

Also helping out is Katherine (Kat) Plint, from Laidley, a professional counsellor who established the 'Hannah's Foundation' in 2007 after the tragic drowning of her daughter. Her experience and enthusiasm are invaluable in helping the disaster victims get back on their feet and start to rebuild their lives. Greatly appreciated are vouchers of up to $200.00, available from her foundation which she gives the desperately needy to purchase life's necessities. Casey, a teenager from Grantham; Monique's partner Damien who comes to help at weekends (he works in Brisbane all week) and of course Dave himself, have all devoted themselves to the cause. These astonishingly generous, unselfish and capable women are committed wholeheartedly to helping the community as long as they will be needed — which will be for some months yet. And Monique has also set herself to help Dave — who is really in no condition to run his farm the way it needs to be — for the next two years, helping to cultivate his land (with a generously loaned tractor), plant and (in due course) harvest his crops and see them taken to market.

They recall with genuine feeling the time — and effort — it took to gain the confidence of the conservative rural community of the Valley. They found it needed patience and persistence — but above all a commitment to keeping promises. These people, naturally wary of strangers, had experienced so many unfilled promises - and even had been donated goods that proved to be worthless household rubbish — they hardly knew who to trust. Ollie and her team are now unquestionably an accepted part of the community, and when their work is finally over — however many months it takes — they fully intend to retain the links that have been forged during their time when they return to their own homes in Brisbane, and Kat Plint of the 'Hannah's Foundation', will continue to be their most valued contact.

ed weekly supplies

The 'loungeroom'

Handplanted strawberry fields on Dave's farm

MUD-PACK TREATMENT FOR
IPSWICH'S PRESERVED HERITAGE

IPSWICH, QUEENSLAND'S OLDEST PROVINCIAL CITY, IS REGARDED AS HOME BY APPROXIMATELY 170,000 PEOPLE. THE CITY IS RENOWNED FOR ITS RICH ARCHITECTURAL AND CULTURAL HERITAGE, AND THE PRESERVATION OF MANY OF ITS HISTORIC BUILDINGS AND HOMES HAS CONTRIBUTED TO AN INCREASE IN THE TOURISM AND HOSPITALITY INDUSTRIES. IPSWICH HAS PRESERVED ITS EARLY RAILWAY HERITAGE BY CONVERTING THE NOW DEFUNCT RAILWAY WORKSHOPS INTO A POPULAR HERITAGE MUSEUM.

Initially named Limestone, the young township was established in 1827 beside the Bremer River, a short distance from its junction with the Brisbane River, as a convict out-station to quarry limestone. It was renamed Ipswich in 1842, when free settlers began to arrive; and with the mining of coal, the city grew as an important industrial centre, with steamboats and barges transporting the coal and other produce to Brisbane, returning with supplies for the settlers in this largely working-class community. The availability of coal for steam trains, however, led to the development of a rail network and the river transport ceased. Later, depletion of coal reserves, as well as a tragic mining incident, eventually led to a decline in mining, and the city of Ipswich has now become a centre for commerce, industry and education.

In January, 2011, Ipswich experienced an extraordinary flooding event which, although peaking at a slightly lower height than in 1974, did much greater damage on account of the city's increase in population and development.

IPSWICH

WIVENHOE DAM

Brisbane River

Brisbane River

TOOWOOMBA 69KM

Warrego Highway

Bremer River

Bremer River

● IPSWICH

Amberley Air Base

WARWICK 120KM

BRISBANE 39KM

Yamanto

Cunningham Highway

PEAK HOUR IN IPSWICH
WATERWAY

THE BREMER RIVER AND ITS MANY TRIBUTARIES CREATE A NETWORK OF WATERWAYS THROUGHOUT MUCH OF IPSWICH, MAKING MANY AREAS WITHIN THE CITY AND ITS SUBURBS PRONE TO FLOODING.

The excessive rain in the first week of January, 2011 fell on already saturated ground. By January 11th, the floodwaters that had devastated the Lockyer Valley were rushing eastward towards Ipswich, and the overflow from Wivenhoe Dam was surging down the Brisbane River, preventing the Bremer from discharging its waters. Every dam and watercourse in the area was flooded and by January 13th the Bremer River had peaked at 19.4 metres, and one third of Ipswich had become submerged.

With limited warning of the impending event, some residents and businesses were able to move vehicles and property to higher ground. More than 1,500 people were evacuated, as polluted, mud-laden water invaded their homes, snatching up their belongings

and distributing them elsewhere. The city's business centre all but disappeared, its security alarms uttering a wailing protest at the unwanted intrusion, and the new Riverlink shopping centre was severely inundated.

As the waters slowly receded, the despondent residents surveyed the sad wreckage of their homes and began the depressing task of consigning many once-treasured possessions to soggy mounds along the roadsides. Soon, however, thousands of willing volunteers and hundreds of Defence Force personnel poured into Ipswich, offering help and support, including generous donations, enabling residents to face the future recovery phase with fresh courage.

As the Ipswich Mayor said, "We will emerge from this disaster better and stronger."

FLOOD

IPSWICH

- **Dec 2010**
  368mm rain falls during the month

- **Jan 6th 2011**
  A further 250mm of rain has fallen since December.
  Flood warning issued for Lockyer and Bremer Rivers.

- **Jan 9th 2011**
  Significant rain over northern Ipswich rural districts.
  Emergency services activated.

- **Jan 10th 2011**
  Esk inundated for the first time in memory.
  Heavy rain continuing.
  Floodwater approaching Ipswich from Lockyer Valley.
  Wivenhoe Dam's overflow builds up in Brisbane River, causing floodwater to back up in Bremer.

- **Jan 11th 2011**
  Bremer River rising.
  Riverlink shopping centre closes.
  River and creek-side areas flooding.

FACTS

- **Jan 12th – 13th 2011**

  More than 3,000 homes and businesses flood affected.

  Bremer River peaks at 19.4m.

  A third of Ipswich is engulfed by floodwater.

  Half the city is without power.

  Surrounding communities isolated.

  More than 1,500 in eight evacuation centres.

  Ipswich Motorway, Warrego and Centenary highways cut.

  Colleges Crossing impassable.

  Shortage of food and essential supplies.

  Barellan Point flooded from both rivers.

- **Jan 14th 2011**

  Floodwaters receding.

  Centenary Highway and Ipswich Motorway open.

- **Jan 16th 2011**

  Volunteers register at Briggs Road Sporting Complex to help Ipswich clean-up.

  Defence personnel assisting.

- **Overall:**

  44,500 tonnes of rubbish collected.

  More than $300,000 million estimated damages.

MAYOR PAUL PISASALE

Ipswich

IT IS NOT EASY BEING MAYOR AT A TIME LIKE THIS BUT I DRAW MY STRENGTH FROM THE VERY COMMUNITY I AM TRYING TO ASSIST– HOPING TO MAKE ALL THE BAD GO AWAY AND "FIX IT". THIS HAS BEEN A DEVASTATING TIME FOR THE WHOLE COMMUNITY AND OUR NEARBY NEIGHBOURS, BUT IN TRUE AUSSIE STYLE, WE ROLL THE SLEEVES UP AND GET ON WITH IT. MANY RESIDENTS HAVE VOLUNTEERED SO MUCH TIME AND BEEN SO THOUGHTFUL OF EVERYONE'S NEEDS.

At the height on the floods on Wednesday 12 January 2011, it is estimated that more than 3000 homes and businesses in the city were underwater. The general consensus of the day was that "nobody thought this could happen again since we had Wivenhoe Dam". The flood waters peaked at 19.4m on 11 January 2011 compared with 20.4m in January 1974.

With around five per cent of the Ipswich population directly impacted from the devastating flooding of the Brisbane and Bremer Rivers in early January 2011, it was important that we not only had the voluntary army so willing to assist, but that we utilised donations of heavy machinery and equipment and assisted to do the "hard yards" that many residents were unable to access.

In Moores Pocket suburb alone, it is estimated about 70 per cent of the people who live there were affected, in Goodna 40 per cent, in East Ipswich, North Booval and Basin Pocket 50 per cent, North Ipswich a further 20 per cent and around 30 per cent of the businesses in the CBD.

Ipswich City Council has been overwhelmed with offers of donations ranging from equipment and household materials to clothing for our flood affected community. Promises of donations have come from local, State, national and international sources.

When we finally put all the pieces back together of our wonderful City Ipswich, I am sure we will continue to grow and be bigger and better than ever. I am also sure in the aftermath of the flood and devastation, there will be many lessons to be learned and hopefully we can all learn those lessons together. Ipswich City Council continues to work with the insurance companies to get the best possible outcome for our residents.

Mayor Paul Pisasale
City of Ipswich

IPSWICH TRANSIT CENTRE
Ipswich

THE IPSWICH TRANSIT CENTRE COACH TERMINAL IS A PIVOTAL DROP-OFF/PICKUP POINT FOR LOCAL, STATE AND INTERSTATE BUS AND COACH COMPANIES. IT PROVIDES THE LINK BETWEEN RAIL SERVICES AND COACH SERVICES TO DESTINATIONS IN THE IPSWICH REGION, TOOWOOMBA, WARWICK AND BEYOND. LIKE MANY OTHER CENTRES CLOSE TO THE BREMER RIVER IN IPSWICH, IT WAS TOTALLY INUNDATED ON JANUARY, 12TH 2011, AND WAS LEFT WITH A RESIDUE OF THICK MUD AFTER THE WATERS RECEDED. THE CENTRE, WHICH IS MANAGED BY QUEENSLAND RAIL, WAS BASICALLY GUTTED BY THE WATERS THAT FLOWED THROUGH THE BUILDING, AS WELL AS BEING COVERED BY A LAYER OF SILT WHICH HAD TO BE FLUSHED OUT. SIX MONTHS AFTER THE DISASTER, QR IS STILL DEALING WITH DAMAGE AND THE CENTRE REMAINS CLOSED AND IS NOT EXPECTED TO REOPEN BEFORE THE END OF THE YEAR. MEANWHILE A TEMPORARY BUS STOP FOR COACHES HAS BEEN SET UP IN BELL STREET, CLOSE TO THE IPSWICH RAILWAY STATION.

EVERYTHING
LOST

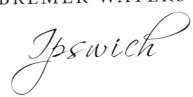

"THERE ARE SO MANY PEOPLE AROUND THIS AREA WHO ARE REALLY STRUGGLING. THEY'VE LOST EVERYTHING —SOME WILL NEVER GET BACK TO NORMAL." AS COL HALL SPEAKS IT BECOMES PATENTLY CLEAR THAT THIS MAN IS HURTING, NOT FOR HIS OWN LOSSES — ALTHOUGH THEY ARE HEAVY — BUT FOR THE RESIDENTS IN HIS CARE IN THE RETIREMENT VILLAGE THAT HE OWNS AND MANAGES. HIS COMPASSION FOR THESE SENIOR CITIZENS OF THE IPSWICH COMMUNITY IS POIGNANT. "THE OLDIES IN HERE, THEY'VE LOST EVERYTHING, NOT COVERED BY INSURANCE AND THEY CAN'T GO OUT AND GET A JOB — THEY'LL NEVER RECOVER," HE ADDS.

Bremer Waters Retirement Village is ideally set, overlooking the Bremer River as it flows towards Barellan Point, where it merges with the mighty Brisbane River. "Resort - style living for the over 55's," it advertises. Who would envisage that such idyllic surroundings could change to a scene of devastation in just a matter of hours?

"We were all evacuated the first night [Tues. 11th Jan.] from 7:30pm," Col explains. "Police came through and told us to get out. No-one thought for one moment that it would ever come this high. But the next day all you could see was kilometres of water." One suspects that, as he speaks, Col is seeing it all again.

"We came back the following morning [Wed. 12th Jan.] The water was up to our waistlines and it was still rising. We went into the Community Centre and got some furniture out — it was all floating. We washed it, dried it. There were objects on the floor that wouldn't float, but the water was so muddy, we couldn't see them and they were tripping us over. Afterwards, we were bashed and bruised. We worked until the water came up to our necks and we had to leave the rest of it. The Piano was floating around, there was a mini-grand down there — that's "history" now," he adds ruefully.

"There was 1.7 metres of water through the top floor of my house," he states. "The Community Centre had 1.7 metres through the top floor. We lost all the ground floor, the pool and the bowls green. Col is now pointing to a plan of all the affected buildings. Two thirds of this property was affected — one hundred homes out of one hundred and seventy-seven."

"They say," he says, "that after a flood you get to know who your friends are. The volunteers' help to clean-up was absolutely fantastic. I've never seen anything like it in my life. People came from Melbourne, Sydney, Newcastle, New Zealand....... all around the place. They were fantastic." We accommodated a few here in the village with the unaffected residents. We fed about 200 volunteers a day. We had people donating all sorts of food and water at our Community Centre. The kitchen had been 1.7 metres underwater, but the volunteers cleaned it up and we got it back up and running — it took two days — and then we got the power back on."

"So we're in the process of rebuilding," Col continues. "The new kitchen has gone in and then we've got the library and the toilet block to rebuild. There is a big gym that will need a complete fit out — all the treadmills are wrecked — a craft room, a salon and a coffee shop, with more toilet blocks needing to be redone. We lost everything in these areas," he explains, "we couldn't get anything out — we didn't have time, management were mainly monitoring residents all day, looking out for their safety."

A tour of inspection of the village reveals horrifying scenes. It is shocking. "As you will notice everywhere, it all stinks," Col says. "It's tough to come back day after day and trudge through all the devastation. Some of our residents have found it very difficult."

"Ten percent of our oldies are now living in their affected homes because they have nowhere else to go. We have done a reduction on site fees as much as we can. The structures of the houses are still sound, so there is no danger to their lives. They will need new plaster, second fix and all appliances. Some of them are living in there trying to put things back as cheaply as they can, just living in the steel frames."

"Fifty percent of the homes are still uninhabited. There are about fifteen caravans all hooked up to power. The residents are still using the damaged showers, they have to bring a light with them if they use them after dark. We've set up our old site office as somewhere for them to go and watch TV together and do their laundry."

Col's kind-heartedness shines through again, as he expresses, "The oldies here, you should see them, I'm doing a barbecue for them tonight. It's hard, you see, some of them have no hope of financially recovering.

They are too old to go out and find a job; others have been retired for a few years and now they're out looking for jobs to pay for their renovations."

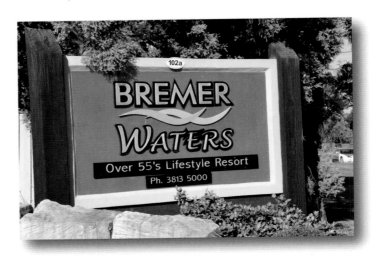

Yes, and while he is setting up his oldies and doing barbecues for them, Col and his wife have their own losses to grapple with. Their own house is trashed, there is nothing left there. The kitchen alone will need a full fit out. Their bed was shifted up with the water, then dropped into the bath as the flood went down. "My wife is feeling it, she's taking it pretty hard. We only got one car load of personal stuff out of my home, that's it." They know they have lost a large portion of their business. The losses of income can never be recovered, "…….but we'll survive somehow," he adds in his optimism.

As part owners of the village, they have sustained losses up to $500,000. The total toll sustained by all the residents is difficult to calculate, but Col estimates it would probably be a couple of million dollars. "We had done a lot of investigations before we started this investment," he informs us. "We thought we might see a one in fifty years' flood, which we did, in 2008. But it's horrifying what we've seen this time."

Col, his wife and the "oldies" will keep on with their struggle to recover. "We're supposed to be made of steel, so you just keep plodding along and don't say too much and get on with it", he concludes.

SOME WILL NEVER GET BACK TO NORMAL

![Llewellyn MOTORS]

LLEWELLYN MOTORS

Ipswich

ARE WE IN THE RIGHT
PLACE?

INTERVIEW WITH JAMES STURGES, GENERAL MANAGER.
THE FLOODS OF JANUARY, 2011 CAUSED MUCH DISTRESS AND LOSS TO THE IPSWICH CAR DEALER, LLEWELLYN MOTORS, BUT IN SPITE OF THE DESTRUCTION THAT THEIR BUSINESS SUFFERED, THE MANAGEMENT OPENED ITS HEART TO ITS STAFF AND TO THE AFFLICTED CITIZENS OF IPSWICH. SUCH GENEROSITY AND LARGE-HEARTEDNESS IN THE FACE OF ADVERSITY IS WORTHY OF ADMIRATION, RESPECT AND EMULATION BY THE IPSWICH COMMUNITY.

The dealership has been catering to the automotive needs of the residents of Ipswich for over twenty years. It markets vehicles from several car manufacturers – Holden, Toyota, Suzuki, Subaru and Hyundai- accounting for some fifty percent of new car sales in the city of Ipswich. Llewellyn Motors also has four service workshops to attend to the maintenance needs of the motor vehicle industry. The principals of the enterprise, Ross Llewellyn and his son Wade, have built the business up, buying up residential properties behind the original premises to construct the service centres, a pre-delivery garage and parts warehouses. The business now covers an area of eight acres.

When a major flood threatened on Tuesday, 11th January, 2011, many of the staff had to hasten home – some because their homes were threatened, and others because they needed to get home before the flooding cut off their access to home. Wade Llewellyn, along with the other principals of the Company, made a decision at 10am that the flood was going to impact the business and the staff. The principals desperately needed assistance if they were going to save their huge stock of vehicles and vital records. They put out a call on facebook and to other personal contacts for volunteers to assist them. The response was overwhelming. People they knew, and some they didn't know, arrived and helped move 600 vehicles to properties on higher ground. Stock on lower shelves in the Parts Warehouse was put up on higher shelves, then servers and phone systems from the administration area, were taken away to safety. They worked frantically from 10am Tuesday till 1am Wednesday, toiling away till the monster flood overtook them.

The floodwaters rose to roof-height in most of the service buildings and warehouses. The havoc caused is almost indescribable. After the waters had receded, workers opened the doors of a service garage, expecting to see a wet and muddy mess, but the sight that met their eyes made them gasp, "Are we in the right place?!" Lounge suites from the upstairs customer waiting rooms were sitting on top of the equipment on the lower floor!

The list of losses for the business is very extensive. An initial estimate of up to $6 million was lost overall, and over 4000 items had to be replaced. All buildings needed major repair work. The Company's insurer, Suncorp, covered most of their losses, a fact that the owners greatly appreciate.

For the recovery phase, the Company principals made an on-board decision to handle it as a three step program:
1: To account for the post-flood situation of each of their staff members;
2: To discover the post-flood situations of families of the staff, and to assist those in need; and 3: To rebuild the business.

This decision was much appreciated by the staff. It took six to eight weeks to get the service areas operational again, so about one hundred service employees had no real work, but they responded to the kindness shown to them by their employers by assisting in the recovery process. The crowning reward for the management's devotion to its staff was a very touching advertisement inserted in Ipswich's local paper by the staff, thanking the Llewellyn management for the caring attitude shown to them.

Thanks to another team of willing helpers, the Toyota sales area was back in operation in just a few days. It was the service areas that took time. Ironically, the last piece of equipment to be replaced was the item that would have been very useful in the earliest stages of the cleanup: the carwash had to come all the way from Germany!

Llewellyn Motors also pledged a percentage of each car sale over the following month to the Mayor's Flood Appeal. This liberal action raised $40,000 for the victims of the floods in Ipswich. Through a relationship that Llewellyn Motors has with Hyundai, two four-ton trucks were made available to the Salvation Army and other community organisations for months after the flood. Perhaps this generous spirit had something to do with the fact that the floodwaters came to within centimetres of owner, Ross Llewellyn's office, but did not come into it; and at Ross' own home, the waters came within centimetres of the floor, but did not enter the house. Whatever the reason, everyone is thankful that this man was at least spared that extra heartache.

Llewellyn Motors is continuing to recover and move forward. The Ipswich community hopes that the business flourishes as a compensation for the liberal spirit that the company has shown to mankind in its need.

Boots left beside road

Bremer River and Riverlink Shops

River Heart - Parklands

IPSWICH

Brisbane Road - Ipswich

Properties underwater

North Booval

Moggill Ferry

River Heart Parklands - aftermath

Ipswich CBD cordoned-off

Bremer River at One Mile - Ipswich

Ipswich CBD

Ulster Hotel

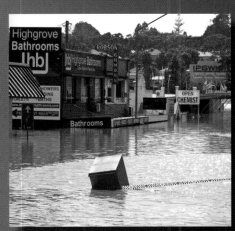

Ipswich CBD

Intersection underwater

TOO GREAT TO
COMPREHEND

BRASSALL STATE SCHOOL IS A LARGE PRIMARY SCHOOL WITH AN ENROLLMENT OF 740 STUDENTS FROM PREP TO YEAR SEVEN, AND APPROXIMATELY SEVENTY STAFF. WHEN THE SCHOOL CLOSED FOR THE SUMMER BREAK IN DECEMBER, 2010, SCHOOL PRINCIPAL, PETER DOYLE COULD NEVER HAVE IMAGINED THE EVENTS THAT WOULD IMPACT HIS SCHOOL BEFORE THE NEW TERM COMMENCED ON JANUARY 24TH, 2011.

On Tuesday, January 11th, the rain was bucketing down when Peter received word that the Ipswich suburb of Brassall was expected to flood. He hastened to close the Summer School of thirty students that was operating at his school during the school holidays. While attending to that matter, he received an offer to sandbag the lowest building in the school, so he stayed and assisted the workers with the task. When Peter left the school at 3.30pm, the creek that runs behind the school had not broken its banks. Peter could not comprehend that enough water could rise to inundate the school.

But the waters did rise. Firstly, they covered the playing fields and then they completely submerged the classrooms that had been sandbagged. Eventually, they engulfed the whole school. When the waters receded, Peter was faced with a very extensive list of damages:

- One hundred and sixty centimetres of water had been through the Administration Block, destroying computers, furniture and all current records of students and staff;
- The same amount of water went through the brand new Assembly Hall complex, which had been completed only fourteen weeks beforehand. The complex included the canteen and uniform shop, both of which were ruined, and the Hall was badly damaged;
- Sixteen classrooms out of a total of thirty were flood-affected. Eight of the sixteen had to be carted away.

- The whole library was lost: the water rose to just above the highest bookshelves, the paper in the books absorbed the water, so not a book was saved;
- The Music Room and all musical instruments were lost;
- All Physical Education equipment was wrecked;
- All resources for reading, mathematics and science were destroyed; Sixty computers — thirty in classrooms and thirty in the library were lost;
- Furniture and cabinetry had swollen and was therefore useless;
- Everything was covered in the filthy mud left by the floodwaters and everything that could float had piled up in the wreckage.

Peter had a mammoth task before him. There were just eleven days left of the school holidays. How could he and his staff create normality out of chaos? It seemed impossible, but he had not realized that the disaster would bring out the best in mankind. Volunteers from a broad spectrum of society stepped into the breach. Hundreds of people came and donated thousands of hours of their time: parents, staff, neighbours, men off the street, members from the RAAF base at nearby Amberley, and groups such as the Buddhist Compassionate Relief sisterhood; all threw themselves into turning the wreckage into an institution suitable for our growing generation to continue their schooling. Anyone who saw the filthy mess would not have thought it possible to have it ready in those eleven short days.

But the school was ready. Teachers began the School year with clean classrooms — some of them temporary demountables — but absolutely no resources. Even the Prep classes had no building blocks or story books. Peter made it a priority to order text books for every child in the school.

The New Assembly Hall

Where did the school go?

Donations have been pouring in and gradually the supply of resources is building up. Six months after the catastrophe, Brassall School still has no library, but a big team of volunteers are working on thousands of donated books. Cabinetmakers are expected during the Mid-Year Break to install new cabinetry in various rooms.

Prime Minister, Ms Julia Gillard, was invited to officially open the new Assembly Hall at Brassall State School on 21st July, 2011. Ms. Gillard responded to the invitation, and in her address to the staff, students and members of the community she said she particularly wanted to come to the Brassall State School because she was impressed with the "remarkable courage and resilience" that the school community had shown in getting the institution "back up and running." She praised the great courage of all who had contributed to the recovery effort and declared it was a "special life lesson, learning to pull together."

Slowly but surely, recovery is taking place.

Photo: Paul Coward
School Children and Official Party

Photo: Paul Coward

Photo: Paul Coward
Left to Right - Prime Minister Ms Julia Gillard - Principal Peter Doyle - MP Shayne Neumann

Playing fields and Classrooms

The Prime Minister opens the School Hall

Staff Carpark

Books!

Collapsed ceiling

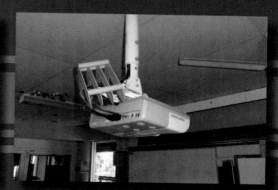
Items that floated - some stuck in ceiling

Note: puddle on chair - silt on others

Our flooded school, the morning after

Library

235

CITISWITCH BUSINESS PARK
Ipswich

THE CITISWITCH BUSINESS PARK IN IPSWICH, IS REGARDED AS AN IDEAL LOCATION FOR THE DISTRIBUTION CENTRES OF: AUSTRALIAN PHARMACEUTICAL INDUSTRIES LTD. (API) AND THE REJECT SHOP LTD., AS IT IS SITUATED CLOSE TO THE JUNCTION OF THREE MAJOR HIGHWAYS: THE IPSWICH MOTORWAY, AND THE CUNNINGHAM AND WARREGO HIGHWAYS. BOTH COMPANIES BUILT HUGE WAREHOUSES IN 2009 AND BEGAN OPERATIONS FROM THOSE CENTRES IN LATE 2009 - EARLY 2010. HOWEVER, THE NEARBY BREMER RIVER ROSE BEYOND ALL PREDICTIONS IN JANUARY, 2011, TURNING THE BUSINESS PARK INTO AN INLAND SEA. BOTH WAREHOUSES AND THEIR OFFICE COMPLEXES WERE INUNDATED BY APPROXIMATELY TWO METRES OF MUDDY WATER, SUSTAINING SEVERE LOSSES OF STOCK AND EQUIPMENT.

The Reject Shop DC was rendered "inoperable" and the Company has been struggling to operate " in a rudimentary fashion" since March. In May, the management announced that they will try to have the DC fully operational by late August, 2011. New equipment has had to be sourced from overseas and buildup of stock has gradually increased. Recovery operations have also involved careful consideration of a flood mitigation plan to reduce the potential impact of any future flooding disaster.

The 19,000 square metre DC for API closed following the January flood, and is not expected to reopen for at least six months — a major blow as the Centre services 900 pharmacies and employs 180 staff. Because this brand new facility was equipped with advanced technology systems for order picking and high-speed dispensing, the losses to the Company were extremely heavy.

Information obtained from websites.

COLLEGES CROSSING
Ipswich

COLLEGES CROSSING WAS A RECREATION RESERVE ON THE BANKS OF THE
BRISBANE RIVER AT CHUWAR, A SUBURB OF IPSWICH. IT HAD A PARK EQUIPPED
WITH BARBECUES, SHELTER SHEDS, A CAFÉ AND A BOAT RAMP AND WAS A
POPULAR SPOT FOR FAMILY OUTINGS.

The entire reserve was more or less annihilated during the floods which saw
the water level rise to over 17 metres with extremely strong currents. The
bridge at Colleges Crossing was closed from mid-December 2010 until late
January 2011 due to floodwater and releases from Wivenhoe Dam. The Ipswich
City Council is committed to restoring the reserve to its pristine condition.

IPSWICH CLEAN-UP

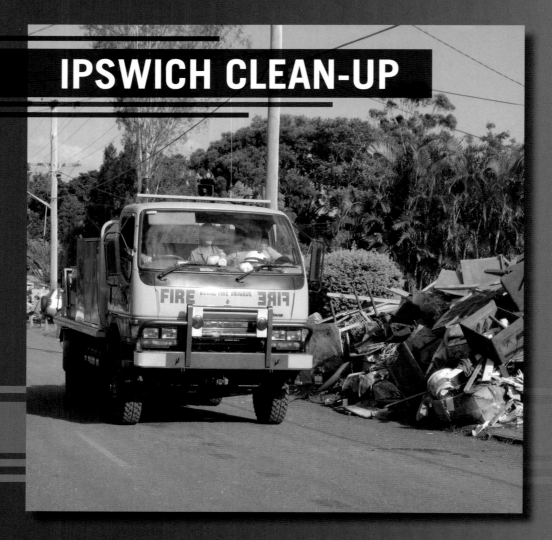

RD CLOSED
to SIGHTSEERS

409·LOP

Pizza Hut

50

Somerset Dam

Caboolture

Burpengary

Bruce Highway

Deception Bay

Dayboro

Narangba
Lake Kurwongbah

Rothwell

Redcliffe

Lake Samsonvale

Kallangur

Clontarf

Lake Wivenhoe

Brisbane Forest Park

Petrie

Bramble Bay

Moreton Bay

Strathpine

Sandgate

Wivenhoe Dam

Bracken Ridge

Albany Creek

Fisherman Isands

Brisbane Valley Highway

Mt Nebo

Samford

Aspley

Nundah

Ferny Grove

Stafford

D'Aguilar Range NP

Brisbane River

The Gap

BRISBANE

Wynnum

Lake Manchester

Mt Cootha

Toowong

Coorparoo

Birkdale
Cleveland

Kenmore

Capalaba

Warrego Highway

Jindalee

Mt Gravatt

Tingalpa Reservoir

Tivoli

Karalee

Darra

Acacia Ridge

Eight Mile Plains

Inala

IPSWICH

Riverview

Goodna

Calamvale

Woodridge

Amberley

Redbank Plains

Browns Plains

240

BRISBANE

RIVER CATCHES
BRISBANE
OUT AGAIN

THE BRISBANE RIVER, WITH ITS BROAD FLOOD PLAINS, COMMANDEERS AN INDIFFERENT PATH THROUGH THE HEART OF THE CITY'S NATURALLY HILLY TERRAIN AND PROVIDES A NATURAL STAGE FOR FESTIVITIES, WATER SPORTS AND ENTERTAINMENTS. A STIMULATING BACKDROP IS SUPPLIED BY AN INTERESTING BLEND OF MODERN AND HISTORIC CITY BUILDINGS, PRESTIGIOUS HOMES, ELEGANT BRIDGES, BEAUTIFUL GARDENS AND LUSH, NATURAL VEGETATION. AT NIGHT THE RIVER TAKES ON A DAZZLING BEAUTY AS VIBRANT REFLECTIONS FROM THE CITY AND THE BRIGHTLY LIT BRIDGES DANCE AND SPARKLE ON THE WATER.

Activity abounds as the high-speed CityCat ferries traverse the winding city reaches amongst a host of yachts and other pleasure craft. Traffic, cyclists and pedestrians present colourful kaleidoscopic images as they come and go continually along the streets and bridges. The tranquil river moves peacefully on as the traffic roars beside it, horns blow, sirens wail and birds overhead call to each other.

In spite of previous flooding, however, magnificent architectural developments and state-of-the-art constructions have continued to sprout along the river banks, but when floods re-visited the city in January 2011, Brisbane watched in helpless horror as its idol rose against it, savagely reasserting its rights to the flood plains and making a mockery of the attempt to tame it with the construction of Wivenhoe Dam.

THIS RIVER WOULD NOT BE TAMED
The construction of the Wivenhoe Dam in the 1980's was prompted by the Somerset Dam's failure to cope with flood waters in 1974, following heavy and sustained rainfall. With the assumption that Brisbane was now flood-proof, developers

have continued to move in and exploit the river's vast potential; amongst other projects, erecting luxurious apartments on the site of the old Tennyson Power Station, which was inundated by the floods in 1974. Many prestigious riverside homes have been built over the last 25 years, often with their own jetties onto the river.

Although late in 2010, large amounts of water had been progressively released from the Wivenhoe Dam, the relentlessly rising floodwaters continued to fill and overflow the dams at an alarming rate, creating an uncontrollable monster that seethed and roared towards Brisbane. For three days the river continued to swell. Many people fled their homes and the city ground to a halt as the CBD was inundated.

As the river peaked on Thursday January 13th, the city looked on in disbelieving shock at the raging river, and the grim reality of the devastation and ruin began to sink in! Shredded vegetation, animals, household goods, water tanks and other unrecognizable debris were swept down the churning, stench-ridden river and, along with pontoons and river craft, were unceremoniously dumped at random, or swept out into the now polluted Moreton Bay.

However, in times of crisis people quickly rally to support each other. Thousands of willing volunteers from near and far and from all walks of life, turned out to tackle the grim task of cleaning up, and to provide support and comfort as well as large donations of money, food and clothing and offers of temporary accommodation. Although countless lives will never be the same again, numerous inspiring stories of unselfishness, kindness, bravery, courage and faith have emerged, showing us a resilience of spirit and a most admirable side of human nature.

Although the water may have subsided and returned to its accustomed bed, Brisbane will need to thoroughly re-examine its relationship with the river, having been reminded once again that history has a habit of repeating itself!

FLOOD

BRISBANE

- **Dec 2010**
  Wettest December in 150 years. Controlled releases from Wivenhoe Dam - which take 36 hours to reach the city reaches of the Brisbane River.

- **Jan 10-12th 2011**
  Average of 286 mm rainfall per day over three days in Brisbane River catchment area.
  River rises.
  Evacuations begin.
  Sandbags made available.
  Power cuts.

- **Jan 13th 2011**
  Brisbane River peaks at 4.46m at 2.57am.
  850 houses along the Brisbane River flooded.
  67 suburbs affected.
  22 CBD streets submerged and many city buildings inundated.
  14,600 homes entirely flooded.
  13,900 homes partially flooded.
  5,200 business properties inundated.
  25,000 residents cut off in western suburbs.
  92 State schools and 14 private schools flooded.
  2m of water through Suncorp Stadium — up to 2nd and 3rd rows of seats.
  3m of water through Brisbane Produce Markets.
  Sections of Floating River Walk torn away and guided to safety by 13 tugs and water police.
  43 Coastguard volunteers clock up 197 engine hours in 6 vessels patrolling the river.
  Port of Brisbane closes leaving 11 bulk carriers out in Moreton Bay.
  Lone Pine Staff worked 55 hours without sleep to save more than 70 koalas and 40 other animals.
  5 out of 10 CityCat terminals destroyed.
  Massive flood plume of silt and debris spreads 30km north-east into Moreton Bay.

FACTS

- **Jan 14th 2011**
  Volunteers, including 800 Australian Army soldiers join the clean-up and emergency support effort.
  70,000 homes without electricity.

- **Jan 15th 2011**
  More than 23,000 people participate in the Council's coordinated clean-up weekend.
  Almost 30,000 tonnes of rubbish is moved.
  More than 220 industrial bins placed in affected areas.
  Waste transported to over 30 temporary dumping locations before being transferred to landfill sites.

- **Costs:**
  Approximately $500 million flood damage – almost one fifth of Council's $2.8 billion budget.
  $137 million to fix the road networks.
  $38 million to restore parks and facilities.
  $70 million to repair damaged ferry terminals.
  $40 million estimated to rebuild floating walkway.

- **Other facts:**
  110,000 tonnes of rotting furniture, food and debris dumped in one week – equivalent to one third of Brisbane's yearly total.
  60 schools, 7 TAFE campuses, 88 child-care centres and kindergartens flood damaged.
  32 Navy divers scour the Brisbane River for submerged debris.
  Marine Safety Queensland salvaged 365 pontoons and 18 yachts that were washed down the river.
  Almost 3,000 properties remained without power for 6 weeks after the floods.
  Further releases from Wivenhoe Dam to guard against further flooding - equivalent to a year's supply of drinking water.

Albert Street - Brisbane City

Riverside clean-up

Riverside Centre

Underground carparks flooded - Brisbane City

BRISBANE CITY

Sweeping up mud

North Quay Ferry Terminal and Victoria Bridge - Brisbane City

Sand Bagging - Albert Street - Brisbane City

Riverside walkway - Brisbane City

Clean-up - Riverside Centre - Brisbane City

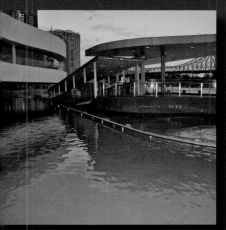

...verside Centre - Brisbane City

Riparian Plaza - Eagle Street - Brisbane City

Police direct traffic - Brisbane City

...agle Street Pier - Brisbane City

Ferry terminals and walkway - Riverside Centre - Brisbane City

Albert Street - Brisbane City

...ity Cycle

Botanical Gardens - Brisbane City

Debris in underground carpark - Brisbane City

247

RUNNING ON
ADRENALIN

"ARE YOU SURE?"... THE BRISBANE CITY COUNCIL HEALTH AUTHORITIES DOUBTED JULIE WHEN SHE TOLD THEM THEIR FAMILY RESTAURANT IN QUEEN STREET, BRISBANE, WOULD BE READY FOR TRADING ONLY NINE DAYS AFTER IT WAS ENGULFED BY FLOOD WATERS. THE OWNERS, JOHN AND JULIE TAYLOR, ATTRIBUTE THIS INCREDIBLE FEAT TO THEIR COMBINED BACKGROUND IN ARCHITECTURE, DESIGN AND BUILDING, THEIR FANTASTIC STAFF TEAMWORK AND A HARDWORKING SPIRIT. JULIE SAYS "I AM A STRONG BELIEVER IN PUTTING THE WORK IN SO YOU GET THE REWARDS" ... AND WORK THEY DID!

It was Monday night, January 10th, 2011, when John, watching the news of the disaster in Toowoomba, realised what lay ahead of them. Their restaurant on the Brisbane River was obviously vulnerable. Tuesday was all hands on deck, John and Julie, their family and all their staff worked until 2am on Wednesday morning. They emptied the linen cupboards, packed box loads of crockery, emptied the cellar, labelled and boxed the non-perishable foods, dismantled cabinets, removed curtains and décor, pulled up carpet and underlay and moved it all into the Admiralty Towers above their restaurant. There was nothing they didn't think of - even the toilets and basins were wrapped in cling wrap to prevent the mud clogging their drains! In a final effort to save everything possible, 8 grown men heaved the custom built 2 metre stove up onto the bench top, and wrapped it with black plastic and a few rolls of duct tape.

As the busy team was working late into the night, they watched the water roar down the Brisbane River at frightening speed taking boats, pontoons, jet skis, large debris, uprooted trees, and personal belongings. Seeing the wreckage from further up the river, was like a creepy prelude to what was about to happen to them. When the Drift Restaurant broke from its moorings at Milton, it too went skiing past; the team could only think "what if that was us?"

By the time they returned on Wednesday morning water was lapping on their front terrace and a catamaran had attached itself to their front railing. Julie recalls seeing countless wandering boats hit the Hotham St Ferry Terminal on the opposite side of the river and sink just minutes later. Water crept under their doors and fish found their way to their terrace area along with place cards and crockery from other restaurants upstream. The water level was steadily rising all Wednesday and predictions came through that it was expected to reach the level of the 1974 floods; this meant that despite all their efforts, all their property stored in the Admiralty Towers was also threatened. They joined forces again and removed everything, distributing it to family and friend's homes.

This predicted level would be over their ceiling and they figured it would have been a loss they physically and financially could not withstand. Finally, when it was all over, posing for a family photo, they prepared to bid adieu to their business of 10 years. Julie laughs as she recounts "What are we going to do with the rest of our lives? We'll let our kids support us – I was delusional! I didn't feel like crying, it was quite surreal - it wasn't raining... There was no real reason to worry – was there?!"

The underground carpark below their restaurant was rapidly filling up with muddy water. As the water swirled around the empty car park the echoing gurgle became a continual unnerving background noise.

John and Julie went to family for dinner, came back that night to check on progress and then again the next morning. The river peaked early that morning, filling the restaurant with over 1 metre of murky water and river mud. Now, it was just a waiting game.

By Friday morning, John and Julie were able to start the overwhelming clean-up. Staff, volunteers, past employees and family "were fabulous, we couldn't have done without them". Mud lay inches thick over everything (including the cling wrap on the basins and toilets!) With high pressure water blasters every wall and floor, inside and out had to be hosed three times over, followed by bleach, detergents and endless elbow grease. Walls needed replastering and repainting. Tiled and timber floors were ruined and needed jackhammers, new concrete, new underlay and more carpet. Power points and fan motors were replaced, and everything needed rewiring. The cellar, the kitchen, the bathrooms, all needed scrubbing from top to bottom, every corner and crevice. The dynamic team worked like beavers and in only 6 days they were ready for the Brisbane City Council Health Inspection. With the approval granted, the Venice Restaurant restocked with fresh food and everything back in place, reopened on Saturday...........January 22nd .

Management of the huge project meant a very hectic 9 days running on adrenalin. John and Julie were physically and emotionally drained and with their restaurant finally ready for business again, they felt they could hand it over to their wonderful staff. Friday night when the Taylors got home, John thought Nachos would be a quick fix to have before they collapsed for their well earned rest. It seemed a good idea, but somehow he put them to grill in the fridge rather than the oven! – the things that happen after 9 nine days without sleep!

IT WAS QUITE
SURREAL

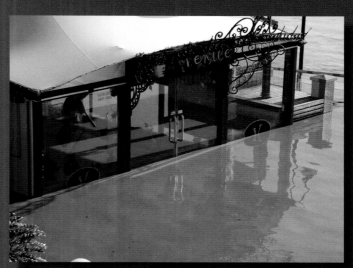

RIVERWALK NUDGED ONTO
NUDGEE BEACH

BRISBANE'S RIVERWALK, AN 850M FLOATING CONCRETE WALKWAY RUNNING PARALLEL TO THE RIVERBANK, WAS COMPLETED IN DECEMBER 2003 AT A COST OF AROUND $15 MILLION. IT CONSISTED OF 250 PRECAST PONTOONS JOINED TOGETHER IN A FLOATING RIBBON, EACH MEASURING 3M LONG BY 5.4M WIDE. EACH PONTOON WAS FABRICATED AS A CONCRETE SHELL, FILLED WITH A FOAM CORE FOR FLOTATION, AND WEIGHED APPROXIMATELY 15 TONNES. THE STRUCTURE WAS MOORED TO CONCRETE PILES. A HYDRAULICALLY OPERATED SECTION OF THE WALKWAY SWUNG OPEN ON A HEAVY STAINLESS STEEL HINGE WHEN REQUIRED, TO ALLOW RIVER ACCESS FOR BOATS MOORED BEHIND IT.

On Tuesday January 11th, as the river began to rise alarmingly, the floating structure was closed to the public, and its gates were opened to allow the free flow of debris. The pontoons floated upward with the rising river and although concerns were raised about the possibility of the walkway breaking loose and causing damage to bridges and riverside properties downstream. to scuttle the walkway at its moorings was considered too dangerous. In the early hours of Thursday morning, as the river reached its peak, a 380 metre section broke free of its own accord and began a potentially destructive journey downstream.

The voluntary and skilful actions of two tugboat operators averted a major catastrophe, and the walkway was eventually securely anchored off Nudgee Beach, in Moreton Bay. (see page 252).

Before floods

Riverwalk as it used to be

Breaking-up

e floods

Under-water

Under-water

issing Links - down near Port of Brisbane

Floating walkway flooded

Tugs to the rescue

Final resting place - Nudgee Beach

251

DOUG HISLOP
Brisbane

THE GATEWAY BRIDGE
SAVED!

DOUG HISLOP, OWNER AND SKIPPER OF MORETON BAY TUGS, AND PETER FENTON, HEAD ENGINEER, WERE CHECKING ON BARGES, WHEN THEY HEARD ON THE 4AM RADIO THAT ONE OF BRISBANE'S MOST IMPORTANT CROSS-RIVER LINKS, THE GATEWAY BRIDGE, WAS CLOSED. IT WAS UNDER THREAT OF DAMAGE FROM A CHUNK OF THE 850M LONG, 5.4M WIDE 'RIVERWALK' - WHICH HAD BROKEN FROM ITS MOORINGS ON THE RIVER BANK AND WAS BEING SWEPT RAPIDLY DOWNSTREAM.

There was no time to waste. With only five minutes before over a thousand tonnes of speeding concrete was destined to smash into the bridge; Doug and Peter just had to act quickly. Despite the dangers, they boarded Mavis the tugboat, and began fighting up-river against the strong current which was racing along at up to 15 knots mid-river, far more rapidly than its usual speed of 1.5-2 knots. When they reached the walkway it was only about 500 metres above the bridge, and floating horizontally across the river.

With no time to communicate or formulate a plan, they went into action. The walkway had to be turned end-on so as to prevent it colliding with the bridge pylons – while the 1000 tonne piece may not have brought the bridge down, in most certainly would have damaged it, forcing its closure to traffic. Battling current and debris the tugboat crew were able to realign the walkway so it could safely go under the bridge. Doug told us "The tugs will only do about 10 – 11 knots; we were really struggling to get up the river. We had to use the eddies on the side of the river, where the friction of the water on the banks slows the water down. We had to get right over against the bank to actually be able to travel upstream. The water in the middle of the river was travelling far too fast; there was no way we could just go against it."

After successfully negotiating the bridge, Doug and Peter continued on down river, their primary concern then being to keep the walkway entire, as it was at considerable risk of disintegrating and creating multiple 30-40 tonnes missiles of destruction. When they reached the mouth of the river, they were joined by two other boats, who assisted them to finally anchor the walkway off Nudgee Beach.

Doug and Peter, "were just doing what they had to do". They insist 'It was not fantastic, brave or courageous.' Yet, for the many commuters who use the bridge daily, it was exactly that. The praises came from all parts of the world. They were nominated for Pride of Australia in the Heroism Medal category. "I'm surprised and honoured," Doug said. "We just went out automatically, and did it. I've worked on the river and in the bay all my life. I was just giving something back to the community."

Walkway undertow

THE WATER IN THE MIDDLE OF THE RIVER WAS TRAVELLING FAR TOO FAST

253

The "Mavis"

Heading downstream

Base of Kangaroo Point cliffs

Debris at Pinkenba

Destroyed ferry terminal

Debris washed up at Flinders Parade - Sandgate

BRISBANE RIVER

Pontoons and boats adrift - Mowbray Park

Maritime Museum flooded

Pontoons around Goodwill Bridge pylons

Upturned cruiser and small boat

Truck trailer in river - West End

cavator at The Parklands - South Bank

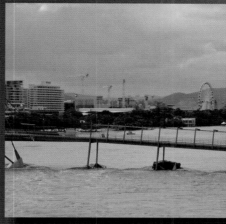

Goodwill Bridge - South Bank in background

Kangaroo Point Parklands underwater

ail of rubbish and debris

Kangaroo Point Parklands

Pontoon and boat adrift

ash washed up at Colmslie boat ramp

Pontoons with boats washed up at Pinkenba

Pontoons removed from water at Sandgate

South Bank

A MIGHTY TOUR OF
DESTRUCTION

Wheel of Brisbane - before

AFTER HOSTING WORLD EXPO IN 1988, SOUTH BANK WAS DEVELOPED INTO PICTURESQUE PARKLANDS AS A GIFT TO THE QUEENSLAND PUBLIC. IN THIS CAPACITY IT HAS BECOME ONE OF THE CULTURAL HIGHLIGHTS OF THE CITY. THE 19 HECTARE SITE BOASTS A MAN-MADE BEACH, CAFES, PLAYGROUNDS, PICNIC AREAS, AQUATIVITY — A HUGE WATER PLAYGROUND FILLED WITH A DIVERSE RANGE OF FOUNTAINS — AND UNPARALLELED VIEWS ACROSS THE RIVER TO THE CITY. THE PARKLANDS ARE EXTREMELY POPULAR, DRAWING CROWDS TO ITS CAFES YEAR ROUND, AND TO ITS WATER FEATURES IN SUMMER, WHILST HOSTING SEVERAL FESTIVALS DURING THE YEAR. IRONICALLY, ONE OF ITS MOST POPULAR DRAW CARDS IS RIVERFIRE, PART OF THE BRISBANE FESTIVAL, A CELEBRATION OF THE RIVER ITSELF.

Locals felt a keen sense of loss as a very swollen Brisbane River engulfed their Parklands and surrounding precincts on its mighty tour of destruction. The once pristine beach and lagoons were filled with sickening sludge, cycleways and walkways disappeared beneath the murky water, which, intent on conquering all in its path, went on and consumed picnic areas and the serene rainforest gardens. Overflow from stormwater drainage systems added to the catastrophe. Incidentally, the most destructive damage occurred beneath the ground, where basement levels, including the underground carparks, electrical facilities, data, offices, and storage areas of businesses in the Parklands were completely inundated.

South Bank Pool - before

A mammoth clean-up effort involved pumping out the filthy water and over 3000 cubic metres of contaminated sand, this process alone took weeks. All hard surfaces required water blasting, a service with which the Queensland Fire and Rescue Sevice assisted, who had between three and six trucks onsite from time-to-time. Gardens had to be restored and infrastructure replaced.

The Parklands have re-opened to the public progressively, as repair and restoration work is completed. Perhaps the greatest indicator of how dearly the city has missed one of its favourite playgrounds, are the crowds who flock to the newly restored facility once more.

Ferry Terminal - before

of Brisbane - during

South Bank pathways - before

South Bank pathways - during

South Bank Pool - after

Terminal - during

The Parklands, South Bank - before

The Parklands, South Bank - during

THE BEER

THAT NEVER WAS

dogstar
South Brisbane

DOGSTAR AND THE BRISBANE FLOODS 2011
THE TRAGIC EVENTS THAT UNFOLDED IN TOOWOOMBA AND GRANTHAM OCCURRED
ON MONDAY. TELEVISION FOOTAGE OF HUGE WALLS OF WATER ENGULFING THOSE
PLACES LEFT A SHARP IMPRESSION. RECALLING THE 1974 FLOOD AND ITS IMPACT
ON BRISBANE CAUSED ME CONCERN — WHAT WAS GOING TO HAPPEN NEXT?

'dogstar's' studio is located in Manning St, South Brisbane, opposite Stefan's
Sky Needle. I am a part-time employee, doing odd jobs and deliveries. Arriving at
work Tuesday, staff had already started moving things up off the floor. We knew
that the studio was susceptible to mild stormwater problems; heavy rain and a
blocked pipe had created havoc about a year before.

We worked all morning to get anything we could off the floor and onto desks, tables
and shelving. We estimated the greatest height of water that might come through
would be about 20-30 centimetres. By midday we had lifted a lot, which meant
that work for the remainder of the day was impossible. So; off home everyone went.
On leaving, I fashioned a piece of thick plastic across the front door and secured
it with gaffer tape and bricks. It came up the door about 2 feet, providing "ample"
barrier for any invading water. Satisfied, I picked up my girlfriend, Kahori, from
work, and headed home, stopping to buy a six-pack (or two) and a bottle of red
(or two) on the way. I envisaged the next day or two would be played out at home,
drinks in hand, over a leisurely game of Scrabble.

I couldn't have been more wrong! Just as I opened my first stubbie, Damian, a
cabbie friend of mine, phoned. Cabbies are great barometers of what's going on
and I always respect the 'oil' from them. His sources told him that there was a
chance that the flood wending its way to Brisbane could approach '74 levels.
Those words gave me a little jolt and I immediately began to worry we had not
lifted everything at the studio high enough. My stubbie was put on the table and
Kahori and I set off for South Brisbane. We phoned our designer, Masayo, to find
out what she wanted put up even higher. "Fabric, save my fabric!" she pleaded.
All of the new season's fabric had recently arrived and was stored largely on racks
under the cutting table, only 40 cms off the floor.

After a bit of effort, we had all of the precious, heavy, new season fabrics up on a
mezzanine that was never built to take that sort of weight. I saw that there was
still so much more that should be up higher so lifted notions of all shapes and
sizes, patterns, computers, workbooks, mannequins, more fabric, and, it seemed,
more of everything, up on top of the cutting table, which was one metre forty high
and really should have been safe. Leaving, I reset the plastic sheeting higher over
the front door. We had done about as much as we could do. Feeling a bit weary
after all the lifting, we were ready to get home and have that beer.

Back home, we made a beeline for the deck and I nestled in ready for a well earned
session. Kahori - who has one of those new-fangled phones that tell you everything
- sat down and proceeded to report that there were fears Southbank was going
to go under. dogstar has a shop at South Bank! I phoned our lovely Orla who has
been with the company for years, for keys to the shop. Orla, like most of Brisbane,
had by this time enjoyed a few 'sherbets', but was ready to help.

I had hoped that we would fit everything from our South Bank shop into the van.
Alas, it was about two vans full. Orla, as chirpy as all get-out, nominated her
house as a storage centre. We carried a huge van load of clothing up the towering
staircase into Orla's house, where we hung them on a teetering collection of
racks. Back to the shop, where we filled our van to capacity again, finally parking
it streets away from the reach of any flood waters. Kahori and I got home for the
third time at about one-thirty on Wednesday morning, by then, too tired to even
bother with the beer.

Early the next day reports were warning that low-lying areas of South Brisbane
were going to go well and truly under, come high tide in the afternoon. It was
apparent that at the studio everything had to be put even higher or completely
cleared out. I had no suitable vehicle for the job, so rang my good friend Sal,
from The Pasta Company. He gladly lent me his huge delivery van and offered us
some storage space. What a relief! Masayo had asked a couple of friends, Juggling
Dan, and Andrei - who is dogstar's computer and peripherals technician - to meet
us at the studio.

The first thing we had to do was heartbreaking. My plastic barrier, surprisingly,
had done a remarkable job of keeping the water out. Unfortunately, the water
was going to get much higher. Begrudgingly I opened the door, in effect allowing
forty centimetres of water invasion rights to the building. It was a terrible sight
watching all that water rush through the completely dry interior of the building.

The safe areas in our building were the mezzanine, the upstairs office and the
top of the fabric bays. Everything had to either be stored in these places or
removed. With water in the studio swirling around our knees, we began. Soon the
mezzanine was straining under the huge burden. The upstairs office area was
full, and fabric and clothing were literally falling off the top level of the racks.
But, still there was more.

Then an amazing thing happened. People came from everywhere to help. Staff,
friends, tourists, students, nearby neighbours - people from all walks arrived.
There was no longer any order to what we were taking out, it didn't matter. Just
get it out! I remember that at one stage we had about fifteen people I didn't
know, ferrying out bits and pieces. The water by this time was about thigh deep.

With Sal's van filled with heavy industrial sewing machines, clothing and fabric, I left for the storage.

On arriving back, the water had reached waist deep, although it had stopped rising quickly. Much of our stuff had been put out onto Manning St, on higher ground. I remember thinking that we would have been completely shot ducks had it been raining - ironically it was a lovely day outside!

Back inside, Andrei was concerned about 'his' plotter. He had spent many hours getting this lovely old dinosaur back to incredible working condition, and he wasn't letting it drown without a fight! We couldn't, however, get its legs off and there was no other way to get it out the front door. I told him he would have to give it up, but Andrei had other ideas. I think he would have chewed the metal legs off with his teeth rather than lose it. I left for a while and when I came back, through dogged determination and a very shonky Allen key, Andrei had removed the legs! So out the plotter went. Somehow in the aftermath, we managed to lose one of its two very large heavy legs, but that mystery is another story!

In the final hours of the evacuation day, more dogstar staff had arrived to help and together we got out as much as we possibly could, with the water finally getting up over chest height. Kahori, Naomi and Orla took the last computers upstairs, with the water in one place up to their necks. Brave little soldiers!

There was still a lot that we couldn't save, but with everyone's help, so much was. Having been in and out of the water all day, I had developed a nasty case of chafe and wasn't moving very well. Ouch! We put the final loads into cars and vans and I got ready to move my car away, only to discover my keys were missing! I was sure I had given them to Kahori a couple of hours earlier. She checked her bag and they weren't there, which meant they could only be in the upstairs office! Chafe-ridden and very unhappy, I trudged back into the murky water, enduring a fifty metre gradual re-drenching as I made my way to the front door, which was neck deep. At that, I heard a whistle. "We've found the keys!" someone shouted. Oh, how they all laughed as I turned around and, even less happy, made the long walk back to dry land.

The next few days were filled with more toil, mud, filth and smell. They were also again filled with lots of help from many friends, staff and strangers - help that has made the recovery easier, and the future for dogstar much brighter. And I did, eventually, have that beer!

Hugh Doessel - background boy

Army, Fire and Rescue - South Brisbane

Clean-up - West End

Brisbane River at West End

Melbourne Street intersection - South Brisbane

SOUTH BRISBANE
AND WEST END

Police at Hill End

State Library and Gallery of Modern Art

Sludge !!

South Brisbane Railway Station

South Brisbane

rdelia Street - South Brisbane

Cultural Centre Tunnel to Museum

Looking towards Glenelg Street - South Brisbane

isbane Convention Centre

Picking up of Rubbish - South Brisbane

Police at West End

est End Clean-up on a large scale

West End Clean-up

West End Shops

WAKE-UP CALL

THE SIGHT OF THE FILTHY WATER DEVASTATING HER SALON WAS OVERWHELMING FOR CHRISTINA, THE OWNER OF GIGI HAIR. "I STOOD THERE IN SILENCE; I WAS JUST IN SO MUCH SHOCK."

On Tuesday 11th, Christina had rung the Council for information on how high the river was expected to rise. Figures were given for the river, but no one could interpret just how this water height would affect her street. After discussing the scenario with a neighbouring businessman, the pair arrived at the conclusion that the water might reach the top step. "We sandbagged the front of the shop just in case, moved all the furniture back and went home…. I wasn't worried at all".

"Obviously, if I'd had warning, I'd have done things differently", she laments. "I just wish someone had said, 'Christina, it's going to flood'." Adding to her sense of security was the fact that friends in the neighbouring suburb of Milton had received a letter of warning from the council, advising them to evacuate their suburb. "We didn't get a letter like that around here", she states, explaining that this led her to assume everything was going to be O.K. In fact, Christina spent the evening frantically helping those friends move all their equipment out, oblivious to the threat to her own salon.

At 2am, on the way home, they stopped by the salon to add a few more sandbags to the pile protecting the front door.

WAKE - UP CALL

At 5am on Wednesday a client, who lives opposite the salon, sent a text message and photo of the floodwaters, which had reached the top step. Christina jumped out of bed and made her way down, not knowing what was ahead. Within half an hour there was water through the salon, and in shock she watched as it quickly rose and consumed her business. Together with a group of friends they salvaged what they could, until the police insisted they get out - a live wire was dragging in the water. Devastatingly, the muddy river peaked at 2 metres inside the shop.

"Thursday was surreal, it felt like the world was going to end; it was just so eerie everywhere." The streets were deserted and the shop shelves, empty. It was 10pm before the army personnel who were guarding the area allowed Christina access to the salon. "It stank, it was disgusting! Sewerage … it was gross, you could smell it for days. The whole place was covered in mud, and everything was just a mess."

Friday dawned, and with it, the clean-up. Helpers had arrived by 6am and within two hours the salon was gutted. Some things were washed and taken to Christina's home garage, where a temporary salon was established. "The support here on Friday was just awesome. It was hard to be sad because the vibe here was really nice." Christina had her moments. "I cried on Wednesday, when the water was still rising and my Mum rang and told me I had no insurance." If it had rained the day it flooded – on Wednesday – the policy would have been honoured. But it didn't. The rain on Tuesday had been torrential; Wednesday was hot and sunny.

She comments, the most stressful thing was the predicament of her employees. "I was really strong throughout the whole ordeal until I started stressing about my staff. I felt so responsible for them. I felt bad they weren't getting full pay," she recalls painfully. "It was so hard working out of my garage, but I was really glad I could do that. It was either that or my girls had to get another job. I couldn't bear that. They are all amazing. They stuck by me – we worked three days (a week) so they had enough to live off."

Rebuilding the shop was a huge undertaking for Christina - both the designing process and dealing with tradies - "I think there was one week when I cried the whole week".

She is indebted to those who helped her through - her partner Keiron, staff, friends, Dale - the patient shop fitter Boost interiors, Redken - a supplier, and clients.

"Everyone just wanted to support us, and so when I got to the point where I thought, 'Oh I want to give up, this is too hard'– I only had to stop and think 'why would you give up, when all these people are supporting you, they believe in you?' "

"I am just so grateful I didn't lose my home.
So many people are worse off."

DEVASTATINGLY
THE WATER PEAKED AT 2M

A SORT OF
DENIAL

IN THE 13 YEARS THAT JOHN AND DONNA HAVE OWNED THEIR COLD ROCK ICE CREAMERY FRANCHISE THERE HAD BEEN PLENTY OF WARNINGS OF AN IMPENDING FLOOD, BUT NOTHING MORE SERIOUS THAN A BIT OF WATER IN THE PARK ACROSS THE ROAD HAD EVER MATERIALISED. SO AS THEY LISTENED TO THE RADIO WARNINGS, THEY WERE IN "A SORT OF DENIAL"; IT WOULDN'T REALLY AFFECT THEM THIS TIME EITHER.

The council had called on local businesses - including Cold Rock - on Tuesday, offering sandbags. Their intention was to deliver them on Wednesday morning. With a high tide expected on Wednesday afternoon, everybody should have plenty of time to prepare. But the water had a mind of its own.......

On that Tuesday, John and Donna worked until 9pm, then took a walk. They noted the water had just started to cross Baroona Road, so piled a few sandbags at the front door and went home to bed. John, normally a heavy sleeper, awoke at 4am, and decided to go and check on the shop. The water was lapping the gutter out in the street, so he put a few things up a bit higher. As a precaution, he wheeled the juke box up the ramp, out of harm's way, and went home.

Returning to the shop with Donna at 5:45am, they discovered water ankle deep through the place. It struck them then - they had forgotten to sandbag the back door. By this time water was coming up through the drains, so the sandbags weren't making any difference, anyway.

All the refrigerated ice cream cabinets were still running – so together they made the difficult decision to turn the power off. There was no hope for the ice cream, it would melt. Being very independent persons, they had resigned themselves to losing everything rather than asking for help. Their small car offered very limited space for goods and chattels, which meant practically sacrificing the entire contents of the shop to the flood waters.

Then, out of the blue, came the volunteers. By 7 o'clock there were so many people not just offering help, but insisting that they helped. Trucks started arriving to ferry the goods. Staff came, people they knew, and complete strangers. "They were pushing us out of the way saying "We'll take it, we'll do it". It was amazing - the community spirit. Lance Armstrong, who conducted a charity ride for the flood victims in the weeks after the event, commented "When Katrina hit New Orleans there were traffic jams with people getting away from the city; in Brisbane there were traffic jams with people coming to help." Truly amazing!

John recalls, "I'd say 'Forget about that', and they'd say 'Oh, no, we'll take it.' One man had a trailer, we didn't know him, but he took a load of our stuff and left us with his phone number – he, and all the others, they were just wonderful people. We have neighbours with the whole underneath of their houses jam packed with our stuff."

They were basically finished when three guys turned up with a ute, asking "What can we do?" There was nothing left except the Juke Box, so John gave them the address and they delivered it. "Everything was there when we finally got home; our driveway and street looked like a Cold Rock Ice Creamery."

By 9.30am the water had crept to 1.2m, continuing upwards until finally it reached 1.8m inside the shop. No foodstuffs were salvaged as no freezer vehicle was available. "Friday was a beautiful day, the skies were clear. We opened the back door and received a severe shock!" The mess was horrible and the smell horrendous. "It was just unbelievable," John recalls. "A three-door fridge had hit the ceiling and come down upside down, everything was churned around. We didn't know where to start, but we were determined we would fix it by ourselves.

As we stood there, stunned, clinging to the couple of brooms and gloves we had brought, we were suddenly pushed aside by the army of people that came in, fully equipped with boots and squeegee mops. A man had a generator and a pressure cleaner. The whole shop was full of sour, melted ice-cream; grown men were retching, almost vomiting, out the back. But within 2 hours, everything was washed out – clean! It was just incredible. There were about 30 people in here, and the council had trucks coming through picking up the debris."

During the clean-up there were people who called by, "We can't help with the mud", but they were offering sandwiches and cupcakes. A church group set up and fed everybody - they were pleasantly surprised because people were turning up and donating to them. The spirit was amazing.

John considers himself fortunate, "There were so many worse off. We didn't get the devastation that they had in the Lockyer Valley, people trying to cling to their babies only to have them ripped out of their arms. It's unimaginable what they've been through. Here we've just had a slow inundation, and an army of people to help us. At the end of the day we were able to go to our own home and put our feet up. We're the lucky ones".

264

ROSALIE GOURMET MARKET

ACTION IT
NOW!

NORRIS LEWIS, PROPRIETOR OF ROSALIE GOURMET MARKET, DESCRIBES HIS FLOOD EXPERIENCE AS "A VERY SIMPLE STORY". SIMPLE? YES! SIMPLE, BECAUSE THEY SIMPLY TOOK NOTICE OF THE BRISBANE CITY COUNCIL'S ADVICE TO IMPLEMENT A FLOOD PLAN – AND SIMPLY BUT METICULOUSLY, ACTED UPON THAT ADVICE.

By the beginning of October, 2010, it was obvious to all that a very wet summer lay ahead. Brisbane City Council had advised its constituents to prepare a flood plan. "The Council, particularly the Lord Mayor, was very proactive. I think he did a terrific job," Norris commented. At Rosalie Gourmet Market, a 'Flood Plan' was carefully and thoughtfully designed – right down to the size and shape of the plastic bags required to cover the bread trays on which the food would be transferred, in the event of a flood. The staff had even practised the art of fitting the bags over the trays.

On Monday 10th January, when Lord Mayor Campbell Newman announced by radio that anyone who had a flood plan should "action it now", Rosalie Gourmet Market Flood Plan was launched into operation. Other local traders, and indeed some of their own staff, thought they were crazy. Norris, however, cognisant of the Lord Mayors engineering background and his training in the Army, felt it was right to heed the warning, and with the help of his staff moved their stock and collected loads of sandbags from the Council depot at Darra.

By the time the waters began to rise on the night of Tuesday 11th, Norris and his colleagues were fully prepared; their plan had gone like clockwork. All stock, machines, registers, and computers had been transferred to other prearranged locations. Only their sixteen heavy refrigerators and some cabinetry remained. The doors and other potential leakage points had been siliconed up, and black builders' plastic covered the shop front. A sandbag levee bank, 1.2 metres high, formed the final barrier. But: even a simple story can develop a complication, and the Rosalie Gourmet Market Flood Story encountered a complication that caused unnecessary distress and loss.

ROSALIE GOURMET MARKET
Brisbane

It was on the Wednesday that disaster struck. "Four young blokes", cruising the flooded streets in a dinghy, "did a donut" out the front of the shop. Norris very graciously allows that it was an accident – ".....they were having fun..."he points out. But, for all their fun, those joy riders wrought havoc on a near-perfect flood plan. The wake from the circling boat sent a large piece of timber spearing through the front glass door of the Gourmet Market and with a surge, the filthy water poured in. The heavy refrigerator cabinets inside became buoyant and tipped over on top of each other. It was a shattering blow to all those who had worked so hard to save the premises.

When the waters receded, Norris and company were able to put the Recovery Stage of their plan into action. Special equipment was hired to dry out the electrical motors of the refrigerators, and, as willing volunteers arrived, specific chores were allocated out.

Just eleven days after the flood, Rosalie Gourmet Market was ready to re-open for business. Health inspectors could not believe it! "They ticked off on it" and went away, but returned the following morning with a more senior colleague and requested to see what procedures had been followed. Norris had actioned the advice of an architect, cleaning and disinfecting his equipment and cabinetry four times with a routine of bleach, ammonium compound and then oil of cloves. Their premises passed the inspection with flying colours.

The laborious task of cleaning up was not without incident. When the twenty-two men working on the project found it impossible to budge a six-foot long refrigerator cabinet, the help of a Bobcat driver who was removing rubbish in the street outside, was sought. The driver willingly brought his machine into the shop and proceeded to lift one end of the monster and shift it into place, while an over-zealous Council foreman screamed "....Stop! Stop! ....you can't do this..." The backhoe driver ordered him to get out of the way [he didn't mention that he'd been given some nice French cheese for his efforts– "You can put that in your book," Norris chuckles]. The foreman became quite agitated and insisted the driver back out of the shop. Norris pleaded with him, to no avail. The rest of the crew – twenty one men- 'went ballistic' and booed the foreman out of the shop! At this, the driver set his machine going and effortlessly shifted the cabinet the remaining few centimetres into place.

Norris believes that his Flood Plan was of huge benefit. He found the trauma of the whole experience psychologically unsettling. Had he not had a Flood Plan, the effects could have been devastating. The plan also meant that the assistance from volunteers was used to the best advantage. Too often, well-meaning and well-equipped volunteers are not fully utilised due to lack of organisation. The efficient and speedy return to business could not have been achieved without the Plan. Cost benefits to insurance companies and relief organisations such as Centrelink would be a fraction of their devastating total, had more people adopted a plan like that of the Gourmet Market. Norris suggests that insurance companies should reward clients who have had the foresight to implement a flood plan, by giving them priority with their claims. Maybe others will feel encouraged to emulate the forethought of these diligent people.

CULTURAL LANDMARK
SWEPT AWAY

A COMMUNITY HAS GONE INTO GRIEVING FOLLOWING THE DEMISE OF THE LEGENDARY DRIFT RESTAURANT - A CULTURAL AND CULINARY LANDMARK WHICH WAS TORN AWAY AND SWALLOWED BY ANGRY FLOOD WATERS. RECENTLY RENOVATED, AND MUCH CELEBRATED FOR ITS SPECTACULAR RIVERSIDE VIEWS, RESTAURANT AND JETTY CAFE, HAD BECOME A LOCAL INSTITUTION. "IN SUCH A SMALL SPACE OF TIME, IT HAD BECOME SUCH AN ENDEARING VENUE WITHIN BRISBANE," OWNER DAVID MOORE SAYS. "WE WERE DOING CABARET, COMEDY, EVERYTHING ... PEOPLE JUST FELL IN LOVE WITH IT, IT WAS SUCH AN UNUSUAL VENUE." BUT IN A MUCH SMALLER SPACE OF TIME, EVERYTHING WAS GONE ....SEEMINGLY THE END OF AN ERA.

So could it all be over for the Coronation Drive entity, ineligible for insurance when a large section of it was ripped from the main structure by unsparing flood waters and swept crashing into the Go Between Bridge. The battered hulk, at the mercy of the raging river, continued out into Moreton Bay, ending its odyssey somewhat unceremoniously, finally washing up at Sandgate, 30 kilometres north of the city. Owner, David Moore, is confident about the daunting task of rebuilding. "I don't know how we'll do it, or what with, but we will do it," he said. "The river has taken the restaurant, but it will never take our spirit."

A popular icon for 22 years, previously known as Oxley's On the River, the restaurant re-opened as 'Drift' in May 2010, and in September it won the Savour Australia, Best New Restaurant award in Brisbane. Less than 5 months later, it had vanished. As the river rose on that horrifying morning, onlookers could barely take in the sight of the Drift Restaurant going under, its white sails consumed by the murky water. It became one of the defining moments of the flood. Thousands watched via television as the attached Jetty Cafe broke free; tables and chairs spewed into the water, joining the amazing array of debris being carried by the current.

Drift Restaurant was designed to remain afloat regardless of the river level as it sits on telescopic pylons. On the afternoon before the flood peaked, 15 tradesmen were frantically working to cut the structure free from the riverbank. "We were sheltered, thinking we were going to raise the venue." Work was slow because power tools could not be used in the water. Then the devastating orders came to evacuate – their lives were in danger. It was possible the sheer force of the flood could sweep the structure down river, a potential safety hazard, so police ordered a halt on freeing it from its moorings.

That afternoon David was advised, in the interests of safety, to open all the doors and windows and let the murky waters flood in - a move designed to ensure the venue would sink. "It was the most gut-wrenching experience because at that time it was like turning off a life support system, where you realised there was no hope anymore," he despairs. Regret that they had dedicated their precious time to cutting the restaurant free from the riverbank instead of saving the contents of the venue overcame him. "We had three days prior to take the grand piano, the furniture, the food, the alcohol or staff records, but we've taken nothing and we spent the whole day lifting furniture and cutting the building rather than taking what we could save. That night I drank like I've never drunk before."

David surveyed the remnant of his beloved restaurant the following morning. "I'm just numb really, and sickened at the thought of my 60 staff. I don't know what to do right now. I know I'll rally myself in the coming days and we will be back and fighting, but right now I just don't know what to do."

The Saturday following the flood saw 150 people gathering to help clean-up. David started with the muddy gyprock walls. "I took my vengeance out on the wall. Everyone just started demolishing it. It was just amazing." Surprised at how upbeat he was - considering his former award-winning restaurant was reduced to a gutted, empty shell, with girders where the walls once stood - everyone kept asking, "Why aren't you devastated?" But it was one of those situations where so many people were giving so much love, support and guidance, adrenalin inspired empowerment helped David to keep moving forward, to take that next step and clean-up. Over 1,600 people helped in the coming days.

Professionals have given the all clear to go ahead with re-building. Many suppliers have been generous, postponing the payment of bills. David is waiting - one of thousands of flood victims - to find out what aid is obtainable from the Government. "I have this absolute faith that assistance will be available, and I have to hang onto that because I think if I don't, I would just be a blubbering mess."

Will the support be enough to see the iconic restaurant spring back to life again? Only time will tell.

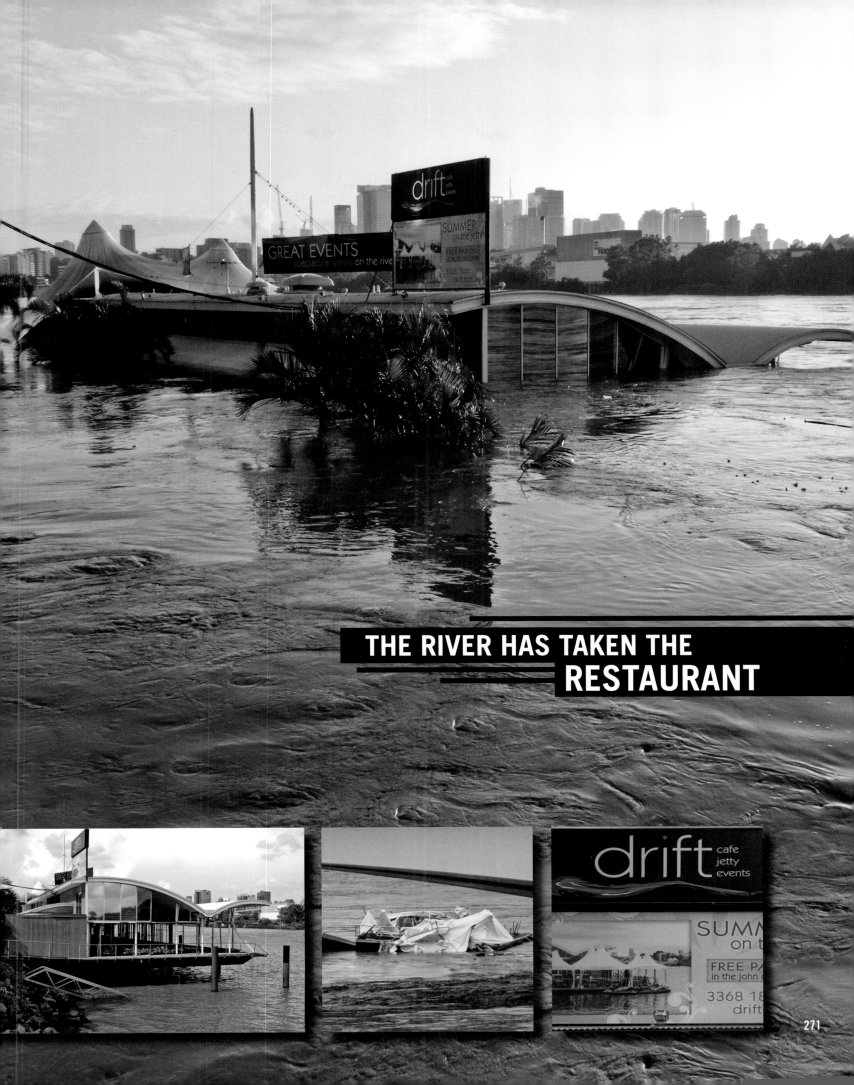

THE RIVER HAS TAKEN THE RESTAURANT

271

Alternative Transport - Rosalie

Brisbane Street - Toowong

Clean-up at Rosalie

NORTHERN SUBURBS

Coronation Drive - Regatta Hotel in background

Torwood Street and Milton Road - Milton

Dixon Street - Milton

Feeding clean-up volunteers - Milton

onation Drive

Two storey houses at Heussler Street - Milton

Train parked - Auchenflower Station

oowong

ilton State School

Lang Parade - Auchenflower

House at Toowong

WORST FLOODING IN
40 YEARS

FOUREX HAS BEEN PART OF THE QUEENSLAND COMMUNITY FOR WELL OVER 120 YEARS — LOCALLY, XXXX STANDS FOR THE QUEENSLAND WAY OF LIFE. THE HOME OF XXXX, CASTLEMAINE PERKINS BREWERY IN MILTON, IS ONE OF QUEENSLAND'S MOST SYMBOLIC SITES AND PRODUCES SOME OF QUEENSLAND'S BEST-LOVED BREWS, INCLUDING THE SECOND-BIGGEST SELLING BEER IN THE COUNTRY - XXXX GOLD.

When Queensland was hit with the worst flooding it had seen in 40 years, the XXXX Brewery was not spared. At the peak of the flood on January 13th, 2.5 metres of water filled the Brewery's packaging area, part of the brewing room and its offices. Looking more like a floating oil rig than a Brewery, the site remained under water for almost three days.

Just 18 days after the flooding the Brewery was once again producing beer, whilst outside the Brewery, XXXX got to work thanking volunteers for their efforts in cleaning up the state — giving away slabs of XXXX GOLD at the end of a hard day's work and alongside the broader business, donating close to half a million in cash and product to recovery efforts.

The 2011 floods and the aftermath that followed was undoubtedly a challenging time for XXXX and the entire Queensland community, but it has also been a time that has shown the strength and resilience of the people who call Queensland home.

Clean-up - muster room

Cordova Street - Milton - looking towards Suncorp Stadium

SUNCORP STADIUM

Photo courtesy of The Courier-Mail - Jan 2011

SUNCORP STADIUM HAS HOSTED MANY EVENTS, NOT THE LEAST OF WHICH WAS THE FAMOUS FLOOD EVENT IN JANUARY 2011. MURKY BROWN WATER SPILLED FROM OVERFLOWING DRAINS TO COVER THE FAMOUS SPORTING FIELD AND REACHED UP TO ROW 5 IN THE SEATING BOWL.

While an attempt was made, as a precautionary measure, to move equipment, some simply could not be shifted. The stadium's electrical, telecommunications and fire systems were under the West Stand, which was inundated with water.

Heussler Terrace - Milton - looking towards Suncorp Stadium

Suncorp Stadium - street side

Wally Lewis statue

Home Dressing Room lockers

Yet there was one who was totally prepared! King Wally stood proud in his snorkel, floaties and goggles surveying the devastation all around.

Despite the soaking, a coordinated clean-up strategy was soon in place and to the joy of many fans the Suncorp Stadium was back in use in time for the Queensland Roar game on the 12th February, 2011.

Suncorp Stadium from Heussler Terrace - Milton

Suncorp Stadium from Cordova Street - Milton

277

BRISBANE HAD BECOME
CHAOTIC

GLENN AND CINDY HAVE NURTURED THEIR BUSINESS FOR 21 YEARS, DEVELOPING IT FROM A SMALL COMMUNITY FOCUSED PAINT STORE TO ONE OF AUSTRALIA'S LARGEST INDEPENDENTLY OWNED TRADE AND RETAIL STORES. THE BUSINESS IS CHARACTERISED BY THE FAMOUS WHITE HORSE 'CHESTER', WHO PROUDLY GUARDS THE PREMISES BY DAY.

"There is so much love in this business. The team we have – we're a little left of centre, we're not mainstream, and somehow it happens for us. We had a fibreglass horse out the front, what has that got to do with paint? Nothing. What did Chester do out there? Well, he just did his thing, he just looked. We got tired of bringing him in and out of the shop each day, and sometimes we thought, 'Oh, stuff it, we won't do that anymore', and customers came and said 'Where's Chester? We expect him to be there and we use him as a landmark for friends!' So we became a slave to that damn horse out the front! Sometimes he needed a touch up and customers asked 'Where's the horse?' and we just said, 'Oh, he's just out in the back paddock'. Customers loved him, we loved him!"

On the night of Monday the 10th, Glenn and Cindy were warned that they could be hit by flooding. That night they moved the stock up a floor and sandbagged madly. Friends lent them a helping hand – they were all running back and forth to Newmarket where sandbags were available. In the dead of night, utterly exhausted by all the unloading and sandbagging, they decided to leave it at one metre off the ground. The following morning, they attempted to raise the 200 pallets of paint product they had. Moving anything out of the store was out of the question as Brisbane had become chaotic, blocked off the night before with the rising water. Nearby industrial areas and warehouses were flooded in.

"We were advised that we'd need about 1.8m of sandbags, so we spent another afternoon trying to get them above that line. In the end none of it was worthwhile. It was irrelevant, a complete waste of time, because the water came through at 3.5m, well over ceiling height. The ceiling collapsed, so it destroyed everything. Anything that's affected by water, like shelving - the timber boards just buckled. At the very top, which is nearly 5 metres high, the condensation built up and it just collapsed in on itself."

In the midst of everything their son left the country. They had known the date was coming for a long time, and they were looking forward to the excitement, lots of hugs and kisses and tears. Instead he was hastily dropped at the airport 5 hours early, or he wouldn't have got there at all. Cindy stayed home with the dogs in case they got stranded.

The water was coming up the drains at the end of the street. Throughout Wednesday and Thursday it just kept rising. "But over those couple of days, we spent most of the time just watching. We could see the building from the walkway...so we saw it drowning... all we could do was watch our life submerge, slowly, surely...it was torturing, and the next day it went even higher."

Glenn describes the aftermath, "On the Friday afternoon I came in here by myself, and I forced open the back door, and it was effectively as though you had spun the store around a few times, and then poured mud all over the top of the lot. The stuff wasn't even recognisable. It was all enclosed, it was hot - and the smell was like nothing I have ever smelt in all my life - mud and toxic sludge.

Glenn tried to prepare Cindy before she took her first look, but it was impossible for her to process the enormity of the devastation. "It took my breath away. It was so big and I felt so dwarfed, so vulnerable...I came in and just said "Oh". There was no floor space; we had to walk on top of everything. Glenn was feeling overwhelmed, he just sat on a tin, staring at nothing. I had seen fully grown men crying down at Rosalie, they could barely hold their emotions back, and little kids that were traumatised, but somehow I stayed composed all day."

"It wasn't until I saw Chester lying in the rubble, ruined, that I crumpled. The little bit of joy and uniqueness about this business was completely destroyed. We had jokingly suspected for a long time that Chester comes to life at night – anything that is left around that nobody owns up to – must be Chester! It was just a little lightness about everyday existence, and the absolute sheer joy that this fiberglass horse gives all sorts of people. Seeing him damaged triggered the emotions that had been slowly building all day, but it was a good release."

"Saturday morning, at the crack of dawn, about 150 people barrelled in the door - some people we knew, but the vast majority we had no idea who they were - all ready to go. They had a human conveyor belt out the front and back. Trucks arrived, a bobcat and a scissor lift just materialised. Our forklift was being worked on by someone, trying to get it going. It was like this entity that had its own heart beat - they took control, they had their little chiefs in charge and got things happening, it was phenomenal."

"I must have walked to the front and back of the shop probably 500 times that day thinking, I should be controlling this, I should be able to grasp this. As well-intended, and as incredibly heart-felt, warming, beautiful, wonderful, and supporting as it was, it was completely overwhelming. All our awards over those 21 years were smashed up in various stages within their frames. They were just being ripped out. I mean it was a practical thing to do, but it was heartbreaking. I was literally frozen, unable to process it all. They tore walls out; they did what needed to be done."

Chester watches over the clean-up after he has been carefully restored

"Then after Sunday we tried to sort out what was salvageable. This was all that was left of our life; we had to rescue anything we could! We were able to recover some things; they were left out the back and we had the army offer to look after them for us. It's amazing how usually you don't take much time to reflect on what the army does for our community, but we came in here one morning at 6, and we were weak, tired and vulnerable. We went out the back, and there they were, all asleep on their camp beds! That was so inspiring and reassuring when everything else had fallen to pieces, we were so grateful to them, I still get emotional about them, unbelievably decent people. They were just lifesavers."

"When we focused on our business, we felt guilty because we wanted to help others; there were hundreds of our customers that lost their homes. One thing I say is that there was too much stuff thrown out. When people are sitting on their milk crates, perhaps they will think 'Maybe I should have kept some of that stuff!' For six weeks they worked extremely long hours to completely renovate the premises and painstakingly restore most of their equipment. "We've been through this and survived - now we can take on anything - we are stronger than ever!" Cindy said confidently.

Bulimba City Cat Terminal

Mud aftermath

Residents sandbagging - Hawthorne

SOUTHEAST SUBURBS

Hardcastle Park - Hawthorne

Businesses flooded - Wooloongabba

Morley Street - Coorparoo

Mowbray Park City Cat Terminal

Volunteers fill sandbags at Balmoral council depot

Bulimba home sand bagged and ready

Bulimba home during flooding

Norman Avenue - Norman Park

Queenslander homes - East Brisbane

Shops at Bulimba

Brunswick Street - Newfarm

City Cycle and Ferry Terminal - Newfarm Park

Eves on the River Restaurant

NEWFARM AND ALBION

Breakfast Creek - Albion

James Street - Newfarm

Street behind Breakfast Creek Road

Sydney Street Ferry Terminal - Newfarm

Brisbane Corso - Dutton Park

Fairfield Road - Yerongpilly

Brisbane Corso - Yeronga

YERONGA AND FAIRFIELD

Park Road - Yeronga

SPCA - Fairfield

Kingsley Parade - Yeronga

Hyde Road - Yeronga

BRISBANE MARKETS
Rocklea

THEY CAME IN DROVES

EVERY DAY, WHILE THE CITY OF BRISBANE SLEEPS, A SMALL ARMY RACES THE RISING SUN TO ENSURE THAT A MOUNTAIN OF PRODUCE IS DELIVERED FRESH TO OUR GROCERY STORES, SUPERMARKETS AND RESTAURANTS. IT'S LIKE A MASSIVE ORCHESTRA COMPOSED OF APRON-CLAD WORKERS MOVING TONNES OF FRUIT AND VEGETABLES TO THE TUNE OF BUSTLING FORKLIFTS AND CLATTERING CRATES. IT ISN'T OFTEN THAT THIS NOISY BUSTLE IS HUSHED: IT HAPPENED IN 1974 WHEN THE GREAT FLOOD INUNDATED THE CITY. AFTER THAT, THE ENGINEERS BUILT THEIR MIGHTY WIVENHOE DAM AND DECLARED THE CITY SAFE.

On Thursday, 10th January, 2011, the unthinkable occurred. The Brisbane Markets were inundated again, the only sound on its great selling floor was the splashing of water against the platforms. Brisbane Markets are huge – over 75 hectares of land at Rocklea, with more than 40 buildings that house the merchants who bring the city's daily quota of apples and carrots. Not only are there dozens of fruit, vegetable and flower vendors, but there are also restaurants, cafés, shops and other affiliated businesses that do what is needed to keep this 'orchestra' running smoothly. One would hardly think that anybody could love such an enormous place, but disasters are strange things; they not only expose the weaknesses of our defences and the cracks in our buildings, they also bring out the best in people. When Brisbane Markets was inundated by floodwaters in January, it was also inundated with offers of help. They came in droves; people who were willing to lend their hands, shovels and heavy machinery to the back-breaking and sometimes heart-breaking job of cleaning up the stinking, rotten mess of spoiled produce, ruined equipment and damaged buildings.

It took days to clear away the filthy black mud that had deposited itself over every surface, worked its way into electrical equipment and clogged up drains. The army came and helped to shovel and sweep the stuff into massive heaps, contractors came with their heavy machinery and removed the towering piles of rubbish, the 'firies' came and hosed everything down. Then there were the 'ordinary' folk - people with extraordinary hearts who came with food to feed the helpers - pies and pizzas, sausages and sandwiches. They came until there were too many to count – just some of the hundreds of nameless, unsung heroes who helped out across the city and across the state when the rains forgot to stop.

Photograph courtesy of *Cpl. Janine Fabre*

Australian Defence Force trucks on standby to assist removal of the mountain of rubbish

Aerial view of the 75ha Brisbane Markets - Rocklea during

Volunteers clear away muddy debris of rotting vegetables

volunteers sort out the mess in the Brisbane
ts Commercial Centre

Photograph courtesy of Cpl. Janine Fabre
Members of the Australian Defence Force assist with
the huge clean-up effort

Mountains of debris are carted away

e January 2011 floods

BRISBANE MARKETS

Submerged Central Trading area at the Markets

Abou Chahla of Garden Verde thigh deep in mud
n flood waters

Pallets are left high and dry on a Market worker's car

The entry to the Markets is a swimming pool!

285

GALVANISED INTO
ACTION

BRISBANE TRUCK CENTRE GENERAL MANAGER LOREN SCHROFF, HAS TWO FAVOURITE STORIES FROM THE FLOOD CLEAN-UP. ON SUNDAY, WHILE ABOUT 40-45 PEOPLE WERE WORKING AWAY CLEANING UP THE DEVASTATED BUILDING, A COUPLE OF LADIES PULLED UP IN AN AUDI Q7 AND CAME IN, GENEROUSLY HANDING OUT BAGS OF FOOD, CUPCAKES AND SANDWICHES; THEIR CAR WAS LITERALLY LOADED WITH FOOD. SHORTLY AFTER, FOUR GUYS PULLED UP IN A UTE WITH A BBQ ON THE BACK, AND BEGAN COOKING UP SAUSAGES AND HAMBURGERS AND HANDING OUT SOFT DRINKS. THEY WERE FROM A FOOTBALL TEAM IN BALLINA, 185KM AWAY. THEN ON MONDAY, THEIR LARGEST COMPETITOR SHOWED UP AND OFFERED TO SEND IN STAFF TO HELP. DUE TO OH&S ISSUES AND THE FACT THAT THEY HAD ENOUGH MANPOWER AT THE TIME, LOREN WAS UNABLE TO ACCEPT THE OFFER, BUT INSISTS THAT IT "SURE WAS A NICE GESTURE". THESE POSITIVE EXPERIENCES AT A TIME OF GREAT HARDSHIP REALLY REINFORCED THE FACT THAT HIS MOVE HERE FROM CANADA FIVE YEARS AGO WAS CERTAINLY A RIGHT ONE.

The hundreds of references to the devastating flood of 1974 didn't mean a lot to Loren, only a relatively new resident of Brisbane. However, the radio announcements warning of extensive flooding, with Rocklea being listed in the top thirty suburbs destined for inundation, got Loren thinking. After a discussion on Tuesday morning it was wisely decided that they should get their trucks off the premises immediately - no small task considering there were over 130 vehicles stored there, and that it was predicted the water would begin its march on their premises that day.

Fortunately, they had plenty of storage space at their Wacol factory, fifteen minutes away, so the mammoth task of shifting the vehicles began. Loren and some others began to line the trucks up at the gate, while fifteen drivers were galvanised into action, beginning the shuttle service. One of the new buses from the showroom floor was used to ferry the drivers back from Wacol to begin the run over again. Working tirelessly all day, the round trip eventually taking two hours due to the increasing traffic on the roads, they moved 120 trucks. When they left at 5pm, there was about 450mm of water at the front gate. As a result of this tiring effort, the vehicle loss was confined to two bus chassis, four new trucks and eight customer trucks, just a fraction of what had been in the yard that morning.

The water peaked during Wednesday night and Loren and some workmates managed to kayak in on Thursday morning for a preliminary assessment of the damage. The water level was still over 2.5m deep, and as they paddled around the back, they were relieved to find that the mezzanine floor on which they had stored as many parts and tools as could possibly fit, had only just gone under water, the thickness of the pallets preserving the goods from any significant loss.

Interestingly, the Ipswich Motorway overpass, which rose like an island from the sea not far from their premises, had five cows and three deer taking refuge on it, their distant habitat obviously inundated.

Saturday was the first day they were able to get back on the premises to begin cleaning up the mess. Loren highly commends his fifty staff, the first of whom arrived at 10am, with the number swelling to forty by 2pm. On top of this, all but three showed up on Sunday, bringing family and friends to assist. Loren didn't underestimate the enormity of the clean-up process, and with high levels of toxicity present, diligently followed strict OH&S procedures to assure the wellbeing of his staff. Four days after the water receded, he dismantled a starter motor for the sake of curiosity - inside it was just a ball of rust.

The office staff's tolerance and cohesion continued for weeks after, working in cramped conditions with inadequate air conditioning, whilst the workshop crews worked from temporary facilities, their efficiency greatly reduced by the inconvenience of not having a fully equipped workshop at their disposal.

As he sits in the upstairs office of the newly renovated building, Loren ponders the many opinions regarding the circumstances of the flood and summarily declares, "it's a natural disaster, and you can have all the inquiries you like, you're not going to change it, and if you're looking for someone to hang, that's the wrong thing to do, but sure, look for ways to do things differently and better for the future."

Photo: Tim Marsden - The Courier-Mail

CHRIS ANGELOS

Rocklea

THINGS WERE GETTING SERIOUS

CHRIS, FROM ROCKLEA, HAS LIVED IN THE SAME HOUSE FOR 11 YEARS. HE HAS POURED A LOT OF TIME AND MONEY INTO IMPROVING IT – EXTENDING AND BUILDING A DECK. FINALLY, NEEDING MORE SPACE TO ACCOMMODATE HIS GROWING FAMILY, HE AND HIS WIFE DECIDED IT WAS TIME TO MOVE ON. THEY CONTACTED REAL ESTATE AGENTS, HAD THE HOUSE PAINTED, AND THE GARDEN BEDS DONE AND WERE JUST ON THE VERGE OF SELLING.

On the day the flood hit, Chris came home from work sick. "I went to bed, thinking 'Oh yeah, it will go away as it normally does, it banks up a bit, then it flows out as fast as it builds up.' About midday QLD Premier Anna Bligh started talking on the radio. She mentioned 1974 so I went outside, it was the first time I noticed anything. Oxley Creek, which flows into the Brisbane River, has this unique feature where it points up the river, and acts like a big scoop for the whole of the Brisbane River. Everything that was coming down the Brisbane River actually started going up Oxley Creek. I started seeing things float upstream, instead of going downstream, and it was then I knew that things were getting serious."

When the water began to lap at the bottom of the property it became fairly evident that nothing would stop it rising. Chris remembers checking the letterbox for the last time, to find a flyer letting them know they should evacuate. They just had time to save photos, PC's and some digital possessions. "To actually sit there and physically watch your house go under by inches, unable to do anything to stop it happening, it's like death by a thousand cuts. I and my little ones are avid readers, and we lost 30 years' worth of books. I had 4 book cases in the house, the books just soaked up the water."

"The man next door drove from Sydney on Monday night. He got up here at about 6 in the evening, got all his belongings out and put them into storage at Beaudesert Road. He thought everything was sweet, until the storage place went under too!" The water came through at almost ceiling height. "The house was just trashed; all the furniture basically lifted up and dropped where it was, so we had the fridge sitting over on its side, lounge suites were pointing up in the air. We started working – 6 of us had the house cleaned 3 hours later. About 10 o'clock the house was empty and 2 hours after that there wasn't one sheet left in this place…just the speed at which we got rid of stuff. Everything was out on the street, and the house was completely bare."

"We had a girl called Vanessa turn up with 6 friends from Melbourne - they got together and said 'Let's go and find someone to help, and they just happened to knock on our door …and stayed for a week. They painted the whole outside of the house!"

"There was a guy with a semi-trailer and he organised his house as a collection point for donated goods. He'd drive up and down the road, with the back of his semi covered in couches, fridges, freezers. He'd pull up and honk the horn, everyone would come out, have a bit of a chat and say what they needed, take it off and away they'd go! It was incredible, the way people responded. If you'd asked me 3 or 4 years ago, where's the sense of community in Brisbane? I'd have said it wasn't there. I think it just lay dormant, and given the opportunity, it absolutely blossomed."

"But now we feel that we're stuck in limbo in plans for our life. We wonder, 'Are we rebuilding a house only to get flooded again?' It's the biggest thing we own, but at the same time it's unsellable, so we're trapped. A lot of the water came from the Lockyer Valley and Wivenhoe, and it was just unable to get away. We've had community meetings, and they're talking about changing Oxley Creek so water can run out. If something good comes out of the commission they've begun, some better planning, it's something."

Photo: Tim Marsden - The Courier-Mail

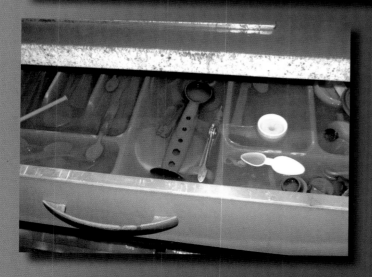

THEY WERE THERE THROUGHOUT THE
ORDEAL

FOR RACHAEL FLETCHER AND LITTLE DAUGHTER BELLA, OF FRENEY ST, ROCKLEA, THEIR STRONGEST MEMORY FROM THE JANUARY 2011 FLOODS — IS THE WAY THEY PROVED GOD'S CARE.

"We saw God's hand in everything," Rachael said, her face shining through tears, as she recounted the heartrending story of facing the possibility of losing everything. "Every day, we stood as close as we could to the edge of the brown ocean which should have been parklands and football fields near our home. Along with many other residents, we were there to get an idea of how bad things really were. During the four days it took for the water to subside, my family could only mentally prepare and pray. One of those days, I prayed for three things specifically; I don't know why I prayed for them, I just did! I prayed for my work laptop, an unworn pair of new joggers to start the year (I'm a PE teacher) and I also prayed for my Bible which was a gift I received after my Baptism.

Despite my belief that God answers prayer, you can imagine my surprise when I got back to find these three specific things all high and dry! Only the bottom cover of my Bible was a little damp — the rising waters had stopped just beneath it and had gone no further!!! I couldn't believe it! I thought, 'O what little faith I have! I should have prayed for everything!' This was just the start of many ways in which my Lord showed, and reassured me, that He was going to be with me throughout this experience."

The waters rose 4.5m to the windowsills of their highset unit, making it uninhabitable and forcing Rachael and Bella to find a new home. But the impact was softened by the amazing support of the Christian community she belongs to. They were there with her throughout the ordeal of cleaning her unit and finding and furnishing a new one - making it into a home for Rachael, her daughter and their precious bird, Parry. It was an anxious time for Bella as she faced the possibility of having to give up Parry if the new landlord didn't allow pets.

"One of the most difficult things in the whole experience was not being able to do anything, but pray and wait - wait for the waters to reach peak, wait for the waters to subside, and wait for a new unit/house to be approved," Rachael recalled. "But even before I became too worried, my pastor was on the phone asking how we were and if we needed a place to stay. He added that he had a crew poised and ready to help when required - which was an enormous relief.

As soon as I heard my neighbour had gotten through to our units, I took my mum to have a look. It smelt like a swamp; there was mud covering everything including most of our possessions. I did not know where to start. Luckily, as I looked around, my friend rang. She said she would come and pick up clothes and bedding. She distributed them to women from church, to wash and see what was salvageable."
"My pastor called again, and we arranged to start 'cleanup' the next day at 9.30am. I arrived to find everything already in full swing - I felt left behind! There were council workers and volunteers busily helping; sorting and piling the rubbish! Someone had already thrown my dryer out even though I still had clothes in it! Luckily we were able to get them out before it was buried beneath the rest of the stuff.
"It was just incredible, the amount of help we received. Everyone was working, people were driving around dropping off food and beer. You'd expect to hear of this in a small country town but to see it in a big city is truly encouraging!"

They tried to salvage anything that could be cleaned - "We did, because it was ours; it may not be a lot, but we had worked for it and it was important to us."

During - Rachael's unit on the left

Rachael's unit after flooding

The experience of watching the council machines pick up the destroyed household contents was devastating. "It was like 'mission clean-up' – one minute whole, the next minute squished beyond recognition. It was upsetting because even though they were ruined, they were still mine."

Rachael's Church had an impromptu voluntary offering for those in the Church who were affected by the flooding. Enough was raised for Rachael to purchase new appliances and furniture. "It was like being on the Oprah show... I would go out to do something, returning to find surprise after surprise! Even our beds were made, and fridge and cupboards restocked." All Bella's school needs were donated, and when word got around that she had lost most of her toys, presents arrived as if it was her birthday! This was overwhelming for the six year old!

"I wanted to take my toys with me, [when packing our bags to evacuate] but Mum told me I had to take only clothes! I took about three soft toys but lost all my Bratz and Barbies. I had to chuck them away. People gave me some more, but a lot were old.....except for two, one real pretty one and one other. People gave me a lot of creative stuff too, and I thought, awww, I was expecting toys!!"

Rachael's final words sum up her overall impression of the time......... "God uses bad situations for good. Even before we could think about things, they were being done. It was a demonstration of the Christian Spirit. I don't know how people could get through without God."

THE LOGISTICAL
NIGHTMARE

JOHN GROSSMAN, DEALER PRINCIPAL OF MERCEDES BENZ COMMERCIAL VEHICLES, PONDERS HIS FIRST JOB AS AN APPRENTICE FOR BROWN AND HURLEY WITH CONSIDERABLE IRONY. DUE TO START IN FEBRUARY 1974, JOHN TOOK A CALL FROM THE SERVICE MANAGER AT THE END OF JANUARY REQUESTING HIM TO COME IN AND START WORK IMMEDIATELY. MEMORIES OF HIS FIRST JOB, HOSING OUT THE FLOOD AFFECTED WORKSHOP WHILST VIGOROUSLY DEFENDING HIMSELF AND NEW WORKMATES FROM RATS, SNAKES AND OTHER CREATURES SEEKING REFUGE FROM THEIR WATERLOGGED HABITATS, CAME RUSHING BACK WHEN HE FINALLY MADE IT BACK INTO THEIR ROCKLEA WAREHOUSE AFTER THE FLOODS RECEDED IN JANUARY, 2011.

John freely admits that he doesn't have many memories of the 74 flood other than his workshop cleaning experience, and that he honestly didn't think it would happen again, his sense of security strengthened by the continual promotion over many years, of the Wivenhoe Dam as the failsafe preventative measure to keep Brisbane from the dangers of her namesake river.

Even as they frantically moved every new truck they could during Monday, John continually questioned his sanity, the stress of the logistical nightmare pressing on him by the minute. He had advised his staff early in the day that any who were at risk of not getting home, or any whose properties may be threatened were welcome to leave, so he was left with about half his staff and 200 vehicles to move, the 5 minute trip taking 40 minutes, due to the gridlocked traffic created by many other business in the area doing the same thing.

By Monday night they had moved all the new vehicles to premises kindly offered to them and went back to the office to put everything up on the tables and to shift as many spare parts as possible to higher shelves. The next morning, John arrived to find the water waist deep across the showroom floor, and after a quick call to the Melbourne Head Office, began to dismantle the main frame computer and put it up above the eaves of the building.

On Friday, after the water had receded, it was a sorry sight that greeted them. Just weeks earlier, they had consolidated all their paper records and made provision for them in purpose-built storage units. The paper had become a sodden mess, with more resemblance to a giant paper mache creation than the carefully filed records that they began as. The walls had been stripped of interior linings, revealing bare framework, the ceilings had collapsed and the furniture was strewn all around the building. "I wouldn't have believed there was so much current" John laments,

as he describes the situation, "it looked like the whole inside of the building had been put in a blender and then tipped back out."

In the workshop, there were nine customer vehicles in various stages of repair, and interestingly, when the clean-up began they discovered there was not a drop of fuel left in any of the vehicles' fuel tanks and no oil left in any of the gearboxes or diffs, it had all floated out as the water inundated everything in its path.

John speaks commendably of their German insurers, who flew four assessors out to view the carnage and make the call on approximately $8 million of damaged spare parts, second hand vehicles and other equipment and furniture. This is separate to the costs of rebuilding the premises and all the costs of relocating and operating from temporary premises. It is interesting to note the insurance company have advised they will not re-insure the Rocklea premises for flood cover! John saves special mention for his focussed staff and the way they have responded since the flood, operating out of multiple sites, temporary premises, borrowed workshops and even the back of service vans with great toleration and devotion to the job at hand. It has been no small task to co ordinate the company's needs for premises, telephones, IT and even power supply, and despite many hours of frustration and daily unexpected setbacks, John has achieved the difficult task of getting the business back operating again to fulfil the needs of their customers.

3.8m bridge Rocklea

Chep Pallets

Vehicles and property at Rocklea

ROCKLEA AND SURROUNDING SUBURBS

Ipswich Motorway - Rocklea

Flooded Houses - Rocklea

Flooded Machinery

Rocklea Businesses

Flooded Businesses - Rocklea

Flooded Service Station - Richlands

Matilda Service Station - Rocklea

Rocklea from the air

Rocklea Street

Garbage Trucks

Sewrage Treatment Plant

JANUARY 2011   JANUARY 1974

KANGAROO POINT DOCKS

JANUARY 2011   JANUARY 1974

YERONGA

JANUARY 2011   JANUARY 1974

WILLIAM JOLLY BRIDGE

JANUARY 2011   JANUARY 1974

CORONATION DRIVE - TOOWONG

BRISBANE CITY - EAGLE STREET   JANUARY 2011   JANUARY 1974

SOUTH BANK - VICTORIA BRIDGE   JANUARY 2011   JANUARY 1974

VICTORIA BRIDGE   JANUARY 2011   JANUARY 1974

SOUTH BRISBANE   JANUARY 2011   JANUARY 1974

IT HAPPENED SO
FAST

DANE AND KRISTY WOODS

Chelmer

INTERVIEW WITH DANE AND KRISTY WOODS — A YOUNG COUPLE WHO LOST EVERYTHING AT CHELMER.

IT HAPPENED SO FAST AND WITHOUT WARNING. WE AREN'T FROM AROUND HERE; MY HUSBAND IS FROM NEW ZEALAND AND I AM FROM SYDNEY, SO WE DIDN'T KNOW ANYTHING ABOUT FLOODS. ALTHOUGH IT HAD BEEN RAINING FOR WEEKS AND OUR YARD HAD WATER POOLING IN IT, WE THOUGHT WE WERE SAFE, AS OUR HOUSE WAS QUITE HIGH SET.

About six months before we were married, I was diagnosed with severe rheumatoid arthritis. I was in so much pain I had to have fluid drained from my knees and steroid injections to even be able to walk down the long flight of steps to meet Dane on our wedding day. Five days later we moved into our first home together; a rented cottage in Harte St, Chelmer. In January 2011, after nearly a year together, our lives turned another totally unanticipated corner when almost everything we owned was lost in the flood.

On the afternoon of the 11th, after months of rain, our neighbours started frantically packing up their belongings. We wondered why everyone was panicking so much. We'd had no warnings of floods right here. We checked the river and it hadn't even broken its banks! The water would have to get really high to affect us. My boss's wife suggested that we load the car with important things, in case of emergency. Dane, was on leave from the Defence Force at the time, and I, packed up my laptop with our wedding photos on it, our books, insurance papers and other small valuable things and took them over to my boss' place at The Gap. But nobody else warned us, nothing from authorities saying, "You had better get out; your house is in danger!" We set the alarm for 2:30am just in case. Were we being overcautious? We decided it was better to lose a few minutes sleep than lose our home. We didn't expect anything serious. But the river rose, and kept rising.................

I woke when the power shorted at 2 am. Something was wrong! From the patio, even in the pitch darkness, I could see a strong reflection of the sky, the house, and the trees in the lake that was our backyard! Unable to believe my eyes, I turned on the light and saw the water. It had silently risen all through the hours of darkness and was now at the top of the clothesline.

Dane yelled, "We've got to get out!" We only had 10 minutes to escape, it was rising so quickly. I was instantly awake, filled with adrenalin, panic stricken. We

collected anything we could fit into the car - the more expensive stuff - and left. While I was grabbing those last few things, Dane had checked out the road, only to discover both exits were already submerged. Driven by desperation we broke down a fence and, mounting the kerb, roared through two front yards and around the corner.

Sometimes you look back and wonder what could have been done differently. We regret that we didn't warn others early that morning. But there was no time, everything was happening so quickly. It was surreal! I was so frightened; I didn't think we would be able to get out. We drove up and down streets trying to leave the suburb. Water was everywhere. Our entire suburb was under siege by a silently rising ocean. Dane was on the phone as we tried to negotiate our way out. I was yelling, "Get off the phone, just go!" Eventually we found our way to Sherwood, and then to a carpark in Indooroopilly. What do we do now? We don't know many people well enough to just land on their doorstep in the middle of the night with a carload of belongings, a dog, and no home! We decided to call a friend in Toowong. They put us up for the rest of the night, then we ended up going to my sister-in-law's place on the Coast. There was nothing more we could do in Brisbane. We kept watching the news — every time the helicopters went over the flooded suburbs we'd be saying, "There's the top of our house!!! Can't see the house next door though…." It was scary, so unreal.

The floods peaked on Thursday. Twelve to thirteen feet of water came up through our house. There was no structural damage - the water just rose vertically.

Can you imagine your house being filled with mud and water, shaken, and drained? Nothing prepared us for what we found on Saturday when we returned. The mess!! The filthy, smelly muck! Even inside the cupboards! The glass cupboard was still

full of water and floating glasses, so as soon as I opened the doors – CRASH. In the back yard, junk was everywhere. A playpen - I have no idea where that came from, we don't have kids - floor linings, boogie boards, chairs, pot plants, a window pane. None of it was ours, yet our towels stayed pegged on the clothesline! It was all one colour......muddy brown.

We had about 40 volunteers come through to help clean and scrub up the house. It was no longer a home – just a worksite. I stood there saying, "Yep throw that out, no keep that." Because of my arthritis, I couldn't lift anything. But when you find stuff like school reports in the clean-up you just sit there and look at them.... The community spirit was amazing, everyone wanted to help. Strangers were in my house, yet I could trust them. There were funny moments; because of my arthritis I had a sharps container and needles were strewn all through the house! I was saying to people, "It's ok, it's just for arthritis!" We cleaned them up pretty quickly! We had to try and clean-up a lot of stuff rather than throw out as we knew we weren't covered by insurance. Still we lost so much – vacuum cleaners, ironing boards, paintings, all our furniture, washing machine, stereo's etc. My braces guards were in the bathroom and they're gone, with the moulds. It's about $1000 to get them replaced. We lost our marriage certificate, my husband's birth certificate, passports, medical records, and our sense of security.

 Rheumatoid arthritis is stress related; consequently my joints swelled, my hands were red and puffy; I was in agony. All my medications were lost, except a couple of day's supply that I had saved. Rheumatoid goes away when the stress goes away but things were bad for a few weeks there!

NRMA aren't covering what we lost. They weren't even apologetic. They called it a sunny day flood because the water entered the premises on a sunny day! After six

WE'VE GOT TO GET OUT!

months of fairly constant rain, we had one of the sunniest days that Wednesday! We are lucky - we saved a few things. We are only starting out, so we had no old family treasures to lose, but so much is irreplaceable. We can't get our medical records back, our x-rays or operation reports. We have tried to write things down but you can't remember everything. I have learnt to keep books for everything –important passwords, that kind of thing.

To make matters worse, we were robbed soon after we moved. My wallet went. It wasn't easy getting my licence replaced with no marriage certificate or passport. Fortunately working at a bank meant I got the keycards replaced to use for ID. My workplace has a fund that helped us to start again. My boss refurnished our living area. The Army helped us too; they bought us a fridge which is essential for my medications.

Even though there are many worse off than us, we will carry the scars for a long time. I washed clothing and bedding for days trying to get rid of that terrible flood odour. I can still smell it in things. I think I'm over-sensitive to it!

This whole experience has caused our priorities to completely shift. When I went back to work I went through all my drawers and threw heaps out.   When you lose everything, you realise there's so much you don't actually need....... We have learnt so much from this – I am going to be over prepared from now on – ready for anything!

299

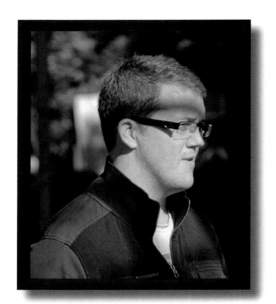

FLOODING WAS
IMMINENT

WATCHING THE NEWS ON MONDAY EVENING, JANUARY 10TH, 2011, DAVID KEERS WAS SPELLBOUND AS HE SAW IMAGES OF CARS AND HOUSES BEING WASHED AWAY IN THE GRANTHAM AND TOOWOOMBA REGIONS. THE NEXT MORNING, WHILE HAVING HIS HAIRCUT, THE BARBER ASKED HIM THE USUAL, "AND HOW ARE YOU TODAY?" DAVID ANSWERED, "YEAH, I'M FINE – I'M JUST HAPPY MY HOUSE ISN'T FLOATING DOWN THE STREET." HE LITTLE THOUGHT THAT IN LESS THAN FORTY-EIGHT HOURS, HIS HOUSE WOULD SUFFER TOTAL INUNDATION.

In the leafy Brisbane suburb of Graceville with the Brisbane River flowing past their backyards, one of these homes belonged to David and his wife, Trish, who had moved in with their two little children just thirteen months before January, 2011. They were pleased with their purchase – the neighbours were friendly and there was a "community feeling" in their neighbourhood.

Going to work after his haircut, David was startled by Trish, on the phone to say flooding was imminent and that Graceville was under threat. Although they knew that their house was flooded in 1974, they did not believe the flood would reach their home this time.

David immediately headed for home. On his way, he called at his parents' home, in another riverside suburb, Tennyson, which was on higher ground. As they watched the fast-flowing river, a boat went floating by, they contacted the Water Police to report it, but as the day progressed, boats were floating by every few minutes, and their reaction became, "Yeah, there goes another one".

Returning to his own home, David with Trish agonised over what to do. Was evacuating really necessary? Then David noticed a neighbor loading his possessions onto a truck, who told him, "We were here in 1974 and we're getting out now". So David and Trish also secured a truck and loaded their possessions into it. While they were doing this news came through that flooding was now predicted to be worse than 1974! How thankful they were that they already started to remove their belongings! Friends and family turned up to lend a hand, and soon they had transferred most of the contents of their home to David's parents' place. By evening David had done his last load, and exhausted, he thankfully sat down to a hot meal at his

parents' home. As he ate, his conscience started nagging at him – he had a truck available and his house was almost empty – what about the other poor folk in his street? He quickly finished his meal and went back and helped his neighbours move what they could.

On Wednesday morning, David was unable to return to Graceville, as the road was already cut by floodwaters, he realised then that his home was indeed in big trouble. There was nothing to do but wait and see, which was not easy!

When the floods had receded enough they were able to see the sorry state of their home. It was the lowest in the street, and the worst affected. The waters had been up in the roof, some ceilings were sagging, others had fallen in. The collapsed ones were gyprock, the sagged ceilings were the older asbestos sheeting. Removing the asbestos was a problem, but friends with asbestos removal licences helped, and the Army also helped in its disposal.

They were overwhelmed with the number of volunteers who helped with the cleanup. Friends, relatives, the Army and complete strangers were not afraid to toil in the mud and filth. He did not even find out the names of many of them, and he remembers one man who helped him that came from Perth. He had taken some of his annual leave and flown across the continent to volunteer his help! Another man arrived on David's doorstep a week or so later, reconstruction was just beginning, he had a handyman's business in New South Wales and had come up to Brisbane to volunteer his services! David very gratefully accepted them.

Six months after the disaster, David and his family are still living with his parents. His family, friends and church have all been active in assisting him practically and financially. The whole experience has drawn the neighbourhood even closer together. David and Trish decided to raise the house – they could not bear to think of renovating their home and then have the floodwaters go through it again. It is now half a metre above the 2011 flood level, which means they will have to negotiate twenty-five steps when entering or leaving their home! But they can rest assured that future floods will not wreak the havoc of the floods of January, 2011.

COMPLETE STRANGERS WERE NOT AFRAID TO TOIL IN
THE MUD AND FILTH

David's House after flooding January, 2011

David's House -now raised

Bins at Graceville

Clean-up - Verney Road - Graceville

Clean-up at West End

BRISBANE CLEAN-UP

Flood damaged home

Flood ruined

Flood ruined piano

Loader helps move rubbish

eaning Up !!

Eager helpers

Feeding the volunteers

ud being swept away

oading ruined possessions

Loads of rubbish were removed

Many offered free food and drinks as their contribution

WOW Sight and Sound - Oxley

Worker at Chelmer

Waterblasting off mud

BRISBANE CLEAN-UP

Temporary rubbish tips were set up at parks, railway stations and other locations to hold the thousands of tonnes of ruined possessions

Streets full of ruined belongings

Street clean-up - Chelmer

Mattresses

aterblasting a house that went right under

Volunteers and their equipment

Thousands of volunteers travelled by public transport to h

treets lined with eager volunteers

stove and other ruined possessions

Residents show their appreciation for assistance
with clean-up

Removing water damaged plasterboard - Jindalee

WIVENHOE
AND SOMERSET

D'Aguilar Highway

CABOOLTURE 119KM

Lake Somerset

Toogoolawah

SOMERSET DAM

Mount Byron

Brisbane Valley Highway

Esk

Lake Wivenhoe

BRISBANE 88.9KM

D'Aguilar National Park

WIVENHOE DAM

Mount Nebo

IPSWICH 53.2KM

Fernvale

Brisbane Forest Park

DAM CATCHMENT AND RIVER SYSTEMS

LEGEND
- Catchment Border
- State Forest
- Protected Areas
- Urban Areas

NAMBOUR

CALOUNDRA

NANANGO

SOMERSET CATCHMENT

Bribie Island

WIVENHOE CATCHMENT

SOMERSET DAM

Moreton Island

Toogoolawah

Upper Brisbane River

Mount Byron

CABOOLTURE

Lake Somerset

NORTH PINE CATCHMENT

Esk

Lake Wivenhoe

NORTH PINE DAM

WIVENHOE DAM

D'Aguilar National Park

North Stradbroke Island

Mount Nebo

Brisbane River

Fernvale

Brisbane Forest Park

BRISBANE

Lockyer Creek

TOOWOOMBA

Gatton

Bremer River

IPSWICH

Laidley

Lake Moogerah

308

Catchment areas in Square Kilometeres

	1	2	3
North Pine			348
Somerset		1503	
Wivenhoe	5554		

Somerset Dam

Wivenhoe Dam

SOMERSET DAM

EARLY SETTLEMENT OF THE BRISBANE RIVER VALLEY. IN THE EARLY 1800'S THE LAND ALONG THE BRISBANE AND STANLEY RIVERS WAS FOUND TO BE PARTICULARLY SUITED TO CATTLE FATTENING, HOWEVER, THE FIRST WHITE PASTORALISTS TO OCCUPY THE BRISBANE RIVER VALLEY WERE WARNED BY THE LOCAL ABORIGINES THAT MAJOR FLOODING WAS NOT UNUSUAL.

Between 1857 and 1903, these pastoralists experienced both crippling droughts and severe flooding, which resulted in huge losses of cattle and crops as well as homes, farm buildings and equipment that were washed away in floods. Many miraculous escapes and rescues from floods were recorded. Some people had to shelter on rooftops, in spite of the fact that their houses were built on ten foot (three metre) stumps. Some clung to trees for hours, making ropes from their clothing to reach higher branches, and as the waters began to recede, one farmer awoke in the morning to find eight black snakes in his bed!

All these experiences clearly demonstrated a need for both drought-proofing and flood-proofing measures. After much discussion it was Henry P. Somerset, a South African who had migrated to Queensland in 1871, who suggested selecting a site on the Stanley River for both water supply and flood mitigation purposes, and the Somerset Dam site was selected by the Bureau of Industry in 1932.

SOMERSET DAM IS BUILT

A township for construction workers was set up, named Somerset after H. P. Somerset who was then the member for Stanley in the Queensland Parliament. It had all the facilities necessary to provide for workers and their families for the years it took to prepare for building the dam, and by 1937 the number of employees had swelled to 450. Preparatory ground work began in 1933 and the pouring of the first bucket of concrete on Thursday, 28th October 1937 was celebrated with free liquid refreshments at the canteen!

Work on the dam was suspended during World War 11 and not resumed until 1948 and although the main construction had become operational in 1953, the final works were not completed until 1958. The dam wall was tested during the 1955 flood in which the spillway was topped and the eight spillway crest gates and two low-level sluice gates were opened for the first time. Two thousand acres of farmland were flooded, at the time, causing extensive damage; this flood and the subsequent one in 1974 showed that the dam was not able to prevent the flooding of Brisbane during extreme rainfall incidents.

STATISTICS

Situated on the Stanley River, near Kilcoy, Lake Somerset covers an area of 4,400 hectares at full capacity, drawing from a catchment area of $1503 km^2$. Its full supply capacity is 379,849 megalitres and the flood mitigation capacity is an additional 155,000 megalitres. The dam wall is of mass gravity type construction in which 203,000 cubic metres of concrete were used. The wall is 305 metres long, and the thickness at its base is approximately 41 metres. The eight radial gates on the spillway each measure 17.97 x 7.01 metres. The top of these gates is 53 metres above the wall's base foundation.

The arrangement of radial crest gates, sluice gates and regulator valves is shown in the following diagram.

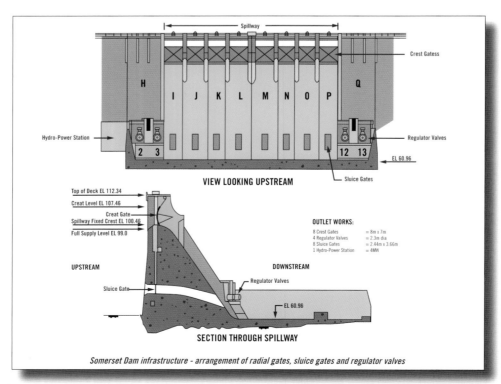

Somerset Dam infrastructure - arrangement of radial gates, sluice gates and regulator valves

The small hydroelectric power station at Somerset has a capacity of 4,000KVA. It was commissioned in 1953 and completed in 1959.

SOMERSET DAM

WIVENHOE DAM

ANOTHER DAM WAS REQUIRED IN THE BRISBANE VALLEY. IT HAD BECOME CLEAR BY THE 1950'S THAT ANOTHER DAM WOULD BE NEEDED IN THE BRISBANE VALLEY BOTH TO SUPPLEMENT BRISBANE'S WATER SUPPLY AND IMPROVE FLOOD MITIGATION. LAND ADJACENT TO THE BRISBANE RIVER, BELOW ITS JUNCTION WITH THE STANLEY RIVER, WHICH HAD FED THE CATTLE INDUSTRY WAS NOW TO BE TAKEN OVER BY WATER. ACQUISITION OF LAND BY THE WIVENHOE DAM COORDINATING COMMITTEE COMMENCED IN MARCH 1973 AND 28,000 HECTARES WERE RESUMED INITIALLY FROM 128 LANDHOLDERS.

WIVENHOE DAM IS BUILT

Design of the dam works started in 1974, with the first contract being signed in 1977. A channel to divert the Brisbane River was made in its right bank, and was completed in 1978, by which time the construction of an embankment across the river had begun. A township providing accommodation for 750 personnel was built, the children from the town travelling to Fernvale for schooling. By September 1983, water storage commenced and the dam structure was completed in 1985, which included the installation of a 79 tonne gantry crane, five steel spillway gates and the construction of a multi-purpose hydroelectric power station. The power station is situated between Lake Wivenhoe and the Splityard Creek Dam, involving water being pumped to the upper storage of Splityard Creek Dam, and the flow, when reversed, driving the turbine generator to generate electricity. Two earth and rock fill saddle dams were also constructed on the left bank (looking downstream). The Brisbane Valley highway was redirected to pass over the dam wall.

STATISTICS

Lake Wivenhoe is more than twice the size of Sydney Harbour. It is on the Brisbane River upstream from Fernvale, with a surface area of 10,750 hectares when full. The catchment area is 5554km^2, which is 40% of the Brisbane River's total catchment. (50% of The Brisbane River catchment is below Somerset and Wivenhoe dams). The zoned earth and rock fill embankment structure is 2.3 kilometres long and 50 metres high from foundation to crest. At the top, the main dam embankment is 10.0 metres wide. Over 4 million cubic metres of rock fill were required for the embankment, and about 140,000 cubic metres of concrete were used to construct the spillway, which is 60 metres long. The storage capacity of the dam is 1,165,238 megalitres with an additional 1,450,000 megalitres flood mitigation capacity. The five steel radial crest gates are among the largest of their kind in the world, each measuring 12 metres wide by 16.6 metres high.

The arrangement of Wivenhoe Dam's radial gates is shown in the diagram.

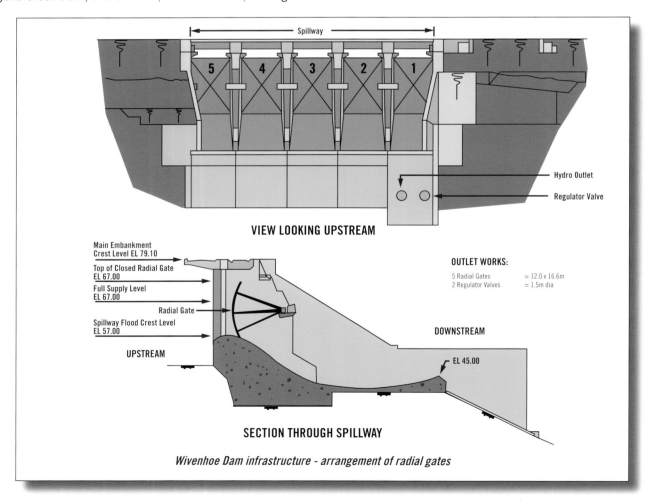

Wivenhoe Dam infrastructure - arrangement of radial gates

RECREATION AT THE DAMS
BOTH SOMERSET AND WIVENHOE DAMS OFFER A GREAT RANGE OF RECREATIONAL ACTIVITIES AND HAVE FACILITIES FOR CAMPING, BARBECUE AND PICNICKING, WITH EXCELLENT OPPORTUNITIES FOR FISHING, SWIMMING, BOATING AND WALKING.

OPERATION OF SOMERSET AND WIVENHOE DAMS
Both Somerset and Wivenhoe Dams are dual-purpose storages, serving as a water supply to much of South East Queensland, and providing flood mitigation benefits to areas prone to flooding along the Brisbane River below Wivenhoe Dam. If, in the event of heavy rain, Somerset reaches capacity, water may be released downstream to Wivenhoe Dam. The dams are operated in tandem during flood events to maximise their flood mitigation capabilities, by which the outflow of floodwaters is regulated by carefully monitored controlled releases of water through the flood gates. Ideally, the dam is cut back to full

supply level as soon as possible before the onset of another flood event but if the catchment continues to fill before the dam can be reduced, its flood mitigation capacity is limited. Consideration must also be given to the structural safety of both dams, which will not sustain unlimited overtopping.

Wivenhoe Dam, an earth and rock fill dam, has a 165m wide auxiliary spillway constructed in 2005 to improve its capacity to withstand flood events. This consists of a three bay "fuse plug spillway" at the right abutment. The fuse plugs, when activated in association with the spillway gates, are designed to erode away, allowing more water to be released from the dam, thereby reducing its risk of failure. The radial gates, sluice gates and regulator valves are Somerset's water release methods; being a mass concrete dam, it is able to withstand limited overtopping.

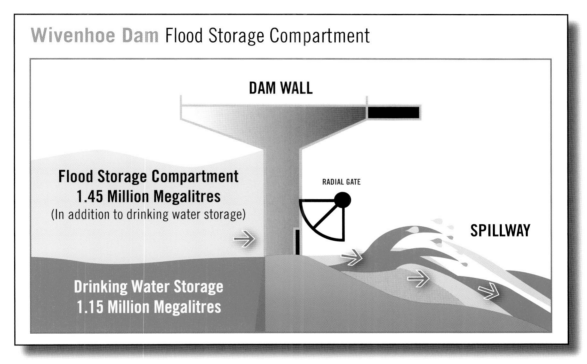

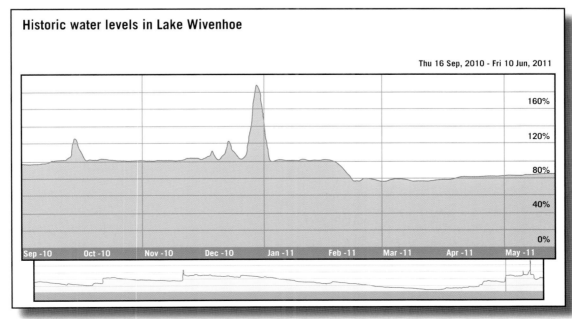

WIVENHOE SMALL HYDRO
ENVIRONMENTALLY SUSTAINABLE HYDRO POWER LOCATED IN
SOUTH EAST QUEENSLAND

ABOUT STANWELL
Stanwell is a Queensland Government owned corporation
with an energy portfolio comprising coal and hydro facilities
throughout Queensland. Currently, Stanwell trades more than
30 per cent of the State's electricity requirements.

STATISTICS
Capacity	4.3 MW
Greenhouse Gas Savings	21,000 tonnes per year
Powered Equivalent	43,000 x 100 watt light bulbs
Commissioned	2002

*Wivenhoe Small Hydro is located
at Wivenhoe Dam, 75 Kilometres
north-west of Brisbane, in South
East Queensland*

ABOUT THE PROJECT
Wivenhoe Small Hydro is located beneath one of Wivenhoe
Dam's five spillway slots and operates 24 hours a day, seven
days a week. This clean, green power generation facility
captures water released for other primary purposes, without
commanding dedicated water releases. The water passes
through a butterfly-type turbine inlet valve and into a 4.3
megawatt (KM) Francis turbine.

It produces electricity at 6,600 volts, which is increased
to 33,000 volts through an on-site transformer that feeds
into Queensland's electricity grid. The 4.3 MW facility was
commissioned in December 2002 and represents an investment
of $7.5 million.

ENVIRONMENT
Hydro-electric generation (using the energy of moving water
to drive generators) is one of the cleanest and most efficient
methods of producing electricity. Wivenhoe Small Hydro
captures water released for other purposes and, therefore,
has no effect on the flow of water downstream. Operation of
the hydro does not emit any greenhouse gases and it is one
of the few power generation facilities in Queensland able to
supply green power.

WATER SUPPLY
Wivenhoe Dam is owned by Seqwater, which is the major
supplier of untreated water to local government and industry
in South East Queensland. The dam consists of a 59-metre-
high, 2.3-kilometre-long, earth and rock embankment built
across the upper reaches of the Brisbane River

COMMUNITY AND TOURISM
Wivenhoe Dam is a popular tourist attraction, offering a
range of activities and recreational facilities. The surrounding
Brisbane River Valley is abundant in wildlife and is a designated
koala habitat. For more information about Wivenhoe Dam and
surrounds, please phone the Lake Wivenhoe Tourism Centre
on (07) 5427 8100.

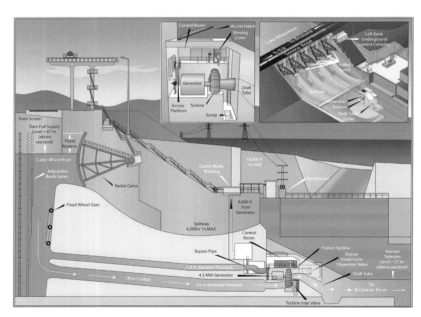

LOCKYER CREEK AND THE BREMER RIVER
The Lockyer Creek and Bremer River catchments are not
controlled by Somerset and Wivenhoe dams, but contribute
to the Brisbane River downstream from Wivenhoe. During
controlled releases from the dams, consideration must also
be given to the concurrent intensity, duration and distribution
of rainfall occurring in those catchments.

In the 2010 - 2011 floods, Lockyer Creek and the Bremer
River were severely affected by flooding and contributed huge
volumes of water into the Brisbane River below the dams, which
significantly contributed to the flooding of Brisbane. It is thus
clear that Somerset and Wivenhoe, although having major
mitigating benefit, are not sufficient to flood-proof Brisbane.

314

Information sourced from Stanwell Co. Ltd.

WIVENHOE DAM

SOMERSET DAM SPILLWAY IN DROUGHT 2006

SOMERSET DAM SPILLWAY DURING FLOOD 2011

SOMERSET DAM

SOMERSET DAM DURING DROUGHT 2006

SOMERSET DAM DURING FLOOD 2011

THE SPIT - SOMERSET PARKLANDS DURING DROUGHT 2006

THE SPIT - SOMERSET PARKLANDS DURING FLOOD 2011

WIVENHOE DAM SPILLWAY IN DROUGHT 2006   WIVENHOE DAM SPILLWAY DURING FLOOD 2011

WIVENHOE DAM

WIVENHOE DAM DURING DROUGHT 2006   WIVENHOE DAM DURING FLOOD 2011

WIVENHOE DAM WALL AND GATES DURING DROUGHT 2006   WIVENHOE DAM WALL AND GATES DURING FLOOD 2011

THE JANUARY 2011 FLOOD EVENT WAS UNPRECEDENTED IN THE HISTORY OF WIVENHOE, SOMERSET AND NORTH PINE DAMS AND RIVALS THE LARGEST FLOODS IN THE REGION'S RECORDED HISTORY.

As the owner and operator of the dams, Seqwater played an integral role in managing and responding to this flood event.

Seqwater operated the dams in accordance with the Manual of Operational Procedures for Flood Mitigation for Wivenhoe Dam and Somerset Dam, and the Manual for North Pine Dam, with staff managing a highly complex, rapidly changing and challenging situation, involving multiple variables and scenarios.

MANAGING THE DAMS DURING THE JANUARY 2011 FLOOD EVENT

The January 2011 Flood (the Event) at Wivenhoe and Somerset Dams began on Thursday 6 January and concluded on Wednesday 19 January 2011.

In the 28 days prior to the beginning of the event, rainfall in South East Queensland had been well above the December average and three separate flood events had occurred at the dams. Flood releases from Wivenhoe Dam occurred on most of these days and as a result of the rainfall, the catchments were near saturation and primed to generate runoff.

Each flood event is different as rainfall events vary in intensity, duration and distribution over the catchment. Only rain which falls upstream of Wivenhoe and Somerset flows into the dams. This is approximately 50% of the Brisbane River catchment. Manifestly Wivenhoe and Somerset cannot provide any flood mitigation benefits for rain that falls below them.

At the beginning of the Event, virtually all of Wivenhoe and Somerset Dams' dedicated flood mitigation storage volume was available for use.

Seqwater's Flood Operations Centre (FOC) was mobilised at 7.42am on Thursday 6 January. At this time 24/7 staffing commenced at both the FOC and the dams.

The flood event at Wivenhoe Dam involved two distinct flood peaks occurring 30 hours apart.

The first, on Monday 10 January, was similar in nature and magnitude to the comparable flood flows of the 1974 flood event. The combined mitigation effect of Somerset and Wivenhoe Dams ensured this first flood caused no damage to urban areas or dwellings downstream of the Brisbane suburb, Moggill.

However, to achieve this, Somerset and Wivenhoe Dams' flood storage compartments were allowed to fill significantly by this first flood peak.

Intense rainfall directly on and near the Wivenhoe Lake area on Tuesday 11 January contributed to the second flood peak. This was also similar in nature and magnitude to the 1974 flood flows.

Scale of the January 2011 Flood Event

Wivenhoe and Somerset Dams

- Can be categorised as large to rare

- The Brisbane River Event is comparable with the flood of 1893, and resulted in almost double (190%) the comparable volume of inflows of the 1974 flood

- The maximum inflow rates for each of the two flood peaks are estimated to be around 200-230% of the comparable flow rate from the 1974 event

- The Bureau of Meteorology (BoM) define the Event as a major flood for the Brisbane River

- During the Event, some rainfall stations in the Brisbane River catchment recorded rainfall estimates beyond the credible limit of extrapolation (Annual Exceedence Probability of 1 in 2,000 years) for durations between six and 48 hours.

North Pine Dam

- Can be categorised as rare

- Maximum inflow rate more than double the largest previous flow rate into the Dam ever recorded (records commenced in 1916)

- Total inflow was 94% of the Dam's total storage.

The impact of intense rainfall at this critical stage, was worsened by the fact it fell directly on and near the Lake, thereby immediately raising the lake level.

Wivenhoe Dam rose more than 1.5m (from 73.40m to its peak of 74.97m) over a 15-hour period on Tuesday 11 January. Accordingly, the second flood peak could not be completely contained within the Dam without risking its structural integrity. In line with the Manual, water releases from Wivenhoe early

in the Event also took into account the significant flood flows from Lockyer Creek and the Bremer River and sought to keep the combined flow below the level where urban damage would be sustained downstream of Moggill. Dam outflows that would cause urban inundation were delayed for as long as possible until it became apparent no other option was available without risking the safety of Wivenhoe Dam.

Given the event's magnitude, damage to urban areas downstream of the dam was unavoidable. Even if water releases had not been made, damage would have still occurred given the volume of flows from Lockyer Creek and the Bremer River into the Brisbane River.

FLOOD MITIGATION BENEFITS

Wivenhoe dam provided clear flood mitigation benefits during the January 2011 Flood Event. The peak outflow from the dam was approximately 40% lower than the peak inflow which meant that, just below the dam, the maximum hourly flow rate in the Brisbane River was reduced by around 40%. Although North Pine dam is not designed for flood mitigation, its storage reduced peak outflows to a maximum of 82% of inflow rate.

The peak flood height measured at the Port Office gauge in the Brisbane CBD was 4.45m and it has been estimated this peak height would have been approximately 2.0m higher without Wivenhoe. Based on the available damage curves (from Brisbane City Council's flood damage tables – river PMF tab), this projected reduction in the flood peak height resulted in:

- Significant reductions in the potential for the loss of life
- Monetary savings in regard to property damages in the order of up to $5 billion
- 14,000 fewer properties being impacted.

Not only did the dams provide clear flood mitigation benefits, Seqwater also successfully maintained drinking water supplies to the South East Queensland water grid during the event. This was achieved despite significant issues including power outages, limited access, poor raw water quality and damage to physical infrastructure associated with Seqwater's water treatment facilities.

(All information sourced from Seqwater website and Seqwater's January 2011 Flood Event Reports available from www.seqwater. com.au)

Damage to Wivenhoe Spillway viewing paltform and surroundings as result of large releases from the dam after 2011 floods

Wivenhoe Pocket - downstream from the dam - areas devoid of vegetation due to dam release water after 2011 floods

RESCUE, RESPONSE AND RECOVERY

322

THE RESCUE, RESPONSE AND RECOVERY TO THE 2010 — 2011 FLOODS THAT DEVASTATED QUEENSLAND WAS AN INCREDIBLE DISPLAY OF COMRADESHIP, SELFLESS TOIL AND LABOUR. THE INITIAL RESPONSE, AT THE HEIGHT OF THE TRAGEDY, WAS NOTHING SHORT OF AMAZING. ALL OF THE EMERGENCY SERVICES WERE DEPLOYED: FROM POLICE, FIRE AND RESCUE AND AMBULANCES, EXTENDING TO SES, COAST GUARDS, SURF LIFE SAVERS, SWIFTWATER RESCUE, EMQ (EMERGENCY MANAGEMENT QUEENSLAND) AND OTHERS.

Along with these was the Australian Defence Forces which launched Operation Queensland Flood Assist, a complex multi-service response to the 2010-2011 Queensland floods. Comprising of units and personnel from the Royal Australian Navy, Australian Army and Royal Australian Air Force not only from Queensland, but right across Australia, the units offered their assistance both at the height of the disaster, and also helped in the massive clean-up and recovery operations.

323

Most photos supplied by Australian Government Department of Defence

MARK KEMPTON

EMQ Helicopter Pilot

HEROES
STEP UP

GRANTHAM! ...... PEOPLE ON ROOFTOPS WAVING...... SHIPPING CONTAINERS....... TRUCKS .... CARS.....AN AEROPLANE SWIRLING PAST IN THE WATER; BIG TREES ROLLING AROUND LIKE TOOTHPICKS, CRUSHING BUILDINGS - SMASHING THEM LIKE NUTS IN A NUTCRACKER. A MASSIVE, RAGING, BROWN TORRENT, FAR AS THE EYE CAN SEE.... AND THE SMELL- EVEN 100 FEET UP IN THE AIR YOU CAN SMELL IT. WHERE ARE THE BEAUTIFUL FIELDS, GREEN ROLLING HILLS, MEANDERING STREAMS?

I've flown over the Lockyer Valley a thousand times, and know it like the back of my hand, but on January 10th, 2011, I could not believe what I was seeing.....

In my 26 years as a pilot, I have never had a day like it – and neither had our crew of the day, [winch operator Darren "Parso" Parsons, rescue crewman Mark Turner, intensive care paramedic Illya Selmes, doctor Glen Ryan, and myself, Pilot in Command]. We had received a couple of routine jobs early that morning, but we were unable to take off early in the day because the cloud base was so low. When the weather improved we were able to rescue two patients in Kilcoy which was totally surrounded by water. As we were returning the Police Inspector in Toowoomba called… "Look, Toowoomba has just been flooded, the main street has been inundated – you need to get up there and help!" I had to tell him, "Sorry, we have two patients on board, and the weather's so bad – we couldn't make it to the top of the range – but we'll reassess later." We took the two patients to the Princess Alexandra Hospital, returned to base and were in the process of

refuelling when we got another call, "Go to Grantham, it has just been slammed with water ….!" I knew that because Grantham is low-lying, we could get there by sort of scud-running up the valleys, which is what we did.

We set out for Grantham at about 4.30pm - a 15 minute flight. As we reached the township all we could see was an inland ocean of filthy water. Things were being smashed apart in front of our eyes, buildings destroyed, large water tanks rolling around in the brown muck, and boats being pushed along on the surge of water rushing through. Cars, trucks- every imaginable piece of debris- massive trees were hurtling through the town like torpedoes. It was unbelievable. An aeroplane from the local airfield was swept into the side of a shed. And amongst it all were groups of people on houses. Every building still standing had terrified people huddling on it, waving at us, desperate for our attention. We circled the town looking for anyone in more imminent danger than others, wherever we looked, people on rooftops were waving frantically. "We are going to have to work this out logically," I rationalised with the crew. So to ensure we didn't miss anyone, we started at the western end of town because the wind was blowing from the east, working from rooftop to rooftop, loading up then transferring to safe, high ground.

It is far more efficient for a helicopter to hover into the wind. Our first family, the Mahon's – John and Kathy, their daughters Jess and Andrea, and Andrea's little boys, Liam and Lachlan were up on their roof. The boys with floatie rings around

their arms - see page 198 John couldn't actually get onto the roof; he was hanging onto the guttering in water up to his neck, with debris and snakes floating past. We took Liam and Lachlan first, then Jess, Andrea and Kathy. John was wildly pointing to his neighbour Dave, who, with an injured leg, was in grave danger. With Dave on board we were fully loaded - the back of the helicopter full of traumatised and exhausted people. We took them, along with our paramedics, to high ground, and then returned to the township. It was an hour before we got back to John because we had to prioritise our rescues to those in even worse predicaments. We flew over and waved to him several times to indicate where we were heading, and check that he was still OK. Our team has maintained contact with the Mahon family; we feel we made a connection with them that day. (See page 198)

Often as we approached a house, the people on the roof would indicate someone else who was in a more perilous situation – someone clinging to the guttering of a collapsing roof, or frantically grasping a tree branch. At one point I said to Parso, our winch operator, "What's in those trees that those people are pointing at?" None of us could see a thing! Then as we came closer, the trees were buffeted by the helicopter rotor downwash, opening the branches slightly, and we could see a little head! Mark Turner, our rescue crewman, went down in what was probably the most dangerous episode of the day. He was swept under the trees and vanished – and we feared that either he, or the cable, could get tangled, and that we would have to cut the cable and leave Mark down there, ceasing all operations. But after he had been out of sight for what seemed like an age - probably only a few seconds - I said, "Don't cut him yet - let's wait a bit, then winch him in - see if we can get him back." Which we did and out he came with a survivor, and immediately announced he would have to return as another person was there as well! Ken and Fran Arndt, an elderly couple cheated death by clinging to trees as their ute was swept away, had been hanging on for two hours before we arrived. – see their story on page 200.

A similar thing happened again later in that day. As we were rescuing a group off a roof, they pointed to what looked like a bunch of shrubs on higher ground which when we flew nearer proved to be a person huddled there: Stacey Keep. She was pregnant, totally bedraggled, in pain and totally distraught, upset and in shock. As Parso carried her in he did his best to reassure her, "Oh, you're having a baby, you are going to be alright."
"I've just lost my baby," she sobbed uncontrollably.
"What do you mean? You're pregnant!"
"I have just lost my 22 month old daughter, she was swept out of my arms just before you came."

She was beside herself, devastated. For us it was absolutely heartbreaking - it still cuts me up. But we had to keep going; there were a lot more people we had to attempt to save.

We just kept on winching, filling up the aircraft, delivering the survivors to a farm just outside Grantham. The owners were typical country couple – showed a great Aussie spirit. They opened their house to 43 people that night; they were all through it, lying everywhere. Grantham has held a fundraiser since, to help them replace the sheets and bedding and everything else that was ruined.

We were able to rescue 28 persons in 2 ½ hours, and one cat! That was one light moment amongst all the sadness! We can't take animals on board the helicopter, so lots of pets had to be left behind. But this little black kitten sprang up and caught onto a lady's dress as she was being rescued, and clawed its way up her! Our crewman and the lady were 60 feet up in the air with the kitten clinging on. By the time they got up to the aircraft the cat was almost in her lap! Parso said "no pets!" and I said "mate, that cat deserves to live!"

We were running out of fuel and there were still people on rooftops as far as the eye could see. It was getting dark and as we had no radio contact with our base; I called the pilot of the nearby Channel 10 helicopter, and asked him to radio our base to mobilise a second helicopter urgently. We left with heavy hearts – we just couldn't speak as we returned to base with just over 5 minutes of fuel left. It was just too much for us, an emergency helicopter crew to leave that scene, with so many people still in peril. The second chopper rescued a further 15 people, but that's a separate story – see page 328. Our only comfort is that we did the best we could, and between our two crews we managed to save 43 lives. Even in retrospect I look at it with wonder. I can't believe we winched 28 people in the 2½ hours from when we left base till we returned. Each winching takes about 4 minutes, but it takes a lot longer than that to go down the winch cable, assess the situation and secure a person in the strop. Our weight limit allowed us to carry up to 10 people, including crew, in each load. What we achieved is nothing short of miraculous.

The second day [Tuesday 11th January] I was at the base by 4.30am. I collected another crew - Rod Morgan, Dave Turnbull and paramedic Jason Jones, and by 5.00am we were en route to the Lockyer Valley. Suddenly a line of thunderstorms came through – half an hour of non-stop torrential rain - forcing us to land and wait at the Gatton Showgrounds until it was over. We transported the police up to Murphys Creek that morning and were the first people to see the devastation there. The water had come down the escarpment, smashing everything as if

EMQ Helicopter stopped on Warrego Highway

with a giant Gerni gun. The devastation was horrendous and complete. We were actually told to look for a man stuck on a roof in a place called Tent Hill, a little town nearby. With floodwaters obscuring landmarks - our maps were useless. One of our crewmen was able to use his iPhone – he dialled Google Maps, and, there in the cockpit, we were able to follow its directions. Arriving at the address only to find that no one was on the roof, we circled the area for another hour or so, to ensure we hadn't missed him or gone to the wrong place. We flew over so many properties that were totally surrounded by water. People would come out, wave to us and give us thumbs up to let us know they were OK. One man flashed his torch and waved frantically, so we went down. He was concerned about his father and brother-in-law, who lived further up the road; he had been unable to contact them. We invited him aboard to check their place. They came out waving to indicate everything was OK, so, greatly relieved, we flew him home. We conducted similar tasks most of the morning until refuelling became urgent.

As I was working with the night-shift crew, we really needed to be relieved. I organised the day relief to come to Amberley Air Force Base where we planned to land, refuel, do a crew change and finish for the day. But, as we were heading back to Amberley, tracking along the Warrego Highway, another severe line of thunderstorms came through. With continuous lightning and bucketing rain I had to fly at about 200-300 feet above the ground, as the fuel level was too low to enter the cloud then attempt an instrument approach and landing. Every creek, river, stream, and drain was overflowing – water was everywhere; if I landed in a paddock we would surely be washed away! So I pulled into a hover with all the lights ablaze, the traffic moved over, and we landed on the westbound lanes of the highway, where I shut down the engines to wait the weather out.

It was then my wife Julie rang to tell me water was pouring into our house at Yeronga, one street back from the Brisbane River! The flood hadn't begun in earnest yet, but the house was already filling up. I thought panicking, "If water hits there like it did in Grantham, they are going to be trapped – it will be a disaster!" I'd seen too much! So I told her to grab our boys, Lachlan, 14, and MacKenzie, 12, and get out! When the weather improved a little we took off, but only reached tree-top height before being forced down again. You can imagine my state - worrying about my family. We'd done all we could out at Grantham, Helidon, Forest Hill, Murphys Creek, things weren't life-threatening now. So I called up the day crew, "Come up here and relieve me, at least, and preferably, all my crew," which they did. Then, because it would be hours before the RAAF at Amberley could release any fuel for State use, our engineers brought four or five drums from our Archerfield base in their personal vehicles, and pumped it into the helicopter by hand, right on the highway. But, it was some three or four hours before the aircraft could take off, the weather was so atrocious.

I returned by car to base, debriefed, then left. "I have to go, my house is flooding!" When I arrived there was water inside, and we managed to salvage items from the lower floor. Then the flooding started in earnest, with the water continuing to rise through Wednesday and into Thursday morning, when the river peaked. Our lower level was inundated to two metres but thankfully our upper level wasn't affected. We had no flood insurance- after all, with Wivenhoe Dam, Brisbane was never going to flood again, or so we were told! We had Rainwater Inundation coverage but not Flood Cover - we thought there was no point.

It was devastating, but we were alive. At the end of the day we can rebuild the house. What makes a home is family, friends and neighbours and the times we spend together. We will be able to do that - for some folks in Grantham, that will never be an option again.

By the weekend, people were coming down our street, looking for where the helicopter pilot lived! They had seen an interview we'd done in front of our flooded house, and wanted to assist. It was just fantastic. A busload of SES also turned up to help, which was great. They were shovelling the mud, ripping the plaster off walls... it was a quagmire, a horrible mess. And they were ready to help all our neighbours too.

About six weeks after the flood we invited everyone who had helped us to our home, about 80 people in total. We also invited John and Kathy Mahon from Grantham and their family (see page 198). We called it our warehouse, or bomb shelter party, because we had no plaster on the walls, no kitchen - there was nothing there! It was basically a building site! We had a barbeque, with some drinks. That was our way of thanking everyone for being so generous and helping us out when the chips were down. It was good for everyone having the Mahon's come down, and it was great to see the little kids running around. Liam, 5, and Lachlan, 3, after their horrific experiences; still not saying too much…..We also had them come to the base along with some other survivors to spend a day there when we had a bit of a reunion. The kids sort of came out of their shells then, and now apparently they are drawing pictures of helicopters with a rope hanging down, saying, "We have our own personal rescue helicopter pilot – Mark Kempton!" They have been drawing little stories for us as well!

Now we are waiting for the repairs. We are all a bit stressed and worn -out. The crowds have gone. Our street is like a ghost town, people waiting for insurance and on tradesmen. It's only been 3 ½ months since it happened, but it seems like 3 ½ years! I have been on both sides of it – not only have I rescued people but I have been rescued and can empathise with those who have lost their homes, the grief, the loss of that period of time, the upset in their lives. People say "you're

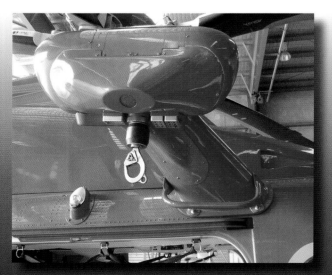

EMQ Helicopter Winch

Footage from EMQ helicopter – Mark Turner performing rooftop rescue in Grantham not so badly off, there are others a lot worse off than you!" I say to them, "Look, I know what you mean, but you know I can't possibly feel better because someone is worse off than me." Our pain is the same as everyone else's. It doesn't matter if you live in a little shanty or a mansion – it's still a home.

I have learnt so much from this event. We all live busy lives; the world is such a busy place. Julie and I have two sons, and she runs a cake business – we were so busy we hardly had time to wave to the neighbours. But in the last three months I've spoken to and spent more time with them than I have in all of the last ten years! Experiences we've been through together have clarified what's important in life. It's not houses, possessions or things - it's the people and the time you spend with them; that spiritual contact you have with people around you. My wife and I discuss this a lot - we're so glad we can spend time together. It's been life-changing for us - a real 'Ah-ha' moment; you know, waking us up to what really matters. We've had a real focus change.

The attention our organisation received since Grantham is amazing, The Prime Minister has spoken in Parliament about what we did, the Premier and the Minister for Emergency Services have congratulated us. Our team is very proud of what we achieved, managing to help so many people. I was invited to the NAB Australia Day Flood Fundraising Day (SES), a Gala Ball in at the Convention Centre. EMQ has received awards for the Goodridge Hoist International Rescue of the Year, the Shepherd SAR Conference Rescue of the Year, presented in the UK and USA, as well as the Helicopter Association International Rescue of the Year. A lovely lady

who bakes ANZAC biscuits and sends them all over the world, to Afghanistan, to Iraq, to people anywhere who display the Australian Spirit – decided this year to send some to our base here! People have sent donations which we have put into our donation pool for Emergency Services and Flood Relief. I am very pleased for EMQ. We work for the Government, without promoting ourselves. My flight suit is going on permanent display at the museum as part of a memorial telling the story of the 2011 Floods. All this recognition is terrific but we do it for the people of Queensland; Emergency Medical Service, Search and Rescue, Emergency Disaster Rescue – anything that you can do with a helicopter; we're there to help.

We cannot forget those few days in January 2011, the dreadful waters, the disaster of the Lockyer Valley - Wivenhoe Dam needing to release water..............but life goes on. May no such disaster befall Queensland ever again!

rk, Julie, MacKenzie and Lachlan Kempton

PM Julia Gillard, Mark Kempton and QLD Premier Anna Bligh

327

EMQ Helicopter Pilot

NO
HESITATION

COMMANDEERING A PIECE OF EQUIPMENT WORTH $20 MILLION IS NOT A COMMON OCCURRENCE FOR MOST OF US, BUT FOR PETER ROW, IT FORMS A MAJOR PART OF HIS LIFE. AS PILOT OF A RESCUE CHOPPER FOR THE PAST 17 YEARS OF HIS 23 YEARS FLYING, HIS CAREER HAS BEEN AN INTERESTING ONE – AND CHALLENGING.

A team it truly is – consisting of himself as Pilot, an aircrew officer who seconds as a navigator and communicator, a rescue crew officer who rides the winch wire, and very often senior medical registrars, consultant doctors, and intensive care paramedics – and together they had seen just about everything......from natural disasters to medical emergencies and everything in between.

Then came the 10th January, 2011.......and a few "firsts" for this wonderful team.

On that tragic day, the drenching rain made fresh mockery of rain gauges and records, and a steely resolve and fight for survival began.

In the Operations room of EMQ Rescue, Peter Row had gathered with Senior Base Air Crew Brett Knowles and rescue Crew Officer David Turnbull – when the message came loud and clear that all hell had broken loose in Toowoomba and the Lockyer Valley, and that urgent response was required to rescue many in peril.

Immediately, Peter recognised fresh challenges ahead......Yes, this is when those years of training pay dividends. Faced with the prospect of a rescue mission of daunting proportions, he and his team did not hesitate in answering the call to action. Peter knew the terrain of the Lockyer Valley – so he and his team equipped the helicopter for winching, and set off for Grantham.

Low cloud and heavy squalls of wind and rain meant the only option was to fly beneath the cloud cover, following well known roads. Peter recounts his first glimpse of the area, "Everywhere beneath the clouds was an ocean of water, an absolute ocean!" Where roads, train lines and housing communities should have been was just an inland sea.

Hovering close to the ground in a helicopter while your team mate is down on the winch is difficult at the best of times, let alone in the awful weather of Jan 10th. Looking for visual reference through the windscreen quickly became an exercise in futility because of the squalling rain, so Peter had to look through the chin bubble and out the door. Visual reference is vital to hold the craft in a hover. And then came an interesting "first" for this team.

Winching a baby to safety was something they hadn't been faced with before. Not having a strop for the baby, ingenuity prevailed, and mother and baby were winched to safety with the baby cradled between mother and David.

Up to 5 at a time, and a total of 43 that evening, were winched to safety between the two rescue helicopters.....................and then came Kristy.

Freshly plucked from a rooftop and now sitting in semi darkness in the back of the helicopter, Kristy was reliving the last terrifying hours. As the wall of water descended like an express train on both herself and her husband, Kristy had looked frantically around for something to cling to as her husband ran off down the road to save their dogs. There was nothing to grab as the raging torrent engulfed them both and swept them away in an instant. As the current carried her along like a rag doll, Kristy was washed up against a power pole and literally wrapped around it. The force of the water was pinning her in position and she was drowning. She was convinced she had seen the last of her husband and that she too was about to become a sad statistic of that fearful event.

Then the pressure of the water eased!!!!!

Freeing herself from the pole, she was again swept at colossal speed – this time towards a huge steel gate. Fate would have been certain had the gate not collapsed in front of her under the pressure of the raging torrent and she passed over it without harm, into the front yard of a home.

Struggling for survival, Kristy was washed into a little eddy near the front stairs. There, half way up the front stairs of the house, hanging on for dear life and gasping for air, Kristy noticed that others were climbing up on to the roof. After she had regained some of her strength, she was helped up by the little petrified band that had sought refuge on the roof top, and watched as the angry torrent mercilessly swirled by.

Eventually airlifted to safety by Peter Row and his fantastic team, she sat cold and wet in the back of the helicopter, overcome by helpless despair.

As the team continued their rescue mission, Peter commanded with urgency "we are starting to run low on fuel and have to go" – the enormous search lights on the side of the chopper beamed down in to the murky darkness below – and there from the middle of a tree and mostly immersed in water, a man gazed desperately up at

them, his face pleading "please don't leave me here!!". Peter made the difficult decision......... "We can't leave him there, he's in the water – lets winch him up."

As the gentleman appeared at the top of the winch cable, there was a scream from Kristy!!!!!! "It's my husband" and she launched from her seated position, wrapping her arms around him. Such was the embrace that the crew had to prise them apart to get the strop off!!! What a truly wonderful reward for the poor traumatised lady who had struggled so long and hard for survival against mountainous odds!!!!!

After dropping this last group off to higher ground, it really was time for the rescue team to head back to Amberley for refuelling, but there was one more challenge for them that night. A severely traumatised Stacey Keep, whose baby had been torn from her arms by the mighty current, needed transport to a hospital as soon as possible. Peter and the crew flew her to a waiting ambulance at Amberley. The rescue team refuelled and went back to their Archerfield base.

It is commonly accepted that one hour of chopper flying is equal to three hours of driving. On the following day, Peter did nine hours of flying, which equates to 27 driving hours. Throw in other challenging variables such as low cloud, squalling showers, low level dodging of powerlines and hours of hovering, and it would be reasonable to say that Peter had done the equivalent of 35 hours driving that day. Mental exhaustion is hardly an apt description!!!!

Peter reflected back over the day. This was no ordinary disaster. True, he had rescued people before in two's or three's, but never so many in one night!!!!! There was little they - or anyone - could do for those who had disappeared in the swirling current other than hope, pray and search. As the hours lengthened, the stark reality seemed to settle in; some were not coming home again, and some may never be found. Weeks later a BBQ was organised and Peter and his team had the opportunity to meet again with some of those they rescued on that fateful day. For Peter and the crew, this meeting brought a sense of closure. The distraught faces they saw coming up the winch rope will always be with them, but to meet and greet those they rescued in more familiar and happier surroundings proved good therapy.

One thing is forever certain. For Peter and his crew, the events of Jan 10th were something they had not seen before, and have absolutely no desire to ever see again.

Rescue 510 Brisbane based crew

EMQ Rescue Helicopter

Grantham residents and helicopter crew

GIVING THEM A
LIFT

LIEUTENANT COLONEL
TIM J. WITENDEN
Black Hawk

INCESSANT HEAVY RAIN ENDLESSLY SATURATED THE LAND UNTIL IT COULD TAKE NO MORE. MUCH OF QUEENSLAND WAS ALREADY REELING AS COUNTLESS BUSINESSES, HOMES AND LIVES WERE IN RUINS. EVERY DAY BROUGHT FURTHER TALES OF DESTRUCTION AND DAMAGE, AND ALSO OF SURVIVAL AND KINDNESS BETWEEN STRANGERS... BUT NO STORY COULD COMPARE TO THE TRAGIC SET OF EVENTS THAT UNFOLDED IN THE TOOWOOMBA, GRANTHAM AND LOCKYER VALLEY REGION ON THE AFTERNOON OF THE 10TH JANUARY, 2011.

While the nation watched the news broadcasts helplessly in disbelief, others including Tim Witenden (LTCOL T.J.Witenden) were deployed into action. His role as the acting commander at the time, and as a senior ADF officer for the Darling Downs area, meant that he was in the heart of the action that day and the days that followed. Tim had been working in the area in the prior weeks, his task being to evacuate people from the nearby town Condamine. His two Black Hawk helicopters were on 24 hours notice to move. On the morning of the 11th, his team was ready to go.

The carrying capacity of the Black Hawks is immense. Flying time or endurance is about 3 hours with a full tank of fuel and tanker truck refuel points were suitably deployed, so that immediate refueling was available. This made many remarkable feats possible. When asked to comment about the demands of that time, Tim replied, "On the 11th of January we lifted 193 out of Condamine, 56 out of Laidley, plus 24 hoist rescues in weather conditions that grounded just about every other aircraft in southeast QLD. The crew were pushed well and truly beyond their normal limits, and I think they did an incredible job."

The hoist rescues gave Tim and his crews constant challenges. So many factors had to be considered, so many things were against them. For many persons, it was their first flight in a helicopter, let alone a hoist rescue. The rain was still driving hard. Everybody was extremely cold and wet. Emotions were running high — fear of the situation they were in; terror of being hoisted; sadness about leaving their property to the mercy of the water; anxiety about the fate of others who were missing. Additionally, the hoists were designed for army personnel, full grown men, not children.

The complexity of their most trying hoist rescue is recounted by Tim and Rob Nelson (CPL R.Nelson): "We arrived at a two storey house, where the water was just below the carport roof. It was probably a single car size, a really small spot to hoist down to. Rob went down the line, we landed him onto the roof and we ended up pulling 6 people off, 4 kids and a couple of adults. One of them was a grandmother."

Rob takes up the story, "It was well and truly dark. The helicopter couldn't hover too low as the roof wouldn't have lasted if we had got any closer; it was just a little dodgy carport type of thing. It crumpled every time I walked on it — a really unstable structure, especially given the body and volume of water that was passing underneath it.

The little kids were hysterical. When I tried to take the youngest first, the little 3 year old girl was absolutely terrified and as I tried to get her out the window she kicked me in the head. I had to get the mother to hold her while I got her in the sling, and then I just carried her, fighting me as she went up. It was too risky to send the children with the parents, as it would be easy for them to fall out of their arms in an ill-fitting sling and unfamiliar situation — so I had to take them myself, one at a time.

The grandmother was a bad risk as she had just had a major operation on her lower back but with the water threatening to engulf the house, we had no option. She was a very well built lady, but I got my arms around her, supporting her weight as best I could, so that it wouldn't fall on the strop. I considered using the sling I was wearing to make a more stable platform, to help take the pressure off her back, and then I saw a car get swept past the house, and suddenly there was no way in the world I was going to disconnect. I thought, 'If that car hits the leg of the carport, I'm in the drink and that's the end of the rescue!'"

Despite the odds, the rescue was a complete success, like so many others this highly skilled rescue team performed in those desperate hours. Everybody, including the grandmother, managed to walk out of the aircraft unassisted. Rob recalls "She even gave me a hug!"

A Black Hawk helicopter containing Forest Hill residents departs for Gatton

Forest Hill residents board for transfer to Gatton

Queensland police board a Black Hawk for transfer to Gatton

A Black Hawk helicopter lands at Forest Hill to transfer residents to Gatton

Army Aircrewman guiding Forest Hill residents

331

All photos supplied by Australian Government Department of Defence

IT WAS JUST IN TIME

MAJOR NATHAN COYLE

Black Hawk

IT WAS THE LAST LIFT OF THE DAY. AWAKE SINCE 4:30AM, AT THE END OF A HIGHLY STRESSFUL AND DEMANDING 9 HOUR CONTINUOUS FLYING STRETCH IN THE WORST WEATHER HE HAD EVER FACED, ARMY BLACK HAWK HELICOPTER PILOT, MAJOR NATHAN COYLE, AND HIS RESCUE CREW, STROVE TIRELESSLY TO SAVE JUST ONE MORE LIFE.....

The water just kept rising. It was devouring entire streets and houses, yet amongst the buildings and household debris was something far more important – human lives. Working against all odds, and in complete darkness, the rescue helicopter crew made their final evacuation.

"We had transferred to Night Vision Goggles, which is the most difficult way to fly. The sound of weeping filled the helicopter. You can talk about kids screaming, but adults sobbing is something else. Then Andy (Aircrewman Sergeant Andrew Bryson) spoke up –'I have some bad news for you'.

Severely fatigued, and low on fuel, I inwardly screamed, "What else? What else could go wrong now?" Andy continued. "Old mate in the back tells us his neighbour, an elderly lady, also needs rescuing." My watch said 9:30pm. We were in total darkness, and we had strict orders not to do any night flying. But could we fly away, knowing we were so close, and leave someone behind?

I called up our commander Lieutenant Colonel Witenden. 'We have been notified of one more person. Can we try? If I can't find her straight away we are just going to have to leave her.' LTCOL Witenden ordered us to perform the rescue, and then return immediately. The other helicopter BLHK220 had departed, so we were now on our own. Had we needed to put out a Mayday, the only communication contact we had was an emergency centre located in Melbourne – who a least promised us a SAR (search and rescue) if we didn't return to base by a given time!

Relying on directions from the elderly neighbour; we soon reached the house. The first thing that met my dismayed vision was power lines running parallel to the house. The lights were on, which meant that they were live. Hovering, we considered our options. The hoist could easily swing into those live power lines, killing the people on it instantly, we in the helicopter would be OK. We had to figure out an alternative plan - and fast.

The water was right up against the floor boards, and there was a set of stairs rising out of the water straight to the front door, no balcony or landing. Some live wires were going into it, near the one solitary entrance. Incredulity kicked in. 'You're kidding aren't you? "This has

to be the hardest thing we have ever done!' Brand new co-pilot LT Warren Wilton described this as "Baptism By Fire".

Thankfully Aircrewman Sergeant David Hill was on the ball. He spotted a mound of soil ten metres from the front door, where we could put Andy down safely. With much difficulty we eventually landed him on the spot. We were now effectively reduced to a three person crew, as Andy disconnected from the wire and strop and hence from all communications, and disappeared into the house."

ANDY

"I left my night goggles in the helicopter so as to not get them wet or broken (the Army doesn't appreciate that!), then separated from the aircraft. The water was chest deep and I couldn't see. Not being a strong swimmer, it took me some time to work my way to the steps through the myriad of obstacles in the water and get to the door.

I hammered loudly on the door without getting any response. I could see the lady pottering around inside, putting things in a little bag. As she was very elderly – and obviously deaf - I realised I would just have to walk in, and risk frightening her, which I did. I hastily advised her that her house was about to be flooded and I was here to rescue her, she promptly informed me she wasn't coming, as her daughter was driving down from Toowoomba to pick her up! I tried to explain that her daughter would need a boat, but she refused again, as she couldn't afford a bus fare. I enlightened her 'It's not a bus, it's a helicopter.' She replied, 'Well sorry darling, I definitely can't afford a helicopter!'

I managed to persuade her into agreeing to come – (I hadn't yet mentioned the winching!), when she dashed off to the kitchen. She had remembered her manners and thought she had better offer me a cup of tea! Meanwhile, the others were anxiously waiting in immense agitation - with only 20 minutes worth of fuel remaining, all of which we needed to get back to base at Amberley.

Frantically relenting on our 'no bag' rule, I took the things she was holding, shoved them into her hand bag, I thrust the sling around her and just bodily dragged her out. I had been in there 15 minutes - an eternity to the helicopter crew. As we were finally winched in, one-and-all heaved a collective sigh of relief – it was just in time!"

Black Hawk and Sea k
sports ground to Laidl

I TRIED TO EXPLAIN THAT HER DAUGHTER WOULD NEED A BOAT

A Black Hawk helicopter lands at Forest Hill to transfer residents to Gatton

Two Black Hawk helicopters assist in Forest Hill transfer

...ers transfer residents from Laidley

Guiding local residents to Black Hawk at the Laidley sports ground

Helping local residents transfer to Laidley hospital

Sea King

SEA KING CHOPPERS TO THE
RESCUE!

THE SEA KING, A LARGE HELICOPTER IN THE SERVICE OF THE ROYAL AUSTRALIAN NAVY, IS USED IN SEARCH AND RESCUE MISSIONS AS WELL AS A VARIETY OF OTHER TRANSPORT ROLES. IT IS ESPECIALLY VERSATILE, BEING ABLE TO CARRY HEAVY LOADS, FLY AT LOW ALTITUDES AND OPERATE IN MOST WEATHER CONDITIONS.

Commander Paul Moggach, in charge of 817 Squadron, was working with Police and Emergency Services during the floods at Roma in early January 2011. On Monday 10th, they received an urgent call to come and support the desperate rescue efforts being undertaken in the Lockyer Valley, following the devastating episode of extreme flash-flooding, already described in this book. It being too late to reach the Valley before nightfall, they decided to leave at first light the following day.

Their take-off next morning was delayed, however, because of the terrible weather conditions, but eventually they got moving, refueling at Oakey in the late morning, and arrived at the Lockyer Valley. There they encountered the worst weather they had ever flown in. At one point, one of the aircraft made a forced landing on a property north of Gatton, to wait out the violent thunderstorms and driving rain.

Their first task was to help in the evacuation of the entire population of Forest Hill, in the face of atrocious weather and limited visibility. The two Sea Kings assisted two Black Hawk helicopters from the Army Aviation Centre, Oakey, and a couple of smaller helicopters to air-lift the flood-bound residents to the Gatton sports ground. They also did evacuations from the town of Laidley.

The Sea Kings visited Grantham in between work at Forest Hill and Laidley. Commander Moggach and his team were able to assist in the evacuation and rescue of traumatised Laidley locals, until fading daylight made further operation impossible.

One dramatic rescue involved a man who had been washed out of his canoe whilst attempting to row across the swollen Laidley Creek. One of the pilots spotted him amongst the debris in the churning water, and diverted the aircraft so that a crewman could be winched down

in an attempt to snatch him out of the water. But the man managed to grab onto a tree and climb up into it, clinging on for dear life. The crewman was then winched down to the tree and, with great difficulty, persuaded the terrified man to let go of the branches and be drawn up into the aircraft. This operation was extremely dangerous for the crewman, but without his action there would have been very little chance of survival for the man struggling in the swiftly flowing, debris laden water. Apparently he had already been swept under the railway bridge and survived - which was a miracle!

During the following days the Sea Kings operated out of Amberley, assisting the Army, the Queensland Police Service, SES and Emergency Response Teams with logistics and reconnaissance work within the Grantham and Murphys Creek areas. In the end there were three Sea Kings and some twenty-five people involved with them, assisting the military, diving units and other ground crews in painstaking searches of the area.

A week later, their tasks completed, the Sea King crews were released from the operation and returned to their base, glad to have been able to assist, but never wanting to witness another disaster on the scale of the Grantham tragedy.

A Sea King helicopter lands at Forest Hill to transfer residents to Gatton to escape rising flood waters.

Assisting Forest Hill residents to be evacuated to Gatton

Local residents board at the Laidley sports ground for transfer

Leading Seaman Aircrewman James Inglish assists Forest Hill residents

Sea King picking up survivors at Forest Hill

335

All photos supplied by Australian Government Department of Defence

Army helps at Suncorp Stadium

Army picking up the anchors from the marina for the Moggill ferry

Army soldiers clear mud off roads at West End

DEFENCE ASSISTANCE

Army soldiers clear the Rail Bridge at Grantham

Street clean-up at Graceville

Navy Sailors assist with clean-up at Karalee - Ipswich

One of the many parks used as temporary dumps

Army soldiers load a truck with damaged possessions at Chelmer

Clearance divers search Brisbane River for sunken debris

Army truck - Brisbane

Tri-Service uniform deployed to Operation Queensland Flood

Most images supplied by Defence Force

Prime Minister Julia Gillard views floodwaters around Rockhampton

Soldiers conduct a search at Postmans Ridge

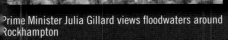
Street clean-up at Chelmer

General Mick Slater and The Honourable Julia Gillard MP Prime Minister of Australia

Queensland Premier Anna Bligh at Grantham

Photo supplied by Australian Government Department of Defence

The Honourable Julia Gillard MP Prime Minister of Australia and Qld Premier Anna Bligh shake hands with Army Personell at Grantham

The Honourable Julia Gillard MP Prime Minister of Australia at Grantham

Her Excellency Ms Quentin Bryce AC Governor-General of the Commonwealth of Australia at Grantham

SUPPORT FROM MEMBERS OF OFFICE

The Honourable Julia Gillard MP Prime Minister of Australia and Qld Premier Anna Bligh visit Bundaberg

Rescuing stranded pets

Pam Bartlett-munt
A dry spot !!

Water Dragon

Oh Deer, looks like we have to swim !!

Beetles and spiders

Escape !!

HOW THE ANIMALS FARED

THE FIRST RUSH OF FLOODWATER CARRIED AWAY AND DROWNED MANY ANIMALS BUT SOME WERE ABLE TO BE RESCUED AND THERE WERE SOME REMARKABLE STORIES OF PETS AND LIVESTOCK REAPPEARING, ALIVE, MANY KILOMETRES DOWNSTREAM.

Most large animals survived however, by moving unassisted or being driven to higher ground.

Even insects such as ants, beetles and cockroaches managed to stay above the flood until the water dropped — although without question vast numbers of such creatures would have been swept to oblivion.

Kangaroo

Cow swimming

Stranded ants

What's going on in my house?

Cows marooned on Ipswich Motorway

Doggy paddle !!

Snake

Swimming horse

Some arboreal animals — birds, possums and the like — which are rarely affected by floods — lost homes and lives where trees lining waterways were uprooted and washed away by the ferocity of the flood.

Waterfowl and other aquatic species some of which were surely swept downstream by the first rush of the floodwaters, were mostly able to survive; this water dragon and even snakes (which can all swim) managed to stay alive. Water rats and platypuses of course can stay snug in their burrows for many days during a flood.

When the floodwaters recede the real capacity of our wildlife to recover will be demonstrated. Adapted as they all are to Australia's extremes of nature — drought, flood and fire — the survivors waste no time to make good their losses and repopulate their rejuvenated habitats in the shortest possible time. By the anniversary of these floods, even the most astute observer will be unable to detect any negative effect of the flood on them.

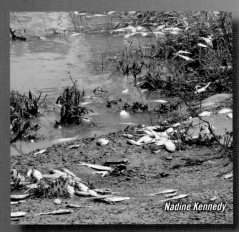

Fish out of water !!

Literally - a drowned rat!!

Horses move to higher ground

Cockroaches scrambling onto any high ground

THE QUEENSLAND FLOODS COMMISSION OF INQUIRY

AS THE VICTIMS OF THE QUEENSLAND FLOODS OF DECEMBER, 2010 AND JANUARY, 2011, BEGAN TO COUNT THE COST OF THE APPALLING DISASTER THAT HAD OVERTAKEN THEM, QUEENSLAND PREMIER, THE HON. ANNA BLIGH LAUNCHED AN INDEPENDENT COMMISSION OF INQUIRY INTO THE FLOODS ON JANUARY, 17TH 2011.

The magnitude of the disaster was unprecedented. At its worst, three quarters of the State of Queensland was flood-affected, including eighty six Queensland towns and cities - one expert compared it to "all of France and Germany going under water". A death toll of over forty is horrendous. A damages bill, although estimated to be $13billion, may never be fully calculated and the emotional cost is impossible to calculate. Thousands had to flee their homes, and tens of thousands of homes were flooded. Ninety two Queensland schools were flood-affected to varying degrees and up to half the State's road network, including major highways, were damaged. Recreational areas and parklands have been devastated. The loss to coal producers was at least $1billion and $2billion worth of agricultural production has been ruined.

It is imperative that everything that can be done, is done to prevent a catastrophe of such vast proportions from ever occurring again. The inquiry is necessary to expose those causes of this calamity that were within the capacity of people to prevent, and to recommend all feasible measures that must to be put into effect to avert the recurrence of the events of January, 2011.

The Premier stated that the year-long commission of inquiry would have the full powers of a royal commission and an interim report would be provided by the commission in August, 2011, and that a final report would be presented in twelve months. However, on May, 26th, the commission was granted a five and a half week extension for the final report, making February, 24th 2012 the due date for the presentation.

The inquiry is being led by Justice Cate Holmes and being supported by two deputy commissioners – former police commissioner, Jim O'Sullivan AC and international dam expert, Phil Cummins. Two Queensland barristers, Peter Callaghan SC and Elizabeth Wilson, have been appointed as counsel assisting the inquiry. An allocation of $15million has been made to cover costs.

The inquiry held its first public hearing on February, 10th 2011. In her opening remarks, Justice Cate Holmes referred to "the enormous task ahead of her".

TERMS OF REFERENCE:
The Commission of Inquiry will investigate and report on:

(a) The preparation and planning by Federal, State and local governments; emergency services and the community for the 2010-2011 floods in Queensland;

(b) The performance of private insurers to meet their claims responsibilities;

(c) All aspects of the response to the 2010-2011 flood events, particularly measures taken to inform the community and measures to protect life, private and public property including:
- immediate management, response and recovery
- resourcing, overall coordination and deployment of personnel and equipment
- adequacy of equipment and communication systems, and
- the adequacy of the communities' response.

(d) The measures to manage the supply of essential services such as power, water and communications during the 2010-2011 flood events

(e) Adequacy of forecast and early warning systems particularly as they related to the flooding events in Toowoomba

(f) Implementation of the systems operation plans for dams across the State and in particular the Wivenhoe and Somerset release strategy and an assessment of compliance with, and the suitability of the operational procedures relating to flood litigation and dam safety

(g) All aspects of land use planning through local and regional planning systems to minimise infrastructure and property impacts from floods.

INQUIRY SUBMISSIONS
In April, the Inquiry began moving from one affected region to another, hearing submissions from lay people, emergency services personnel, police and emergency response centres as well as experts in hydrology.

The Commission held hearings in Brisbane, Ipswich, Toowoomba, Emerald, Dalby, St George, Goondiwindi and Rockhampton. It will continue to hear submissions till November 2011.

When the inquiry heard submissions in Ipswich in May, 2011, it was told that many locals suffered from what is known as "the Wivenhoe Syndrome" – they believed that the Wivenhoe Dam would prevent another flood of 1974 proportions.

Local farmers living in the shadow of the Wivenhoe Dam have praised the management of the dam in coping with the extremely high rainfall – 160 millimeters in two hours, for example – which fell on already-waterlogged ground in the Lockyer Valley region during the days preceding the flood. The farmers say that the dam saved Brisbane from a flood which would have outstripped the 1974 flood levels, but that the dam releases exacerbated the flood damage to the areas in the lee of the dam. It was submitted, however, that fifty percent of the Brisbane catchment is below the two dams.

is still possible for the Brisbane and Bremer Rivers to flood.

Dam safety chief, Mr. Peter Allen explained in his submission that this year's event was unusual in that it had two distinct inflow peaks only thirty hours apart. The second peak was the cause of the flood which inundated 15,000 properties in Brisbane and caused the inundation of 3,000 properties in Ipswich.

Several submissions have been made that Wivenhoe Dam should be used primarily as a flood mitigator rather than a water storage facility, the argument being that flood mitigation is the more critical purpose for the dam, even though its water was critical during the drought of 2008-2009. Several statements have been submitted regarding the adequacy of forecasts and warnings. In Brisbane, the number of homes to be door-knocked for flood-warnings, tripled in a day from 10,000 homes to 30,000. Practically speaking, it became an impossible task to door-knock so many homes in the limited time available.

An independent review of the Brisbane City Council's handling of the floods has recommended permanent flood markers on key roads and more comprehensive local warnings – the recommendations were presented in full to the Brisbane City Council and were then submitted to the Commission of Inquiry.

In Rockhampton, a Banana Shire Councillor in a nine page submission highlighted the primitive communications available to emergency workers. He stated that landlines failed and emergency workers were forced to rely on mobile phones.

In Toowoomba, environmental engineers submitted that early warning systems for flash flooding with automatic update needed to be implemented. Also in Toowoomba, a private meteorologist submitted that it should be legal for private meteorologists to warn the public about potentially deadly floods. Currently, private meteorologists are not legally able to issue public warnings.

INTERIM REPORT
The Commission handed down the interim report on 1st August, 2011. T he report is presented in a volume comprising over 250 pages. The Commissioner has meticulously considered the issues that triggered the inquiry.

The report recommends that Seqwater should review all arrangements for the operation of dams during flood events, by 30th September, each year. Recommendations for warning systems are extensive, covering the installation of more flood markers and the assurance that residents and businesses fully understand the impact of predicted flood levels on their properties. The Bureau of Meteorology (BOM) is advised to strive to develop working relationships with all councils and dam managers, particularly for the purpose of exchanging information. The BOM is also advised to identify amateur, but creditable weather-watchers and to establish means of communication with them.

Power distributors are advised to review network switching options before the next wet season and to provide generators in areas that could become isolated.

To protect life, the Queensland Government is advised to provide a public awareness campaign about dangers of floodwaters. Queensland Fire and Rescue is advised to increase its number of swift water technicians and to equip appliances with more flotation devices.

The Commission supports the development of an All Hazards Information System for ease of communication in the event of a disaster.

Every local government susceptible to flooding is advised to ensure that, before the next wet season, it has a workable disaster management plan and to conduct community awareness education programs.

The efficacy of mobile phones has been raised and it appears that the emergency services could be advised to resurrect the two-way radio as a reliable form of communication.

Two crucial issues that have not been touched upon, as yet, by the inquiry – namely, the insurance claim issue and planning laws – are expected to be considered in the latter part of the year. It is anticipated that the inquiry will venture into these potentially inflammatory areas of community concern when it reconvenes on 19th September.

Three weeks have been set down for hearings in Brisbane, and then the inquiry will move on to Bundaberg, Maryborough and Gympie, returning to Ipswich for another hearing on October 19th and 20th. It will finish public hearings on October 27th, in Brisbane.

It is clear that Commissioner Cate Holmes is ensuring that no issues regarding the handling of the floods are being overlooked. The public now looks forward to February, 2012 when the final report is to be released by the Commission.

ACKNOWLEDGEMENTS

When we come to thanking and acknowledging all those who contributed to the Flood Horror and Tragedy publication we feel totally inadequate to convey our appreciation. This book is not the product of one person or even a group of persons, but by a community. It includes previously unknown persons, victims of tragedy, survivors, local people, community leaders, emergency personnel. It is not an inquest into the floods. It is a collection of stories, pictures, experiences, dramas, ponderings and reminiscences from recovering communities, united to provide a moving memento of the floods of December 2010 and January 2011.

Sincere gratitude is extended to all those who were so ready to share, contribute and provide stories and photographs for the book.

Her Excellency Ms Quentin Bryce, AC Governor-General of the Commonwealth of Australia
Ainsworth Motors, Gerard Bellgrove
Angelos, Chris
Arndt, Ken & Fran
Australian Defence Force
Banasiak, Cnst. Michael
Barron, Brett
Bartlett-munt, Pam
Bartley, Lynn
Behne, Sgnt. Paul
Big Dad's Pies-Toowoomba, Vicki Townsend
Black Hawk, Lt Col Tim Witenden
Black Hawk, Major Nathan Coyle
Bloomfield, Phil
Bowen Tugs and Barges, Doug Hislop
Brassall State School, Peter Doyle
Bremer Waters Retirement Village, Colin Hall
Brisbane Markets Ltd, Vanessa Kennedy
Brisbane Trucks, Loren Schroff
Bunch, Linda
Bundaberg Chainsaw, Keith Iseppi
Bundaberg News Mail
Burch, Larry
Bureau of Meteorology
Burraston, Karen
Campbell, Garry
Cartmill Riding School, Jane Sayer
Castlemaine Perkins Pty Ltd
Citiswich Property Owners
Cold Rock Ice Creamery, John & Donna Weatherhead
Collison, David
Condamine Pub, Shane Hickey
Condamine SES, Bill & Glenda Power
Corbett, Jill
Cullen, Neil
D'arcy, Elizabeth
Dionysius, Malcolm
Dogstar, Hugh Doessel
Dolzan, Tracey
Downs Group Training, Darren McDonell
Drift Restaurant, David Moore
Emerald Auto Glass, Kay Schulz

EMQ Rescue, Mark Kempton
EMQ Rescue, Peter Row
Fabre, Cpl Janine
Feldhahn, Dan
Fitzroy Hotel , Anthony Higgins
Fletcher, Rachael
GEO. Cossarts, Rob Mercer
Gigi Hair, Christine Avolio
Glenoch Angus, Roger Boshammer
Gray, Michelle
Guerin, Thomas
Hales, Katherine
Harm, Ken
Harper-Heyns, Shannon
Harrold, Jodi
Harvey Norman-Dalby, Ian Brassett
Herwin, Murray
Hetherington, David
Hill, Terry
Inscape Photography, Paul Coward
Ipswich City Council Media Manager, Allan Roebuck
Ipswich Mayor, Paul Pisasale
Joubert, Ann-marie
Keers, David
Kennedy, Nadine
Knights Laundry, Jenny Regal
Knott, Mike
Laws, James
Liosatos, Judi
Llewellyn Motors, James Sturges
Macek, Robert
McDonald, Judy
McDowell, Cheryl
McGuire, Danny
McLeod, Rosemary
Mahon, John & Kathy
Mans, Ollie
Marsden, Tim
Marshall, Stephen
Mary River Marine Supplies, William Brown
Mechielsen, Lyndon
Mercedes Benz Commercial, John Grossman
Midtown Marinas, Ray Foley

Muddy Waters Café, Michael Cox & Mia Poulos
Murray's Art and Framing, Peter Granfield
Newspix
Oberhardt, Steve
Paint Place-Milton, Glenn & Cindy Stringer
Phillips, Stephen
QLD Police Service-Media & Public Affairs Branch
Reeves, Snr Sgnt Graeme
Rigney, Sally
Riley, Bruce
Ripcord Skydivers, John Friswell
Rosalie Gourmet Markets, Norris Lewis
Rowe, Sue
Rowes Furniture
Seqwater
Sea Kings, Commander Paul Moggach
Sheppard, Leeroy
South Bank Corporation
Sparkes, Rebecca
Spinnaker Bar and Restaurant, Brett Jensen
St George Mayor, Donna Stewart
Stanwell Corporation Limited
Steele's Bakery, Brad & Gail Steele
Steel Rudd Towing, Bob Malone
Stevemic Meats, Machiel Heyns
Sugden Kerr, Stephen Jurgs
Suncorp Stadium
Telstra Shop-Gympie, Lauren Blackburn
The Black Group, Craig Black
The Coffee Club-Toowoomba, Kate Stevens
The Courier-Mail
Trapp, Annette
Vale, Michael
Van Straten, Peter & Marie
Venice Restaurant, John & Julie Taylor
Wallace Motel and Caravan Park, John Kennedy
Warburton, Marty
Weston, Neville & Catherine
Williams, Kellie
Winton, Lachlan
Woods, Dane & Kristy
Wooler, Grant & Mabel

We extend our gratitude to many other people and organisations who assisted with this publication and to those who may have provided stories and photographs which have not been printed in the Flood Horror and Tragedy book.